Automotive Service Management

Principles into Practice

ANDREW A. REZIN
Columbus State Community College

Upper Saddle River, New Jersey
Columbus, Ohio

Library of Congress Cataloging-in-Publication Data

Rezin, Andrew.
Automotive service management : principles into practice / Andrew Rezin.
— 1st ed.
p. cm.
Includes bibliographical references and index.
ISBN-13: 978-0-13-199863-6 (alk. paper)
ISBN-10: 0-13-199863-3 (alk. paper)
1. Automobile repair shops—Management. I. Title.

TL153.R46 2009
629.28'72068—dc22 2007047251

Editor-in-Chief: Vernon Anthony
Acquisitions Editor: Wyatt Morris
Associate Managing Editor: Christine Buckendahl
Editorial Assistant: Christopher Reed
Production Coordination: Satishna Gokuldas, TexTech Inc.
Project Manager: Holly Shufeldt
Design Coordinator: Diane Ernsberger
Cover Designer: Bryan Huber
Operations Specialist: Laura Weaver
Director of Marketing: David Gesell
Senior Marketing Manager: Jimmy Stephens
Marketing Assistant: Les Roberts

This book was set in Stone Serif by TexTech Inc. It was printed and bound by Bind-Rite Graphics. The cover was printed by Phoenix Color Corp.

Pearson Education Ltd.
Pearson Education Singapore Pte. Ltd.
Pearson Education Canada, Ltd.
Pearson Education—Japan
Pearson Education Australia Pty. Limited
Pearson Education North Asia Ltd.
Pearson Educación de Mexico, S.A. de C.V.
Pearson Education Malaysia Pte. Ltd.

10 9 8 7 6 5 4 3 2 1

ISBN-13: 978-0-13-199863-6
ISBN-10: 0-13-199863-3

BRIEF CONTENTS

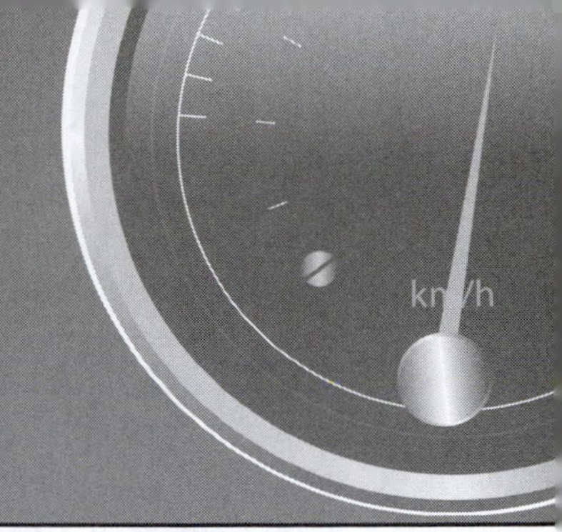

CONTENTS

PREFACE

Automotive service is a very complex business. It is rare that a service management employee has the luxury to specialize in just one area. Just as in most small businesses, a manager in automotive service is expected to be a jack of all trades. As a result, an effective service manager must possess a wide range of knowledge and skills to effectively address daily challenges, skills ranging from accounting and advertising to customer relations and scheduling—and beyond.

In addition to the diversity of knowledge and skills required, there are few industries where employees perform under more pressure than automotive service. The automobile that you purchase or lease is the second largest investment that you will probably make in your lifetime. The sheer dollar value makes your car an important commodity, but a car's value goes beyond that. Not only does the average person invest heavily in his or her car, he or she depends upon a car more than any other purchase. The public's extreme dependence on an automobile as a key to maintaining their way of life makes keeping a car in proper running order essential to maintaining their lifestyle.

Whether you own a mansion in the countryside or share a small apartment in the city, you could wake up any morning with problems ranging from an air conditioner that doesn't work to a leaking faucet. Even though these problems are upsetting, you can still go to work, go to church, go shopping, go out to eat, and have a social life while you're waiting for the technician to schedule a visit to fix your problem. That is not true when you have a problem with your car. Without reliable transportation you can't get anywhere, and loss of use of your car may even result in the loss of your job—your means of income to support your family, your home, and your lifestyle. This scenario is not rare. It applies to just about everyone you know. Now, that is high stakes!

This book is an effort to share my 30-plus years of experience in the automotive service industry. It is an overview of what I believe are the basic knowledge and skills needed to succeed in this challenging business. It will not provide you with all of the answers to all of the situations that you will encounter in the automotive service industry, but it will provide you with a broad-based foundation upon which to build a fruitful career.

The book is divided into the following sections:

- Section 1: Service Operations
- Section 2: Management Styles
- Section 3: Management Strategies
- Section 4: Financial Measurement
- Section 5: Organizing and Managing Your Efforts
- Section 6: Customer Relations
- Section 7: Employee Relations
- Section 8: Marketing, Merchandising, and Selling Service
- Section 9: The Legal Issues and Responsibilities

Supplements

To access supplementary materials online, instructors need to request an instructor access code. Go to **www.prenhall.com,** click the Instructor Resource Center link, and then click Register Today for an instructor access code. Within 48 hours after registering you will receive a confirming e-mail including an instructor access code. Once you have received your code, go to the site and log on for full instructions on downloading the materials you wish to use.

Acknowledgments

Special thanks to my wife, Shelley, and my entire family whose patience and lifelong support have allowed me to undertake this project and my lifelong career in the field that I dearly love, automotive service.

I thank Mark Hambaum; Timothy Gilbert, Northwood University; Drew Carlson, Cosumnes River College; Carl Eric Anderson, Fullerton College; and Tom Grothous, University of Northwestern Ohio, for their assistance with the text review of the original manuscript.

I also wish to thank my friends and business associates at Germain Motor Company, Ricart Automotive Group, Clintonville Auto Repair Service, Boyd's Goodyear Tire and Service, and Midwestern Auto Group in Columbus, Ohio, for allowing us "free access" to their facilities to shoot the photos for the book.

And, finally . . . thanks to all of those who I have worked with and learned so much from during my automotive career. Without your friendship, support, and examples, I would have had nothing to write about!

I hope that you enjoy the journey and that it provides you with a solid foundation for a long and prosperous career in automotive service. I hope you enjoy it nearly as much as I have enjoyed my association with this industry and the great people that I have been privileged to meet and work with over the years.

—ANDREW A. REZIN, PH.D.

ABOUT THE AUTHOR

Andrew A. Rezin, Ph.D., brings a unique perspective to the subject of service management based on his diverse automotive background. Drawing upon twenty years of private sector experience working for major automotive manufacturers and as a manager in large retail service departments, combined with his more recent experience as college instructor and department chair, he provides a unique and informed perspective based on real-life experience of the critical topics students need to be successful in the modern automotive service industry.

SECTION 1

SERVICE OPERATIONS

The automotive industry plays a very important role in our economy and our lives. Automotive service plays an essential role in the support of this mammoth industry. There are many resources required to provide the proper service environment. These resources include the buildings and equipment required to perform service. They also include the human resources needed to staff and operate repair shops. Service departments are far more than a place where a technician repairs vehicles. Many support functions need to be performed to meet customer needs and qualified personnel are needed to perform these essential tasks. The interplay of all of the physical and manpower resources in automotive service forms a complex system that needs to be expertly managed and directed. The service manager is the individual who is primarily responsible for orchestrating and coordinating the complex operations that make up the service system.

CHAPTER

1

The Automotive Service Industry

CHAPTER OBJECTIVES

- To understand the size and current state of the automotive service industry in North America and globally
- To recognize the challenges facing those in the automotive service industry in developed countries and also in underdeveloped nations
- To identify the major types of repair organizations that comprise the service industry
- To compare and contrast the unique benefits and challenges of the different types of repair organizations

KEY TERMS

service departments
independent repair shops
service chain stores
service stations
fleet

Introduction

Wherever you live, wherever you travel, automobiles are there. The worldwide market for automobiles continues to grow in leaps and bounds. In developed countries there are, on average, currently more than two vehicles per household and this number continues to grow. Currently, there are over 200 million cars registered in the United States and another 25 million in Canada.

In developing countries, access to individual transportation is a major focus as they work to build their economies. Today there is hardly a location on earth where there are no cars. It is estimated that there are over 600 million vehicles running on roads worldwide today. So there is a very large and constantly growing need for a robust automotive service industry to keep them running.

The State of the Industry

The demand for vehicle service continues to grow faster than the supply. The U.S. Department of Labor (USDOL) indicates that in the United States alone there are currently more than 818,000 automotive technicians and 249,000 bus, truck, and diesel technicians (Bureau of Labor Statistics, USDOL, May 2005). There continues to be a shortage of qualified technicians. Further, future USDOL projections indicate that the shortage will continue to grow as the current population of technicians ages and retires faster than they can be replaced by entry-level technicians. They also predict that by 2012, annual demand for technicians will grow by 12.4 percent. These labor trends are not unique to the United States. Similar shortages abound across the globe. A 2005 report from the British Columbia Sector Council (Canada) reported that

> Twenty-seven percent of employers have at least one unfilled position for a qualified journeyman automotive service technician. There are reasons for this shortage but there are also solutions . . . Industry needs to act now to avoid an employment crisis.
>
> *(Automotive Training Industry Association, July 2006)*

A similar chronic shortage continues to be the cause of alarm in Europe and around the world.

> Propelling the increases for service productives is the well-known skills shortage in this area. And the 369 respondents to the 2006 *Pay Guide* survey reported a high turnover of service staff—essentially technicians and mechanics—and difficulties filling these positions.
>
> *(Retail Motor Industry Federation, 2007)*

At the same time that nations with more mature, well-developed automotive service industries are struggling to find qualified employees, developing countries around the world not only struggle to find technicians and other service employees but also travel to the United States and other nations seeking insights for building an automotive service infrastructure. For example, many delegations from China have toured U.S. educational institutions in recent years to understand how our service infrastructure operates and to learn what they need to do so that they can manage the explosion in demand that they are currently experiencing.

These technician shortages are a clear example of the global issue of increasing demand and growing shortages. The automotive service industry is more than just technicians, however. There are critical needs in all service support positions. National data indicates that technicians occupy 52 percent of the total jobs in automotive service careers. According to 2005 data from the U.S. Bureau of Labor Statistics, the production support activities needed in service operations account for 48 percent of the total jobs in the industry. The total need for service personnel is roughly twice that indicated for technicians. Management and sales-related jobs (for example, service advisors) account for about 15 percent of the support positions in service organizations. The 2 percent of all automotive service employees that are managers are responsible for guiding and directing the other 98 percent and are accountable and responsible for 100 percent of the final results. In this book we will focus on the skills and responsibilities needed to guide and direct that 98 percent.

Service Market Segments

There are five major market segments in the automotive service industry. They are

- New car and truck dealerships
- Automotive repair and maintenance shops
- Automotive parts, accessories, and tire stores
- Gas stations
- Fleets

Each of these major market segments poses unique characteristics, needs, and challenges for employees. Let us briefly explore each of them.

New Car and Truck Dealerships

According to the Bureau of Labor Statistics, automobile dealership service departments account for about 40 percent of the total automotive service market (USDOL, 2005). Dealerships play a unique role in the automotive service industry. As the only factory-approved sites for warranty repairs, dealerships are solely responsible to make all of the warranty repairs to vehicles. Because of this mandatory specialty, service work in new car and truck dealership **service departments** has historically been dominated by warranty repairs.

Service Departments

Dedicated service facilities that are a part of all new car and truck dealerships; the sole warranty repair stations that perform general maintenance and repairs as well.

Because of their close ties with a specific manufacturer, dealership service departments specialize in the maintenance and repair of the specific make and models that they have been awarded an exclusive franchise to sell and service in their market. Because of this agreement, they are solely responsible for the warranty repairs of that brand of vehicles in their area. As part of this close tie with the manufacturer, these service departments have access to the latest technical support data on those models. Thus, historically, even when maintenance and customer-paid work is involved, they tend to limit their work only to their manufacturer's products.

In recent years, because of dramatic improvements in product quality, dealership service departments, which were originally built to support huge volumes of warranty work, have begun to look for other sources of work to sustain their large operations. As a result, dealership service departments have become more engaged in retail sales of repairs and preventive maintenance.

Whereas two decades ago many dealerships generated 60 percent or more of their total business with warranty repairs, this percentage of total work has significantly declined. Recent industry trends indicate that the volume of warranty repairs is less than half of what it was just ten years ago. As a result of this decline in warranty repairs, dealerships have shifted their focus to the highly competitive retail service business. Even though their total market share of retail repairs and maintenance still hovers in the 20 to 30 percent range, in most markets dealerships are making a concerted effort to increase this market share.

Another unique trait of dealership service departments is that they are a small part of a much larger organization. Dealerships are a group of diverse operations all working under one roof. The six major departments in dealerships (new vehicle sales, used vehicle sales, service, parts, body shop, and car leasing) are commonly managed and operate as unique and separate subcompanies within the organization.

Although the service department is only one of six profit centers of the overall dealership operation, it is essential to dealership stability and profitability. Dealers depend on service as an essential profit center that produces a steady source of income that they can count on to pay the bills each month.

Automotive Repair and Maintenance Shops

Independent Repair Shops

Single-purpose service shops that are not affiliated with a specific manufacturer or product; perform service and repairs on a wide range of vehicles.

Unlike dealerships, automotive repair and maintenance shops are **independent repair shops** that operate as single-purpose organizations. Their sole purpose is to repair and service vehicles. Independent shops range in size from locally owned one-bay proprietorships to large multibay shops that are comparable in size to some of the local new car dealerships. In most cities the number of independent service shops is much larger than the number of dealerships.

Automotive repair and maintenance shops do not have a built-in business as do new vehicle dealerships. They cannot depend upon the consistent flow of manufacturer-paid warranty repairs. Conversely, they do not carry the liability and burden of being the sole source for resolving some of the difficult new vehicle problems. Their singular focus is customer-paid work. Nationally, automotive repair and maintenance shops account for slightly more of the total service business than dealerships. In addition, they generate more than double the amount of customer-paid service of their dealership counterparts.

Unlike dealerships that focus on servicing only one make of vehicle, automotive repair and maintenance shops are not tied to any specific manufacturer. They work on all makes, models, and years of vehicles that come to them for service or repairs. To be successful, their technicians must be jacks of all trades. However, it is not uncommon in any city to find some shops that have chosen to specialize in a specific segment of the market (such as domestic, European, or Japanese vehicles).

One of the greatest challenges to the nondealership organizations in automotive service is access to technical information and training. The manufacturers open their books only to their franchised dealers, providing those dealers with the latest specific technical information; this poses an ongoing challenge to others in the service industry. The nondealership organizations must actively seek out information on a broad array of vehicles and vehicle systems, yet their access to manufacturer technical data and specifications is limited. While this is a major challenge, over recent years the rapid expansion in access to technical information, primarily through the Web, has been of great help to improve this situation.

Automotive Parts, Accessories, and Tire Stores

Major regional and national **service chain stores** have been the outgrowth of some of the larger parts and service retailers over the years. Much like car dealerships, these companies house several unique departments. Whether their core business is tires, mufflers, batteries, or general parts, the service operation is most often only one profit center among several. There, however, are many ways that these organizations are similar to their smaller automobile repair and maintenance shop cousins than they are to dealerships.

Service Chain Stores

Stand-alone service centers that are part of a group of independent repair shops, owned and operated in conjunction with a major provider of parts or accessories.

These service departments generally work on all makes and models of vehicles. They also work with limited access to manufacturer technical information. One unique benefit that they possess, however, is that they are part of a much larger network of shops. Because they are part of a large group of identical shops in varying locations, they can share information, training opportunities, and even equipment and tools across different sites to become more efficient.

Although some exceptions exist, large chain operations tend to be "semi-specialists." That is, they intentionally limit their range of work. For example, if they are part of a major tire store chain, they may choose to focus primarily on tires, suspension, and brake repairs. Although they may accept some minor repairs to some other car systems, they will most often completely, and by the company's edict, steer clear of heavy mechanical or electronic repairs or troubleshooting.

Gas Stations

Although gas station repair shops have been an institution in automotive repair since the automobile's introduction over a hundred years ago, their numbers have declined significantly over the past decade. Today they employ just over 4 percent of the total number of automotive technicians in the United States. This is primarily because of the difficulties in keeping up with the technology and the high cost of specialized equipment, tools, and training. In the limited space that most gas stations can provide (typically one to three service bays), the cost to equip the shop is often prohibitive.

These small businesses face the same challenges as the automotive repair and maintenance shops but with only a fraction of the space and production capacity to make them profitable. Unfortunately, because of these trends, many of the existing **service stations** have converted their service bays into convenience stores. As new gas stations are built, they are rarely designed as service stations, their previous common name and description. They are most likely to begin life selling gasoline, soft drinks, chips, and other convenience items rather than venture into the highly competitive automotive repair business.

Service Stations

Gas stations that also provides automotive service repairs and maintenance.

Fleets

Fleet service operations are departments within companies or governmental agencies that maintain and repair only those vehicles that are owned or leased by that particular company or agency. These shops do not accept business from the general population. Their sole responsibility is to keep as much of

Fleet

A group of vehicles that are owned and operated by a company to support its business operations.

their fleet up and properly running at all times as possible. These fleets range widely in size and variety of vehicles serviced.

Many corporate fleets limit the number of makes and models of vehicles that they service at any one time. This helps to simplify their needs for technical information and allows them to become specialists in working within their unique market. Fleet service departments are support functions of an organization in another primary business. Therefore, the composition of their pool of vehicles is dictated by the business that they are engaged in. For example, the fleet of the local transit authority may have several makes and models of vehicles in its fleet at any one time. With rare exception, however, the composition of the fleet will normally be dominated by buses. Likewise, a fleet service working with the state police will specialize in preparation, maintenance, and repair of police cruisers.

Fleet services, like their other nondealership counterparts in the service industry, struggle to obtain technical information. There are exceptions to the rule, however. Because many of the larger fleets purchase large numbers of new cars or trucks every year from major automotive manufacturers, they may request and be granted special privileges by these manufacturers. This may include access to the manufacturer's latest technical bulletins and service manuals and even access to direct training from the manufacturer. Some of the largest of these fleets are even granted the status of becoming local warranty service centers, which allows them to perform their own warranty-reimbursed repairs in-house.

SUMMARY

In this chapter we learned about the size and importance of the automotive service industry today and into the future. The need for automotive service is very large in North America and around the globe. Many countries report a shortage of qualified technical workers in the automotive service industry, and this shortage is growing at an alarming rate. This growth in the need of service workers is not limited just to the developed nations. It has more recently taken on greater importance in many of the developing nations.

The automotive service industry is divided into five distinct types of service operations: dealership service departments, independent repair shops, chain stores, gas stations, and fleets, all of which experience unique challenges in the marketplace. Now that you have a general idea of the size of the business that you are getting into, let us explore in detail what it takes to build, maintain, and staff a service operation.

PRACTICING THE PRINCIPLES

1. Which of the following service operations may be authorized to perform manufacturer warranty repairs?
   a. fleets.
   b. independent repair shops.
   c. tire stores.
   d. chain stores.
2. Automotive parts, accessories, and tire stores may provide vehicle service but it is likely to be
   a. low priced.
   b. limited in areas of service provided.
   c. poor quality.
   d. all of the above.
3. The type of shop that is most likely to have access to the latest manufacturer bulletins and technical information is
   a. new car dealership.
   b. large fleet.
   c. new truck dealership.
   d. all of the above.

4. Which type of service shop is least likely to provide service to all makes and models of vehicles?
   a. independent repair shop.
   b. tire store.
   c. new truck dealership.
   d. chain store.
5. Even though the demand for service continues to grow, the one type of shop that is rapidly vanishing is
   a. tire store.
   b. chain store.
   c. service station.
   d. parts store.
6. According to reports, there are more than __________ vehicles in operation worldwide.
   a. 6 billion.
   b. 835,000.
   c. 2.6 million.
   d. 600 million.
7. Automotive technicians make up __________ percent of the total number of employees in automotive service shops in the United States.
   a. 52.
   b. 67.
   c. 48.
   d. 75.
8. There are more than __________ automotive technicians currently in the United States.
   a. 800,000.
   b. 250,000.
   c. 1,500,000.
   d. none of the above.
9. Shortages of qualified technicians have been reported in the United States and
   a. Canada.
   b. Europe.
   c. China.
   d all of the above.
10. One of the greatest challenges to the nondealership organizations in automotive service is
   a. being price competitive.
   b. access to technical information.
   c. access to factory technical training.
   d. a and b.
   e. b and c.

CHAPTER

2

Physical Resources

CHAPTER OBJECTIVES

- To identify and lay out the physical facilities necessary for an automotive repair shop
- To identify the equipment and tools necessary for operation of an automotive repair shop
- To be able to calculate the total investment in facilities, equipment, and tools required to properly equip a repair shop
- To calculate the total investment required to properly equip and operate an automotive repair shop

KEY TERMS

physical facilities
repair stalls
storage space
support space
administrative area
special tools
communications equipment
computing system

Introduction

If asked to list the resources needed to run a successful repair shop, a typical automotive technician would likely answer with one word: *Me*. Although the automotive technician is an essential part of any automotive repair shop, building and maintaining a successful repair operation requires a far more complex mix of resources and assets. In this chapter, we will look at the physical resources needed to operate a repair shop, which include everything from the physical facilities to the service equipment, tools, and also other considerations that are a part of outfitting a typical repair shop.

Facilities

Physical facilities are required to operate an automotive service business. These facilities are the land and buildings that provide a suitable physical environment for conducting business. The need for suitable facilities is especially important for an automotive service operation. Because of the nature and complexity of the automotive service business, the investment required to provide these physical resources is substantial. There are some very important factors that must be taken into account to provide facilities for any automotive repair shop.

Physical Facilities
The land and building that provide a suitable physical environment to conduct business.

General Facility Guidelines

A successful automotive repair facility must be large enough to house the cars being repaired and should occupy a convenient, accessible, and easy-to-find location. The ideal facility for an automotive shop

- Is large enough to handle an average day's business
- Is visible and easily accessible to customers
- Has adequate external space for customer parking and vehicle storage
- Has adequate space for repair support services (write-up area, locker rooms, parts storage, business office, equipment storage)
- Has adequate space for customer services (customer entrances, a waiting area, and restrooms)
- Provides a neat, clean, and professional customer friendly environment

Although it is important to address all of these criteria when selecting or building a facility, it is important to approach all brick-and-mortar investments cautiously and conservatively; do not overdo in any of these areas. Whether you rent, lease, or purchase them, facilities are fixed assets, and therefore are very difficult to change or dispose of rapidly. As a result, they continue to be an expense whether the business is good or bad—even when the shop is not open. When planning your investment in facilities, keep in mind the need to provide a facility for efficient operation and keep fixed expenses to a minimum.

Facility Needs

The guidelines listed above are good starting points for choosing a facility, but your ultimate choice must address the need to support repair and customer services essential to your business. We will now discuss each of these needs your facility must fulfill, as well as their importance.

Repair Space

Repair Stalls
The physical space, each stall typically measuring 12′ × 25′, that is set aside to provide adequate room to repair an automobile.

The typical service shop dedicates the majority of its facility space to the **repair stalls.** Each stall must provide room for the car and a reasonable workspace surrounding it so that the technician has sufficient space to easily access all the car's systems. Because a standard midsized car measures 6′ × 16½′, the average size of a repair stall is 12′ × 25′ (300 square feet). A stall of this size is large enough to accommodate light-duty trucks as well. A shop that repairs smaller import vehicles and/or sports cars can reduce the stall size to 10′ × 20′ (200 square feet). Because most automotive manufacturers now offer products in several classes—from subcompacts to full-sized sport-utility vehicles (SUVs)—however, planning for a more spacious and flexible 12′ × 22′ stall is a wiser investment.

Providing access to each of the repair stalls is as important as setting aside adequate space for the stalls. Stall access is often provided by means of two overhead doors and a large drive-through aisle that runs the entire length of the shop. The aisle must be long enough to provide access to each stall yet wide enough to allow vehicles to be turned and driven in and out of the stalls. This layout is very common, especially in areas where the seasons change dramatically. The two overhead doors provide adequate access for vehicles while limiting entry to the facility. This increases building security and reduces the direct effects of the weather inside the shop. Figure 2-1 shows examples of basic repair area layouts.

In milder climates, individual overhead doors lead directly into each repair stall. Whereas this layout reduces the total square footage required under the roof, it adds to the risk of theft and increases wear and tear on the

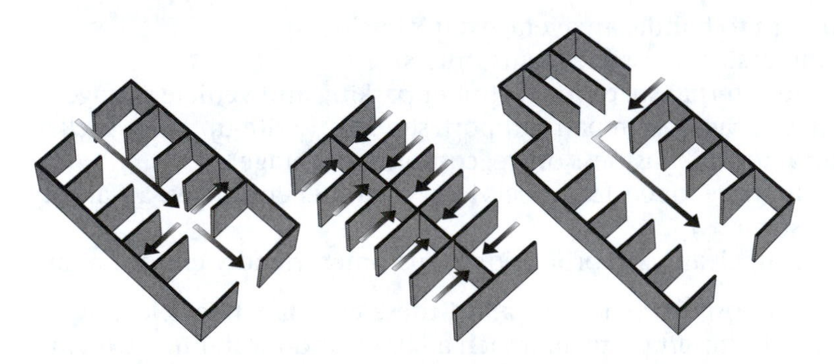

Straight Drive-Thru Layout   Drive-In Bay Layout   L-Shaped Layout

Type of Lift	Min Space	Ideal Space
Surface-Mounted	12 ft. × 25 ft.	13 ft. × 25 ft.
In-Ground	11 ft. × 25 ft.	12 ft. × 25 ft.

Figure 2-1 Basic repair area layouts

building (most often in the form of frequent door repairs). The mildest climates, such as the desert Southwest, often feature open-air facilities housed under roofs suspended over concrete slabs. Shops in such environments experience a unique set of climatic obstacles: instead of contending with cold temperatures and rain, they must deal with extreme heat and dust storms.

Storage Space

Storage Space
The physical space required to house equipment, tools, and supplies.

The repair space must also include adequate **storage space** to house the equipment and tools typically shared by the technicians (such as a brake lathe, wheel balancer, valve grinder, and other special tools), and it must be easily accessible from any part of the shop. At the same time, storage space for shared equipment must provide adequate security to prevent loss or damage to these expensive tools. The shop layout must also allow sufficient room for each technician's toolbox. Professional automotive technicians own and regularly use a large variety of tools. These tools are stored in large rolling toolboxes. These toolboxes range in size from a small 26″ × 19″ box for entry-level technicians to more extensive and specialized sets of up to 6′ × 2½′. Locating storage space for toolboxes close to the repair stalls provides technicians with easy access to essential hand tools.

Drainage

An important, but often overlooked, point is to make sure the shop floor provides adequate drainage. Two common methods of drainage include sloping the entire floor toward a central floor drain trough, or locating a variety of drains throughout the repair space. Drainage is essential for cleanliness and, more important, safety. Hundreds of cars drive in and out of the shop every day, causing an accumulation of road grime. Incidental fluid leakage or spills involving antifreeze, oil, and other fluids further contribute to dirty, slippery, and unsafe floors. The shop owner must anticipate and plan for these conditions in the design and preparation of the repair facility.

Support Space

Support Space
Facilities required to conduct functions that are not directly involved in the primary activity of automotive repair.

Now it is time to discuss the rest of the shop—the **support space** in the facility that is not directly involved in repair. Although a shop may be adequate without one or more of these areas, you should always consider them when developing an automotive service shop layout. In most cases these support services require space equal to at least one-half the size of the repair shop.

Employee Facilities

The nature of the repair business makes the employee facilities among the most essential supplemental areas in a service shop. To keep the vehicles that they work on, the shop, and themselves clean and neat, technicians require ready access areas where they can clean up and change clothes when needed.

Technicians must be able to change quickly and conveniently from street clothes into work uniforms. Because they work with hazardous chemicals such as oils, greases, cleaners, and solvents; they also need an accessible space that allows them to clean up quickly and thoroughly. Most technician locker rooms in mid- to large-sized shops therefore include employee restroom and shower facilities, a changing area with individual lockers, and a large multistation washbasin. The importance of these facilities for shop safety and customer satisfaction cannot be overstated.

Parking Lots

The facility should include adequate parking that is clearly marked and visible from the street. The customer parking area should be paved, well lit, and provide easy access to the service facility. Providing convenient parking sends a strong message to customers that the shop is aware of their importance and makes every effort to take their needs seriously.

Although the parking area represents a smaller investment than a building, it is not an insignificant expense. The parking area must have adequate space for the cars of current and potential customers, as well as for all vehicles currently being repaired and those being stored temporarily while awaiting service. In addition to paying for acreage and improvements (such as lighting and paving), the owner must also ensure that the entire facility and all cars on the property are safe and secure. Repair facilities commonly employ alarm systems and security fencing around areas where cars awaiting service are parked.

Detailing/Wash Rack

Most shops include an area for cleaning customer vehicles. Such a service is highly recommended for increasing customer satisfaction. This area might consist of a simple one-stall space where a porter can handwash vehicles before returning them to customers. Many mid- to large-sized shops, however, now feature full car wash and car detailing areas in an attempt to provide a full-service shop that can meet all the customer's needs in one stop.

Administrative Area

Running a service facility involves performing not only repair tasks but also administrative tasks, such as work distribution (dispatching) and the handling of customer paperwork and payment (cashiering). Employees in small shops may perform both administrative and repair duties, whereas larger facilities may hire separate personnel to handle these tasks. Regardless of the size of its staff, a shop must have an adequate **administrative area** to perform these needed services. Larger shops must set aside office space to house service management and general business management (accounting) personnel. Because these management personnel perform duties that require the ability to work quietly and without distraction, their offices may be located out of the normal traffic flow.

Floor space allocated to perform general business functions of the company or department.

Parts Sales and Storage Area

Although not all service shops have their own parts department, all but the smallest shops maintain an inventory of common parts and supplies. Keeping an inventory of commonly used parts frees a shop from depending on a third party to deliver the parts needed for repairs, thus making the shop more efficient and productive.

Many larger independent shops and those associated with dealerships carry enough inventory to act as retail parts outlets. This inventory requires investments in both the inventory and the additional physical space needed to store those parts while still making them easily accessible to the service personnel. Often this means that the shop will maintain two separate parts counters: a wholesale counter accessible to the technicians and a separate retail counter that is accessible to customers.

Parts Inventory

Building and maintaining a parts inventory is a large investment that requires careful consideration and even more careful monitoring. Because parts in stock tie up a significant amount of space and money, the shop owner needs to consider carefully the size and scope of the parts to be inventoried. After all, parts sitting on the shelf are not generating income or a markup or profit. Unlike the equivalent amount of money in a bank, they do not generate income—instead, they depreciate. The longer a part sits unsold on the shelf, the more likely it will remain there; even if it does sell, it is more likely to sell at a reduced price. Still worse, the longer the part remains unsold, the more likely the part will become obsolete and unsellable.

Even the smallest parts department must emphasize accurate and thorough record keeping, tight inventory management and control, and a strict policy to control obsolescence. Computer-based inventory control and management systems help provide the information a parts manager needs to stock only inventory that is in demand. They can also provide sufficient warning to allow the manager to dispose of nonselling inventory before it becomes obsolete and valueless. Once a shop has committed to keeping a parts inventory, it should consider the option of using this inventory as a means for generating additional income by opening a retail parts sales counter. Such a move can significantly increase the sales of common parts and will help generate profit and offset the cost of inventory. It is critical for the shop owner to assign a capable employee the responsibility of managing the inventory and overseeing the shop's investment in this area.

If you decide to maintain a parts inventory, there are two methods to help assure that the parts will be sold rather than just sit on the shelf: comprehensive inventory control and obsolescence monitoring. Commonly available as computer-driven programs or services, these tools provide the management information needed to keep only inventory that is in demand and provide warnings to allow disposal of nonselling inventory before it becomes obsolete and valueless.

Customer Space

An automotive service shop's reputation rests not only on the repair service it provides but also on the overall impression the shop leaves its customers. A clean, organized, and physically appealing facility can attract additional business as surely as a dirty, disorganized, and unappealing business can drive customers away.

Customer Entrances and Write-Up Area

As in every other retail purchase transaction, the first impression that the customer has when they enter your service facility typically sets the tone of the overall customer experience. The shop should feature a clearly marked and easily accessible entrance that leads customers to a write-up area where employees can attend to their needs. The write-up area is typically the site of the first face-to-face contact between the customer and the service advisor. The write-up area should provide a clean, well-lit, and quiet environment where customers can comfortably discuss with the advisor the reason for their visit and raise any questions or concerns that they may have. Because this face-to-face transaction leaves a lasting first impression on the customer, the write-up area must reflect a clean and professional environment.

In most climates the write-up area should also include a covered space where customers can enter or exit their vehicles while being protected from the weather. Such a space allows the customer and the service advisor easy access to look over the vehicle and assure a common understanding of the customer's concerns and the planned services. This additional inside facility space can greatly improve customer relations and satisfaction and easily justifies the added cost to provide the space.

Customer Waiting Area

Providing customers with a waiting area is an important part of demonstrating concern for their needs. You can demonstrate your concern for customers' needs by making available separate customer restroom facilities and a customer waiting lounge that are clean, well lit, and isolated from the repair space. Because customers may choose to wait for minor services and repairs, the facility should feature a comfortable place for them to sit, read, or watch television while they wait for repairs to be completed. Many shops today accommodate the mobile businessperson by providing telephones or wireless Internet access so that customers can conduct business while waiting for repairs. These additional amenities provide shops with a competitive edge.

Tools and Equipment

Special Tools
Tools that have been designed for a very specific purpose and application.

The total investment in the physical resources needed to open and operate a service shop does not end with the lease or purchase of an adequately large facility. Once the facility has been located, it must be outfitted with sophisticated diagnostic and repair equipment and **special tools.** Although every technician possesses a large rolling toolbox filled with tools worth thousands of dollars, their investment pales in comparison with what the owner must invest to properly outfit the shop. In this section we will look at the typical tools and equipment required in a service shop.

Tools

Although technicians make a significant investment in their own personal and hand tools, they expect shops to provide a wide array of specialized and commonly shared general-use tools. These include large tools used in diagnosis and testing of vehicles, such as charging system testers, cooling system testers, and electronic diagnostic scopes. Shops typically provide these tools because of their considerable cost and the frequency with which they are used. Most shops possess only one or two of these expensive and highly specialized diagnostic tools, which all technicians at the shop share.

Real World Application

Shop owners and technicians often disagree over which tools the shop should provide and which ones the technicians should buy for themselves. Deciding what tools and equipment the shop should purchase and what should be purchased by individual technicians is always difficult. As you can imagine, when there is any doubt, the technicians would prefer that the shop purchase the equipment.

When I took the position as service director at a large dealership, I had to develop a reasonable set of guidelines to govern this important issue. Based on my work experience with many well-run shops, I arrived at the following rule of thumb: "If it fits in your toolbox, you buy it!"

Using this rule of thumb, a technician should purchase small hand and power tools that can be stored in his or her toolbox and take such tools along if he or she changes employers. Larger shared tools, such as pieces of diagnostic testing equipment (charging system testers/diagnostic scopes), by contrast, are appropriate investments for the shop.

Special tools constitute a notable exception to this rule. Although the individual pieces of special tool kits often are small enough to fit in a technician's toolbox, the entire collection of these rarely used yet essential tools is too large to be in the possession of any single technician. Further, manufacturers often require the shops that work on their products to purchase and own specific sets of these specialized tools.

A shop also typically provides additional specialty tools, or shop tools, specifically designed for certain products that the shop services. Dealership shops or highly specialized shops may need to make significant annual investments in special tools designed to service a particular product or product line.

Equipment

Shop owners make an even larger investment outfitting the facility with the basic equipment required to provide proper repair services. Although technicians often take the fact that the company buys these basic pieces of equipment for granted, this equipment is a substantial investment for the shop owner. Some examples of the most basic pieces of equipment common to all shops, whether full-line dealerships or local muffler and brake shops, are

- Centralized power exhaust system
- Adequate lighting
- Air compressor
- Air distribution system
- Electrical outlets
- Work benches
- Hydraulic press
- Floor jacks
- Bench grinders
- Vehicle lifts

Depending on the types of work a shop performs, the shop may need a wide range of additional equipment. Some of the most common big-ticket items specific to each major automotive repair area are

- Engine mechanical: cooling system tester, cooling system flush machine, valve grinding machine, oil drains, mobile crane, precision measuring equipment (run-out gauges, micrometers), torque wrenches;

- Automatic transmission (A/T): A/T fluid exchanger, precision measuring equipment (dial indicators, micrometers, depth gauges), torque wrenches, pullers, presses, pilot tools;
- Manual transmission and driveline: transmission jack, differential jack, bearing press;
- Steering and suspension: alignment machine, wheel balancer, tire mounting machine, strut compressor;
- Brake systems: brake lathe, power bleeder;
- Electrical systems: charging system tester, battery chargers, short finder, multimeter;
- Heating and air-conditioning (A/C): A/C recharging/recycling system, electronic leak tester;
- Engine performance: diagnostic testers, digital multimeter, code reader, timing light, oscilloscope.

Communications Equipment

Communications Equipment

Telephones, intercoms, and other equipment that improves employee interaction.

No shop can exist if its employees cannot communicate effectively with one another as well as with their suppliers and customers. To address these basic communications needs, a shop should have **communications equipment,** such as a commercial telephone system with multiple incoming lines, fax machine, and line-transfer capabilities. In addition, an intercom and internal paging system can help improve internal communications among employees. A large shop may also employ an automated system to distribute and deliver internal documents. For example, some shops use a vacuum-operated tube to route repair orders and other important paperwork quickly from the write-up area to the dispatcher and then on to the cashier's office.

Computing Equipment

Computing System

The electronic data gathering, organizing, and processing equipment required to support the business operation.

Regardless of its size, a fully equipped shop needs a **computing system.** A small shop may require only a single, Internet-connected personal computer to allow online communication with vendors and customers. Larger facilities with many employees may need an in-house mainframe computer, or a system of networked personal computers, to perform essential functions, such as inventory control, personnel and payroll management, and accounting. Shops increasingly are moving from traditional paper repair orders to paperless electronic repair order systems. An electronic system allows instantaneous transmission of the information from the service advisor to the dispatcher, technician, and, finally, to the cashier. The following is a list of common computer-based operations in a modern shop and the employees or departments that handle these operations:

- E-mail (all employees)
- Inventory control (parts department)
- Appointments (service advisor)
- Repair order writing/preparation (service advisor)
- Work distribution (dispatcher)
- Documenting performed work (technician)
- Repair order tracking (service advisor and management)
- Invoicing and billing (cashier)

- Management reporting (manager)
- Accounting (business office)

Planning Your Investment

Entrepreneurs commonly are optimists, with high ideals and even higher aspirations for success. Business research, however, indicates that most new small businesses fail within the first six months. The most common cause of new business failure is not the lack of a great idea, a great product, or a great service, but rather overoptimistic initial projections and lack of initial capital. In other words, the problem is overprojecting business and overspending at startup. It is unreasonable to expect to survive in a competitive market such as automotive repair without providing levels of services and benefits comparable to your rivals. It, however, is just as difficult to survive if you get too deeply in debt by trying to run before you walk. The owner and management personnel must develop a clear vision of the long-range needs and potential of the company while also being prudent in their initial investments and realistic about their strategies and prospects for growth. A successful entrepreneur slowly and steadily builds up to long-term goals and does not formulate plans based on dreams of instant success.

A balance of optimism, enthusiasm, drive, and conservative business planning is essential for survival. Therefore, it is critically important that management be keenly aware of the dangers of overinvestment or even premature investment, especially in fixed assets. The prudent manager or owner must be cautious and carefully evaluate which decisions are right for now and which should be delayed for the future. Continue to reach for your dreams, but plan for your company to survive long enough to see those dreams become a reality.

Real World Application

Be careful what you ask for. Having the best-equipped shop is the dream of every manager. Before you decide to make a major investment or even ask your boss for approval to do so, however, you need to think it through carefully. Many companies have invested themselves right into bankruptcy by buying too much, too soon.

In my first job in retail service management, I had the great fortune of having a general manager who allowed me to run "my" shop, but was quick to make me face the tough questions and justify to him and the owner why I wanted to make changes or major expenditures. In my enthusiasm as a new, young manager, I excitedly told him about the new alignment machine that we "just *had* to have." He calmly, but seriously, looked me directly in the eyes and asked, "What can you do with this equipment that we cannot do now?" He followed that by a second, and more pointed, question, "How much additional business will this piece of equipment generate, and based on that how long will it take to pay for itself?"

His questions stunned me. I was not prepared and did not have good answers to address his concerns. I needed to go back and do a careful analysis to answer them. This, however, turned out to be some of the best advice I ever received to help me determine the value of any investment, whether professional or personal.

As a responsible manager you need to analyze thoroughly before you consider making a major investment. Careful research is required. This will lead you to make a sound decision and a plan to generate a return on any new investment that makes it a good business decision. It is important to realize that in many cases, the cost of an investment in fixed assets (tools, equipment, additional space) is the tipping point that transforms a previously profitable operation into a money-losing one.

SUMMARY

After a general overview of the many and varied resources that are essential to start up and operate an automotive repair shop, it is clear that from the physical resources viewpoint an automotive repair shop is a complex business. Significant investment is required to provide and adequately equip the facilities required to succeed in today's highly competitive automotive service industry. Much care and consideration must be given to make business decisions in these important areas.

The physical facilities of an automotive service business require a well-thought-out and planned combination of buildings and land. These facilities must then be built or modified to provide adequate space for repairing cars and for other purposes. Providing space for the essential nonrepair support services must also be a part of the plan.

An efficient repair facility, however, is more than a building and land. It is not functional until it is outfitted with sophisticated technical equipment and tools required to repair vehicles. Further, additional equipment and tools must be added to allow the service support personnel to do their jobs effectively.

All these factors must be carefully considered and planned for to build an efficiently functioning and competitive shop in today's marketplace. Each resource must be provided in the right amounts to meet the market needs without overbuilding and overspending. The investment required to build or rent and properly equip a shop is substantial. The cost to equip the shop further adds to that investment. The financial risk involved is substantial.

PRACTICING THE PRINCIPLES

1. A typically sized shop repair stall is
   a. 200 square feet.
   b. 300 square feet.
   c. 400 square feet.
   d 500 square feet.
2. Along with the technical tools and equipment needed in a shop, you must also have which of the following to be able to function in today's market
   a. phones, computers, copiers, fax machines.
   b. guard dogs, security police, fire engines.
   c. tools and equipment.
   d. all of the above.
   e. none of the above.
3. Those essential functions that must be performed above and beyond actually working on cars are called
   a. business expenses.
   b. nonproductive workers.
   c. lot boys.
   d. support functions.
4. Beyond having enough space and doing quality repairs, a shop should.
   a. have curb appeal.
   b. have adequate signage.
   c. project a professional image.
   d. all of the above.
5. A support area that can require a significant amount of facility space and an investment of financial resources but directly helps to speed up the repair process is
   a. a good telephone system and fax machine.
   b. parts inventory and storage.
   c. a good shop drainage system.
   d. a clean service drive-thru area.
6. Which of the following could you possibly eliminate to save money?
   a. some of the overhead doors.
   b. a customer entrance.
   c. a parts storage area.
   d. all of the above.
7. You cannot fail to plan for which of the following pieces of equipment in a shop?
   a. an alignment rack.
   b. a diagnostic scope.
   c. a car wash.
   d. an exhaust system.
8. If you were looking to open an eight-bay shop in your town, what is the minimum size of building (square feet) that you would need to fit the repair area only?
9. Based on Question 8, what is the minimum building total square footage that you would look for to house your entire shop operation?
10. Your new boss has charged you with coming up with an equipment budget for her brand-new two-bay tire store. She has told you that the shop will be doing front-end alignments as well as tire mounting and balancing. Using the Internet and/or any other sources of your choice, provide an item-by-item budget for the major pieces of equipment that the shop will need.

CHAPTER

3

Manpower Resources

CHAPTER OBJECTIVES

- To define the different job positions that are needed in the service shop
- To explain the job responsibilities of each of the service employees
- To distinguish the unique combination of knowledge and skills needed to perform each of the service jobs.

KEY TERMS

service cashier
dispatcher
claims administrator
flat-rate manuals
shop foreman
service advisor
lead technician
porter
parts specialist
technicians
customer relations specialist
service manager
service director

Introduction

The most valuable resource of any company is its people. The automotive service industry is no exception to this rule. Although the owner must make a substantial investment in facilities, equipment, and tools, the product of the service shop—labor sales—is not generated without a host of qualified, motivated employees. In this section we will look at the different job responsibilities that people must perform in an efficient automotive repair shop. To gain a better understanding of the diversity of talents and skills that are required in the automotive service shop, we will hone in on the varied responsibilities that employees in each of the jobs must shoulder and the types of knowledge and skills that they must possess to effectively perform their respective jobs.

Not all shops can afford to have one or more people doing each of these individual jobs. The job titles and descriptions listed in this chapter are an example of how the work may be distributed in a large automotive service operation. Depending on the size of the organization, the number of people performing the different jobs within the service shop will vary greatly. In a small, two-bay service station there may be a total of only three employees. In a mega-dealership service department there may be 80 to 100 employees. No matter how large or small the size of the shop, however, all of these job responsibilities must be performed for a shop to compete in the marketplace.

In a small shop, individuals need to be flexible and perform a variety of different jobs. In a large shop, there will be one or more individuals assigned to do each separate task. In some companies, large or small, the job responsibilities may be recombined in different ways. All these tasks, however, must be assigned and completed in all service shops, small or large. As you will learn, service is not simply a matter of fixing cars.

Service Cashier

Job Responsibilities

Service Cashier
Person responsible for collecting payment from customers upon completion of repairs and for the final processing of payments and repair records.

The **service cashier** carries out some very important functions in the service operation. The general responsibilities of the service cashier are to

- Review and calculate the service invoice
- Notify customers once the repairs are completed
- Maintain a filing system for paperwork
- Greet the customers when they arrive to pick up their vehicles
- Process payment for the repairs
- Provide the customer with copies of service records and a receipt for payment

The service cashier is extremely important to the success of the service operation. The cashier has face-to-face contact with customers. Therefore the impression of professionalism and caring that the cashier leaves with the customer strongly influences the impression the customer has of the entire service organization. Because the cashier's meeting with the customer is the final step of the service process, the cashier has the unique responsibility for leaving the last impression on the customer. The outcome of this encounter can strongly influence overall customer satisfaction and markedly affect the customer's decision to return for service in the future.

Skills and Abilities Required

As indicated by the list of tasks given earlier, the service cashier must possess a wide range of skills to be effective. These skills include those in the fields of accounting, filing, organization of paperwork, cashiering, and direct customer communications.

Dispatcher

Job Responsibilities

 **Dispatcher**
Evaluates repair order information and assigns the repairs to technicians with the goals of meeting stated deadlines and making the best use of the available technical skills.

The **dispatcher** is the one who manages the daily workflow in the shop and is responsible for the distribution of work throughout the shop. In a typical shop environment the repair orders, when written up by the service advisors, are forwarded to the dispatcher. The dispatcher is held accountable to know what work has been promised, the number of technicians available and the skills they possess, and the available amount of time each technician has available. Ultimately, he is responsible to get all the work out correctly and on time every day.

The dispatcher's ability to assign the right work to the right people at the right time has a profound impact on the productivity of the shop and of the individual technicians. The shop's entire workload—the paperwork and the demands of the customers, the technicians, and the managers—funnels through him. Even though few customers ever come in direct contact with a dispatcher or even know that such a job exists, their satisfaction and the ultimate success of the shop lie in the dispatcher's hands.

The dispatcher must also think on his feet. More often than not, situations change unexpectedly in the shop. Some of the situations a dispatcher may face on a typical workday include: the technician that the shop is counting on becomes ill, the job that should have been simple turns out to take three times than what was originally anticipated, the parts that are usually in stock have to be purchased and delivered from across town on short notice. The dispatcher's success and, ultimately, the shop's success depend on his readiness and willingness to adjust on the fly and make the necessary changes in the work schedule to make the best out of what resources he has available.

Skills and Abilities Required

The dispatcher must be highly organized. He touches and significantly affects every single transaction that goes through the shop daily. His decision-making ability determines how efficiently the shop runs and, therefore, the shop's productivity.

Although the dispatcher does not have to be an expert technician, he needs to have a good working knowledge of the technical aspects of automobiles. Only with this knowledge, and a clear understanding of the capabilities and skills of each of the shop's technicians, can he effectively decide what to prioritize and how to distribute the work to maximize shop efficiency. In addition to this technical knowledge, he also needs to possess a keen ability to organize, reorganize, and adapt to changing situations.

The dispatcher needs to maintain his composure and ability to think logically under pressure. Because of the high likelihood of changing situations and encountering unexpected delays, he needs the focus of a chess player—to think many moves in advance and willingly accept the challenge when an unexpected situation arises.

Claims Administrator (Booker)

Job Responsibilities

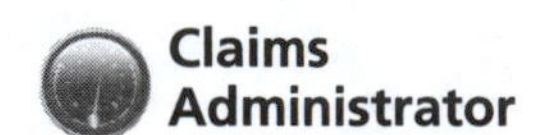

Claims Administrator

Person responsible for determining the proper labor operation codes, assigning flat-rate times to a repair order, and processing technician pay based on the explanation provided on the repair document.

The **claims administrator** is responsible for evaluating the repair order and determining what the technician should be paid for the repairs. In some organizations the term "booker" is used as the description of this job because the primary task of a claims administrator is to evaluate the repairs done and pay the technician by making out a pay slip that goes on the technician's weekly payroll record (book).

This job is very complex because the administrator does not normally have face-to-face contact with the customer, who identifies her service requirements; the service advisor, who has written the repair order stating what needs to be done; or the technician, who actually performs the repairs. Claims administrators must depend solely on the repair order documentation. Through reviewing the written explanation of the customer's repair requirements, the notations from the advisor for the work that was approved, and the technician's explanation of what was done, the claims administrator has to evaluate the facts and make decisions. What was requested? What was authorized? What was done? How much is the repair worth (in labor hours)? At this point the assignment of labor hours may sound arbitrary, but it is not. The service administrator has several tools to help him in his decision-making process.

Automotive repair shops depend upon independent authorities to provide them with books of labor standards time guides that they can use to make sure that they are charging the customers a fair and consistent price for a needed or requested repair. This ensures that the customer is charged a fee that is related to the actual time that the repair will take and is comparable to what other customers will be charged there or at another competitive shop in the area. Further, these labor standards assure technicians that the amount that they will be paid is fair and consistent.

There are several labor standards time guides. Every shop will have one set of these guides to establish the average time to be charged and paid for all customer-paid labor operations. If the shop also performs warranty work (dealership or fleet), the manufacturers will require the shop to use a unique set of manufacturer-produced guides that is specific to their products.

Flat-Rate Manuals

Books that provide labor job descriptions and standard times allowed to perform those repair operations for most common repairs.

The labor standards time guides, often referred to as **flat-rate manuals**, are complex and cover thousands of repair operations with unique sets of labor times for various vehicle makes and models. These guides provide make- and model-specific information because the design of different vehicles, and therefore the time required to access and service systems on those vehicles, varies greatly. Each of these manuals is comparable in size and complexity to a large dictionary. Because of their continued growth in size many companies now also offer these time guides in CD or DVD format. To be effective at claims administration, the administrator must be very comfortable using these manuals quickly and accurately.

The ability of the claims administrator to effectively perform this task is essential to the success of the service shop. If the administrator is not thorough in his research and in proper assignment of labor operation codes (especially in warranty reimbursement claims), the claim payment will likely be rejected. Further, if his documentation is not thorough, the amount of labor that the shop can legitimately claim and therefore charge the customer or manufacturer will be reduced. This will cause the shop and the technician to earn less than they have rightfully earned for the services performed.

Skills and Abilities Required

The claims administrator requires an individual who is very detail oriented. Although the administrator must be fluent in his understanding of the systems of a vehicle, he is not required to be a technician. His responsibilities are first, to read and understand the information received from the customer, service advisor, and technician. Then, he has to search through the flat-rate manuals and, if necessary, technical bulletins to identify repair operations that best match up with what was done.

The ability to accurately and thorough research the manuals for every claim presented to him is essential. The administrator must be willing and able to spend time learning to completely understand the flat-rate manual information system, so that he is comfortable with doing research in these publications. The claims administrator is responsible for assigning labor times and operation numbers for every vehicle that passes through the shop. In order to process this volume of paperwork daily, the administrator must quickly look up and decipher information and then post it completely and accurately. The skills needed closely parallel those required by a librarian (research), service advisor (technical understanding), and accountant (working with numbers and preparing precise documents).

Shop Foreman

Job Responsibilities

The **shop foreman** is the on-the-field coordinator of the day-to-day activities in the repair shop. The foreman works with the technicians in the shop, assisting them with diagnosis of difficult problems. He provides guidance and additional brainpower and a second set of hands to assist experienced technicians. He provides on-the-job training for younger, less experienced technicians. The foreman works with service advisors to help verify and pinpoint the cause of customer complaints to assist them in developing a reasonable estimate of the cost of repairs. He often is actively involved in the most difficult technical problems that the others in the shop are unable to resolve. Overall, he assists in the coordination of the resources in the shop to keep repairs moving and ensure that employees are productive. Finally, in many cases, he is responsible for double-checking repairs before a car is returned to the customer to verify (quality check) that the repairs have been completed correctly. In a shop working under a team system or support group structure, the function of the shop foreman may be performed by a team leader or lead technician of each work group.

Shop Foreman
Responsible for overall technical supervision of shop operations including assisting in diagnosis and repairs across the shop as needed.

Skills and Abilities Required

The shop foreman must possess a very high level of technical skills. Further, he needs not only to know how to perform repairs accurately and completely but also to have an in-depth understanding of the why of repairs, an understanding of the underlying theory of operation of the various systems. He does not necessarily have to be the fastest at performing repairs but must be the best at fixing them right the first time. A great deal of his time is spent assisting others in doing this and then verifying that this goal has been accomplished.

The shop foreman must be a good communicator. He must know more than how to make the repairs and why; he must clearly and consistently help others to learn these principles. To do this, he must be a good teacher. He must demonstrate how to do the job the right way. His reputation for thoroughness, accuracy, and excellence has a profound effect on the quality of the overall production of the shop. He must be the living example of these attributes.

Service Advisor

Job Responsibilities

Service Advisor
The main customer contact in the service department responsible for determining customer needs and wants and preparing the repair order document.

The **service advisor** is the front line employee and the face of the company in the automotive service shop. He is the one that the customer contacts and works most directly with throughout the repair process. He *is* the company in the eyes of the customer. The service advisor's major job responsibilities are to

- Respond to customer inquiries on the telephone, online, and in person
- Schedule appointments based on the availability of resources to perform the repairs
- Write up repair orders to accurately reflect the customers' concerns and requests
- Perform general diagnosis of complaints through observation and questioning
- Recommend needed services to customer based on time, mileage, and observation
- Prepare accurate repair estimates and obtain customer approval to proceed with repairs
- Notify the customer of repair progress
- Verify the completion and accuracy of repairs and bills

The service advisor must possess a wide range of skills and abilities in order to perform all of these tasks. The most important of these skills is the ability to be highly organized and to communicate clearly and concisely with customers and fellow employees. The service advisor must have a good working knowledge of automotive systems.

The advisor is often called upon to be a translator of sorts. He is required to communicate with the customers in a level of technical language that they can understand. This ability enables him to probe the customer for important details that will assist in verifying and pinpointing the real concerns and needed repair issues. He must communicate in more technical terms to the technician, providing general guidance on what needs to be repaired. Further, once the root cause of the complaint has been identified, he is again responsible to translate the technical information from the technician back into layman's terms so that he can explain to the customer what is needed and why.

In addition to the technical knowledge, the advisor must also possess a great deal of sales and marketing skills. He is the main contact point for suggesting and selling needed maintenance items to the customer. He is also responsible for putting together an estimate for repairs to address the customer's concerns and calling the customer to explain the expected cost of repairs and obtain approval to proceed with the work. This often takes a great deal of customer relations skills and salesmanship skills.

Skills and Abilities Required

The advisor's job requires him to perform a wide range of functions. Because of the range of activities that he must consistently perform, the service advisor must possess organizational and time management skills. The typical advisor will interact with 30 to 40 customers each day and write up, follow up, and process about 20 repair orders each day. This requires that he be very organized and able to multitask.

Lead Technician

Job Responsibilities

The **lead technician** is the normally the most qualified master technician in the shop. Depending on the organizational structure, the shop may not have a lead technician but rely solely on the shop foreman to perform the lead technician's responsibilities. Whereas in a shop that pays each technician based on individual performance there may be one lead technician, in shops working under a team system or support group structure there will generally be one lead technician per group or team. In a team or support group shop, the person in this position may also be referred to as the "team leader."

Lead Technician
Technician responsible for resolving the most difficult concerns and directing the efforts of less experienced technicians.

The lead technician is the jack of all trades and an ace at accurately diagnosing a wide range of problems. He typically works with two sets of responsibilities: resolving the most difficult problems and guiding and directing others within his work group to efficiently resolve the more simple problems.

Skills and Abilities Required

The lead technician must possess a great deal of technical expertise. He also generally has extensive industry experience that gives him real-life knowledge to complement his theoretical understanding of the principles and practices of automotive repair. It is rare for anyone to be selected as lead technician unless he or she is ASE Master Certified and has a minimum of five years of full-time field experience. Further, the lead technician is typically the most heavily trained individual in the shop, having been selected to attend and pass most of the update training seminars supported by the repair shop or manufacturer.

A high level of knowledge and skills are essential to be a lead technician, but unless he is capable of sharing that knowledge with others, he is ineffective. He needs to be a leader. He needs to lead the team by setting an example of dedication and high work standards. He also needs to have the ability and willingness to help provide local training to fellow employees that will improve their productivity and that of the entire organization.

Porter

Job Responsibilities

Porter
Moves and cleans vehicles and assists in general upkeep of vehicles and the shop as directed.

Although the responsibilities of a service **porter** may vary from shop to shop, the service porter is typically responsible for performing tasks such as

- Shuttling customer vehicles from the service write-up area back to the storage lot
- Providing rides to customers to get them to work or home while their car is being repaired and bringing them back to the shop once the repairs are completed
- Cleaning and/or detailing customer vehicles after repairs and new vehicles before retail delivery
- Shuttling customer vehicles back to the service pick-up area from the storage lot when the customer arrives to pick up the vehicle
- Running errands to pick up customers, parts, tools, and equipment as needed to support the overall flow of work in the shop
- Doing miscellaneous chores around the shop, including housekeeping duties

Skills and Abilities Required

Although the porter's job does not require a great deal of previous training or education, it is, nonetheless, a very important part of assuring the smooth flow of production in the shop, the timely completion of work, and the positive attitude of customers about being properly cared for when they come in for service. To do this wide variety of tasks well, the porter must have a good driving record, a pleasant personality to deal with co-workers and customers, and the ability to be a self-directed worker. He has to be an individual with multiple abilities and a desire to follow tasks through to a successful completion.

Parts Specialist

Job Responsibilities

Although not all shops have an internal parts department, all automotive service shops need to have access to parts to perform many common repairs

REAL WORLD APPLICATION

Many shops, unfortunately, view the position of porter as a dead-end job. It is, therefore, also the position in a shop where management spends the most time and effort addressing attendance issues and in dealing with high employee turnover.

Fortunately, shops that are more progressive have found out that the porter position is not a dead-end job; it is a good steppingstone from which to cultivate long-term employees. After all, if you are looking to have to train someone in-house to do the right things the way that you want them done, why not start with someone that you know who has already demonstrated some basic employability skills through his attendance and positive attitude?

What a shop typically wants when they decide to grow their own employees are individuals with the ability to learn, the desire to get ahead, the commitment to show up consistently on time ready to work, and who are dedicated to long-term employment in the organization. Who is better qualified to have demonstrated these characteristics than your porter?

and, therefore, often employ a **parts specialist.** The parts department may range from someone who simply contacts local parts stores to identify parts and may, on occasion, run to pick up parts to a full-scale parts operation that inventories hundreds of thousands of dollars of mechanical and collision repair parts and is, in its own right, a profit center within the company. In the case of the complete internal parts department, parts specialists are responsible not only for identifying and providing the proper parts, but also for forecasting the needs so that the company's inventory is able to fill most of the needs of the service department.

Parts Specialist
Identifies, locates, provides, and properly prices out parts as needed by the service technician.

In general, the function of the parts specialist is to assist in identifying what parts are needed to perform the repairs for a specific application and to have them available in a timely manner. Without accurate identification of the right part and availability at the right time, the amount of delays that are likely to occur will cost the shop profit and, very likely result in the loss of many customers.

Skills and Abilities Required

The parts specialist must be detail oriented. The ability to consistently identify the correct part to fit the right vehicle requires thoroughness and accuracy. He needs to research parts manuals very quickly to consistently pinpoint the right part. He must then locate the part and provide it at a reasonable price in a timely manner. Causing delays in providing the parts will cost the shop income because of unproductive waiting time and may ultimately result in the loss of the job and/or the customer.

In a shop that has an internal parts operation, the parts specialist must develop and maintain a real-time system of inventory control. This system not only organizes the parts by location so that they are easily found, it maintains a dynamic database of demand and availability that is an essential management tool to keep the inventory up-to-date so that it can meet current shop demands. The parts specialist must possess business analysis and accounting skills because there is a significant investment that is tied up in the parts on the shelves. Unless he or she is able to regularly analyze and evaluate the inventory patterns and make changes to keep the inventory relevant to the shop's needs, the inventory will become obsolete resulting in a significant financial loss to the organization.

Technician

Job Responsibilities

The automotive **technicians** in the shop are the heart of the shop. They are the only productive employees in the shop. Now, before you get defensive about this statement, please understand its intent. Because the service technicians are the only ones who are directly responsible for *producing* the sole major product that the service shop sells—labor—they are the only productive employees.

Technicians
Individuals responsible for verifying customer concerns, pinpointing the cause, and resolving the customer automotive repair concerns in a safe and timely manner.

The primary responsibility of the service technicians is to perform specific diagnosis to verify the complaint and pinpoint the cause. Based on this information he is responsible for developing an estimate of cost and time needed to resolve the concerns. Upon receiving approval, he performs the necessary repairs, verifies that the work completed has resolved the customer concerns, produces a detailed written record of what was done on the vehicle, and makes sure that the vehicle is returned to its original condition of cleanliness.

Skills and Abilities Required

Most shops require that technicians possess a minimum of high-school technical training or its equivalent in direct industry experience before being hired. The best preparation to become a service technician, as endorsed by all the major automotive manufacturers and the U.S. Department of Labor, is the completion of a post–high-school automotive technical program of technical and academic training.

Many individual shops require that technicians earn ASE certification in the repair specialties that they work in and then keep those certifications up to date. Further, because of the rapid and constantly changing technology in the automotive industry, technicians are expected to attend annual training provided by manufacturers, tool and equipment providers, and outside training organizations to maintain knowledge of current and emerging vehicle systems. The willingness and commitment to lifelong learning is an essential ingredient to the long-term career success of the service technician.

Customer Relations Specialist

Job Responsibilities

Customer satisfaction is a key to repeat sales and the ultimate success of any service operation. Therefore, many service shops contact customers after a service visit to ensure that they had a satisfactory experience and to identify and resolve any problems. This function may be performed internally or performed by an outside service.

Contacts customers after they have picked up vehicles from service department to assure that they are satisfied with their service experience and resolves or refers upward any questions or concerns.

The **customer relations specialist** takes a proactive approach to assuring customer satisfaction. This is in contrast to the old-school philosophy where satisfaction was assumed unless a complaint was received. Shops have learned that by taking a proactive approach, they can head off most major problems and learn about and resolve minor ones that might never have been reported but that could have resulted in the end of a relationship with a valued customer.

Skills and Abilities Required

The customer satisfaction specialist will generally contact customers using the telephone. Also, she is likely to occasionally encounter an upset customer who may even be verbally abusive. Therefore, essential skills for an individual in this role are excellent people skills, customer complaint handling skills, and general telephone etiquette and communication skills.

Service Manager

Job Responsibilities

Service Manager
Supervises, motivates, and directs all personnel in the service repair department.

The **service manager** is responsible for the smooth coordination of all of the jobs and functions in the repair shop. Unlike what occurs in most Fortune 500 companies, management of a service department is not handled by a

Real World Application

The value of performing proactive customer relations activities, such as customer service follow-up contacts, cannot be overstated. Experience from both the wholesale (manufacturer) viewpoint and the retail (dealer or service shop) viewpoint indicates that when a customer is dissatisfied and seeks a resolution, it is important who the customer perceives as the one making the efforts to resolve his or her concerns.

If the customer feels that he has to go to an outside agency (such as manufacturer, Better Business Bureau, or local TV station) to get the proper attention to his concerns, he will have strong positive feelings about that agency but most likely will abandon the shop that caused his problem once it is resolved. On the other hand, if the local shop has created an environment where the customer feels that the shop has reached out to identify the problems and is willing to resolve them, the customer perception of the shop is much different.

Rather than this incident being an indictment that the shop is incompetent and uncaring, it can be changed to one of "we all make mistakes" and result in the customer's willingness to give the shop a second chance. Because repeat customers and their good will and person-to-person testimonials about your company are the best advertising, you can get great value by instituting activities that resolve customer concerns and leave them with a positive perception of your company.

group of specialized managers who each has a narrow field of expertise and responsibilities.

The automotive service manager is not a specialist; he is required to be a generalist. He is responsible for possessing and exercising a variety of skills that span the entire range of managerial talents and abilities. The service manager's main functions are coordination, motivation, and leadership. He is the head coach, and, in many organizations, upper management expects the service manager to be, in effect, operating his department as a company within a company.

Skills and Abilities Required

Unlike large corporations, where the various management tasks are clearly divided among a crew of managers that work in narrow job responsibilities (such as customer relations, marketing, sales, financial planning), the service manager, in effect, likes the sole proprietor of a small business. He must possess a wide range of skills and abilities to perform a variety of tasks on a daily basis. These tasks include, but are not limited to

- Operational and strategic planning
- General management and leadership
- Financial measurement and analysis
- Organization and time management
- Customer relations and complaint handling
- Employee relations, hiring, discipline, and firing
- Marketing, merchandising, and sales
- Workplace safety and other legal issues

Service Director

Job Responsibilities

The title and responsibilities of **service director** often only occur in larger repair shops and dealerships. The responsibilities of the service director are, in

Service Director
Supervises, motivates, and directs all personnel in the service department, body shop, and parts department.

many ways, similar to that of the service manager. The major difference, however, is in the scope of responsibility. Whereas the service manager is only responsible for one profit center, the service department or repair shop, the service director is responsible for the oversight and operation of three distinct and very unique profit centers: the service repair shop, the parts department, and the body shop.

Skills and Abilities Required

The knowledge, skills, and abilities of the service director include all those identified for the service manager. He has to do everything the service manager does, but on a larger scale. In addition, regardless of his previous area of expertise that has allowed him to rise to this level of management, he must develop and maintain a solid working knowledge of the unique characteristics and finer points of the three different departments under his control. He needs to be an excellent leader and mediator to maintain a sense of fairness and balance between the operations and the egos present in all these operations. Finally, he needs to possess the political savvy and discretion to interact with the other directors and supervisors within the organization and with the owners to advocate on behalf of his departments.

SUMMARY

The service repair department is a very complex system. To run efficiently, it requires personnel with a wide variety of skills and abilities. Although the service technicians are the only ones in the shop who actually produce the "product" of the service shop—that is, labor sales—the skills of the technicians must be supplemented by a supporting cast that can perform the other needed tasks.

Even with the best technicians ready, willing, and able to perform the repairs, very little happens in a shop unless the support activities are effectively conducted. Service advisors need to be there to answer phone inquiries, to make appointments, and to greet the customers and write up their repair requests when they arrive. Similar to the advisor, who is the public face of the service operation, those providing the other essential support services are as essential in making the service experience positive and profitable.

Every shop needs to provide this entire range of services to remain competitive. Although in small shops several of the jobs listed may be combined and performed by a single person, they, nonetheless, must be done. Every shop, no matter how large or small, needs to be customer friendly and efficient in order to be successful. It takes the entire range of jobs and skills discussed to ensure that it happens consistently.

PRACTICING THE PRINCIPLES

1. The owner of the company has received a customer complaint indicating that the cost for her recent repairs was far more than the initial estimate. Which service employee is responsible for preparing a complete and accurate estimate?
   a. the service advisor.
   b. the service manager.
   c. the technician.
   d. all of the above.
2. When questioned about her overall customer satisfaction, the owner says "I really do not know for sure, but I very rarely receive any calls from upset customers." Which of these statements is most likely to be true?
   a. The shop has a very high level of customer satisfaction.
   b. The shop does not have anyone doing customer follow-up contacts.

c. The service manager is doing a good job of hiding the customer complaints.
d. Two of the above choices listed above are likely to be true.

3. Joe, the lead technician, is very dissatisfied. He storms in to see Ralph, the owner. "I am underpaid and underappreciated. I am the only productive employee around here and yet you say that you cannot afford to pay me more. Why don't you just get rid of some of the other nonproductive people and just pay me what they earn?" A likely response from Ralph should be
   a. "Joe, I need those other people to help do all of the other work that needs to be done besides simply fixing cars."
   b. "Joe, I agree that you are the only one producing labor sales, but without the others there would be very few cars here for you to work on."
   c. "Joe, you can make yourself a raise faster than I can by simply producing a few more flat-rate hours each day and that will make us both happy."
   d. All of the above.

4. Every service shop should have someone responsible for customer satisfaction follow-up contacts because
   a. you have got to have some sort of job in the shop for the owner's son to do.
   b. customers usually tell you when they are not happy with their repairs or their bill.
   c. customers usually will not tell you if they are unhappy, they just go somewhere else and tell their friends.
   d. you need to be sure that most of your customers are not satisfied.

5. The service director needs to possess a wide range of skills including
   a. a working understanding of the three departments under his control.
   b. being a highly skilled diagnostic technician.
   c. ability to handle the most difficult customer and employee concerns.
   d. both B and C.
   e. both A and C.

In Questions 1–5 match the job titles with the description that best fits their job duties and indicate your choice on the line provided to the left of the job title.

____ 6. Dispatcher	a. distributes work to shop
____ 7. Customer relations specialist	b. processes final payment for services
____ 8. Automotive technician	c. contacts customers to assure satisfaction
____ 9. Service advisor	d. performs service repairs
____10. Cashier	e. prepares the customer repair order

CHAPTER

4

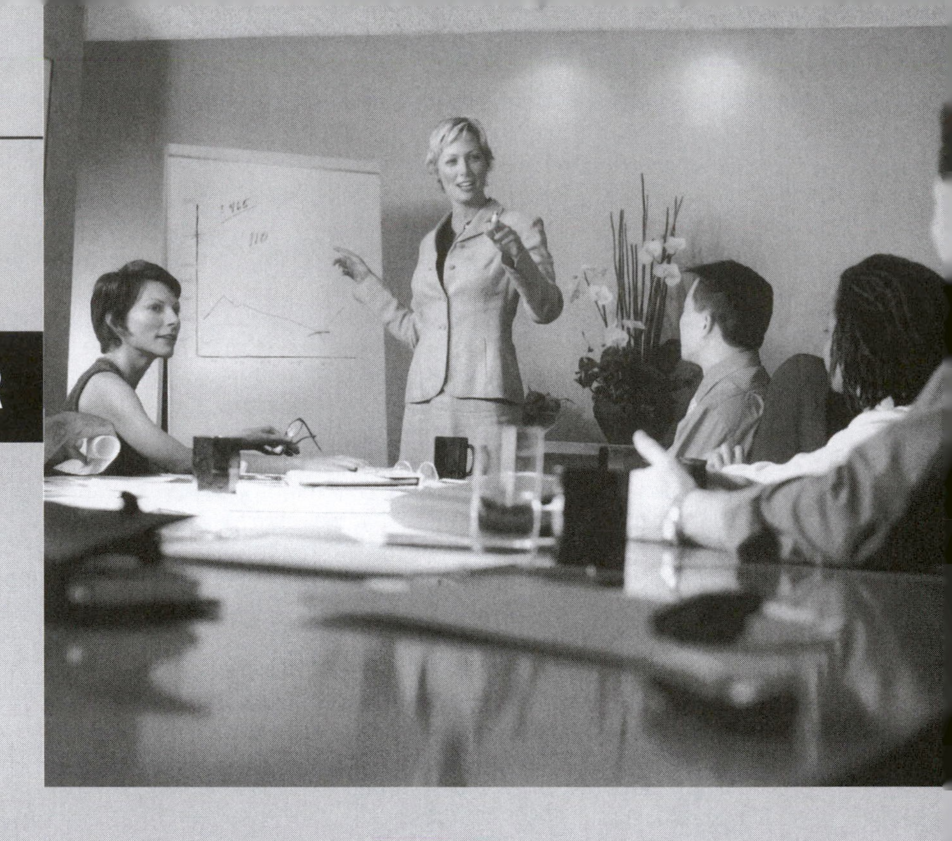

The Service Workflow

CHAPTER OBJECTIVES

- To define the traditional management view of the service operation
- To explain the service operation when viewed as a system
- To differentiate the steps in the repair process
- To develop and chart the flow of work as it proceeds through the service operation

KEY TERMS

traditional view
systems view
inputs
process
outputs
feedback
systems thinking
repair process
appointment
reception
work distribution
work performance
quality assurance
invoicing
warranty administrator
delivery
cashiering
follow-up
flowcharting

Introduction

If you ask an automotive repair shop employee to describe the shop's organization and how the shop works, he would probably start off by giving you a list of all the employees and their job titles, who reports to whom, and who is in charge of what. That very typical viewpoint of the organization is based on the traditional organization chart. In this chapter we will look beyond names and titles so that you can begin to see a much more exciting way of looking at the organization, as a living, operating system. We can then expand on that idea by diagramming the typical workflow of a service transaction. Viewing things in this manner, I hope that you will develop a different view of how the organization actually works and how to better monitor it, manage it, lead it, and assure its success.

Traditional Management View

When someone asks you to explain your company or the department you work for, your first response would likely be to explain in terms of its organizational chain of command. In an automotive service repair shop (such as a dealership service department), you might describe the department as shown in Figure 4-1. In the **traditional view**, an organization is defined by its organizational chart, which is a necessary tool for defining the hierarchy and politics of an organization. It outlines the basic chain of command within the company's structure. It graphically portrays the path of authority and how decisions and authority flow down through the management hierarchy to the workers on the floor.

Traditional View

Looking at the organization based on its organizational chart and job titles within the organization.

The organizational chart does very little to explain the day-to-day operations of an organization, however. Knowing the organizational chart may

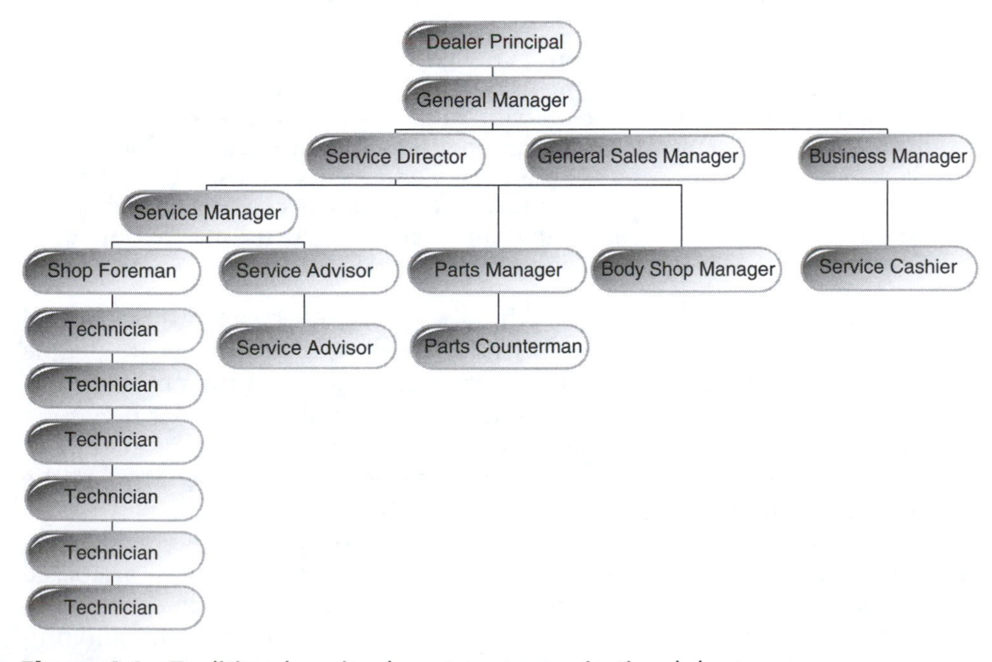

Figure 4-1 Traditional service department organizational chart

help you to know whom you, or a customer, should go to complain to *next* if you are dissatisfied, but it does nothing to help unravel the mystery of why things did not, or do not, work properly. Because the organizational chart does not explain how work actually gets done it is really of little value in helping you to problem solve and correct performance problems within the organization.

This most commonly used management view has one additional weakness: it is solely focused on people. This is not meant to imply that the people are unimportant. People are the most valuable asset any company has. It is shortsighted, however, when any organization looks at the operation based *only* on people. When a company sees itself and its performance as solely a function of the people that it has, there can be some really great news—or there can be some really bad news. If the company succeeds all of the credit is given to the employees (generally the supervisors who led the team), but when it fails, the blame falls solely on the employees.

Let us look at this management approach a little bit more closely. Is it really fair? Have you ever been in a situation where you were blamed for something that was beyond your control? If the situation was beyond your control and was really nobody else's fault, how could it have happened? Why were you held accountable? The answer is that in the traditional view of management, people are viewed as the solution—and also the sole cause of every problem. In this management approach, failure to perform is *always* a people problem. Here is an example.

> Joe has just been hired as service advisor at Mel's Service. He is one of two advisors working at this shop that employs 24 technicians. During his first few days on the job, he notices that work seems to be very slow. He is only getting about ten customers to write up each day, and the technicians seem to be grumbling constantly about the lack of work. They are all sitting on their toolboxes after lunch with nothing to do. Each time the boss comes by Joe sees the disgusted look on his face. He hardly says a word to anyone. Joe asks his fellow advisor if he treats all the advisors like this. She indicates that she has only been there for a month.
>
> Finally, Joe's feelings of job insecurity get to him. He asks the boss to sit down during his lunch break to talk about "things." Joe very cautiously approaches the topic of his concerns with the low morale and low performance of the shop. It does not take long for the boss to get Joe's message. He responds, "Well, that's why I hired you. I've been through five service advisors in the last year trying to finally find someone who can really sell service and get this shop back to running the way it did in the past. I believe you're the man to turn it around, Joe. I hope you agree. Now get back to work!"

Based on this example it appears that Joe's boss may be using a traditional management approach; he believes that all successes or failures are people issues. It sounds like he has tried over and over again to fix the problem (five advisors in one year)—or, at least, he has tried the only thing that he knows how to do. He clearly believes that failure to perform is a people problem. His pattern of behavior also indicates that his first rule of management is "Get the job done, or else!" What other possibilities are there?

As we have previously discussed, the traditional view of the organization and the traditional style of management that often accompanies it are based solely on the performance of individuals. Is there another way? In the remainder of this chapter we will explore a different management viewpoint and philosophy that takes into account factors that go beyond mere personalities and personal skills. It views the operation as a system and considers the fact that some of the problems that occur may go beyond people issues.

The Systems View of an Organization

Systems View
Looking at the organization based on the workflows within the organization and taking into account the inputs, processes, and outputs of these workflows.

The **systems view** looks at the organization of a department by how work flows through the department. It is *not* based on the management hierarchy. It is based on the belief that although people play important roles in the system, the way things are organized and the way the work flows (or fails to flow) have a profound effect on overall performance.

An example of this can be seen on an automobile assembly line.

> All of the parts flow in from various points and join up with the cars as they slowly but smoothly progress down the line. Each worker performs his individual task, such as bolting on the mirrors or installing the seats, and all of these individuals work in concert. It is like a symphony with everyone playing his or her part—until something goes wrong. Because all the work flows down one well-defined path—the assembly line—a blockage or delay at any point from start to finish can stop "the music." All it takes is for the worker at station number 250 to run out of the proper lug nuts to fasten the right front wheel onto the car. The car cannot continue down the line and drive off of the end of the line with only three wheels on it!

In the previous example, the traditional management approach would be to blame the people first. After all, they are the ones responsible for making things happen. Using this type of management logic, the blame game could easily follow down the line as follows:

- It starts out as the assembly line worker's fault: "Why didn't he put the lugs on, it is *his* job?"
- Once it is determined that the assembly line worker was not at fault, the blame would be passed on to the person who was designated to keep the parts stocked at the workstation: "Why didn't *he* stock up the lug nut supply box on time?"
- Oh, you say that there were none left in the plant, then: "Why didn't *the truck driver* arrive on time to deliver more lugs?"
- The shipment was late: "Why didn't the supplier's *dispatcher* send the shipment sooner?"
- There was a shortage of stock at the plant. Well, then, "Why weren't the supplier's *workers* able to produce lug nuts faster to keep up with our demand?" and "Why did we choose *him* as our supplier?"

This example is a bit simplified, of course. However, it does make clear a very important point. What is the common link between all of these "reasons" for failure? Look at the italicized words for the answer. The answer lies in the fact that in every case the blame is placed first on the individuals (*he, she, the truck driver, the dispatcher, the workers*, and *the supplier*). Never has any consideration been given to the possibility that the cause goes beyond the individuals involved. In this case, even if it was learned that the supplier's truck had broken down, the next question would have been something like "*Who* was responsible for doing the maintenance on that truck?" Again, it is a 100 percent people-focused trail of accountability and blame.

In this scenario do you see any possibilities that the line coming to a halt was caused by something other than the workers? Are there other factors that might have prevented this stoppage? Is it possible that with some better planning a method might have been devised to allow work to keep on flowing down the production line?

Looking at operations in a much broader sense as a complex system that includes people, other resources, and even the way that the resources are organized attempts to take into account all of the factors that can affect performance. It is often called a systems approach, or systems viewpoint.

Let us take a look at what a simple system looks like. The basic systems model presented in Figure 4-2 shows the major components of any system. Any operation, whether it is an automotive service shop, a production line, a bank, or a college can be viewed as a system.

By looking at an operation or even a complex organization not by how it is structured but rather by how it gets work done, it is clear how things actually operate to produce the products and/or services that are the lifeblood of the organization. There are three basic components of every system. Let us take a brief look at what they are.

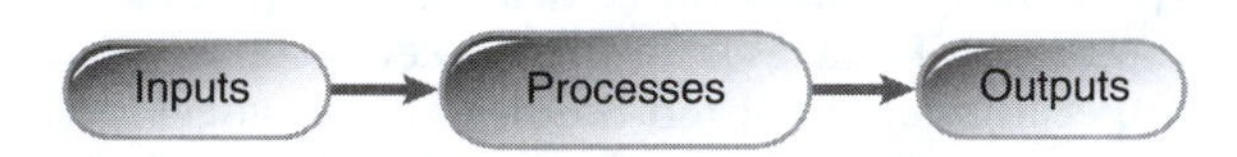

Figure 4-2 Basic systems model

Inputs

Inputs

All of the resources that are required for a system to be able to function.

Inputs are all of the resources that are required for the system to be able to function. Look at the automobile assembly line example again to get a better view of inputs. The raw ingredients, the 20,000 component parts of the car, the tools, the specialized equipment, the assembly line itself, the electricity to power the plant, and the manpower needed to assemble the car are inputs into this system. A shortage of any of these inputs will have an effect on the efficiency of the process—building a car.

The automotive repair process is a bit less complicated than the automotive assembly line. It does operate as a system, however, and requires that the proper inputs (resources) must be available if the repair process is to go forward and we are to produce anything of value. Efficient management strives to assure that the right resources are present in the right quantities at the right time, so the entire operation is more productive and profitable. Later in this chapter we use another management tool, flowcharting, to help you better understand the process and how to analyze and improve it.

Processes

Process

The series of actions and operations necessary to do work (produce a product or service).

Building an automobile is not a simple **process.** However, if you look at the simple systems model in Figure 4-2, you can see that from the big-picture viewpoint that this example follows the basic systems model. When you consider the hundreds of employees involved on the assembly line, the many outside vendors used to build the parts, and all of the employees and vendors that are involved in getting 20,000 parts to the same location and properly installed in the right place at the right time on the right vehicle, it is more than just a system, it is a miracle.

If you take the time to break down each of the activities at each of the places that all come together on the assembly line, you would see that every one of them can be described separately as a system. Each of these simple systems is, in turn, part of a larger, more complex system, which results in the largest system—the assembly plant system.

Outputs

The **outputs** of a system are the products or services that the system provides. In the example of the automobile assembly line the obvious product is new cars. Every system has an output. The output is the system's reason for existence.

Outputs
All of the products, services, and/or information produced by a system.

Automotive repair shops do not build anything. They do not produce a product. So what is their output? Their output is service. It is repairing vehicles to meet customers' requirements. Whether it is a satisfactory 30-minute oil change in 25 minutes or an overhauled engine that runs properly and is back on the road, as promised, in 10 days, both are examples of automotive service shop output.

Advanced Systems

The advanced system model (Figure 4-3) should look familiar to you. The core of the model is the basic systems model discussed earlier and shown in Figure 4-2. There is only one addition to the basic model, the addition of a feedback loop. This feedback, which is often overlooked, is an essential ingredient of continuous improvement. Let us discuss feedback a bit further.

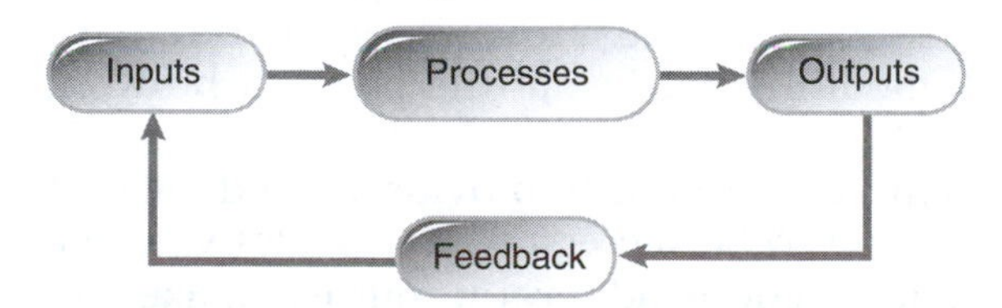

Figure 4-3 Advanced systems model

Feedback

You cannot make things better unless you know that they are not good. This is simple to say, but difficult to do. Many companies believe that they address this concern adequately: after all, they have a well-marked and well-lit customer service desk. Unfortunately, waiting for customers to verbally complain is not the only, or most efficient, way to find out what you need to change to provide quality products and services and, therefore, have satisfied customers. We will discuss this topic in greater depth in Chapter 19.

The idea of adding a **feedback** loop to the system takes the information gathered from being a by-product of the system that rarely occurs and is more rarely acknowledged into being information that is expected, counted on, and valued. Along with producing the intended product or service, you will also receive some form of feedback about whether you met the customer's expectations.

Feedback
Information generated as an output of the process that is used as an input for future work.

By intentionally taking this output (feedback) and funneling it back into the system as an additional input (information), you create an environment where you can constantly and consistently make things better each time through the cycle. The feedback may be positive, which reaffirms that you should continue doing things exactly the way you are currently doing them. It might be dissatisfaction that indicates that there are serious flaws in your processes. By acknowledging these problems and rapidly resolving them, you can save countless customers and countless dollars in warranty claims, returned products, and bad press. Actively seeking and using feedback is the best strategy to improve efficiency and overall customer satisfaction.

Systems Thinking

The beauty of looking at things as systems is that this method of looking operations and processes can be universally applied across a wide range of activities and industries. Further, and more important, by including *all* the resources that come into play, not just people, this perspective helps us view operations from a broader perspective. It gives us the opportunity to identify and fix the root cause of performance problems.

A foundational principle of systems thinking is that 80 percent of all problems are systems problems and only 20 percent are people problems. Using traditional management and organizational viewpoints, our only approach to improving performance is dealing 100 percent with a minor cause (20 percent), people. **Systems thinking** is a more holistic approach to viewing operations and performance. It allows you to improve existing systems and design new ones that will flow smoothly and increase productivity. It is based on looking at the organizational workflows and the resources required to make the processes within them flow smoothly, not just at the people who work within them.

Systems Thinking
An approach to viewing operations and performance based on workflows and the resources needed to make them work, not just the people who work in them.

The optimum goal of the systems approach is to provide a workflow that will allow our systems and our people to be successful. It provides valuable insights to help us move in the right direction and stay on course to make sure that we reach our objectives and prevents us from destroying our most valuable asset, our employees.

THEORY INTO PRACTICE 4-1

CASE

As a technician and then the shop foreman at a local shop, you have seen the shop go through five service managers in the past 3½ years. In each and every case the story is the same: "He came to us highly regarded but he just could not get the job done so we are going to have to replace him." The owner then turns to you and asks, "I would like to see you take over the job here as service manager. Interested?"

1. You decide

Based on the information provided in this chapter, what do you think is the reason the shop has had a high turnover of service managers?

2. You decide

Based on the information presented earlier, what would you want to see changed before you could feel comfortable taking the job as service manager?

The Repair Process

In Chapter 3 we discussed the different people who must come together with a variety of skills and abilities to make the automotive repair service operation work. Now we will move a step further and look at automotive repair as a process. The **repair process** takes into account each of the steps that must be completed to move from the start, where the customer determines that he needs or wants service, to the end, where we made sure that the repairs were done correctly and the customer is satisfied. In its simplest form the repair process goes through the following steps:

Repair Process

The series of steps or tasks necessary to resolve a request for service.

- Appointment
- Reception
- Work distribution
- Work performance
- Quality assurance
- Invoicing
- Delivery
- Cashiering
- Follow-up

Let us briefly discuss each of these steps to ensure that we understand their importance.

Appointment

Most repair shops work primarily on an **appointment** basis. This is done so that the shop can be certain that they have the resources available to quickly and efficiently provide services once the customer has arrived. Once the customer has determined that there is a need or desire for a service or repair, his or her first action is to contact the service shop to arrange a convenient time to have services performed. The majority of appointments are made by phone. However, some customers still prefer to come by to make an appointment face-to-face. Further, as Web-based communication continues to become more widespread, many shops are beginning to offer online appointment scheduling. Because we continue to move toward a more "wired" society, this trend is sure to continue to grow.

Appointment

A prearranged date and time to have service performed.

Reception

At the prearranged date and time, the customer arrives at the shop for the service appointment. During the **reception**, the responsible shop employee meets and greets the customer and gathers necessary information about needed services and repairs. This step in the process is important for customer satisfaction because it is during this (typically) face-to-face meeting that service personnel have the opportunity to discuss the requested services directly with the customer, verifying that they have an accurate and thorough understanding of what the customer needs and wants. Further, and no less important, it is at this time that the shop and the customer come to an initial agreement about what the cost for repairs will be and when the repairs are expected to be completed. All of this information is documented on the repair order.

Reception

The meeting, greeting, and initial contact between the customer and the service department in which the concerns and other requests for service are verified and an initial estimate provided.

Work Distribution

 **Work Distribution**
Scheduling and assignment of repair jobs to specific technicians based on careful evaluation of priorities and available physical and personnel resources.

Once the repair order has been generated, it is passed on to be evaluated and assigned. The **work distribution** step in an efficiently operated shop is much more than merely handing out the next repair in the stack of orders. The quality and quantity of repairs that the shop is able to perform each day is directly related to management's ability to maximize their resources. This means that they intentionally plan to match up their people, their time, and their space so that they can achieve maximum productivity.

In an automotive service shop work distribution may be done manually, using a dedicated work-routing system or may be done using an automated system. In either case, it is done by striving to assign each technician to the work he does best. As a result, technicians produce more work in a day with fewer errors, the shop sells more service in a day, and the customers are more satisfied because they get their cars back sooner and with greater assurance that they are fixed right the first time.

Work Performance

 **Work Performance**
The process of verifying customer concerns, performing specific diagnosis, and performing repairs to resolve the customer's concerns.

Now that we have gone through the preparatory work, it is finally time for something productive to occur. It is time for the technician to finally do what the shop is in business to do—fix cars. During the **work performance** stage of the process, the technician, using the repair order as a guide, verifies the customer's concerns, diagnoses the vehicle to verify the cause, and performs the needed repairs.

Although the technician is the one primarily responsible for performing repairs, they rarely do this in isolation. Often the technician will require external information, parts, equipment, or additional approval from the customer to quickly and accurately complete the repair. Once the repair is completed, the technician is responsible for verifying that the customer's concerns have been resolved. Finally, he must write up a detailed explanation of what he found and what he did to resolve the customer's concern before he passes the repair order on for processing.

Quality Assurance

 **Quality Assurance**
The act of verifying that the customer's concerns were addressed and resolved and that the vehicle is in proper condition to be returned to the customer.

Before the customer is notified that the repairs are completed, it is customary that the shop verifies that the work completed has addressed the customer's concerns. The technician performing the repairs typically starts this process by double-checking his work before he turns in the repair order as complete. Once he has done this, the repair order, complete with his comments, is routed for verification of the repairs.

Depending on the structure and size of the shop, the verification of repairs may be done by the advisor who wrote up the repair order or by a shop foreman or **quality assurance** technician. The function of quality assurance is to verify that the repairs have successfully resolved the customer's concerns and that the vehicle has been returned to the condition in which it was received.

Invoicing
Complete and accurate documenting of what was done including explanations, assignment of operation codes (as needed), and final pricing of the repair order.

Invoicing

There is an old adage that holds true in the automotive repair business: "The job is not complete until the paperwork is done." **Invoicing** includes three main operations that are required to accurately and completely prepare the paperwork: reporting what was done, assigning repair operation numbers, and calculating the final bill.

Documenting what was done to repair each of the customer's concerns or requests is started by the technician, who writes his explanation. He is not, however, the one responsible for determining the value (charges) that are assigned to his efforts. In an effort to assure fairness and consistency of pricing, another service employee is generally responsible for looking in the flat-rate manual and assigning the job's flat-rate time.

If the repairs are done under manufacturer warranty, then invoicing includes looking up and coding the order with specific operation numbers required by the manufacturer to obtain reimbursement for the repairs. Because the difficulty and precision required in looking up and accurately preparing documentation for warranty reimbursement are high, large dealerships that perform a large volume of warranty repairs may employ a specialist, typically called a **warranty administrator**, who has sole responsibility for looking up and properly assigning warranty labor operations and then tracking warranty claims for payment.

Warranty Administrator

Individual responsible for looking up and properly assigning warranty labor operations and tracking warranty claims for payment.

Once the labor operations and labor times have been established and documented, it is necessary to prepare a pay ticket that will pay the technician for his or her time and completely price out the labor, parts, and other supplies that the customer is to be charged for the repairs. Finally, the charges are compared against the approved estimate to be sure that they fall within the amount approved.

Delivery

Reviewing with the customer that vehicle repairs are completed, what has been done to address their concerns, the price for those repairs, and making final arrangements for pick-up of the vehicle.

Delivery

The **delivery** step may sound like it is out of sequence, but it is not. It is critical for customer satisfaction that the customer clearly understands what has been done, what has been approved, and what the charges are before she is asked to settle up the bill. Once the work is completed and the charges calculated, the shop should notify the customer that the car is ready to be picked up and review the work done and the total charges due at pick-up. If there are any misunderstandings or concerns, these should be resolved before the customer arrives to pick up the vehicle and pay the bill.

Cashiering

Providing customer with a copy of the bill and an explanation of services performed, handling payment and issuing a receipt for payment.

Cashiering

Cashiering is the last face-to-face step of the transaction. Having already reviewed the repairs and charges with the shop, the customer arrives to pick up the vehicle and settle the bill. She is given copies of all repair documents detailing her requests and concerns, what was done to address each one, and a detailed cost breakdown for each item along with a receipt for payment.

Follow-up

Contacting customers after completion of repairs and customer pick-up to verify that they are satisfied with the services provided and making arrangements to resolve any questions or concerns, if they exist.

Follow-up

Follow-up is a post-repair activity that is intended to verify that the customer is satisfied with the repairs. This step is typically performed one to three days after the customer has picked up the car from the repair shop. Having given the customer adequate time to drive the car to verify that the repairs are satisfactory, the repair shop contacts the customer (usually by phone) to assure that she is satisfied. If there are any concerns or questions, the follow-up information is then channeled back to the shop immediately, so that the shop can make arrangements to address the concerns.

THEORY INTO PRACTICE 4-2

CASE

As a service manager you have a top technician who has a great deal of difficulty getting along with the other workers in the department. She is constantly complaining that she is underpaid and that she is "the only one who really produces any work around there and makes the shop any money." Based on the information provided in the last section

1. You decide

Is she just complaining, or is she right? Why?

2. You decide

How might you approach her to improve her attitude?

Real World Application

As a manager it is your job to get things done. Many managers take the traditional approach of winning, and losing, with people. The shortcoming of this viewpoint is that it makes one big assumption—that all results, good or bad, are caused by people. Therefore, it is reasonable to blame poor performance on people and punish them accordingly. Did you ever feel that you were in a situation where the results were beyond your control? Was it because of someone else above you? Was it because of a lack of information or resources or time? How did it make you feel?

As a manager and leader, you are responsible not just to get things done but to provide an environment where things can be done. This includes not only having the right people on the staff but also providing them with a good work system and the tools necessary to succeed.

You *do* win with people, but, as a manager, failure to perform is most often your responsibility, not theirs. You are responsible for creating the proper environment, providing the necessary tools, and inspiring your people to perform. If your department fails to reach its goals you are the one who is ultimately accountable.

Charting the Workflow

In Chapter 3 we reviewed the manpower requirements of the repair service shop. In this chapter we just looked at the repair process and the individual steps that each repair transaction must go through from start to finish. To further our understanding of how all the resources come together and how a typical shop actually operates, we will now move forward and use the personnel and repair steps to chart a typical transaction. This can be done using a graphic-based method called **flowcharting.**

Flowcharting

A graphical representation of the flow of work as it progresses through the major steps involved in a workflow.

Why flowchart the system? Most of us in the automotive repair field think better and learn better when we can see something, touch it, feel it, and, ultimately, understand it. It is the way that our brains work. The whole idea behind flowcharting the repair process is to help you "see" how it works. Once you can "see it" in action, it should help you to better understand it and be able to identify possible problem areas and make the changes necessary to improve them.

Flowcharting helps to analyze how the work actually gets done in the system. It diagrams the flow of work from person to person and task to task as the transaction moves through the process, from the customer's first contact with the shop to the end of the follow-up call that verifies that the customer is very satisfied with the quality of the repairs.

Graphically portraying the flow of work helps to identify and analyze problem areas. It should help you to see areas where the flow is slowed or comes to a stop. These bottlenecks may be caused by a lack of people performing an important task or simply by timing. If too many customers, too many cars, too many repair orders, and too many bills all arrive at the same place in the shop at the same time, the flow of work slows down dramatically. Identifying these bottlenecks is the first step in helping to resolve them to improve the flow and productivity of the shop.

Flowcharting Basics

Before we flowchart the service transaction, we should understand the common symbols used for flowcharting. These symbols are the universal language of flowcharting. Just like words in any language, they are commonly accepted symbols that everyone using flowcharts accepts as having a specific meaning. The basic symbols are (Figure 4-4)

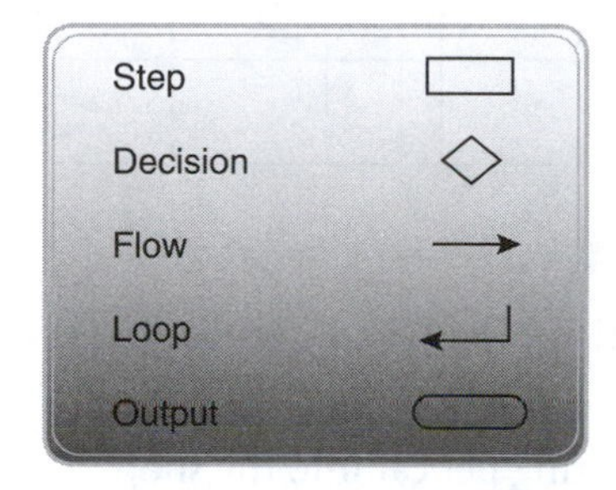

Figure 4-4 Flowcharting basics

- *Step*—A step is designated by a rectangular box. This box represents a specific action that takes place in the process. An example of a step in the repair process would be road testing the car to verify that the repairs were completed correctly.
- *Decision*—A decision is designated by a diamond-shaped box. This box represents a point where the flow can go in two or more directions depending on the results. An example in the repair process would be: Is the car fixed? Y/N. The proper next step would be different depending on the answer to that question.
- *Flow*—The movement through the process is indicated by lines with an arrow at their end. The line represents the process moving from step to step, decision to decision, and the point at the end of the arrow designates the direction of the workflow. An example in the repair process would be anytime when the repair order moves, such as when the order is written up and moves from the service advisor and is given to the dispatcher.
- *Loop*—A loop is a line combined with an arrow heading back toward any previous step of the workflow. Any time that we need to double back to repeat a step again, a loop is required. An example in the repair service process would be when the repairs are quality checked and found to be incomplete and the car needs to be returned to the technician for further repairs.

- *Output*—The symbol for an output is an oval or rectangle with rounded corners. This indicates an ending point or a product. In the repair process an output would be the successful completion of the repair.

Now that we have a basic understanding of the language of flowcharting, where do we put them? The answer is simple. We put them on a chart. The chart is a matrix that shows the job titles down its left side and the individual steps in the repair process across the top (Figure 4-5).

Task / Employee	Appointment	Reception	Work Distribution	Work Performance	Quality Assurance	Invoicing	Delivery	Cashiering	Follow-up
Service Advisor									
Dispatcher									
Technician									
Parts Specialist									
Shop Foreman									
Cashier									

Figure 4-5 Workflow chart

Now that gathered all the tools together, it is time to chart a service transaction. Here is the scenario.

> Marge Jones calls in and makes an appointment to bring her car into the shop on Tuesday for an oil change and to check out a strange noise that happens every time she applies the brakes. On Tuesday morning she arrives on time and speaks to Hannah, the service advisor. Hannah greets Ms. Jones and verifies that she wants an oil change and that the noise appears to be coming from the right front of the car and only happens on hard braking, but it seems that the car stops fine with no pulling to either side. After writing up the repair, Hannah gets Ms. Jones to verify that the information is correct and complete and gives her a preliminary estimate for the oil change and tells her that because her car is only five months old with only 4,360 miles on it, that the repair to the noise should be covered under her manufacturer's warranty. Hannah then sends the completed paperwork on to Dave, who dispatches the shop's work. Dave assigns the car to Heather to check out the noise and perform the oil change. Heather verifies the complaint and finds that there is a broken retainer clip on the right front brake pad. Because this is a faulty part, it is covered under warranty. Heather gets the parts from Fred in the parts department and replaces the defective pad. She also completes the oil change and road tests the car. She then completes the paperwork. When the completed repair order returns to Hannah for her to call Ms. Jones, she calls over Jerry, the shop foreman, and asks if he can road test the car again to be sure everything is all right, because Ms. Jones is one of their best customers. After his road test Jerry comes in and notifies Hannah that the car is fine and Hannah prepares the paperwork. She calls Ms. Jones and gives her the good news that the noise is fixed and that the only charge is for the oil change. Ms. Jones can come and pick up the car any time before 7 P.M. Ms. Jones arrives at 5:30 P.M. to pick up the car, pays the cashier, gets her receipt, and drives home.

On Wednesday afternoon the cashier calls Ms. Jones to make sure she is satisfied. She is satisfied.

You have the entire sequence of events. The first task in flowcharting is to break down the sequence of events into the individual steps that occur.

Sequence of steps:

1. Ms. Jones calls in and makes an appointment with the advisor, Hannah.
2. Ms. Jones arrives and the advisor, Hannah, writes up her car.
3. The paperwork then goes to the dispatcher, Dave.
4. Dave assigns the work to Heather, the service technician.
5. Heather diagnoses the cause of the problem and needs to get a new part from the parts department.
6. Heather goes to Fred, the parts specialist, and gets the new brake part.
7. Heather completes the repairs and the oil change and sends the completed paperwork to Hannah.
8. Hannah reviews the paperwork and asks Jerry, the shop foreman, to quality control the car.
9. Jerry road tests the car and verifies that the car is fixed and returns the paperwork to Hannah, who prepares the invoice.
10. Hannah calls Ms. Jones, telling her the good news, the total charges, and advises her that the car is ready to be picked up.
11. Ms. Jones arrives at the dealership and speaks to the cashier, and pays her bill, gets her receipt, and drives off with her car.
12. The next day, the cashier calls and verifies that Ms. Jones is satisfied.
13. END—Mrs. Jones is another satisfied customer, who will undoubtedly return and also tell her friends what a great job the repair shop has done.

That was a pretty simple and straightforward repair and it took a total of 12 steps. Many repairs are not quite so simple. How many steps might they take? Let us take these 12 steps and chart them in Figure 4-6, to see exactly how the workflow looks.

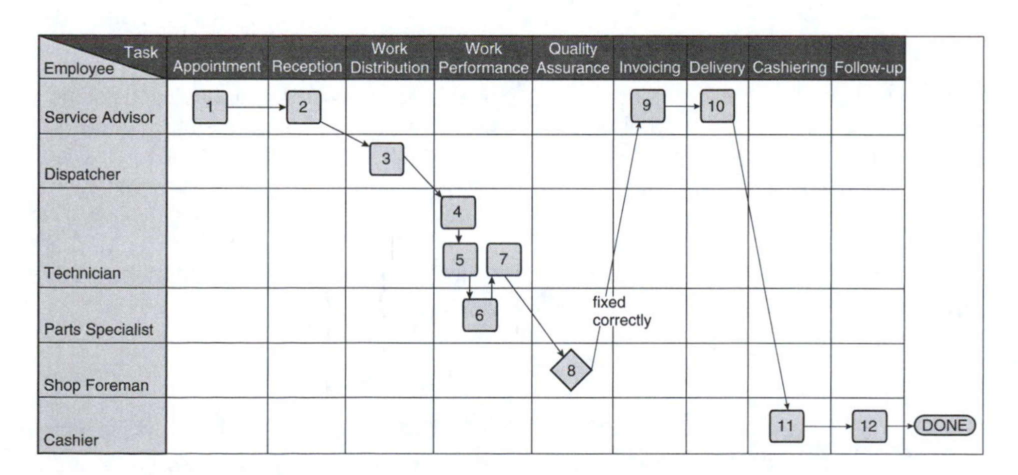

Figure 4-6 An example of a repair workflow

The 12 steps that we have identified for this repair give us a much clearer picture of how the workflows on a regular basis in the shop. It really tells us quite a bit about the shop's operation. Take another look at the chart. It tells us who the essential people are for each service transaction. It tells us the individual procedures that we require for each transaction. It tells us who is responsible for which action.

Before we end this chapter, let us take a brief look at ways that putting the workflow down on paper might come in handy to help you better manage your shop. Here are some examples of how the knowledge that you have gained from charting the workflow can be useful to you:

- Helping you to develop job descriptions that document assigned job responsibilities
- Identifying potential bottlenecks in the shop where the workflow slows down, thereby reducing productivity
- Reassigning job tasks and seeing the potential impact on the rest of the shop
- Creating help wanted advertisements to recruit employees
- Evaluating the possible effect of adding additional people to your shop

THEORY INTO PRACTICE 4-3

CASE

As a service manager you find that customers are always complaining that when they arrive to pick up their cars, the paperwork is not ready.

You decide

Is this a people problem or a systems problem? How would you know?

SUMMARY

In this chapter we have looked at automotive repair as what it is—a complex system. Fixing cars is a process involving a variety of resources. We discussed the physical resources in Chapter 2 and the manpower resources in Chapter 3. Now we have explored how to put all the resources together into an efficient system.

Because the lifeblood of the service shop is producing labor hours, the essential workflow, or process, in the shop is the repair order process. Therefore, we have explored ways to document it, look at it, and analyze it so that we understand it better. To effectively manage a service operation, you must have a clear and thorough understanding of the process and the flow, so that you can constantly monitor and evaluate the system. Through this thorough understanding, you will be able to make the best decisions to identify and resolve problems and to continually improve the system to make it more efficient and productive.

PRACTICING THE PRINCIPLES

1. An area where the flow is slowed or even comes to a stop is referred to as a
   a. traffic jam.
   b. plug.
   c. bottleneck.
   d. corkscrew.

2. The step in the repair process where the repairs are verified is called
   a. quality assurance.
   b. cashiering.
   c. bottleneck.
   d. work performance.

3. The step in the repair process where someone notifies the customer what was done, what the charges are going to be, and arranges for them to pick up the vehicle is
   a. invoicing.
   b. cashiering.
   c. delivery.
   d. all of the above.

4. The step in the repair process where the customer is questioned to verify what their concerns are is
   a. work performance.
   b. appointment.
   c. traffic jam.
   d. quality assurance.

Use Figure 4-7 to answer Questions 5–10.

5. Who is responsible for the delivery step of the transaction?
   a. technician.
   b. dispatcher.
   c. cashier.
   d. service advisor.

6. Who distributes the repair orders to the technicians?
   a. dispatcher.
   b. service advisor.
   c. shop foreman.
   d. cashier.

7. Who makes the final decision of whether the repairs are done correctly?
   a. dispatcher.
   b. service advisor.
   c. parts specialist.
   d. shop foreman.

8. You have been receiving more complaints lately that the phones are not getting answered quickly enough—there is too long of a delay to get waited on—and that the paperwork is never ready on time. You have 18 technicians and three service advisors. What more can you do? Worst of all, the complaints do not seem to be directed toward any one individual but seem to be occurring throughout your shop. Where do you think the bottleneck is most likely to be occurring?
   a. dispatcher.
   b. service advisor.
   c. parts specialist.
   d. shop foreman.

9. Using the information in the chart along with what you learned in Question 8, what task might you reassign to someone else? Why?
   a. quality control.
   b. work performance.
   c. follow-up.
   d. work distribution.

10. Using the information in the chart along with what you learned in Questions 8 and 9, who would you suggest perform that task? Why?
    a. dispatcher.
    b. service advisor.
    c. shop foreman.
    d. cashier.

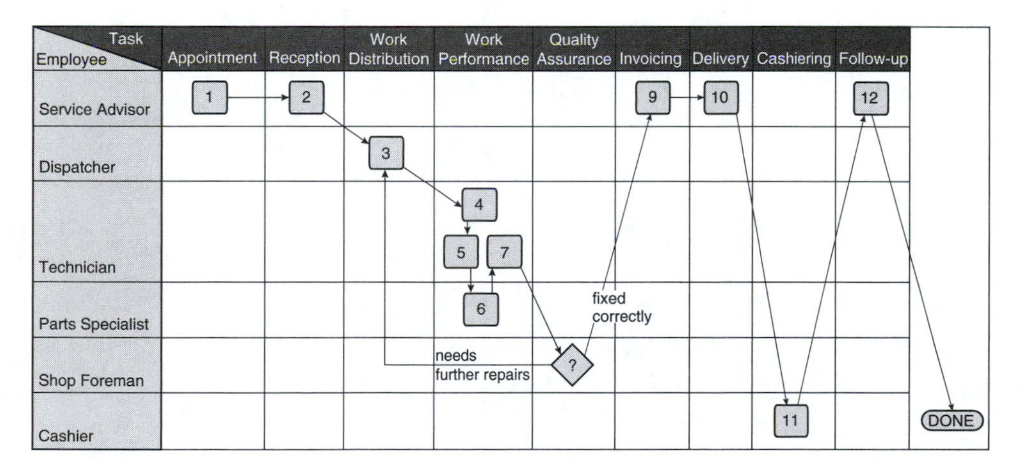

Figure 4-7 Workflow example for Questions 5–10

SECTION

2

Management Styles

Just as there is no one person who is the perfect employee, there is no one way for all people to manage in all situations. This section will begin by providing a background on the recent history of management philosophies and practices. It will introduce a range of management styles a manager may adopt to supervise a department. The strengths and weakness of each style will be presented and discussed. The differing styles will be contrasted and compared with the goal of helping the manager identify the style that fits him or her and the organization the best. Finally, we will explore overarching principles and values that should guide your actions as a responsible and ethical supervisor.

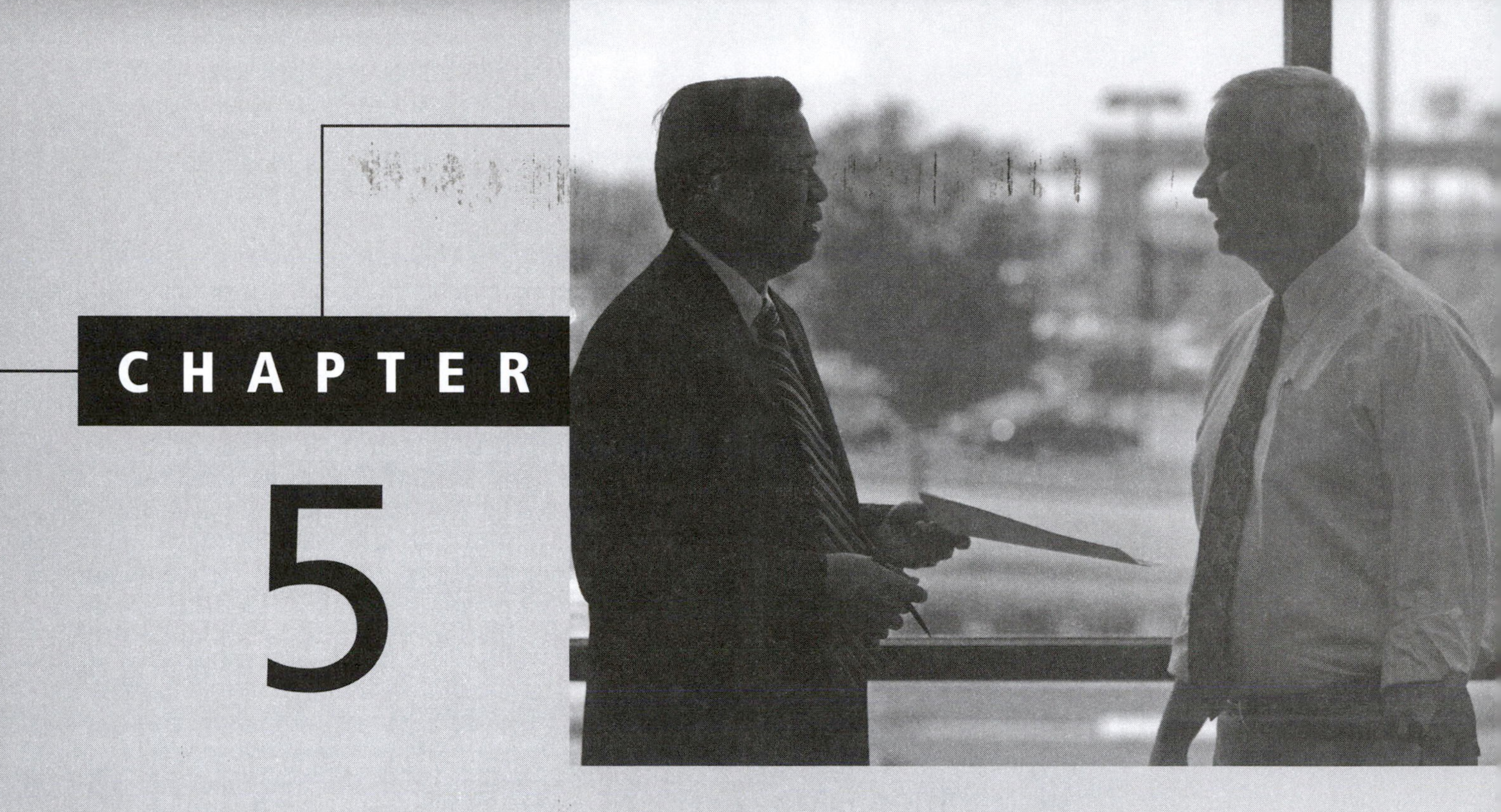

Classic Management

CHAPTER OBJECTIVES

- To identify the basic philosophies of traditional management
- To examine the role of management in traditional management systems
- To examine the role of labor in traditional management systems
- To analyze the changes that scientific management made to traditional management
- To identify the management concepts of management by objective (MBO)

KEY TERMS

traditional management
consistency
Frederick Taylor
scientific management
George Odiorne
MBO
objectives
task oriented
objective oriented
leadership
compliance

Introduction

The *Merriam-Webster Dictionary* defines *manage* as "to handle or direct with a degree of skill: to make and keep compliant." Although this definition may seem dated, it expresses a concept of the purpose and responsibilities of management that has existed for centuries. Shepherds, for example, still manage their flocks using the techniques developed millennia earlier—directing the sheep to do what the shepherd (manager) feels is in his best interest and, from his perspective, the best interest of the flock. Modern businesses often use this same approach when managing unskilled or low-skilled labor. Supervisors tell the employees what to do (give them direction) and make sure that they comply with those directions (keep them in line). Is this approach really any different from the role that a shepherd plays to his flock? In today's world the skills required to effectively manage are very different. Let us take a look at how management has evolved from these simple roots to its current state as we explore classic management theories and practices.

Traditional Management

Traditional Management

Management theory in which managers direct and make all decisions and employees are additional hands, feet, and bodies to assist management.

Traditional management theory is an outgrowth of the Industrial Revolution. The major shift in how goods were produced resulted in the need for a change in the way that production was managed. Before this time the majority of goods were produced in small quantities by highly trained craftsmen. Now, the introduction of factories that could produce goods in mass using low-skilled workers changed the work environment, and management, forever.

The general management principles of traditional management can be traced back to the late 1600s. However, although he did not invent the concept, it is Adam Smith who is given credit as the person responsible for defining the principles and practices and making them widely available. He did this when he published his analysis of modern capitalism "The Wealth of Nations" (Smith, 1776).

Traditional management theory creates distinct divisions between the roles and responsibilities of labor and management. Labor performs the role of the extra hands, extra legs, extra strong backs that, when directed toward a specific task, multiply the productive capacity of effective managers. This theory proposes that coordinating and directing the work of large numbers of people, a manager can produce a great deal more work than he could possibly achieve alone, and the collective work will be of the same quality as work done by a single talented individual. The key principle is working *through others:* the effective manager becomes the brains of the entire workgroup, and the employees become extensions of the manager. Managers do not consider employee ideas or suggestions as part of this process; often they discourage such input. Although management in this model considers employees incapable of making sound decisions, it assumes they will develop into productive bodies under the careful guidance of a skillful manager.

Traditional management principles limit the employee's responsibility to producing and/or delivering the company's product by doing their assigned tasks as directed by a manager. In a traditional assembly line, for example, the manager's goal is to produce workers who can consistently perform very simple repetitive tasks over and over again. This approach enables the manager to train a large number of people in a short period of time. For an assembly line worker

Real World Application

The automotive industry that we work in today is, to a great part, based upon the implementation of traditional management principles. Henry Ford used these principles to develop his assembly line system, build the Model T, and forever change the future of the automotive industry. The assembly line production system that he pioneered not only improved consistency but also lowered the skill requirements, so that the assembly workers no longer needed to be craftsmen with a wide range of skills, just additional sets of hands and legs that could learn to perform one repetitive task. As a result of breaking down the process into these small bits, Ford was able to dramatically lower costs and build a car that the average American could afford. Were it not for this innovative approach, automobiles might still be only affordable to the very wealthy.

Although the assembly line is a graphic example of how the traditional system worked, you can apply the same example to someone who is selling a product or answering a phone. If people do not see the relationship between their part in the process and the results, they will not feel responsible for producing quality results. After all, it is not their job.

in a 1970s auto manufacturing plant, this might mean doing nothing except installing the lower screw on both headlight bezels of every car or truck that came down the line. Although the work was not difficult and paid quite well, few employees found it satisfying or fulfilling. Because each employee performed one small, unskilled task out of the thousands required to produce a car, few felt much accountability for the overall quality of the finished product. Reflecting traditional management theory, early auto manufacturers assigned managers the responsibility for judging the quality of the finished product. Inspectors strategically placed along the line oversaw each process and, to the best of their ability, decided which processes were acceptable and which were not.

Fears of the Traditional Manager

Those who have grown and developed in a traditional management environment have learned to live in a situation in which they are responsible for everything. They, therefore, are expected to take all the credit when things go well and take all the blame when things go badly. Therefore, under the more basic approaches to traditional management, it is common to find supervisors who are concerned about power and accountability. These supervisors are worried that they will lose their power if things do not go well. If all goes well they are proud of their accomplishments . . . if things fail they likely will feel that it is the fault of their employees that they directed "perfectly" but who just did not "seem to get it." It does not seem fair, does it?

There are three major fallacies of traditional management that reduce the efficiency of managers under this system. They are summarized in the following three questions:

- *Delegating:* If I delegate responsibility, am I giving up my power?
- *Decision making:* Am I not the manager because I am most qualified to make the decisions?
- *Controlling:* What if one of my employees does it well—will he or she take my job?

Let us discuss the logic, or illogic, of these three fears.

Delegating Traditional managers are very hesitant to delegate responsibility. Their logic goes something like this: "I am responsible for everything and will be blamed if things do not go well. If I delegate responsibility to my employees am I not giving up power? What authority will I have to make sure they do things correctly and on time if I am powerless to stop them and redirect them?"

The answer to their concerns is, "Yes, that is true, you will give up some of your power. However, if you do not share responsibility and trust them, you will be spending all your time monitoring and watching them, waiting for them to make a mistake. If all your energies are wrapped up in that type of close scrutiny, how will you get anything else done? If you are so tied up that you cannot get anything else done, how is your managing them any more efficient than you simply doing the job yourself?"

Decision Making It is hoped that the manager has a unique combination of training, intellectual capacity, and previous experience that make him best qualified to direct the group. This, however, does not indicate that the employees have no ideas. Going back to the extreme case of classic management (remember the shepherd?), this might be true in some cases. However, in most business cases the employees have a unique perspective on operations, opportunities, and efficiencies. Further, they do not feel respected or fully engaged in their work unless their involvement is at a much higher level than that of being merely an extra set of hands.

Getting input from employees provides fresh perspectives. It provides differing viewpoints that either support and validate the current direction or give rise to new and improved ways to avoid errors and improve efficiencies. Finally, simply by the act of asking for input, employees feel more appreciated and are, therefore, more likely to feel more involved and motivated to help achieve organizational goals.

Controlling If you involve employees, it is inevitable that some may rise to the top and become successful. They may even show the potential to become better managers than their current manager has been. However, rather than being a drawback, this is really a strength.

An innovative and strong manager begins his work by looking diligently to train his replacement. By doing so, he engages his workers and inspires them to reach to new heights of involvement. As a result the productivity of the entire operation is maximized. When the operation becomes exemplary, the manager is the prime candidate within the larger organization to be promoted, leaving his successor to take his old position. It is not a win-lose, but clearly a win-win strategy for mutual success.

Traditional Management in Automotive

In the automotive repair industry, as has historically been the case in many technical fields, the best producer in the shop is often elevated to the position of manager. The goal of the business is production, satisfied customers, and, most important, profitability. Therefore, this line of reasoning makes perfect sense. The supervisor or owner sees someone in the shop that produces the most and the best quality, and wonders, "What would it be like if all my employees were like him?" Being practical, however, the owner realizes that it would be too difficult to find and hire all the top technicians in the town. "After all," he reasons, "even if I did, the cost would be astronomical. Is there another way to achieve the same goals?" In response to this dream, the owner reasons that although he cannot clone his "top gun," maybe he can spread the wealth by having him share his knowledge, skills, motivation, and desire with the others: "Let me put him in charge!"

Scientific Management

Frederick Taylor

The father of the scientific management theory.

Frederick Taylor was a mechanical engineer in the early 1900s who was passionate about finding new and better ways to improve efficiency and consistency in manufacturing. The value of his findings was not limited to manufacturing. They also could be applied to other areas of business. As a result, his writings were widely read and accepted. Because of his contribution to the theories of management, Taylor has been acknowledged as the "father of **scientific management**." His principles of management continue to be widely applied to management in every aspect of business today worldwide.

Scientific Management

A more scientific and systematic approach to breaking down the work process, making sure that every employee knows their small part in it and then managing to assure that work is consistently performed.

Frederick Taylor aimed to increase efficiency and consistency in the workplace and create a new environment that would bring greater prosperity for both employers and employees. He identified several key problems with the traditional work environment and argued that more scientific and systematic management could overcome them. Taylor summarized the common workplace concerns that he felt were at the root of inefficiency:

- Laborers' concern that working too hard would lead to increases in productivity that would put many of them out of work
- Defective systems of management that encouraged employees to work slowly (a phenomenon known as *soldiering*) to protect their common financial interests
- Unscientific rule-of-thumb methods—arbitrary rules based on past practice, not scientific evidence, that were accepted in every trade—that reduced the efficiency of the workforce

Consistency

Results are the same or with very little variation from the established standard.

Taylor confidently predicted that increased productivity would result not in unemployment but rather in increased prosperity. Further he felt that managers could boost productivity with a minimum of additional effort by placing a greater emphasis on increasing the efficiency and **consistency** of the workplace. Achieving greater consistency required changing the role and approach of management. This change was a more scientific and systematic approach to breaking down the work process, ensuring that every employee knew their small part in it, and then managing to assure that it was consistently performed.

A major obstacle that Taylor identified, soldiering, refers to the observation that productivity in a workplace tends to find and maintain a natural balance if all employees are paid at the same rate. If slower workers get paid the same as faster workers, it does not take long until faster workers, seeing that they receive the same pay, same benefits, and same recognition as the slower workers, begin to realize there is no incentive to work harder. Although management might hope that the example set by the faster workers would inspire slower workers to push harder, the opposite consistently occurs. The productivity of the faster workers declines until the entire group achieves a single pace at which they can all work together, like a column of soldiers marching at the same pace.

Finally, Taylor believed that management asked employees to do too much. He asserted that most of the employees did not have the knowledge or skills to do their jobs completely or consistently. Therefore, one should expect their work habits and the consistency of their production to be less than optimal, because they lacked the capacity to do all that management asked of them. In his book *The Principles of Scientific Management* (1911), Taylor wrote: "great gain, both to employers and employees, which results from the substitution of scientific for rule-of-thumb methods in even the smallest details of the work of every trade. The enormous saving of time and therefore increase in the output which it is possible to effect through eliminating unnecessary motions and substituting fast for slow and inefficient motions for the men working in any of our trades can be fully realized only after one has personally seen the improvement which results from a thorough motion and time study, made by a competent man."

Frederick Taylor believed that a solution existed to cure all of these ills of the workplace, which appeared to be universal across all types of businesses and locations. He saw a more systematic and scientific approach to management as the solution to these problems. In many ways, his proposed solution was elegantly simple. He proposed that managers reduce employee expectations about the variety of responsibilities and tasks they would perform and assign them only those tasks that fell within their limited capacity. Management should limit each employee's activity to performing only those tasks for which the worker was hired. Managers should also assume responsibility for making all other business decisions and arrangements and for addressing any issues or difficulties that arise.

Taylor's organizational concept envisions the workplace as a large orchestra, with employees playing the roles of the musicians under the leadership of a conductor, who represents management. The conductor sets the pace, starts and stops the play of each of the instruments, and makes decisions about who plays what, when, and how. The musicians accept the conductor as the person solely responsible for making all of these decisions. This allows the musicians to concentrate on what they do best—playing their unique instruments to the best of their ability. The result is a symphony of consistently beautiful music made possible by creating an environment where both management and labor can excel. As Taylor stated, "No great man can (with the old system of personal management) hope to compete with a number of ordinary men who have been properly organized so as efficiently to cooperate" (Taylor, 1911).

Using this orchestral metaphor, Taylor's scientific management philosophy sought to create a harmonious work environment, as each worker had a clearly defined small part to play, and improved efficiency occurred through the ability of all the workers to play their small parts consistently. This method made a major contribution to the achievement of consistent quality and productivity. However, by breaking down each employee's role into such a small, simple, and finite part of the whole process, employee morale was severely compromised. No longer did employees act as craftsmen who could clearly see the results of the many hours that they spent plying their trade. They were now just an interchangeable part in the process with limited ability to even appreciate the value that each individual added to the final product. Whereas Taylor's theory markedly improved efficiency, it failed to improve on the low employee morale that was a carryover from traditional management practices. Instead, it increased it.

Management by Objective

George Odiorne, one of the strongest proponents of management by objective (**MBO**), defines MBO as "a strategy of planning and getting results in the direction that management wishes and needs to take while meeting the goals and satisfaction of its participants" (Odiorne, 1965). In its most general sense, MBO functions as a plan to help both management and employees achieve their goals. Odiorne adds that MBO requires "a blending of individual plans and needs of managers toward a *large-scale accomplishment within a specific period of time*" (Ibid., 1965). Therefore, MBO not only aims to meet mutual goals, but also involves setting up a system that clearly defines a specific timetable for achieving accomplishments along this path.

George Odiorne

A major proponent of the management by objective (MBO) theory of management.

MBO

A management system based primarily on outputs that blends individual plans and needs of managers toward a large scale accomplishment within a specific period of time.

Objectives

Well-defined aims or goals.

According to MBO theory, everyone within an organization must commit to a focus on the following items:

- *Objectives*—MBO focuses primarily on outputs. The system requires clearly defined **objectives** and a universal commitment by all employees to achieve the stated organizational objectives.
- *Time strategy*—Employees must achieve objectives within the stipulated time limitations without exception.
- *Total management*—Managers must coordinate the efforts of individuals to achieve common goals. Success depends upon clearly communicating goals and objectives and obtaining employee commitment to supporting them. Sharing a common understanding of goals and objectives helps to reduce frustration and minimize lost effort while the organization strives to achieve maximum productive capacity.
- *Individual motivation*—Although the core objectives in an MBO system focus on the needs and desires of the organization, managers seek employee input and consider the needs and goals of the employees when planning objectives. In return, the organization expects employees to support organizational goals and commit to carrying them out.

Comparing Management Approaches

Management by objective and scientific management share many common traits. Both systems try to minimize lost motion and lost efforts. Both try to systematize the work by assuring that everyone is doing things the one right way. MBO, however, deals directly with one of the major drawbacks of scientific management—lowered employee morale. Let us discuss this and other differences between the two methodologies in more detail.

Scientific management and MBO differ dramatically in their approach toward individual employee involvement in the planning and execution of the management plan. Taylor's foundational philosophy is that the employees should not be expected to make decisions about what to do and how to do it because they are not capable, and therefore they are purposefully excluded from any planning processes. Employees are carefully instructed what to do and when. In MBO the employees are intentionally and actively involved in developing objectives and timelines. In doing so, this philosophy expects a higher level of commitment to these shared goals and therefore higher levels of consistent performance.

Although MBO's primary focus is to identify organizational goals based on the needs and objectives of management, it purposefully solicits input from employees to assure that their needs are met. This method seeks to ensure the long-term success of employer and employee alike, by defining goals and objectives and by setting up a structured process for defining, pursuing, and achieving operational goals along the way. This assures the ultimate success of the overarching organizational goals. As a result, in an MBO system management can reasonably expect the following:

- Employees are more motivated because they have participated in planning and carrying out the plan.
- Fixed timelines will increase the likelihood of completing projects by their deadlines.
- Employees clearly understand the goals and objectives of the company.
- Morale is higher throughout the organization.

Let us consider how scientific management and MBO might differ when applied in the real world. A traditional manager using the scientific management approach likely expects the following:

- The manager will clearly and very specifically define the individual tasks employees will perform.
- All employees will carry out these tasks in exactly the same manner.
- Employees will not deviate in any way from the specific directions they receive.
- Employees will not question or try to improvise upon the assigned directions.
- All employees will work as interchangeable parts in a complex system.

The hallmark of this approach is *consistency*.

In addition, the manager in the scientific management system does not expect employees to be involved in any way in the development of objectives: developing and assigning tasks is solely the responsibility of management. Whenever the actual production varies from the intended output in either volume or quality, it is the responsibility of management to identify the variation, determine the cause, and take proper corrective action. In this model the employees are extra sets of hands to help extend the abilities of the manager to produce more of what he or she would produce. The manager controls all activities and is responsible for all activities and results. This is clearly an environment where the responsibility of management is vast and that of labor is minimal. Management sees its role as the one making all the decisions and being accountable for all results (good or bad), and its relationship with the employees as one of simply pushing them to work harder/faster/more efficiently. Employee responsibility remains solely **task oriented.**

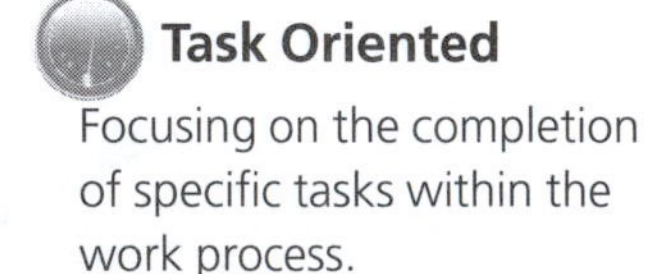

Task Oriented
Focusing on the completion of specific tasks within the work process.

In the work environment using MBO, the approach and responsibilities of management toward their job, the organization, and the employees would be dramatically different. Although the overarching goals and objectives of the company still come from top management, developing strategies, objectives, and timelines to consistently meet these goals is achieved through the involvement of the employees with management. The hallmark of this system is that both management and employees are involved in the development of an ***objective-oriented*** strategy to achieve consistent and lasting success.

Objective Oriented
Focusing on broader objectives rather than on the details.

Because both the manager and the employees understand and feel a sense of responsibility for achieving the goals and deadlines, the work environment is more one of mutual gains than of management versus labor. Employees begin to feel a vested interest in the success of the operation. After all, they helped to define the objectives. Their level of involvement in the organization as a whole has risen to a higher level because now they are valued as being more than an additional set of hands. Their minds, their concerns, their needs, and their expertise have all been considered in developing a plan that they share with management. Although management still guides, directs, and assigns tasks to assure consistency and is ultimately responsible for achieving objectives and deadlines, this responsibility is now more shared throughout the organization.

Leadership (Goal Orientation)

Whereas a manager using Taylor's scientific management is *task oriented* and a manager using Odiorne's MBO is objective oriented, a manager who is a leader is *goal oriented*. A leader not only assigns tasks or delegates them, he or she also delegates the responsibility that goes along with the task. **Leadership** has become the focus of a great deal of the evolution of management theory over the past 20 years.

Leadership

A management theory based on a higher level of involvement of employees in the management process, delegating tasks but also delegating authority and responsibility.

A leader sets himself apart because he

- not only delegates tasks but also delegates responsibilities
- not only involves employees in planning by getting their input, but involves them in the ongoing decision-making process
- knows that a key to success is to get "buy-in" (commitment) from employees for any action or plan
- gets others to do what is needed, by being a living example—he walks the talk
- not only encourages, but expects employees to be involved

We will spend more time investigating the principles of leadership in Chapter 6.

Compliance

Strict adherence to rigid rules or specifications.

SUMMARY

Traditional management principles date back far before the twentieth century. Many businesses still operate using this theory of management. The traditional approach defines management as providing expectations and rules and then monitoring performance. The shepherd who leads his flock by making all the decisions for the entire herd is the classic model of the traditional manager.

In the early twentieth century Frederick Taylor, through his scientific management theory, made sweeping changes to the classic management philosophies, as he tried to improve consistency of operations, planning, and results by instituting controls and deadlines. Taylor attributed inconsistent work performance to the belief that workers lacked the capacity for decision making. He believed that management needed to provide employees more specific guidance to correct this shortcoming. Scientific management theory proposed that the entire burden of decision making must rest on management. However, by providing clear and consistent direction and requiring rigid **compliance** based on scientific principles, the consistency of work performance and the resulting output could be improved from traditional methods. Scientific management was a huge success and was eventually adopted by a wide range of businesses.

Management by objective (MBO) took the evolution of management theory further by involving employees in planning. In the broadest sense, MBO focused on setting clear goals and specific deadlines and improving efficiency by adhering to well-defined performance objectives. Its allowance for employee input was an enhancement to previous management approaches, where managers manage and workers work and generated increased employee support for institutional goals.

We closed the chapter with a brief introduction to the principles of a leadership-based approach to management. This most recent stage in the ongoing evolution of management theory continues to spread and forms the basis of much of the current wave of new management styles. We will explore leadership in greater depth in Chapter 6.

PRACTICING THE PRINCIPLES

In Questions 1–3 match the management theory with the orientation that best defines it.

_____ 1. scientific management	a. goal oriented
_____ 2. MBO	b. objective oriented
_____ 3. leadership	c. task oriented

In Questions 4–6 match the management theory with the individual that is most closely tied to that approach.

_____ 4. traditional management	a. Frederick Taylor
_____ 5. MBO	b. Adam Smith
_____ 6. scientific management	c. George Odiorne

7. If you were managing in a shop using the (MBO) approach you would expect your people to
   a. carry out all tasks in exactly the same manner.
   b. not vary in any way from the specific directions given.
   c. not question or improvise upon the assigned directions.
   d. none of the above.
8. The management system that expects employees to be involved in the decision-making process is
   a. management by objective.
   b. leadership.
   c. scientific management.
   d. all of the above.
9. MBO is
   a. a structured output-focused strategy.
   b. based on management making all the decisions alone.
   c. a system in which objectives are expected to be met all the time, on time, every time.
   d. both a and c.
10. The major event in history that resulted in the need for the development of traditional management is
    a. the French Connection.
    b. the Industrial Revolution.
    c. the Italian Connection.
    d. the Dark Ages.

REFERENCES

Adam Smith, *An Inquiry into the Nature and Causes of the Wealth of Nations*, 1776.

Frederick W. Taylor, *The Principles of Scientific Management* (New York: Harper Bros., 1911), 5–29.

George S. Odiorne, *Management by Objectives* (New York: Pitman, 1965), 55.

CHAPTER

6

Being a Leader

CHAPTER OBJECTIVES

- To compare the differences between management and leadership
- To examine the key characteristics of leaders
- To recognize the importance of building relationships
- To assess the benefits of building upon strengths as a leadership strategy to help anyone reach his or her potential

KEY TERMS

manager
leader
authentic
lead by example
credibility
respect
commitment
motivation

Introduction

Manager

One who directs the actions of a group, primarily through orders and instructions.

Leader

One who guides a group, primarily through influence and positive example.

There is a major movement in the theory of management that encourages supervisors to become more than **managers**—to become **leaders.** The question, however, is not whether to be a manager or a leader, but how to become both. Traditional management theories that were discussed earlier (see Chapter 5) teach that the supervisor must manage people and physical resources to maximize production and profitability. However, more recent theories of management broadly support the notion that people respond much better to being led rather than being managed. Thus, an effective supervisor in today's marketplace must have the dual skills of managing resources and leading people. We will explore the concept of leadership in more depth in this chapter.

What Is Leadership?

Leadership is not a set of principles or practices that is only practiced by management. Throughout our lives we have all seen many examples of formal and informal leadership . . . and very likely followed them. Although each of our experiences has been different, here are some of the common leadership experiences that you may have encountered from the early stages of your life:

- The person on the playground who was able to get you to play on the slide rather than on the swings.
- The person who got the group together to play a pick-up game of baseball or to go bowling.
- A member of the swimming team, track team, or football team who encouraged you to join the team.
- The person who was pursuing an education to prepare for a career and encouraged you to do the same.

Have you ever experienced something like this in your lifetime? What was different about these people and about what they did? These people did not try to bribe you or sell you something that they were not interested in themselves. Rather, they were enthusiastic and committed to a particular direction and action. It was this enthusiasm that you found exciting. It helped you to decide that you wanted to be a part of it. When the group decided to go along and play on the slide or play baseball, this person was right there with you, shoulder to shoulder, playing and enjoying the experience. By their presence and enthusiasm, they made the experience more fun. By inspiring the team members it is likely that you all achieved more than you would have otherwise. These people were not managers, bullies, salesmen, or even adults—they were leaders.

Even though leadership is a highly desirable trait for effective managers, it does not come with, nor require, position. The examples described earlier demonstrate this clearly. Leadership is not limited to, or by, position. Anyone can be a leader, and we all should aspire to provide leadership in those areas where we have a passion and commitment. Let us take a deeper look at this very important trait.

Management versus Leadership

As we discussed in previous chapters, classic management is highly task oriented. It focuses on guiding and directing. Leadership is a much more goal-oriented approach. The following examples compare and contrast some of the key differences between the two approaches:

- A manager assigns tasks. A leader delegates responsibility.
- A manager makes decisions and tells the employees what to do. A leader involves people in the decision-making process, and they do it together.
- A manager makes decisions. A leader builds buy-in and, thus, motivates employees to want to achieve mutual goals.
- A manager says, "Do what I say." A leader says, "Do what I do."
- A manager expects people to comply because he or she SAID so. A leader expects people to *see* the vision and inspires them to do what they can to further it.

As you can see from this comparison, management refers to guiding and directing actions and tasks and allocating resources. It is for this reason that we must learn to take supervision to a higher level. We need to understand and practice the key principle that: *we must learn to manage resources and lead people.*

Leadership Traits

Becoming a leader requires more than learning and practicing a variety of skills. In order to effectively and consistently lead people you must be

- Authentic
- Credible
- Exemplary
- Respectful
- Motivational
- Inspirational

Building on Strengths

Anyone who is intentionally motivated toward getting ahead and maximizing his potential will take a hard look at self-improvement. This is a quest to look inward and better understand who you are and what your strengths and weaknesses are. There are many seminars you can attend, and there are many evaluation tools that will help you to identify your strengths and weaknesses. You have probably already heard about the Myers–Briggs type indicator[1] and DiSC®[2] as two of the most commonly used personality type assessments.

It is important to know yourself so that you can understand how others see you. You cannot relate well to other people if you are unaware of how they perceive you, your actions, and your motives. Further, you need to become committed being aware of and adapting to your shortcomings that may become major obstacles to building positive relationships with others.

Beyond knowing who you are and what your strengths and weaknesses are, it is important to determine what you do with this knowledge. Armed with an improved awareness of their strengths and weaknesses, many people set out to focus the majority of their efforts on how to cover up their weaknesses. They may even expend a great deal of time and effort in trying to build up those areas, hopeful of turning their weaknesses into strengths. This attention to self-improvement is certainly superior to doing nothing, but it just may not be the best use of your time and energy.

The best use of your time in becoming self-aware and improving your performance can be found in identifying your strengths and using them. This strategy is the exact opposite of the more traditional approach of working on your weaknesses but deserves serious consideration. You have probably heard of Gallup, the organization that conducts polls on everything from who will be the next president to where the best place to live is. Their 25 years of research of successful leaders and managers (Buckingham and Clifton, 2001) indicates that your strengths are your strengths and your weaknesses are your weaknesses. What? Your strengths are your strengths? Your strengths are more than abstract concepts, they are who you are. Each of us possesses innate strengths. This research further indicates that those who are the most successful and the most satisfied know their strengths and learn to maximize them and to use them to their advantage. They work to their strengths rather than spending their time and effort covering up their weaknesses.

It is not that addressing your weaknesses is unimportant. You do need to be aware of your shortcomings and try to minimize them so that you can keep them from becoming handicaps to building relationships. However, rather than trying to make yourself into what you are not, the best use of your time and energy is to maximize what you are.

This is very much like what any very successful athlete does. Although you can train and practice to become better at anything, it probably is not the best use of your time as a 5′6″ adult to spend all of your time learning to dunk a basketball if your goal is to play in the NBA. Although you may succeed, putting all your efforts into a skill that you will rarely be able to use in a game and that will not earn you a position on a team is not the best use of your time and energy. Rather, identifying and developing your strengths such as your vision, your speed, your ability to shoot a jump shot would be more likely to help you to achieve your goal (playing in the NBA). Practicing hard to improve your three-point shot, your passing and dribbling skills, or your ability to identify defenses and call plays will help you to maximize your strengths. By doing so you are far more likely to raise your performance significantly to a level where you are one of the best in your areas of expertise.

Authentic

Having consistency between your words and your actions.

Lead by Example

Inspiring others to follow by demonstrating the desired traits or actions.

Having said all of this about knowing yourself and building upon your strengths, you might ask, "But what does this have to do with being a leader?" Actually it has major implications in developing your ability to be **authentic**, genuine, and to **lead by example**. But the most important use of this knowledge is its application to those with whom you work.

As a leader and a manager, your success is ultimately dependent on your ability to get the most out of your people. Certainly for people to work to their potential, they have to be in an environment where they are willing and able to push to their limits. They need to be given the proper tools so that they can get the most out of their abilities. The best way to help them to get the most out of their abilities, to get the most out of themselves, and to feel the greatest amount of satisfaction is for you to help them identify and use their strengths.

Just as in the example of the 5′6″ basketball player, your employees can expend their efforts either at trying to be what they are not or at recognizing what they are. Your goal as a leader is to help to unlock their potential, and you can best do this by developing your ability to see their strengths, helping them to see those abilities, and then, together, doing whatever you can to help them play to their strengths. Then you need to help them to make the connection between their abilities, their desires, their motivations, and your (mutual) work.

— Real World Application

In the automotive shop the key measure of success is in the ability of the team to produce the maximum amount of repair work, done right the first time, consistently. Proper distribution of work (who does which jobs) is essential to achieve maximum shop productivity. Shops vary greatly in how they distribute work. Some do it in the simplest form, in which the next job that comes in goes to the next technician that is available.

This system may seem the fairest to the customer and the technician. After all, this customer came in first; therefore her car should be the next in line, right? And, from the perspective of the technician, that technician is the next one who needs work to do, so it is the fairest to give the job to him, right? Let us consider whether this is really the best for both, or even either, of the two parties involved.

When a customer brings her car for repairs, she has three goals in mind: get it done right, at the lowest possible cost, and as quickly as possible. In other words, her goals are accuracy, affordability, and speed. To test whether the simplest form of the system is the best for the customer we need to test the results against these three criteria: 1) Out of all the technicians in the shop, do we know that the first available technician is capable of performing the repair correctly (accuracy)? 2) Do we know that this technician has the knowledge and skills to accurately diagnose the cause the first time, thereby reducing the chance for unneeded repairs or parts, or lost time (affordability)? 3) Do we know that this technician can get the repair done the fastest (speed)? Answers to the question "Is this the best course of action?" may range from "I'm sure" to "absolutely not." Let us look at the issue from the technician's viewpoint.

When the repair order is given to the technician, what are his goals? He is there to earn a living. He does this by being able to accurately diagnose and repair vehicles in as little time as possible. Realistically, his performance goals are the same as the customer's. The only difference is in the rewards. Both the customer and the technician want accuracy and speed. The technician is not as concerned about affordability but, in the long run, wants the customer to feel that she received a good value so that she will come back for future repairs; so the technician wants to ensure that cost of repairs is competitive. Based on these criteria, do we know that just because this technician was next in line he is likely to achieve these three goals? Not necessarily. Now, let us look at the big picture.

In the scenario just described, the method for handing out the work does not provide any assurances that it will meet either the customer's or the technician's needs. However, this approach is not uncommon and is still in practice in many shops. It is the classic method that many shops have operated with for many years.

To better assure that the criteria of accuracy, affordability, and speed are consistently met, the shop does have some choices. If the shop management is keenly aware of the strengths (skills/knowledge/abilities) of each of its technicians, it can improve shop performance by matching up these strengths to the needs of the particular repair job. Thus, the shop assigns the work to the technician who is most capable of making the repair quickly and accurately and in a timely manner.

This approach makes this customer, and all their customers, happy because it increases the likelihood that all (or most) customers will reach all three of their goals. It also satisfies the technicians because they are able to fix more cars, feel more satisfied and confident in their ability, and make more money. Finally, it is the best overall solution for the shop because it assures satisfied customers and the continued flow of customers, which will keep the shop busy and profitable well into the future.

Building Relationships

Leadership is a two-way relationship. You may choose to lead, but you are not a leader unless you have followers. Those who follow must choose to do so and must be comfortable in accepting you as the leader. Without commitment at both ends leadership does not happen.

Leadership is an informal agreement among all parties that they feel a level of comfort and mutual benefit to proceed in a certain manner. It is not dependent upon position but upon credibility, respect, and commitment. As described at the outset of this chapter, we have all chosen to defer to the lead of someone else at some point in our lives. However, within the framework of the supervisor–employee relationship the goal is to cultivate and develop an ongoing relationship and informal agreement that allows the interaction between you, your employees, and co-workers to transcend the limitations of management and reach new levels of performance and mutual satisfaction.

Credibility
Acting in a consistent manner that allows others to believe or have faith in you.

For people to trust a leader, they must consistently see that individual demonstrate attributes that earn their respect and trust. **Credibility** is an essential attribute that is the foundation of building this type of relationship. The only true way to build credibility is through sustained and consistent action. People must see that you mean what you say. The best way for them to see this is to observe what you do in your everyday life. The term commonly used in quality improvement to describe that you do what you say is to "walk the talk." That is, what you do is consistent with what you say you believe. This consistent agreement between your words and your actions helps people to build confidence that you really mean what you say.

Respect
Holding in high regard or a rank of honor.

Once people know who you are and where you are really coming from, they begin to relax and feel comfortable with making a personal judgment regarding your actions and values. Do they **respect** those beliefs, values, and attitudes? It is important to understand that this leadership is not a religion. They do not have to "convert" and give up their beliefs. They do not have to become one of you. However, it is essential that between the positive attributes and actions and the consistency you demonstrate that they respect your position. This is essential because they must respect you in order to trust you and will not truly allow you to lead them until you have earned their trust.

Commitment
A firm agreement to completing a task or adhering to a principle or rule.

The final step in the process is obtaining **commitment.** Because leadership is a voluntary relationship, those involved in traveling the path together must willingly submit and consent to be a part of the team. Through building credibility and earning their respect and trust, your employees and co-workers know what they can expect then they can decide that it is something that they can willingly embrace. Not until this point is reached can they finally make a wholehearted commitment. You may wonder, "Well, that's really nice in an ideal setting, but who can wait that long to build voluntary commitment? I have to get things done today. This is just too idealistic." Whereas I fully understand your impatience and frustration in considering this as the only way to lead, rest assured that whenever and wherever possible it is the best way in the long run to guide and direct any operation.

It is important to understand, however, that some situations do not allow you to build consensus and commitment. The obvious example is the unexpected "fire." Whether physical or symbolic, if the shop is on fire, this is not the time to discuss and gain input, to consult, and to build commitment. It is the time to get out of the building! However, even in this extreme case, you would hope that you have built sufficient credibility with the employees that when you walk out of your office screaming "There's a fire! Get out of the building now!" your employees believe you and follow your lead without questioning your motives and, thus, hesitating to act.

Inspiring People to Action

The goal as a leader is to go beyond—having people await your direction for each step. The ultimate goal is to gain their wholehearted commitment and to inspire them to act. Once they have achieved this level of trust, your performance as a leader is virtually unlimited and will very likely exceed your wildest dreams. This is the true path to achieving excellence and performing at the leading edge, being seen as the living, breathing example that others turn to as the benchmark of performance and excellence.

Leading at this level is called "higher ground leadership" (Secretan, 2004). Reaching this level of leadership requires that you inspire your people by appealing to a higher purpose—their higher purpose—their hearts and souls. This may sound all too idealistic, but it does make practical sense.

Think about your work. Have you ever had a day when you worked a really long day and came home tired but, at the same time, felt pumped up and exhilarated? On the other hand, do you recall days when you did not work nearly so hard but left at the end of the day feeling drained, like someone had simply pulled the plug and let out all of your energy? What is the difference? In the first case, what did you do? Chances are very good that you spent all, or at least most, of your time doing something that you felt good about, something that you felt was important, something that made you feel good about yourself. You did *meaningful* work that made you feel as though you had a purpose and had done something of real and lasting value.

Now, think of the other day. Many workers can easily share more examples of the latter than they can of the former. If you consider what you did on a day when you felt completely exhausted, it was probably something that seemed tedious and uninspiring. You put in the effort and met the goal but did not feel it was really important.

Now, wouldn't it be great if you could feel like all of the time and effort that you put in, every day of your working life was exhilarating? Do you think that all of your employees (or at least most of them) would choose to work that way too? Well, then, do it! Although there will always be a need to do busy work, becoming an inspiring leader and fostering a group of inspired workers who see enough value in what they do so that *they* choose to put their best effort into it consistently is the ultimate goal. Give people more than a reason to work—give them a passion to work.

What About Those "Who Won't Be Led"?

It should always be your goal to provide an environment where each employee has the opportunity to succeed and to be inspired and dedicated. However, in spite of your best efforts to lead, guide, counsel, and inspire, the performance of an individual just may not meet your requirements at times. What should you do then? You can let everyone else pitch in to help, but is that really fair? You can dismiss the individual in question, but is that really the best solution?

It is unfair, in the long run, to allow someone to continue to fail and bring down the organization. It does nothing for their morale or their future to allow them to wallow in failure. It is unfair to sentence the rest of the crew to having to work harder and overproduce to compensate for the shortcomings of a colleague. It is not that he or she a bad person; he is in the wrong place and you owe it to him and the organization to do what you can to get him out of this bad situation.

Jim Collins, in his book *Good to Great* (Collins, 2001), uses a powerful analogy of getting the right people "on the bus" to provide us with inspiration about how to deal with these types of personnel issues. As a manager and leader you are responsible to the organization and to your co-workers for getting the right people on the bus. That is, to hire and retain the people with the right knowledge, skills, abilities, and attitudes to help maximize the productivity, profitability, and overall success of the organization.

Beyond getting the right people on the job, it is critical that you work to get the right people in the right role. It is critical that you know your people *and* your operational needs well enough, to be able to consistently match up the right people with the right jobs and responsibilities.

However, occasionally you find that you have the wrong person in place. Is it that you misjudged him in the first place? Did you hire the wrong person? Did you put him in the wrong position? Or did he change? In the final analysis the cause is not important. What is most important is that you recognize that a problem exists and that you do something to resolve it.

The most difficult part is acknowledging the problem. Once you have overcome this hurdle, the problem becomes one of determining the proper course of action. The best course of action in all but the severest personnel problem situations is to advance through a consistent and steady process of progressive discipline.

Progressive discipline, as the name suggests, is not limited to a set pathway to punish. It is, in contrast, a system that provides for and assures that a consistent and fair approach is taken to communicate with employees. The goal of this approach is to provide every opportunity to rectify substandard performance. It is, clearly, more of a plan for corrective action than for continued discipline. Additional discipline, up to and including dismissal, exists only as the last resort. We will look at this very important personnel management process in depth in Chapter 24.

Real World Application

You may believe that people cannot be motivated and do not want to work. Maybe you are missing the point of resistance. Maybe it is not that they will not, possibly it is a combination that they cannot (do not feel capable and will not admit it), or they are simply resistant because they do not feel they have a choice. The following real-life story illustrates this point.

The manager of a department noticed that although his team worked well together and had a commitment to the overall operation of the department, at times some assignments just did not get done or if they got done they were done reluctantly and halfheartedly. After all, he reasoned, there are always some tasks that are necessary but not fun. The best way to deal with this problem has always been to dole them out evenly across the board and let everyone share the tedious tasks. That is the fairest way, isn't it?

Based on informal conversations with employees he sensed that possibly those "tedious" tasks were not really so troublesome for everyone. Perhaps they were more of a problem for some than they were for others. If this were true, maybe it was possible to find a better way to approach this. He decided to include his employees in the process and try a new approach.

At their annual planning meeting, he decided to try a different approach this year. He started by conducting an open brainstorming session. He asked the employees to list all of the important tasks that the department needed to accomplish during the coming year to be successful. The manager stayed in the background, writing down the tasks on the chalkboard. When it appeared that they had exhausted their supply of ideas, the manager stopped, looked at the board, and said, "You realize that this is a pretty big list and that the only ones who can do these tasks are the people here in this room."

The manager then asked the employees to go around the room, choosing the tasks that they were willing to accept responsibility to accomplish. After everyone had volunteered for as many items as he or she felt comfortable doing, there remained a significantly smaller, yet still substantial, list of unclaimed items. The manager turned again to the group, saying, "Does anyone here believe that I can do all of these things?" They somewhat reluctantly acknowledged that this was impossible. He then asked, "Let's go item by item and make a decision about the remaining tasks. If no one thinks that a certain task is essential, then we will just cross it off the list. If you think it is essential, we will decide together who is willing to take it on."

The end result of this exercise was that the department was more aware of what needed to be done, helped to develop the priorities of the department, and had a say in selecting how they would be of service. They all felt better about their ability to choose and to be able to do what they were most comfortable contributing. The final result was the most productive and smooth-running year in recent memory for all concerned.

Leading 24/7

Leadership is more than an action; it is an entire philosophy of operation. Not limited to size or stature, position or rank, it is a frame of mind. It springs from an individual's dedication to a strong set of beliefs and their internal **motivation** to do all that they can to carry these beliefs forward. You cannot fake it, you must *be* it. People will know the difference. That is why people rally around the genuine and credible inspirational leaders and shy away from the paper tigers.

Motivation
The guidance, principle, or belief that causes a person to act.

Leadership permeates one's entire being. It cannot be put on or taken off like a suit jacket or tie. Being a true and complete leader means that this philosophy, this approach to life, permeates all that you do, both personally and professionally.

The truly effective leader's belief system is so strong and such an integral part of who he or she is that it guides his actions in his personal life, whether dealing with personal life issues or in interactions with friends and family. Further, in the work environment it affects management style and the means and methods of interacting with co-workers. It has a profound influence on all decisions that will affect the current and future operations and initiatives of the organization.

After all, everything and everyone that we interact with are to some degree intertwined. We cannot totally compartmentalize our private life, our personal life, or our work life. Because all of our actions are based upon our beliefs, values, and passions, these common threads show forth in all that we do. People see us mostly by what we do, not what we say. It is by these proofs that they choose who they trust and who they will follow. Because being led is a voluntary act, it is only by setting a living example that others will allow us to achieve an effective leadership role.

SUMMARY

Leadership is a philosophy for guiding and directing the future of an activity, a department, or an organization and is distinctively different than that used in traditional management. Leadership is an action, not a job title or position. It is an effort to guide, direct, motivate, and inspire others to willingly participate in the initiative at hand. Leadership can just as easily come from within the ranks as it does from supervisors.

Most important, people often feel that they have no choice whether or not to be managed. However, they must freely choose to be led, and by whom. The dynamics of leadership are substantially different than those of management.

The key rule to follow to raise your level of supervision from management to that of leadership is to remember to *manage resources and lead people.*

Finally, the road to effective leadership is built upon developing relationships with co-workers. It is imperative that you understand who they are and appreciate their potential and their inner motivations if you are to successfully engage them in the work. With this knowledge, it is possible to work together to maximize their strengths and, get the best out of everyone, for their self-worth and satisfaction and for the ultimate positive effects that it will have on their performance and that of the organization.

PRACTICING THE PRINCIPLES

In Questions 1–6 match the job titles with the description that best fits their job duties and indicate your choice on the line provided to the left of the job title:

_____1. Manage	a. inspire others to action
_____2. Lead	b. genuine
_____3. Credible	c. demonstrating desired traits
_____4. Exemplary	d. the reason to act
_____5. Motivation	e. direct to take action
_____6. Authentic	f. believable/consistent

7. Toby, the service manager at Pyramid Motors, tends to be an old-school manager. He feels that he is the boss and that his job is to tell his employees what to do and to make sure that they do it right, and do it now. Which of the following characteristics most closely fit Toby?
   a. inspirational leader.
   b. leads by example.
   c. traditional manager.
   d. all of the above.

8. Learning to identify and build upon existing strengths is most likely to result in
   a. lower employee morale.
   b. confused and unmotivated employees.
   c. poor quality products and services.
   d. none of the above.

9. The best methods to inspire others to action are to
   a. rule with a firm hand.
   b. be a living example.
   c. earn their respect.
   d. assign very specific tasks only.
   e. both b and c are correct.
   f. both a and d are correct.

10. You can get the best out of your fellow employees if
    a. you get them to do what you want them to do.
    b. you get them to want to do what is needed.
    c. you get them to stop thinking and just do it.
    d. you do it all yourself.

NOTES

1. Myers–Briggs Type Indicator, Myers Briggs, MBTI, and STEP III are trademarks or registered trademarks of the Myers–Briggs Type Indicator Trust in the United States and other countries. Contact the foundation at coordinator@myersbriggs.org.
2. DiSC® is a registered trademark of Inscape Publishing, Inc.

REFERENCES

Buckingham, M. and Clifton, D., *Now, Discover Your Strengths* (New York: The Free Press, 2001).

Collins, J., *Good to Great: Why Some Companies Make the Leap . . . and Others Don't* (New York: Harper Business, 2001).

Secretan, L., *Inspire: What Great Leaders Do* (Hoboken, NJ: John Wiley & Sons, Inc., 2004).

The Complex Role of Management

CHAPTER OBJECTIVES

- To define the major roles of the manager as being a position holder, judge, and conduit within the organization and to the outside world
- To identify the qualities of a respected manager and an efficient manager
- To value the importance of delegating tasks, responsibility, and accountability

KEY TERMS

position holder
judge
conduit
respect
efficient
delegate
responsibility
accountability

Introduction

Many lectures have been delivered and articles and books written on the subject of management. A majority include how-to solutions on the best way to manage. Some even promote a twelve step canned recipe: "just mix these ingredients, add water, and stir." A few reluctantly admit that they cannot cover the entire range of management theory and, therefore, provide tips and tricks on how to do one part of the job better. However, there are no two management scholars, advisors, or practitioners who wholeheartedly agree on how to completely define and *do* management. Even if they could come to some form of agreement, they would still be highly unlikely to practice it the same way. This, I believe, is because of two very important truths:

1. Management is a very complex and ever-changing enterprise, because it is focused on working with the most unpredictable, and constantly changing ingredient known to man—other men and women.
2. Management is inexact, and good management better resembles a work of art than a science project.

In response to these two truths, in this chapter we will explore and discuss some of the major areas of activity and responsibility that comprise management. This will help you build a better frame of reference of the wide range of knowledge, skills, and actions that you need to effectively exercise to become a successful manager.

An Ever-Changing Enterprise

Unlike the stability of working on a finite piece of machinery, working with people, in the marketplace, and in our society is changeable. For example, even though a fuel injection system may be highly complicated, with many interacting parts, it has what I would call *constancy.* Each part on various systems of a particular make and model is designed to fulfill the same function, operate in the same manner, and interact with the other parts in the assembly in the same way. For that reason it is possible to learn the components and functions of the system and, thus, be trained to troubleshoot, diagnose, and repair the system consistently. This does not imply that the repair is simple. However, although there may be a variety of symptoms and resulting causes that generate a system failure, they are predictable. Because the system and its parts follow very specific and predictable rules and roles, the system has constancy.

Dealing with people management, the major skill set of service management, however, is highly inconsistent. Unlike the fuel injection system, the "component parts" are all unique. That is why we call them individuals. Not only are they each unique with complex values, attitudes, and life experiences, they are constantly changing in response to external influences. These factors, such as their personal and professional relationships, and what is happening in the world around them, are unpredictable. Although you may be able to anticipate some changes, very often we are at the mercy of random, unexpected acts and circumstances that we could not possibly foresee.

More Art than Science

In Chapter 5, we explored some basic management philosophies. One of them was the scientific management movement of Frederick Taylor. Because of his frustration with the inconsistency of management and, therefore, operation of organizations, he attempted to break management down into a scientific, consistent, and repeatable system. With his principles he helped people to realize that through systematic approach, management and the organization's production could be made more stable. However, although scientific management was able to result in a more consistent approach, it was not able to control the environment.

The dynamic changing environment that you live and manage in requires that you have a broad knowledge base and are perceptive, energetic, and flexible if you want to succeed. You have to be able to see what is in front of you, identify it, choose the proper tool, and then respond appropriately. Unlike the technician who sees an identical fuel injection system to the one that he saw yesterday, you are more like the painter who goes to paint a landscape. Even though you may have chosen the location and know the general surroundings, you cannot predict the clouds, the color of the sky, the exact weather, the birds and animals in advance. That is, there are many variables that you cannot anticipate or control. Rather, to be successful and accurate in depicting this scene, you have to bring your entire palette of colors and assortment of brushes and then be prepared to use the proper tools and paints to respond to "what is." It is for this reason management is said to be part science, part magic, and requires a lot of hard work and good luck.

The Major Management Roles

Managers function in several realms of activity every day and at every moment. A manager is a position holder, a judge, and a conduit. Managers continuously function to fulfill one or more of these three roles. They must remain flexible in understanding the importance of and the distinction between these three major areas of responsibility and be willing and able to fluidly move from one to another at a moment's notice. Let us briefly explore these three unique roles.

Position Holder

The manager's position, or job title, tells everyone, both inside and outside of the organization, that he is the person accountable for a well-defined area of the total operations. A manager is more to employer, employees, and the public than the individual that holds the title. The manager holds a vital role in the operation and success of the enterprise. As a **position holder** of authority and responsibility within the organization, the manager hopes to command the respect of his co-workers by the merit of his character and behavior. However, the position that he holds carries with it a requirement of positional respect. It is hoped that people will respect the manager as both an individual and a position holder. However, it is absolutely essential that all involved respect the manager for his positional power. Without this respect, the manager becomes totally impotent and unable to effectively guide and direct the operation.

An individual as described by the official rank within the hierarchy of the organization that he or she occupies.

Upper management looks to the manager as the one who is able to put management's plans into action and guide those on the frontlines to successfully

Real World Application

After taking on the new role as service director in a large dealership, I quickly understood that there was some discomfort in sorting out the relationship between the employees and the new manager. I had previously worked with these employees for five years as their district manager representing the manufacturer. This was a collaborative relationship, and many of us had become friends as we worked together to resolve difficult technical problems. Now the roles had changed, and I was their supervisor. The question became "What is the proper way to deal with our relationship?"

After much soul-searching, I sat down with the technicians and had a short heart-to-heart with each of them during their evaluations. I expressed my concerns about the growing discomfort that both sides were feeling with this new relationship. I summed up my concerns as follows:

> I am your friend, and I am your boss. I would hope that we can continue to be friends and that we can continue to respect each other as individuals. However, things have changed now that I am your boss. As your boss I expect and require that you respect my position within the organization. I hope that you can continue to respect me as an individual. However, you need to clearly understand that I am your boss, first and foremost. That is not an option.

In so doing, I set down clear guidelines that positional respect was a mandate and personal respect was desired. The guidelines put into clear focus the expectations that I had for the behavior of the employees, and to this day many of us continue to be good friends long after we have moved on into other positions and career paths.

implement that plan. The manager has been put in this position because of his unique knowledge of this particular grassroots operation within the organization. Because of this knowledge, he is expected to fully understand how the business works, how it should work, and how to keep it running most effectively. The manager is also expected to be best capable of translating the needs and desires of upper management into operational decisions that will further those requirements within the specific unit.

The employees look to the manager as both their guide and their advocate. As a guide the manager is an example. Further, the employees look to the manager to direct their efforts so that they do the right things the right way, resulting in success and positive results for all.

One of the most important roles of the manager is as the advocate of his workers to upper management. They expect the manager to communicate with management on their behalf, making sure that their department receives the proper resources and support that it needs. Thus, the manager's role allows them to keep on doing what they do best while the manager makes sure that their needs are met and their concerns are heard.

To the public, the manager is the company. When dealing with the manager, customers expect that the manager is able to make decisions, cause actions, and get results. They expect that the manager is their direct line into the company and that he possesses the ability to commit the organization and its resources and to mobilize those resources to address customers' issues and concerns. Just as they see the manager as the mouthpiece of the company, they also see him as the visible example of what the company is and what it stands for. Based on their perception of the manager and the impressions that he conveys to them, the customers make wide-ranging decisions about how they deal with the company and even whether to continue their relationship with the company.

Judge

Judge
The role of being relied upon by others (employees) to make decisions on behalf of the group.

Work units frequently call upon their managers to make decisions—small and large—on their behalf. This role is much like the role of a **judge** in court. The skills necessary to consider the facts and consistently make right decisions are fundamental to being an effective manager. Managers are called upon to be umpires, referees, and even fortune-tellers. They are expected to make the correct decision on a moment's notice, and to get it right every time. Seems unreasonable, doesn't it? Yes, these expectations may be unreasonable, but are often expected and are a good reason to be prepared. Thus managers must develop proper skills and knowledge to maximize the accuracy and consistency of decision-making ability.

Real World Application

Through more than 30 years in a variety of management positions in corporate settings, in dealerships, and in education, I believe that one of the best management training courses that I ever took was spending a few summers as a Little League umpire. What does that have to do with managing a service department? A lot more than you might expect.

People, whether they are your bosses, employees, or customers, expect you to be decisive. When they come to you for a decision, they expect that you will quickly and confidently make the call—the right call—in a timely manner. If you balk at making a decision, they think you are unsure about making decisions. Is it because you do not know? Or is it because you do not have the authority to make a decision? Or are you simply afraid to take risks?

As I indicated earlier, the best training and repeated practice that I experienced to help me along this way was umpiring. Go ahead, try it. Stand behind home plate some day and call the balls and strikes, whether it is for five-year-olds or for major leaguers. It doesn't matter. You will learn two things. First, everyone involved expects a speedy and accurate decision. Your worst enemy in this situation is indecision. Second, and probably most important, once you have made the call, you need to let it go and not let it influence your future calls. You will not always be 100 percent right, but if you try to make up for a bad call you will just follow one error with an endless string of additional ones.

A word of caution is, however, in order. By this very meaningful example, I do not mean in any way that you need to rush to judgment, making speed more important than accuracy. Business decisions are a bit more complicated than whether the ball is over the plate and between the letters and the knees. It often may take a bit longer to make the correct decision.

However, you can, and should, follow the two rules of umpiring.

Rule 1: Make the simple calls on the spot and the harder ones as soon as you are confident that you have enough information.

Rule 2: Let your decision go once it is made. Try not to make up for mistakes of the past by adjusting future decisions the other way. If you do, you will be spending more time trying to remember how you need to adjust your next call to even out things rather than focusing what is really important—what is the right decision for this situation, this time.

If you are serious about improving your skills as a manager, I encourage you, if time and opportunity permit, to volunteer as an umpire. Whether you do it for a day, a week, or a lifetime, I am confident you will find it to be a valuable training experience for your career in management and a good community service along the way.

Although there are many situations where the manager's decision-making skills are tested, three major areas, although different, are integral parts of management responsibility: planning and allocating resources, negotiating, and problem solving.

It is doubtful that you will ever work in an organization that has unlimited possibilities, unlimited potential, and unlimited resources. Therefore, an important skill set of the manager is the ability to make decisions on where to best use the limited, and sometimes even scarce, financial and human resources to the organization's best advantage. Decisions of this type are forward-thinking decisions that will help the organization to set the right direction and then consistently make the small decisions that keep the organization on this path to ultimate success. We will discuss long- and short-range planning and decision making to learn more about the principles governing this type of decision making in Chapters 9 and 10.

When things do not go as planned, whether because of errors or unforeseen events, it generally becomes the responsibility of the manager to identify, investigate, and develop a course of action to resolve the concern. This role as a key problem solver requires the manager to be able to investigate the situation uncovering all the relevant facts while being able to sort out and disregard unnecessary information. The manager should identify the different possible courses of action and determine the best one. The manager has to do this keeping in mind the short- and long-range goals of the department and the organization.

In many organizations, effective planning and a philosophy of proactive continuous process improvement do not exist. In such organizations the manager can be find himself in the position much like that of a fireman. That is, spending unreasonably high amounts of time putting out fires. That is, making temporary fixes to problems that could have, and should have, been resolved. Until the organization invests time and resources to anticipate problems and continuously improve processes, these situations will continue to occur. Later, in Chapter 12: "Continuous Improvement," we will explore this topic in more depth.

Effective negotiation is a foundational skill that is regularly called upon in every manager. These skills are used in interactions with your supervisor, managers of other departments, your employees, your suppliers, and your customers. As long as resources are limited and people have differing opinions and goals, negotiation will always be an essential skill. Negotiating is the ability to find a mutually acceptable solution that meets the different needs of all the parties involved. It requires listening, understanding, and the willingness to compromise, with the objective of finding a win-win solution whenever possible. More detailed examples of some of the strategies that are useful in successful negotiation are presented later in Section 6, Customer Relations.

Although being a decision maker is an essential part of being a manager, taking on the role of being *the* decision maker is a dangerous trap that every manager must be careful to avoid. There is a large difference between the two. Even though you will always find employees who are ready to second-guess your decisions and criticize the results, it is very likely that you will find that many of these employees are reluctant, when given the chance, to make the decision themselves. Why is this so? Because they do not want to take the responsibility that goes with making a decision. Everyone wants to be a hero, but few want to be held accountable.

Many are just not willing to accept the responsibility for their decisions. You, as a manager, are required to accept that responsibility. You should not allow employees to abdicate responsibility for their actions, coming to you every time for even the smallest decision. If employees are to be effective and productive in their roles, you, the manager, should be able to delegate not only tasks but the decision-making power and accountability that go with that role, so that employees have the resources they need to do the whole job. You cannot "sort of delegate" or "partially delegate." You have to totally delegate both the responsibility and the accountability, and with this delegation goes the expectation that employees will make the small decisions along the way.

Those with big egos might find it fascinating that their employees circle around them to make every minor decision. They might even have the misconception that this shows how indispensable they are to the department and the organization. Little could be further from the truth. For, it is not until you are able to have your employees understand and embrace taking full responsibility and accountability for their jobs, that you will be able to effectively manage.

Conduit

Conduit
The role of communicating information to other places and areas within the organization.

What is a **conduit?** It is a pipeline that assures that something of value gets from one place to its intended destination. Just as a physical conduit protects the wiring, assuring that the electricity gets from one end to the other consistently and without loss, so an effective manager acts as a conduit for communication taking the responsibility, on a regular basis, for communicating up, down, and across the organization. The manager regularly takes in, transfers, and distributes information on behalf of the company and its employees both internally and externally.

There is a great deal of activity that happens within the organization, the industry, and the market that it operates in every day. The manager plays an important role in monitoring current events within the organization as well as industry trends and changes to assure that the organization as a whole and the individual employees are best prepared to gain maximum benefit from these opportunities.

The manager has to disseminate to the frontlines the information he gathered through meetings with management about the current status of the organization and plans for the future. This is essential for keeping the operations and the direction of the department clearly aligned with the strategic direction of the organization (see Chapters 9 and 10). Without clear and consistent communication of this information, the department can easily become out of alignment with the direction of the company. They may be making ground but wasting their energy heading in the wrong direction. As the old adage goes, "If you do not know where you're headed, be careful, you just might get there!"

Not all the rank-and-file employees attend all the meetings and informal discussions with other departments and with upper management. That would be terribly inefficient. Who would do the work if everybody was tied up in meetings all day, every day? The department manager has, as part of his role, to be the spokesperson of the department. In doing so, he plays an essential role in communicating upward the needs and concerns of the employees. The employees expect him to advocate on their behalf to assure that their needs are fairly considered and addressed. The manager also advocates to upper management, assuring that the department receives a fair share of scarce resources. Finally, he communicates the management directives down to the department, representing upper management, making sure that any important information is passed down to each employee of the organization.

A very important piece of guidance on being an effective conduit of upper management to the frontline employees is ownership. That is, as a manager you are part of management. Therefore, your superiors and your employees expect that when you serve in the role of communicating management directives, you do so as the mouthpiece of management, not as a third party. There is a significant distinction between saying "my boss said we have to . . ." and saying "I've discussed this with the rest of the management team and we have decided that we have to. . . ." In the second example, the manager is speaking on behalf of management; in the first one he is speaking *about* management. Similarly, when the manager takes issues up the ladder to his supervisors, his employees expect the same courtesy and commitment that he is willing to advocate on their behalf and as part of their team, not as a neutral third party who is just the messenger.

Finally, just as the conduit protects and isolates the wires from the outside environment, so the manager does this on behalf of his employees. The frontline workers, technicians for example, have a specific job to do—they fix cars. Anything that diverts their attention and energies from performing this job considerably reduces their productivity and, thus, the ultimate capacity of the organization to produce. As a conduit, the manager protects and isolates the employees from unimportant and unnecessary distractions. This important action helps to maintain high employee morale, preserve their ability to stay focused on their primary task, and, ultimately results in consistently high productivity and profitability.

Qualities of a Manager

Regardless of the industry, the size of company, or the overarching management philosophy, there are some universal qualities that separate well-respected and successful managers from the rest. No matter what the business setting is, for a manager to succeed he or she must earn the respect of co-workers. In addition, with the many and varying responsibilities that exist in all management roles, he or she must be efficient to get the best use out of the most limited resource, time. We will now discuss these two qualities in more detail.

Qualities of a Respected Manager

A manager who enjoys the **respect** of his employees is better able to get the most out of them and to foster a more pleasant and positive working environment. It is through respect for their supervisors in the organization that employees feel they are valued and important. When employees can look to supervisors as a living example of the values and ideals of the organization, they can much more easily buy in to the organizational philosophy. This makes it more than mere words, it becomes very real. Thus, respect for the manager helps to foster greater employee commitment to the organization. This type of positive environment encourages employees to feel comfortable in the work environment, to put forward their best efforts, and to make a greater contribution to the success of the operation.

Respect
Holding or being held in high regard or esteem.

A manager must possess a number of attributes in order to gain the employees' respect regardless of his management philosophy or that of the company as a whole. The ideal manager exhibits the following attributes:

- *Hard working*—Employees do not seem to mind working hard and going above and beyond the call of duty when they feel that the manager is willing to do the same. If the manager is unwilling to put forth at least the same level of effort and commitment that he demands of his employees, they will be less likely to work hard for him.

- *Pleasant*—Employees respond best to a manager that is encouraging, upbeat, and enthusiastic. Being pleasant helps to "pump up" the employees and encourage them to want to perform. Employees in a positive work environment often look to their supervisor for encouragement and direction. When the going gets rough, they look to their manager for that inner strength that allows them to keep the faith and, as a result, helps them to muster up the energy to persist.
- *Honest and upright*—Most employees prefer to work for a manager who establishes clear ethical guidelines and adheres to them consistently. Employees need to know their manager will never ask them to do anything they consider dishonest or expect them to bend the rules to succeed. Even slight differences between the employees' expectations and the manager's standards can create an environment of distrust.
- *Dependable*—Employees look to their manager as the company's accepted model of behavior and performance. They expect the manager to be level-headed; someone they can count on in even the most difficult situations. Managers are also the intermediaries between employees and the remainder of the organization, and an employee's future in the company rests largely in the manager's hands. Because managers wield such influence, employees must trust their managers and know what to expect of them.
- *Consistent*—A manager can build trust among his employees by treating them all in a similar manner, avoiding any hint of preferential treatment. Employees must trust that the manager's decisions are all based on performance and principle, not on personality.
- *Firm*—Employees realize that managers are responsible for getting the job done. Good managers clearly and consistently communicate what they consider important and what they expect of employees. A less direct and firm approach, with vaguely defined expectations, goals, and objectives, too often leads to misunderstandings and general employee dissatisfaction.
- *Organized*—Employees expect their supervisor to serve as a source of guidance, information, and stability within the department. They expect that their manager is keenly aware of organizational, departmental, and individual priorities at all times. They expect that the manager is able to multitask—that is, that he is organized enough to keep track of all the tasks and challenges at hand, at any moment in time, and can deal with all of them simultaneously.
- *Fair*—Both reward and discipline exists within the workplace as tools to help to encourage positive performance and curb negative performance. Employees expect to see both of these methods used, but they need to see that the rewards and discipline are used fairly across all circumstances and all employees using the same standards. Simply put, the reasonable expectation is that the rewards fit the performance and that punishments fit the crime.

Qualities of an Efficient Manager

Efficiency is one of the foundational traits of a consistently high-performing manager. Efficiency speaks of your ability to be an example to your employees of how to consistently get the most out of yourself and provide them a living example of how they can do the same. After all, they all are looking for a good example to follow that will make them more successful too. An efficient manager is characterized by having the following attributes:

- *Goal oriented*—Efficient use of time, energy, and resources starts with having a clear vision of where you are headed and why: establishing clearly defined goals and staying on task to accomplish them.
- *Disciplined*—Staying on task consistently demonstrates an efficiency of motion and effort that is needed to maximize the results of your efforts. An efficient manager concentrates on achieving his goals and minimizes distractions that slow down his momentum or waste energy or time.
- *Self-motivated*—A self-motivated individual knows where he is going and focuses on getting there as soon as possible. The self-starter needs no prods or reminders to spring into motion; he typically hits the ground running and does not stop. His inner drive serves as a strong example and inspiration for those around him.
- *Nose for the goal line*—The old phrase "When the going gets tough, the tough get going" is the hallmark of the efficient manager. His motivation, discipline, and goal orientation keep him pushing until he reaches or surpasses his goal. The efficient manager possesses a clear vision of the goal that helps him overcome difficulties and obstacles that frustrate less efficient employees and keep him from reaching his goal and his potential.
- *Trusting*—Typically characterized as the eternal optimist, the efficient manager knows he can count on others. Because he believes this, he helps motivate and inspire others to live up to these expectations. He is thus able to count on more support from employees to aid him in achieving goals and objectives.
- *Seeks input*—The successful goal-oriented manager is not a one-man show or an egomaniac. The efficient manager realizes that he is the leader of a team that can only win if everyone is motivated to pull together. To build a true working partnership with employees, the efficient manager regularly discusses goals and plans with co-workers, solicits their input, builds consensus for team goals, and helps bolster employee commitment. Getting input and then going in a different direction is not **efficient**, or effective. An efficient manager creates a work environment that is open to input and suggestions, up and down the line. Everyone knows that they are more than just another set of hands, that their input is valuable, and that their commitment is essential for success.
- *Willing to let go*—Delegating assignments and activities to workers is necessary in all management environments. A manager can only truly achieve efficiency when he is comfortable delegating both the task and the responsibility for its completion and trusts that the employees will do their best to accomplish the task. Only when the manager is able to let go can he move on completely to his next responsibility and make the most efficient use his time and energy.

Efficient
Being able to produce the desired results with a minimum of wasted time, energy, or other resources.

Delegating

One of the most fundamental skills needed to effectively manage is the ability to **delegate.** If the manager was able to do everything, there would be no need for workers and no one to manage and lead. In its simplest sense, delegation is

Delegate
To give someone the power and authority to act on behalf of others.

Real World Application

One of the great fallacies of management is that "the boss knows best." Many new managers struggle to understand why employees question their decisions; from their perspective, they do not seem to "get it." I know I did. After all, I was chosen for the position because I was best qualified.

However, the first step toward becoming an efficient manager begins when you realize that you are not managing yourself, you are managing others. You need to be able to see the world through the eyes of your employees if you hope to appreciate, understand, and meet their needs. One of the biggest aids to helping me apply this on a daily basis was learning, and learning to understand, a well-known maxim, often called, "The Golden Rule of Management." Simply, it states

People do things for *their* reasons, not *yours*!

If you are interested in becoming a successful manager, I encourage you to write this down, remember it, and remind yourself of it *every* time you are making a decision. It will help you to keep things in the proper perspective and to find win-win solutions that will earn you loyal customers, happy co-workers, and ultimate success in whatever business you pursue.

the ability to get others to be an extension of management. If you are able to direct the efforts of others so that they become extra eyes, hands, and legs, more work can be completed than you can do alone.

Many managers have risen through the ranks because they were the best at a particular job. Because of their expertise in doing that work, their standards are high and, thus, so are their expectations. Because of their skills, abilities, and their resulting productivity, upper management commonly taps these individuals for management in the hope that they will be able to guide and direct others to follow their example. The company dreams that the result will be a shop full of copies of the manager who will all produce the quality and the volume of good work that the new supervisor has so consistently produced.

However, because of the high standards of this exemplary worker, who has now become the manager, the new manager often quickly becomes frustrated with the workers' inability to do their jobs as well, as fast, and as efficiently as they could do it. As a result, being able to resist the temptation to simply say 'step aside and let me do it' and learning to delegate is one of the most difficult and challenging transitions to make. An effective manager gets the workers to do the job correctly, consistently, and efficiently, thus resulting in the greatest amount of results at the lowest cost.

Responsibility
Being expected to assure that a task or decision is carried out and achieves its expected outcome.

Beyond simply learning to delegate (let go) and direct employees to perform the tasks, there are two levels of delegation that are distinctively different: delegation of tasks and jobs and delegation of **responsibility.** By delegating the task, you make the employee accountable for getting the activity completed. By delegating responsibility, you make the employee accountable for the results and give him the latitude to do what it takes to reach that goal. True delegation requires you to let go and delegate the task and the responsibility. For delegation to be effective, it is also essential that you demand **accountability** from the employees for their actions, successful or otherwise. These are essential skills that every manager must possess to allow him or her the freedom to address the many and varied broader responsibilities that go along with any supervisory position.

Accountability
Receiving appropriate rewards or penalties based on the results of your actions.

SUMMARY

Management is not only a skill; it is more than that. It is a combination of knowledge and skills applied at the right moment in the right combination. When done well, it is more like a work of art than like applying a set recipe. Managers are expected to constantly juggle multiple roles. Their managers, their peers, and their subordinates all look to them. Their role as a position holder, judge, and conduit of information is essential to the smooth operation of their department and, as a result, the organization as a whole. As a result of these high expectations and varied responsibilities, there is always more to do than there is time and resources to do them all. Therefore, the efficient manager is aware of and judiciously chooses how to best use the resources and his efforts to get the best possible results.

With the many duties and responsibilities that a manager is called upon to address it is not possible for any manager to do everything that is demanded of him or her. For that reason an essential skill is learning how to identify and prioritize the demands put upon the manager and to consciously decide which ones will have the most impact and, therefore, where to concentrate effort and attention to get the greatest results.

PRACTICING THE PRINCIPLES

1. When a manager speaks, customers commonly expect him to speak on behalf of
   a. entire industry.
   b. only himself.
   c. the department.
   d. the entire organization.

2. Acting as a conduit within the organization, the effective manager
   a. communicates management information to employees.
   b. advocates to management on behalf of the employees.
   c. isolates the employees from unnecessary information/interruptions.
   d. all of the above.

3. An effective manager is able and willing to delegate
   a. responsibility for assignments.
   b. accountability for the results.
   c. tasks only; the manager is the one who is responsible.
   d. a and b.

4. If your supervisor determines the amount of your next raise based on your performance, you are __________ for your actions.
   a. accountable.
   b. responsible.
   c. rewarded.
   d. all of the above.

5. A key principle in understanding and motivating employees is that
   a. people do things for their reason, not yours.
   b. people do things for no apparent reason.
   c. people do things for your reasons, not theirs.
   d. people always want to make their boss unhappy.

6. List three characteristics of a respected manager.

   ____

   ____

   ____

7. List three characteristics of an efficient manager.

   ____

   ____

   ____

8. The role of a manager in which customers see him or her as speaking on behalf of the company is
   a. conduit.
   b. judge.
   c. position holder.
   d. all of the above.

9. Which statement does not fit with the others?
   a. Managers are always expected to be a conduit of information to their employees.
   b. Managers are always expected to provide information freely to the press.
   c. Managers are expected to communicate employee needs to upper management.
   d. Managers advocate on behalf of their department with other departments.

10. Employees often come to their managers for decisions because they think that
    a. they are not sure what to do and do not want to take the risk.
    b. if the manager makes the decision, then the employees cannot be held responsible.
    c. if the employees make the decision, they might be held accountable for the results.
    d. all of the above are possible correct answers.

CHAPTER 8

Ethics and Stewardship

CHAPTER OBJECTIVES

- To assess the importance of applying ethical standards to the management of an organization
- To examine some of the fundamental ethical principles that relate to working with people
- To recognize the stewardship responsibility of a manager toward the organization, co-workers, and customers

KEY TERMS

ethics
applied ethics
responsibility
truthfulness
honesty
integrity
stewardship
reputation

Introduction

We have explored a variety of principles and practices to guide you as a manager to do things right. But how do you know you are doing *the right things?* That is where values and ethics come into play. A dramatic example of an ethical dilemma is the use of atomic energy. I have this powerful resource available to me. Now, the question is: Do I use it to kill people (the bomb) or save people (medicine)? This is an ethical dilemma.

In this chapter we will explore the general concepts of ethics. What are ethics? And, more important, how do they affect me as an individual, a manager, and a leader? These are some of the questions that you will need to grapple with as you move into a supervisory position. Finally, we will discuss an important opportunity to apply ethics—stewardship.

What Is Ethics?

Everyone makes decisions in his or her life. How do you decide what to do? How do you make decisions in your life? Some decisions may be simple and may not appear to be major issues; some may involve complex issues of morals and values. However, a common factor is that all of the decisions that you make are based on your beliefs and standards. Even decisions as simple as answering the question: What do you want for dinner? may be dependent upon your standards. Because of your personal beliefs, you may not eat certain foods. Although this is a very simple example, it implies that underlying your actions are your values and your fundamental code of ethics.

Ethics is applying your principles and values to your decisions and actions. It goes far beyond justifying any specific action. Developing a code of ethics is a process of determining a code of conduct and the principles underlying that code and then acting in a consistent manner based on those standards. This becomes a firm foundation that helps to guide and support all of your decisions. Further, knowing why you choose those principles and values as the foundation of your actions, you can defend and recommend those rules and principles as guidance for proper behavior to others.

Ethics
An individual's application of his or her principles or values in decisions and actions.

If you know where you stand on a particular subject or topic, that stance is based upon some fundamental beliefs that you hold dear. Although some of your ethical values may be based on your religious beliefs, your ethics are not based solely on religious rules or doctrines. Your ethical values are a comprehensive set of values that you have developed over time that create the guiding principles underlying what you believe in and, therefore, are the driving force in the major decision-making process in your life. They are not an external set of rules, such as a street sign that you should obey or a church rule that you're supposed to follow; they are internal principles and beliefs that are a part of your core being.

For example, if you strongly value diversity, then all of your behavior and decisions will be in agreement with that value. You would make a point to assure that in your hiring practices that you provide open and equal access to all people. In fact, you would most likely be sensitive enough to the issue to make a point to intentionally reach out to a diverse population in the community. This same value would also be demonstrated in your daily interactions with co-workers and friends. Your circle of close friends would likely mirror your values as we all tend to gravitate naturally toward those who share our values.

Your ethical values may come from a variety of sources. If you have been raised in a family that is actively involved in religious practice, the values, moral principles, and rules espoused by your church may be foundational to your personal ethics. However, a formal religion is not the only source for these basic principles. Just because you were taught principles and were required to adhere to them does not mean that you truly believe in them, and that is the true test of your core values. Your values may evolve as you encounter and take a stand on matters of conscience, respect, consequences, or justice. Taking into account all of the thoughts, experiences, and external advice that you have encountered in your life, you formulate a stand on many issues. The foundation underlying the decision to take a stand is your values.

Although it may seem odd, your ability and willingness to take a stand can help you to better understand yourself and what you really believe in. Many of us do not take the time to examine our values. We are too busy living our daily lives to get too philosophical. However, when you absolutely must take a stand on an issue, it is a good time to stop and take stock of why you made your decision. If you made an intentional decision, then the underlying thoughts, principles, and values deep down inside of you were very likely the determining factors in your knowing what was the *right* thing to do. Therefore, developing self-awareness and, in doing so, an awareness of the value system and ethics that are the foundation to your actions is an important part of your personal and professional growth.

Applied Ethics

Now, you might be thinking that sounds all well and good and so ideal and lofty, but what about dealing with this in the real world? Although you believe in being truthful and want to live your life that way, if a customer asks you what you paid your technician or what your actual cost is for the tires you are trying to sell him, being totally truthful and giving him that information is not in your best interest. What, then, is the appropriate use of these principles, values, and ethics?

Ethical behavior implies that you live by a higher standard. Doing what you can get away with is not enough. You feel an inner drive for your behavior and your beliefs to agree. However, there are times when you might apply the rules differently in different situations. How can you reconcile not being totally rigid and allow for some flexibility?

In an ideal world, everything would be so consistent that decision making would be simple. Life, however, is not simple. Neither is decision making. Many of the decisions that we need to make are very complex. It is difficult to apply one standard or one decision universally. We need to consider and make decisions on a case-by-case basis. **Applied ethics** is the real-world application of your core values and principles to the wide range of very different situations that you encounter every day. It is not how you would or should apply them in an ideal situation; it is not how you would apply each particular value in theory. It is how you decide in the complex situations you encounter daily that often involve a complex interplay of many factors and many values all at once. Your ability to apply your ethical values consistently and with conviction is the true test of your core beliefs.

Applied Ethics
The real-world application of a person's core values and principles to a wide range of different situations.

THEORY INTO PRACTICE 8-1

CASE

As a very busy manager in a large shop you have learned that hiring a porter is always a time-consuming task. It is so difficult sifting through the applicants whenever you publicly announce an opening for low-skilled positions. However, as a person that values diversity, you want to ensure that you are providing an opportunity for every qualified applicant. After all, you cannot discriminate.

You decide

In this case, which of the following choices would be your best option?

a. Hire one of your employee's daughters so you can avoid wasting time and money advertising and interviewing many people.

b. Run ads in the local paper and be satisfied that whatever response you get is good enough.

c. Advertise until you are convinced that you have a diverse pool of candidates to interview and consider for the position.

d. Take your friend's advice and hire one of his acquaintances who is a female minority, thereby showing that you support diversity.

THEORY INTO PRACTICE 8-2

CASE

It has just been reported to you that your best technician has been taking home some shop supplies (cleaners, lubricants, fluids) for personal use on some jobs that he is doing after hours. You have always made it clear to your employees that all parts and supplies are the property of either the company or the customer and that the employees have no right to use or take any of them for personal use. In fact, you even reprimanded and fired an employee about a year ago for stealing company supplies. However, you give your employees the benefit of the doubt and normally give them several warnings before you resort to stern punishment.

You decide

What do you do? He is your best technician and this is the first time that this has happened. Yet, you know that the word has gotten around the shop and that everyone is waiting to see how you are going to treat this employee, who is taking supplies from the shop. There appears to be more at stake than usual. You are, with reason, concerned about the impact of your response in this case. What would you do?

a. Give him a stern warning making it clear that you cannot give him preferential treatment.

b. Make an example out of this technician by severely punishing him for this infraction.

c. Tell him in private that although you would normally write anyone else up for this, you are not going to do anything this time because he is your best technician.

d. Because you know that other employees are aware of the situation, reprimand him publicly and suspend him for three days without pay.

Ethical Leadership

Let us explore several key ethical principles. These are core values that every manager should strive to demonstrate in every action and decision. Through knowing, understanding, and exemplifying these values, a good manager can build an ethical foundation for his or her team. Therefore these ethical principles are very likely to guide the actions that your entire organization will exemplify.

In Chapter 6 we discussed that people *choose* to follow a leader. You may be able to manage and require compliance, but you cannot lead people without their consent and their willing participation. We also saw that one of the most important principles of leadership was to walk the talk. There is a need to lead by example if we expect others to respect us as a leader. This alignment between what we say and what we do demonstrates one of the most profound attributes of a leader—credibility.

People are willing to make a commitment, take risks, and go beyond the minimum required when they believe in a cause. Their belief in a cause is dependent on the feeling that they are entering into a two-way trust relationship. They can best reach this higher level of commitment when they see total agreement between the words and the actions of the leader that they have chosen to follow. You are credible when your words and your actions agree.

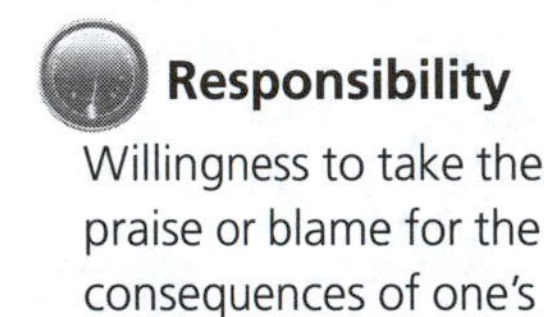

Responsibility
Willingness to take the praise or blame for the consequences of one's actions.

A second major value that underlies a strong management ethical system is **responsibility.** Responsibility is the willingness to take the praise or blame for the consequences of your actions. To be truly responsible, you need to recognize that when you have authority you will be held accountable for making decisions that will affect you and others. Risk and reward are a part of any

Real World Application

As the service manager at a large dealership I received several complaints about cars that had returned within three months with repeat problems after transmission overhauls. Because the technician who performed the original repairs was on vacation, a different technician did the second repair (at the cost of the shop). In two cases I found that the gaskets that had failed were old gaskets; yet both customers had been charged for a complete transmission overhaul, and their bills indicated that they paid for a complete overhaul kit including all new seals and gaskets. How could this be? We fixed the cars at no charge and apologized to the customers.

Upon the transmission technician's return, I confronted him with what had happened. Without hesitation he said that whenever he had to disassemble a transmission to repair a leaking seal or gasket he got a complete kit but only replaced the parts that he could see had failed. I asked, "What do you do with the rest of the parts?" He responded that he kept them in his toolbox as spare parts for the future.

I was very upset. I felt that this was dishonest and unethical. I asked, "The customer paid for a *complete* transmission overhaul, which includes replacement of all seals and gaskets and all you did was to replace one seal and a few gaskets?" He said, "Yes, why should I mess with parts that were not broken?" I responded, "Because that is what you told the service advisor that the customer needed, that's what he called the customer and sold her, and that is what you got paid to do!" He argued that what he did was what he thought was best. I explained to him, "This is far more than a matter of a proper repair—it is a matter of honesty. Our customers depend on us to give them the proper recommendations, and then perform the work that we have recommended and stand behind it. We did not do that in this case." He said, 'Well, you can check around the shop and you will find that other techs do stuff like this every day!'

The result was that we had a shop meeting in which I clearly explained to everyone that we had an ethical dilemma. I made it a strict policy that we needed to be completely open and honest with our customers. If we sold them a complete overhaul, we needed to do a complete overhaul. If we, on the other hand, felt that a simpler replacement was needed and we needed to buy more parts than were used (such as having to purchase a seal kit or overhaul kit), we were not to keep the unused parts. Those parts were the property of the customer and should be returned to the customer along with all the replaced parts.

This was a matter of being open and honest with our customers about what they needed and what we were doing. And, even though it might be difficult at times, we were not going to hide the truth.

business environment. Without risk you will wallow in mediocrity. However, you should take calculated risks while considering the potential impact on yourself and others. Only when these factors have been taken into account and you feel justified that the action plan is in the best interest of all parties can you responsibly make weighty and important decisions.

Contrary to popular belief, there is no such thing as a harmless lie. **Truthfulness** is an essential quality if you expect to command the respect and commitment of employees and customers. Before they choose to follow your direction and guidance they must believe that you will be truthful in the face of any situation. Your reputation depends on it. They will only be willing to consistently take risks if they are absolutely certain that you are telling it to them straight.

Truthfulness
Providing only real and factual information.

A value that may at times be confused with truthfulness is the much more expansive principle of **honesty.** Honesty implies a refusal to lie, steal, or deceive in any way. It goes far beyond what you say; it involves what you say, what you do, and the intent underlying your actions. It requires that you make every attempt to do the right thing.

Honesty
Refusal to lie, steal, or deceive in any way.

Ultimately, when you are able to consistently demonstrate through your words and behavior that you are credible, responsible, truthful, and honest, you have achieved integrity. A person that others see as having integrity is one who is able to demonstrate his values openly and consistently to the point that others see him as being wholly incapable and unwilling to waver on these values. This is one of the highest compliments for someone who is striving to achieve and live an ethical life.

THEORY INTO PRACTICE 8-3

CASE

You are the service manager of a small transmission shop. Your technician comes to you and indicates that the problem with Mrs. Jones' car is that there is an internal leak in the automatic transmission that is causing it to slip in first gear. Because the parts are available only as a complete gasket and seal set, and although Mrs. Jones needs only one seal you are going to have to sell her the labor plus an entire seal kit for $80.

You decide

You know that Mrs. Jones is going to be upset when you tell her about the needed repairs and especially that it is going to cost her $80 for a seal set when all that she really needs is a little O-ring that is worth about $3. Which of the following would you do?

a. Explain to Mrs. Jones that the transmission needs completely overhauled and that the cost of parts is $80 and do not say anything more about the fact that you only need to replace one $3 seal so that you do not get her upset.
b. Install all the parts in the kit because you are going to charge Mrs. Jones for them, so that she will have all new gaskets and seals in her transmission.
c. Explain the cost of labor and parts and very apologetically explain Mrs. Jones that the parts are only available as a kit and that you will be giving her the remaining new parts separately because she has paid for them.
d. Give Mrs. Jones a total estimate, replace the seal, and put the rest of the gaskets in your toolbox along with all the others that you have saved over time so that you can use them in the future if you need them.
e. More than one of the above answers is correct.

The Importance of Ethics

Anyone may believe in the values that we have discussed and demonstrate some degree of success in living these values from time to time. However, it is not until you become aware of these values, acknowledge their importance to you, and make a conscious commitment to use them as guidance for your actions that your actions will consistently reflect your values. This increased awareness of and reliance on these values as a consistent foundation for your actions results in your ability to use these important principles as the foundation of all that you do. This is ethical behavior.

As a manager you are constantly under the microscope as both your coworkers and your customers look to you to evaluate your ethics and standards. Employees and customers alike look for something and someone to believe in. They measure whether you fit that standard based on the values and attitudes that they see you demonstrate on a consistent basis. The foundation of these values and attitudes is your internal awareness of your code of ethics and the degree to which you demonstrate that consistently in your behaviors and actions.

Co-workers, whether they report to you or work in other departments regularly look for guidance, direction, and inspiration. To make a real commitment to the organization, they look for a leader they can choose to follow. Further, as they go beyond merely accepting you as a leader and look for inspiration, they expect that your actions match their high standards and values. Your visible and consistently applied high ethical standards will be essential in helping them to raise their level of commitment to you and to the company.

Integrity
Behavior that upholds a high standard of moral and ethical values.

Customers and external partners, as well, choose to work with someone that they believe has integrity. They expect that they are respected and that they will always be dealt with fairly and honestly. **Integrity** implies that the values are so much a part of you that they are an integral part of who you are and are constant and unwavering. Because you are the company in the eyes of the vendors and customers that you deal directly with, you have to be the indicator of whether the company is credible and has integrity. If they cannot see integrity in the company's actions, their relationship will be tentative at best. They will feel insecure and be wary of getting mistreated. They will not be able to develop and maintain a comfort level in dealing with you and your company unless and until they can feel that you have demonstrated these attributes.

Core values and ethics are not limited to the handful of key concepts and principles that we have presented. These broad principles can and should become the source for you to begin to reflect, consider, and analyze your values and your standards, and in so doing become clearer in understanding your ethical values.

Stewardship

In recent years there has been a growing focus in the business world on the use and abuse of power by managers. The blatant disregard of some employees for those resources that have been put at their disposal has resulted in some of the most momentous cases of fraud, theft in office, and embezzlement that we have ever witnessed.

Stewardship
Taking appropriate care for resources or assets that are under your care and custody.

These recent developments have resulted in a heightened interest and sensitivity of stewardship. **Stewardship** is the act of taking appropriate care for someone else's resources or assets that have been put in your care and custody. Every manager, by the nature of his or her position, acts on behalf of a supervisor, the owner, and/or the board of trustees in this fashion. The very nature of the organization delegating responsibility and authority downward to subordinates, ranging from vice presidents down to coordinators and group leaders, carries with it not only the power to make and enforce decisions, but also responsibility and authority. Stewardship is a major responsibility of every manager.

Because you are a manager, your supervisor or the organization has put at your disposal various assets of the organization with the expectation that you will utilize them to the best benefit of the organization. There are three major areas of stewardship responsibility. The most common is financial stewardship, but your responsibility extends beyond merely watching the money. A second, yet just as important, stewardship responsibility is the responsibility for maintaining the reputation and good name of the organization. Finally, as the supervisor and advocate for your subordinates, you also have a stewardship responsibility for the careers and future of your employees and their families.

Financial Stewardship

Some of the most tangible assets that you have stewardship responsibilities over are the physical resources (shop, tools, equipment) and the budget (company funds) that you can access and use within your judgment as a manager. If you ask about this responsibility, any manager will quickly acknowledge that he or she is responsible and held accountable for the bottom line of their department or operation. But stewardship goes beyond a responsibility for the "bottom line"; it also includes the reasonable and ethical use of resources to achieve that bottom line.

Some of the well-publicized trials of business executives have resulted from managers who were trying to maximize the bottom line. That's their job, right? Yes, but the ethical use of the resources in their care and custody is also their responsibility. That is stewardship. No manager has the right to do whatever it takes. No manager has the right to disregard the rules to achieve success. This is true with their own money and, even more important, with the money and assets of others.

As a responsible manager you are expected to provide direction and use those financial and physical resources that have been put at your disposal in a manner consistent with the guidelines and direction of your supervisors and your organization. You need to manage every resource in a manner that you believe your supervisors would agree with if they were to be making the decisions themselves. This requires that you clearly understand the organizations goals and values to guide you.

How does this set a higher standard beyond strictly staying legal and improving the bottom line? It requires you do not take for granted, waste, or in other ways bend the rules even if the likelihood of getting caught is minimal. "Would the owner approve this if he knew about it?" or "Would the board of trustees approve?" should be the test of your actions. Even further, you might ask yourself, "How would I feel if this was reported on the front page of tomorrow morning's newspaper?"

Just because you can take a few shortcuts does not mean that it is OK to do so. Just because no one will know if I use the company car for personal business or "borrow" some of the shop tools to do some work at home does not make it proper stewardship. Appropriate financial stewardship requires that you exercise the fair and reasonable use of those resources that the company has put at your disposal and under your care and custody.

Reputation Stewardship

 **Reputation**
The commonly held perception of a person's character and values based on their past actions and behavior.

Successful organizations are built upon their public **reputations**. These reputations are earned over a long period of time based on years of consistent performance. In the view of customers you, as a manager, are the company. For that reason your words and actions represent the company and you are perceived as acting on behalf of the company. Customers expect that whatever you say or do is a clear indication of the company's values and beliefs.

If a customer sees a behavior that enhances her perception of the company, you have improved your company's reputation. Conversely, anything that you do or say that lowers a customer's perception can significantly and permanently damage the reputation of the company. Your stewardship of the company's reputation as a frontline representative of the company, therefore, is a responsibility that you must acknowledge and take very seriously. Although it may appear more subtle than mismanaging financial assets, it can have a greater impact on the company's success or failure than the loss or waste of a small amount of money. Stewardship in this regard requires that you take proper care of the trust and goodwill of the good name of the company.

Employee Stewardship

The third and final area of stewardship that you must carefully exercise is that over the well-being of the employees under your guidance as their manager. This area is the one most often ignored. As a manager you are responsible to upper management and the shareholders for the success of your department. When your department meets or exceeds expectations, you and your people receive rewards and accolades. When your department falls below expectations, especially in the long term, it results in upper management decisions that directly affect you personally. The consequences may include increased hours, being passed over for promotions, cuts in pay, and even layoff or termination.

These benefits and consequences not only directly affect you, but also affect the people working under your guidance. Layoffs, reduction in benefits, lack of raises, and even getting passed over for new tools and equipment may all be the result of poor departmental performance. These actions may cause problems ranging from disappointment to a career crisis for your employees.

It is not uncommon to think about how the performance of your employees can either make or break your success as a manager. Because you cannot do everything, to be successful, you depend on their performance. Conversely, as their manager, leader, and coach, your employees' future is in your hands. The decisions that you make directly affect the working environment within which they operate.

You are the steward of the working environment for those employees that you supervise. Global decisions such as pricing, advertising, promotions, pay rates, work distribution, and hiring of other employees can create, alter, or hamper opportunities for them to be successful. Employees work for you and your company and trust that you have their best interest in mind. In return you expect them to feel and act the same way toward you and the company. Your responsibility toward your employees is not to be taken lightly because it can dramatically affect their success at your company and may, in the long run, have a major impact on their entire career, their well-being, and that of their family.

SUMMARY

Ethical behavior is critical to the ongoing success of anyone in business. However, the majority of time and effort are too often so focused on what needs to be done that little conscious effort is ever put into considering why things need to be done. The ethical values of any individual or any organization build the foundation for why they do what they do.

Ethics are more than doctrines or principles. They are your core beliefs. They are how you put your principles and values into action and they provide a solid base for every decision that you make.

Stewardship adds a new dimension to the entire issue of responsibility. It is for this reason that many employees, upon considering the amount of responsibilities that they have to others and to the organization, decide to remain as workers rather than as a manager. However, although the power and authority of managing may sound attractive you cannot use authority alone. There are three major areas of stewardship that all managers must address: financial, reputation, and employee stewardship. With authority comes responsibility, and stewardship is a major responsibility of every manager.

PRACTICING THE PRINCIPLES

1. As a manager you have some degree of responsibility for the financial resources and reputation of the company along with the future of your subordinates. This is called
   a. stewardship.
   b. accountability.
   c. unreasonable demands.
   d. leadership.
2. Ethics is based upon
   a. long-held personal beliefs.
   b. those things that are important to you.
   c. what your religion teaches.
   d. all of the above.
3. Using ethics in a variety of every day situations is called
   a. being a hypocrite.
   b. applied ethics.
   c. living the dream.
   d. none of the above.
4. Being a good steward of your employer's resources means that
   a. you are careful not to get caught.
   b. you do not care about their reputation.
   c. you do whatever it takes to make them money.
   d. none of the above.
5. The application of your principles and values is
   a. empathy.
   b. consistency.
   c. ethics.
   d. inconsideration.

In Questions 6–10 match the definition with the term. Indicate your letter choice on the space to the left of the definition.

	Definition	Term
_____	6. Values are an integral part of who you are	a. credibility
_____	7. You are able to walk the talk	b. integrity
_____	8. You tell it to them straight	c. honesty
_____	9. Willing to take praise or blame for your actions	d. truthfulness
_____	10. Refusal to lie or deceive in any way	e. responsibility

SECTION

3

MANAGEMENT STRATEGIES

Planning and goal setting are essential to obtaining the greatest results from the resources that any organization has at its disposal. Meaningful and reasonable goals and objectives help to keep the entire operation headed in the same direction—the right direction. Building a continuously growing, continuously improving organization is essential to fend off competition and ensure long-term success. With these principles in mind we will explore the multiple levels of planning that are essential to building a clear and comprehensive strategy to achieve your goals. Finally, we will discuss those principles that can help a successful organization to continue to thrive and strive to be better every day.

- CHAPTER 9: Long-Range Planning
- CHAPTER 10: Strategic and Short-Range Planning
- CHAPTER 11: Decision Making
- CHAPTER 12: Quality and Continuous Improvement

CHAPTER

9

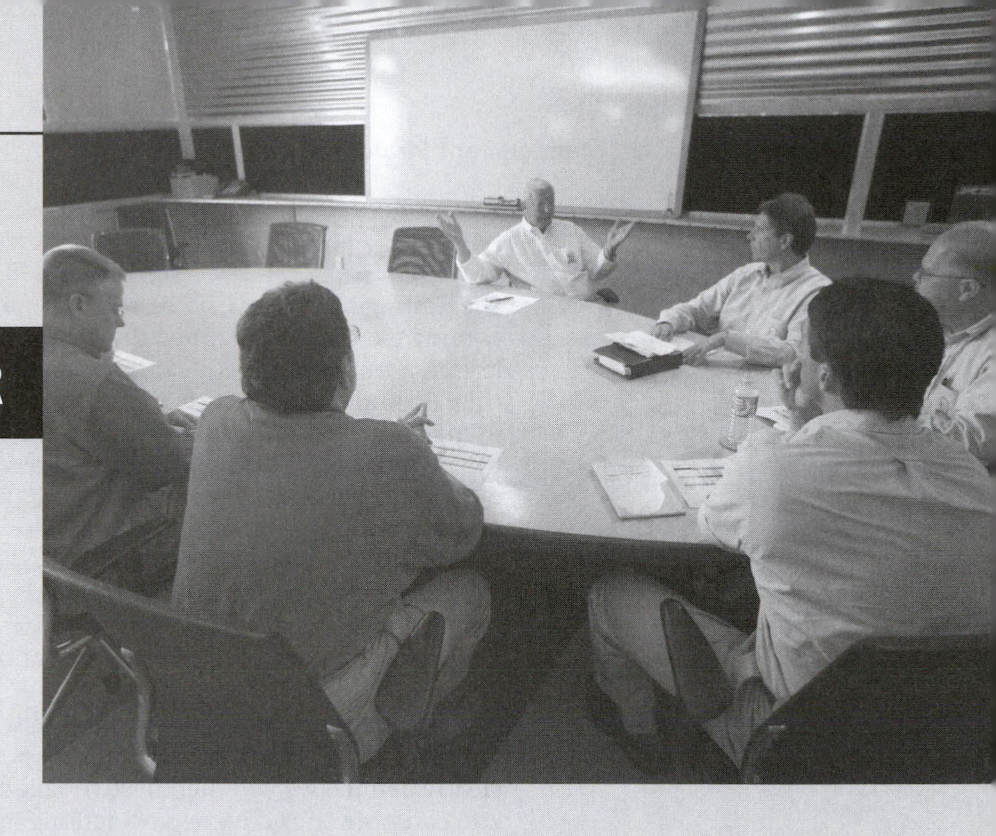

Long-Range Planning

CHAPTER OBJECTIVES

- To identify the foundational principles of long-range planning
- To examine the importance of a vision and mission in the direction of an organization
- To be able to understand the importance of short-term planning and activities in relation to long-range goals

KEY TERMS

vision
mission
values
goals

Introduction

Successful individuals share the common traits of being both focused and committed to a well-defined direction and objectives. Whether it is a business leader, a minister, an educator, or an athlete they all share a passion for what they do and maintain a clear focus of where they are headed. They are, in fact, living their dream. This is a statement you have probably heard a thousand times. But, have you ever stopped to ask yourself: What is my dream? Clarity of direction and purpose is an essential trait of successful individuals . . . and also successful businesses.

In this chapter we will explore how to clarify the overall dream of your department or organization. Once this has been established we will discuss how to methodically translate this dream into reality as you learn to break it down into practical directions, goals, and actions so that all of your efforts can be directed to accomplish it.

The main components in building the big picture future for any organization are in identifying its vision, mission, values, and goals. Once these are clearly defined we will then need to take a look at the day-to-day means to plan and carry out the activities and actions that will assure this reality is achieved.

Many highly motivated people are in too big of a hurry to dig in and get started with the work at hand without considering their ultimate direction. Where are we really trying to go in the long term? What is our final goal and destination? Without a clear vision and picture of the long-term objectives it is very possible that the short-term activities may be taking you, and your organization, in the wrong direction. Long-term planning and the roadmap to success that it provides will help guide all of your actions.

It is essential to step back and take the time to develop this plan first. Long-range planning comes first. Figure 9-1 is a planning funnel that illustrates how these important planning activities relate to each other.

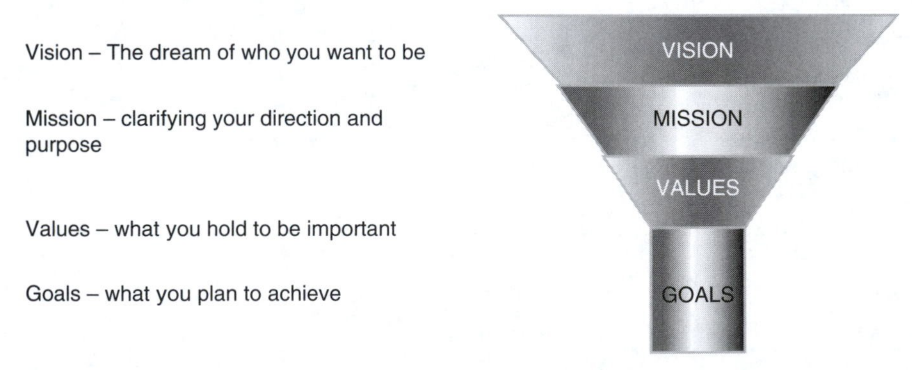

Figure 9-1 Planning funnel

Vision

Vision
The dream of the future that you desire.

Your **vision** is the dream of what it would be like if everything worked out just the way that you want it to be. Yes, I agree that it sounds very idealistic. Yes, you might say to someone with such a vision that he has his head in the clouds. Actually, to create a vision your head has to be above the clouds . . . it is more like the view of the organization from space! Warren Bennis, management guru, defines a vision in this manner

> To choose a direction, an executive must have developed a mental image of the possible and desirable future state of the organization. This image, which we call a vision, may be as vague as a dream or as precise as a goal or a mission statement. (Bennis, 1985)

Those who are more action oriented may want to argue that it is a waste of time to be dwelling on dreams. However, the idea of this big picture is not to *do* the business of the company but rather to be the company's guiding light. The vision creates a framework that can answer the question, If I could build the company from scratch today to be the biggest and best in the world, what would it look like? Only with this type of vision of the possibilities it is possible to align all of your energy and resources toward the ultimate achievement of that dream.

The vision is a dream of what reality could be if there were no obstacles. Why look at it that way? Until you are able to look at the possibilities and see beyond the limitations you will not be able to break through those limiting factors that are holding you back. It would be too easy to set your sights on the easily achievable objectives. However, the true trendsetters, the breakthrough organizations, are those that have learned to see beyond the obstacles and are able to envision clearly how they could be . . . and then muster up the energy to find a way to get there despite the obstacles. Creating a vision requires that you stretch beyond what is easy and achievable.

A vision statement can be as short as a phrase or as long as a paragraph. Usually the vision statement is brief because its goal is to create an image that explains the company's dream. Some examples of a vision statement are

- To be the people's choice of (location) to meet all of their automotive service and repair needs.
- Providing the best solutions to meet the needs of the motoring public.
- (Company Name) strives every day to be the best automotive service company. We do so by living by the old-fashioned values that too many companies have forgotten: providing you with courteous, friendly, and affordable service. We want to become *the* one-stop solution to all of your automotive service needs.
- When people in (city) think of service, they think of _________ Automotive Service Centers.

Real World Application

Have you ever been to a company picnic? Whether it was as a child along with your parents or more recently as an adult it is likely that you've been to one or more in your lifetime. One of the oldest and most common team activities that you're likely to see—and be encouraged to participate in —is the department tug-of-war.

The object of tug-of-war is very simple. All you need are a rope, two groups of people, and a line drawn on the ground. Each group takes its end of the rope and the goal is to pull hard enough to pull the other team over the line. What is the key to success in tug-of-war? Everyone on the team must have a clear vision of what the ideal result is and then be committed to combining all of their energy to pull as hard as they can in the exact same direction. The team that is the best at achieving a shared vision is likely to be the victor.

This would be a good time to take a few minutes before you read on to go on the Internet and spend a few minutes searching for vision statements of a variety of well-known companies. Just do a simple Web search. Enter the phrase "vision statement" along with the name of a major corporation. Reviewing others' statements should help better understand the purpose and structure of an effective vision statement.

The vision, then, becomes the guiding dream of the organization. It can be a powerful tool to inspire everyone. It can also be instrumental in helping to ensure that both current and new employees share that common dream; if they don't, they will not be willing to make the efforts to make the dream a reality.

A clear vision reinforces to everyone in the organization that their efforts are headed in the right direction. It should be a source of encouragement and reassurance when they feel the need to be reminded why they're doing what they're doing. It can also be used to answer the question, Should we be doing this? to assure that their efforts stay on track.

There is a problem, however, with a vision or a dream. You need to have one, you want to achieve one, but you can't *do* one. A vision is far too broad, too long-term, and too general to implement. It, therefore, requires that you break it down into smaller, more focused bite-sized chunks so it can be achieved. The first step in breaking the vision down into more manageable components is the development of a mission.

THEORY INTO PRACTICE 9-1

CASE

You have just come into an inheritance that will allow you to live your dream. You have worked for the past 15 years in the automotive service business and have always dreamed of the opportunity to open your own small independent repair shop in your hometown. You now have the seed money to do just that! You can afford to purchase a piece of property and build an eight service bay shop right on that special corner in town that you've had your eye on.

You decide

As a foundation to building this dream into a reality you realize that you need to have a clear vision of what you want to achieve. After taking some time to think about how *you* would approach this if you had the opportunity, and drawing on the information above on vision statements, please develop a short paragraph that best describes your vision for your new service shop. Once you have written the paragraph, narrow those thoughts further into a vision statement for your new company.

Mission

Mission
The current direction and purpose of an organization.

The **mission** is a clarification of the direction and purpose (vision) of an organization. Although it hoped that all employees can easily share the vision of the organization, it is far too lofty and vague to easily translate into action. It is, therefore, important to be able to begin to break the vision down into bite-sized pieces that can help answer the question of how that vision is going to affect and guide the actions of the organization and its people now. If you refer back to Figure 9-1, the funnel, you can see that as we move from the nebulous vision process into developing the mission it is a matter of narrowing down and more closely focusing and defining just who we are and what we do.

If you know what your dream (vision) is, what are you going to do about it? What direction should you head in in order to be sure that you arrive at this destination? As you move from defining your vision to establishing your mission, you are moving toward breaking down the vision to make it real and achievable and to act as a guide for all of your current and future efforts. Thus, the mission is a clarification of who you are, what you do, what direction you're headed in.

Although it is uncommon for anyone to put their vision on a billboard or widely share it with the world, once the vision has been distilled down to a mission it often takes on the role of being the public announcement of who you are and what you do. It is a long-standing commitment to yourself, your employees, and the world about you. It is a statement of purpose that you gladly and openly express to tell everyone what they can expect from your organization. In fact, if you search for the Web site of any large organization you're likely to easily locate their mission statement.

Mission Statements

As you might guess from the discussion in the previous section, if the mission is something that you're going to use to tell everyone, employees and public, who you are and what you stand for, it is really important that you make it clear. As a result, developing a mission statement is a very difficult task, yet a very important one. The major difficulty is in being precise enough to select just the right words that accurately tell who we are and what makes us unique. Let's discuss how to go about developing one.

A mission statement is generally a short paragraph (no more than three to four sentences) that clearly defines the big goal for your existence. (*Note:* It is probably not a good idea to publicize a mission that says "I want to get incredibly rich and retire.") Although it may be used for marketing purposes, it is more than a slogan. It is, therefore, important to carefully select the words so that they convey the meaning that you intend. Use of marketing jargon is strongly discouraged.

Because the mission statement is the standard by which your organization will be judged, its development should be taken very seriously. All of your employees will be expected to live by it, therefore, it is highly recommended that you get significant involvement from all employees in the development of the statement. After all, you'll expect them to know it, believe it, live by it, and demonstrate it with their everyday performance. (*Note:* In many highly successful, driven organizations employees can recite the mission statement on demand.) This may seem like a lot to ask, but your customers will expect no less than this since you've publicly declared your mission to be your reason for being.

The mission statement is a logical next step from the vision statement. For example, in the section on vision we were working for the company that had developed the vision statement: "When people in (city) think of service, they think of __________ Automotive Service Centers." Assuming that their vision statement is an accurate reflection of their dreams and aspirations as an organization, their mission statement should, then, logically flow from that vision down into a statement of what they intend to do (big picture) to make that vision a reality. In the vision statement the scope of their market was defined as the city that they reside in. The company further indicated that the test of achieving its vision was: when people . . . think of service. Therefore, being first in the minds of the customers is essential. In addition, providing service that will make the company's name the first that comes to mind is also essential. Service, however, appears to be a focal point of the vision and, therefore, is very likely to be the area to better define, describe, and expand upon in the mission statement.

Working to develop a mission statement from this vision statement would require, then, that you further define *how* you intend to become this vision. Service can be defined from several different values: *quality* service, *rapid* service, *high-tech* service, *friendly* service, *affordable* service, *convenient* service, and many combinations of these attributes. The question then becomes how to break down the dream of the vision statement into a group of statements that answer the question How are we going to *be* the vision? What statements are we willing to make that will best explain what sets us apart from the competition? Here are some possible examples

- We will provide consistent, high-quality, affordable service that is unmatched in the marketplace.
- We will maintain competitive prices and convenient service hours to meet your every service need.
- You can count on the fact that all of your services will be provided by certified technicians.
- All of our services are backed by a lifetime no-questions asked warranty.

These promises could then be blended together into a mission statement that goes something like this

> _________ Automotive Service Centers commit to provide unmatched, affordable service to our customers. We commit to do so by providing quality service performed by certified technicians in our state-of-the art facilities, at a competitive price and with convenient service hours that will meet your service needs. Finally, we back up these promises with an unprecedented lifetime no-questions-asked warranty on all services.

Again, I recommend that you take a few minutes now to surf the Web to view a variety of mission statements for some well-known companies. It will help you to get some ideas about how to build your own mission statements.

THEORY INTO PRACTICE 9-2

CASE

Based upon the vision statement for your new shop in Theory into Practice 9-1, it is time to move on to better understand how to define that vision and put it into action.

You decide

Using the vision statement in Theory into Practice 9-1 as a basis, and using the directions provided in this section on mission statements, construct a mission statement for your new automotive service business.

Values

Values
Guiding principles of the organization.

Values are the guiding principles that keep all of your actions and initiatives aligned with your organization. They are, simply put, what is important to your organization. These values will be aligned with your ethics, a topic that we explored in greater detail in Chapter 8. They are standards that are important to you and ones that your customers can count on you to uphold. The illustration in the Planning funnel (Figure 9-1) shows that the values further focus the planning so that the resulting goals are aligned with the organization's core values.

Many organizations approach the same problem or issue. They provide similar products and/or services. The core values of any organization are some of the most important factors in setting them apart from the competition. That is what gives them a unique edge in the marketplace. After all, that is what open-market competition is all about, differentiating yourself in a market where customers can choose from many, yet slightly different, alternatives to meet their wants and needs.

Value statements answer the question What do we stand for? They help to clarify all the guiding principles you operate under. An organization that values diversity and has an open-door policy for employees to encourage open communication across all levels is highly likely to openly communicate these values to potential and current employees and to customers alike. This sets the standards for the company so that employees and customers know how they will be treated under all conditions.

Value statements are, unlike, the vision and mission, generally a short list of statements (sentences) that describe a core value of the organization. We've just covered two possibilities: diversity and open communication. The following is a list of some possible value statements that you might find and/or consider:

- We value truthfulness and honesty. We would rather admit our mistakes to each other and to our customers and use them as a source of learning and growth than to ever condone hiding from the truth.
- We value our employees as our greatest asset. Therefore, we commit to aggressively invest in their professional and personal development to help them to reach their goals and dreams, and, in so doing, make us a better company and a better place to work.
- We value the rich resource of open communication as a tool for all of us to grow and thrive. Therefore, we provide multiple methods to keep these communication lines open and encourage all to actively and openly participate without fear of consequence in the future direction of the organization.
- We value excellence. As such, we strive to hire, develop, and consistently reward those who continue to reach new levels of excellence and, in so doing, set high standards for their co-workers and for the industry at large.

Value statements can be created as a simple list of principles that the organization commits to uphold. The formally published values presented above might be shortened to just include the initial broad concepts as follows.

- We value truthfulness and honesty.
- We value our employees as our greatest asset.

- We value the rich resource of open communication.
- We value excellence.

Another example of how a company might use the brief 'list style' in publicizing their values might look something like this:

________________ Service Center values

- Inclusion and diversity
- Honesty and integrity
- Human capacity development
- Recognition of achievement
- The need to be a leader in the community

Value statements are an acknowledgment of broad underlying principles that guide all of the actions of the company. Many of the value statements may be focused more on the relationship between the company and its employees. This is a good time for you to surf the Web and explore some of the wide variety of value statements that companies that you work with or highly respect express as their core values—what sets them apart from the rest.

THEORY INTO PRACTICE 9-3

CASE

Based upon the vision and mission statement for your new automotive service shop in activities 9-A and 9-B, it is time to personalize the direction of your company.

You decide

You want to make your new service shop a true reflection of who you are and what you truly value. Therefore, it is important that you take the time to develop a set of core values that best reflect your style and your values. This will help clarify what makes your business different from the rest of the industry. With this in mind, please prepare a brief list and/or a short statement that expresses the core values of an organization that you would be proud to own. Remember that value statements may be directed toward your relationship with either employees or the public.

Long-Range Goals

Once the organization has a dream (vision) and a direction and purpose (mission) and has further clarified who it is (values) it is essential to take the next step toward developing a plan of action. into something more specific. You can't *do* a vision or a mission. You can and should believe in your core values, but at some point you need to put all of this into motion. When you sit back and think, OK, I agree that this is who we are and where we need to go now what do we plan to do to get us there? It is time to move toward developing goals.

Goals Practical, measurable, and achievable actions.

Goals are practical, measurable, and achievable actions. In developing goals it is important that just as we have moved carefully and deliberately from the broadest view of the organization (vision) to further clarify it, the types of goals that we are speaking about at this point are big-picture goals. They are broad commitments of what we are going to do to further our vision, mission, and values. There are many courses of action that we can undertake to further these broad concepts. Our long-term goals are those broad actions that we believe are the best way to focus our efforts at this point.

No matter how ambitious we are, we simply can't do everything all at once. If we tried to do that we'd scatter our energy in so many directions that we'd accomplish little and feel like we worked hard and got nowhere. Therefore, we need to prioritize our efforts. We need to decide what the most important things are that we can focus on in the foreseeable future that will best help us to move us forward. These are our long-range goals.

In order for goals to be effective they need to be specific enough so that they become a source for evaluating each of our actions. We should be able to compare our actions to our stated long-range goals to see if we are doing the right things. That is, for example, if we are considering a new initiative, we need to first consider if it is something that we should be involved in. Clearly, if the initiative does not align with our vision, mission and values, it is not who we are and we should not be pursuing it. However, even if it does support vision, mission, and values if it does not support one of our current long-range goals then we should redirect our efforts to something that will support those goals that we have decided are our priorities for now.

Our long-range goals act as a mechanism to help us continually focus and refocus our energies and actions to assure that we are keeping an eye on what we have determined is important at present. The goals of any organization are bound to change over time, but the current goals provide a structured roadmap to guide our current activities. Therefore, they provide the standard against which all of our proposed actions can be tested and determined worthy.

Some examples of long-term goals might the following:

- Be the recognized leader in customer satisfaction of all comparable-sized service shops in the market.
- Achieve and maintain 100 percent industry certification of all technicians within the organization.

Because long-term goals follow from the mission, vision, and values of the organization, an organization with these two goals would be one that has a strong vision of customer satisfaction and quality of repairs. These goals are a statement of two of the actions that they believe will best help them to achieve their vision. This must be so since, even if the goals were worthy in and of themselves, they are not proper goals if they do not directly support the vision and mission of the organization. We will now talk a little bit further about some guidelines to help develop goals.

Setting Goals

Visions are dreams, missions are lofty, but goals are achievable. Two key factors to keep in mind in setting long-range goals are (1) You can't do everything all at once and (2) Your goals must be reasonable and achievable.

When setting up long-term goals it is important that you consider all of the possible goals and then narrow them down to a short list of top priorities. It is not that all of the goals that come to mind are not important and not, at some point, necessary. It is that you can't do it all at one time. Remember, you have to prioritize. You should answer the question, What is the best use of my efforts *now?* Deciding which of your potential goals are most important to tackle now will help you determine which make it to the final list.

As you think of all of the possible goals that you could choose you might identify some that must be completed before others on your list can even be started. Those would very likely rise to the top of your list as priorities to start on right away. Others may just be at the opportune time and may rise to the surface because you have the chance to take advantage of a unique opportunity that may pass. In either case, you need to keep the list manageable so that everyone can feel that they are going to be expected to stretch yet still feel that they can achieve those goals.

That leads us to the second key issue, reasonable and achievable. If the goals are set too low they will meet both tests, but will not help you and your organization to grow as much as you possibly can. On the other hand, overly ambitious goals can be poison to morale and productivity. If the employees know in their hearts from day one that the goals can never be reached they will result in low morale and poor performance. Therefore, reach high—but not too high.

Finally, no goal is achievable if it is a secret! Clear and open communication to all involved is essential to get buy-in, commitment, support, and maximum effort toward achieving all goals. We need to be sure that we are all pulling in the same direction with the same level of effort and commitment if we are to reach our mutual goals.

THEORY INTO PRACTICE 9-4

CASE

Based upon the first three activities that we've completed in this chapter it is now time to start working on goals.

You decide

Please develop three long-term goals for your new company. Please make sure that the goals meet the following tests: (a) they are reasonable, (b) they are achievable, and (c) they are measurable. Please provide the three goals and briefly explain how you will know that they are reasonable, achievable, and how you will measure progress toward their completion.

Tracking Progress

Failure to measure and regularly track progress toward the ultimate completion of any goal, long-range or short-range, is almost certain to doom that goal to failure. Therefore, it is essential that you are able to break down every goal into language that allows you to regularly measure progress toward completion, make the mid-course corrections needed to keep on track and/or get it back on track, and finally, know when to celebrate ultimate achievement. The long-range goals that you select should be the starting point from which you start your shorter-range planning.

SUMMARY

Long-range planning is an essential, yet often neglected, process necessary to set a clear direction for any organization. This big-picture planning helps you to identify and communicate to employees and customers your dream (vision), direction and purpose (mission), and who you are (values). This planning assures that your employees know what your company is all about and where it is headed. Further, it makes a clear statement to the public about what makes you unique.

The final step in the long-range planning process is distilling down the vision, mission, and values into long-range goals. These goals help determine what the most important major initiatives are that the company intends to undertake in the foreseeable future. These goals then form the foundation upon which shorter-range planning and activities can be built. We will discuss the three forms of medium to short-range planning, strategic, operation, and tactical planning, in depth in the next chapter.

PRACTICING THE PRINCIPLES

1. The vision of a company or department describes
   a. their specific goals for the next three years.
   b. your dream for how you'd like it to be.
   c. unreasonable expectations for the future.
   d. more than one of the above is correct.
2. Long-range planning is
   a. essential yet often neglected.
   b. a total waste of everyone's time and effort.
   c. prioritizing efforts for the next six months.
   d. a process that must be done without employee interference.
3. Which of the following statements is incorrect?
   a. Your ethics do not influence your company values.
   b. Your mission is often used public statement of purpose and direction.
   c. A vision statement is very broad and idealistic.
   d. Our vision is the view of the organization "from outer space."
4. A mission statement is
   a. the next logical step from a vision statement.
   b. an explanation of your dream as a company.
   c. a term only used by NASA and *Star Trek*.
   d. all of the above.
5. Along with a vision and mission it is always important that you state your values because they
   a. are a restatement of your core beliefs.
   b. are never influenced by your ethics.
   c. are a way to make people think that you have morals.
   d. all of the above.
6. Long-range goals
   a. help us to focus and refocus our energies.
   b. must be reasonable and achievable.
   c. are priorities items to direct our actions and efforts.
   d. All of the above.

In Questions 7–10 match the definition with the term. Indicate your letter choice on the space to the left of the definition

____	7. Direction and purpose	b. vision
____	8. Principles you hold dear	c. mission
____	9. Your dream	d. long-term goals
____	10. High priority objectives	e. values

REFERENCES

Bennis, W., *Leaders: The Strategies for Taking Charge* (New York: Harper & Row, 1985).

CHAPTER

10

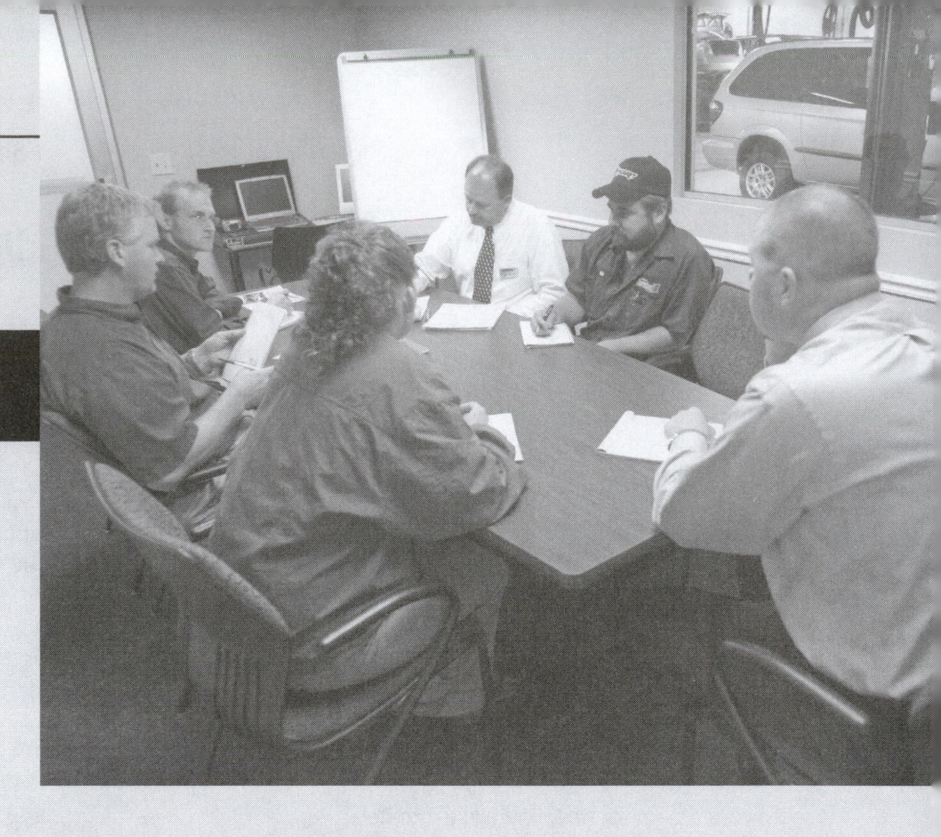

Strategic and Short-Range Planning

CHAPTER OBJECTIVES

- To recognize the importance of medium- and short-range planning activities
- To locate where middle- and short-range planning fit in the overall planning process
- To examine the strategic planning process
- To recognize the value of operational planning in providing flexible support to the overall strategic plan
- To explain how tactical planning can help us adjust our short-term focus and redirect our resources to achieve our goals

KEY TERMS

strategic planning
stakeholders
environmental scan
focus group
SWOT analysis
core competencies
operational planning
tactical planning

Introduction

The importance of planning your future direction cannot be overstated. The old adage, Be careful, if you don't know where you're going you just might get there! makes clear that if you want to work smarter and not just harder you must clarify your intended direction. Once that has been established, it is possible to make sure that all of your efforts, and those of our employees, are aligned. In this chapter we will explore the major levels of middle- and short-range planning and discuss tools, tips, and techniques to help use these planning efforts to build a clear roadmap to future success.

In Chapter 9 we talked about the real big-picture issues of answering the questions as an organization of what we want to be (vision), what our plan is to help us become that (mission), and what the specific objectives (goals) are that we will focus on in support of becoming what we want to be as an organization. Now we will take it down to the level of middle- and short-range planning. This is planning from the three- to five-year level down to that for a year or less. We will look at systematic ways to formulate new goals to support the overall vision and mission and to help make the adjustments needed to keep on pace and on track.

Levels of Planning

Just about every organization does some sort of planning. Unfortunately, many plan on the fly. That is, the tendency is that while all organizations plan activities, fewer expend the effort to plan a year in advance, and very few consistently develop a long-range plan. This seems normal because we all know that we're often so busy with day-to-day responsibilities and problems that we simply don't have the time to think further than the present. Unfortunately, failure to think ahead results in the high likelihood that the present will continue. It has been said that the true definition of insanity is continuing to do the same thing over and over again while expecting different results. If you don't take the time to sit back and plan for the future to be different it is very likely that it won't be!

Rather than work from the most common planning, short-term, to the more uncommon mid-range planning, we will explore the three levels of planning as they should ideally be practiced. That is, we will first discuss building a strategic plan to set the future direction of the organization for the next three to five years and then move to operational planning (one year) to work toward those strategic goals. Finally, we'll discuss the shortest-range component, tactical planning, to discuss the small decisions and mid-course corrections that need to be made on a regular basis to keep us headed toward our longer-range objectives. Figure 10-1 shows how these three levels of planning relate to our everyday actions.

One last factor that you must remember is that strategic planning is not truly the beginning of planning. It is based upon the long-range planning that we discussed in Chapter 9. We need to have vision, mission, values, and long-term goals that define who we are and what we want to be. These long-term ideals and values are implemented through periodic middle- and short-range planning. Planning and adjusting our course in these shorter timeframes allows us to be responsive to a changing world and a changing market while remaining on the long-term course of working to achieve our true vision.

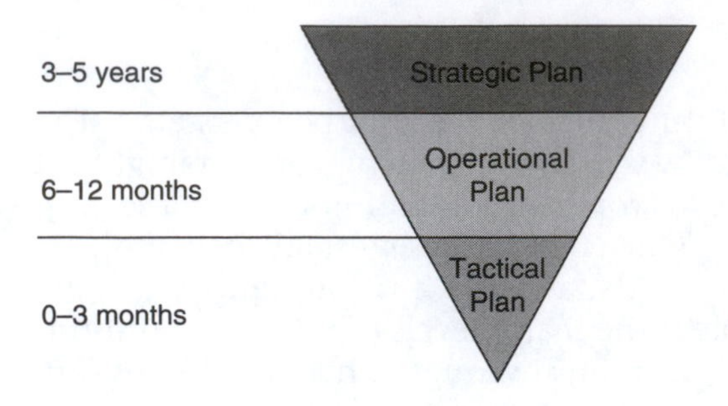

Figure 10-1 Planning model

Strategic Planning

A formal planning process of breaking down the overall vision, mission, and long-range goals into a set of specific strategies and goals that are the focus of activities for the next period of time, typically three to five years.

Strategic planning is a mid-range planning process that should be conducted on a systematic basis every three to five years. Its purpose is to assess the organization's position and identify key goals and initiatives that will best help them move forward during this next period of time, usually three to five years, toward achieving long-term goals. We all know that things change and people change. In many cases when we look at the world around us we look back and realize we could never have anticipated many of the changes that have occurred. One of the primary purposes of strategic planning is to allow the organization to take the time to sit back and look at what has changed over the past several years, to evaluate how those changes have affected the company and its market position, and to be able to take those new circumstances into consideration in making a plan for the near future. At the same time it allows the organization to also adjust to internal changes that have occurred over that time span.

A second, and very important, reason for strategic planning is really spelled out in the term itself, *strategic* planning. Along with evaluating and accounting for changes in the world, the industry, and the market, it is important not to try to do too much. It is not possible to do everything at once. Resources and money are limited. Therefore, it is essential that care is taken to make conscious decisions about where these scarce resources can best be put to use to have the maximum positive effect on company performance. This is the *strategic* use of these resources. That is, actions are taken with a strategy in mind that we believe will use our resources to our best advantage.

Effective strategic planning is not done in isolation. It is not commonly done by one individual, whether that is the owner, CEO, or service manager. It is not a process of sitting down, taking an educated guess about where the company stands, and then making a plan for the future. Along with recognizing that this effort needs to be *strategic,* care and an investment of time and effort needs to go into making sure that the knowledge that we have as an organization about the state of the economy, the market, our company, and our expectations for the near future is sound and is the best projection that we can make at this time. Remember, the strategic plan is the roadmap for our direction and activities for this period. Therefore, failure to do our research and to map out a strategy might result in ending up in the wrong place—and looking back we realize that we wasted a great deal of time and effort and are no closer to our real long-term goals.

The questions that you need to answer in order to develop an effective strategic plan are

- *Situation*—What is the current status of the organization and how did we get to this point?
- *Objective*—Where are we trying to go and what are our ongoing long-term goals?
- *Path*—What is the best route to take to help us to move the furthest from our current situation toward achieving our objectives within this timeframe?

Because of the high stakes involved, it is important to be very methodical in developing a strategic plan. It should intentionally draw upon the collective knowledge of as many stakeholders as possible. Every organization has both internal and external stakeholders. **Stakeholders** are people who have a vested interest in the success or failure of the company. They are your employees, the banker who holds your building mortgage, your customers, your suppliers, your stockholders, your neighbors, your family, and many more. Let's learn about two major tools that are essential underpinnings of developing a strategic plan—environmental scans and the SWOT analysis.

Stakeholders

Those people or organizations that have a specific, vested interest in the success or failure of some event, action, or organization.

Environmental Scan

At first look this sounds like it might be a weather report. Actually, an **environmental scan** is very similar to a weather forecast. Environmental scans are of two types, internal and external. Their intent is to examine the question, What is the state (climate) of the environment that we live and work in right now?

Environmental Scan

An assessment of the surrounding conditions and situations that are likely to affect or have an impact on an organization and its future activities.

The internal scan takes a look at the current state of the organization. Questions must be asked regarding the financial health of the company. Has the company been making a profit? What is the trend over the past several years? What major problems or obstacles does the company currently face? Is the company in a strong position to move forward? What are the pressing needs? The data needed to complete the internal scan is done by gathering information from the employees themselves. Most commonly a great deal of this information is collected from middle management. This should then, however, be verified if possible by gathering input from the workers on the floor to corroborate this data.

The external scan looks at a very different question. Its purpose is to ask what the state of the market is that we are in and plan to be in. In many cases, companies rely upon their employees to answer this all-important question. Although involving employees in this process is necessary, limiting the data to employee input is a big mistake. The point is to know what is going on in the market, not to just think you know what is going on in the market. There is a critical difference between the two. It is important to validate the company's internal vision of what is going on in the marketplace by gathering input from stakeholders external to the company. Your banker, your landlord, your chamber of commerce, your industry association, your suppliers, and your customers would be likely candidates to provide input and guidance in gathering this data.

External environmental scans are commonly done through the use of existing industry panels such as an advisory board. If no such standing

Focus Group

A small group of individuals intentionally selected to represent the broader population who are brought together to obtain their opinions about a specific situation, production, or proposed action.

SWOT Analysis

A formal process that helps to define the current strengths, weaknesses, opportunities, and threats facing an organization, department, or individual.

committee exists, focus groups can be convened specifically for the purpose of obtaining external data. A **focus group** is a small group of individuals that are invited to attend a meeting or group of meetings with the specific purpose of obtaining certain information. In the case of strategic planning, groups from different community or business groups would most likely be invited to participate. The goal would be to get a cross-section of input on the local business climate as well as the perceptions of different customer groups in the market.

SWOT Analysis

Although the name may seem quite foreign, it is actually a very appropriate acronym for its component parts. A **SWOT analysis** is an evaluation of the **S**trengths, **W**eaknesses, **O**pportunities, and **T**hreats facing the organization, department, or individual. Using the information obtained in the internal and external environmental scans as a background, this analysis helps those involved in the planning process to focus in more detail on these four dimensions of the organization. By answering the questions that arise from these four major topics, the organization can more effectively determine where to focus their efforts and resources for maximum effect. Let's take a few minutes to explore each of these areas in more depth.

Strengths

One of the first questions that any organization should ask is very simply: What are we good at? or What do we do well? No one or no organization can be all things to all people. To successfully compete in the marketplace it is very important to determine what makes your business different from the competition. What is it that you can or will be able to do better than the others that will help set you apart in the minds of the customers so that they will make a conscious choice to do business with you.

The strengths of the organization or of the product or service that you sell should be an important focus of your efforts to differentiate yourself from the competition. It is very likely to contribute strongly to successes that you've had to date. Therefore, it should not be forgotten. If a particular strength is, indeed, one of the reasons why people have chosen you in the past then it is something that you need to be sure to celebrate, promote, and maintain to assure your future success.

Weaknesses

In contrast to strengths, this area examines the much more difficult questions of what are we doing poorly? or what is the competition doing much better than we are? Weaknesses may be areas that you are not capable of addressing. They may be unchangeable or too expensive to change. An example would be the location of your shop. Regardless of whether or not identified weaknesses can and should be focused on to improve your performance, they must be acknowledged and addressed and considered.

It has been argued over and over whether it is better to invest your energy in resources to overcome your weaknesses or to invest energy in continuing to build upon your strengths. This can be argued either way. It is important, however, in all instances to be aware of your weaknesses, to acknowledge them, and to consider whether or not you need to focus on them. Failure to acknowledge your weaknesses leaves you vulnerable to attack by the competition. Acknowledgement of your weaknesses makes you a more aware and worthy competitor.

Opportunities

Based upon what you know about your company, your industry, and your market it is important to ask the question of what unique opportunities currently exist that are likely to be the most productive. Whether that is new markets, new products, new customers, or just increased business in your existing markets this is an educated guess at the most likely directions that will yield the greatest results.

Thinking strategically, you don't have unlimited time or other resources so it is important to evaluate the environment and make a conscious choice on where to put your efforts. Therefore, to increase the chances of maximizing the return on your investment you draw upon the information obtained in the environmental scans to make a conscious choice about where those resources would be best invested.

Threats

The last, yet still very important, question that must be asked is, What factors or events threaten our continued success. Your past successes do not guarantee, on their own merit, that future successes are guaranteed. The world and the market continue to change. Therefore, it is important to account for as many of these changes as possible.

It is always helpful to have the comfort level that you have been successful for a long time and that you can always count on your foundational business to keep you afloat. But can you? Common threats that must be acknowledged and addressed may be as uncontrollable as the weather or the current economy. They may be more local issues like changes in local demand for your product or the recent entry of several very powerful competitors. Regardless of how much or how little control you have over these threats it is essential that you take them into account when you do your planning for they will certainly have some affect on your results.

Core Competencies

Once all of the external and internal background data has been collected and analyzed it is important to do one more step before you start to write your plan. You need to refocus yourself on your **core competencies.** Your core competencies are the unique strengths and characteristics of your organization that allow it to do some things better or different than anyone else. Revisiting these innate strengths reminds you to use those assets you do have to your best advantage. It further serves to redirect you from putting an inordinate amount of effort into trying to become something that you are not.

Unique characteristics and strengths of an individual or organization.

Writing the Plan

Finally, after doing all of this extensive preparation it is time to sit down and write the plan. At this point it is important to recall the purpose of a strategic plan. It is to provide a three- to five-year roadmap to focus your efforts toward your ultimate goals and objectives, your organization's vision and mission.

As is the case with any type of planning, there is no guarantee that what you found in the environmental scan and the SWOT analysis is foolproof. No one can see that clearly into the future. In the months following the launch of your plan changes that you did not foresee could alter your future. That is why it is important to draw upon the strategic plan to make even more specific and short-term plans, operational and tactical plans. These further planning steps allow you to make the mid-course corrections that will be essential for you to reach your final destination.

Tracking Progress

As is the case with all plans, it is more than just dreaming. Every plan, especially a strategic plan, requires monitoring and reporting. Each of the goals and objectives must be measurable and definable. That is, you must be able to clearly specify how you are going to measure progress toward accomplishment of your goal. You must also have a clear measure that will allow you to know when the goal has been achieved. This is done by breaking the goal down into an operational definition. An *operational goal* has three key parts. You will know that the goal is accomplished when a specific result (1—the goal) has been achieved (2—by what time) as measured by what result (3—specific target). Based on this you can continue to track progress toward completion of your goal.

No plan is flawless. However, methodical planning sure beats the alternative, failure to plan at all. It is important to remember that failure to plan is planning to fail.

Operational Planning

A process of setting shorter-range goals to support the current strategic plan, typically for the next year.

Operational Planning

An **operational plan** is a short-range (typically one-year) plan that answers the question, What am I going to do this year to support my strategic goals? It is a further clarification of the business strategies and initiatives that you

— Real World Application

No matter how thoughtfully you plan and how hard you work to make that plan a reality there are always situations and events totally beyond your control that may interfere with your best-laid plans. It is for this reason that strategic planning is essential. It allows you to make mid-course corrections to adjust for unforeseen circumstances.

Do you think that you are immune to unforeseen events? Don't kid yourself. What affect do you think that 9/11 had on the American economy? Was it expected? How many businesses, no matter how well they planned, had considered the likelihood of such an event in their forecasting and planning processes? In a more practical sense, if you were a small local auto repair shop, what would the impact be if tomorrow's newspaper announced that one of the largest independent service conglomerates had just purchased the vacant lot directly across the street? It is something that you could not have known, something that you very likely could not have predicted. Yet, it is definitely a factor that would alter your planning from this moment forward!

believe will best help you to work toward your longer term goals and can be accomplished within twelve months or less. As was the case in strategic planning, the shorter the timeframe of your planning, the more practical and concrete the planning is.

Whereas establishing vision, mission, and goals and then moving on to strategic planning are formal processes that involve a great deal of external input, operational planning is generally done as an internal process within the different units of the organization. This is generally done through an informal report requested by supervisors to identify what each employee believes goals and key initiatives are for the coming year. It then allows the supervisors to review the goals, support them, and report them to top management. Furthermore, it gives them an objective basis upon which they can evaluate individual and group efforts for the year.

The real test of the value of any operational plan is the degree to which you can tie its success to the goals of your strategic plan. From this short-term viewpoint you are more capable of breaking the big-picture plan down into very definable activities and initiatives. This becomes the foundation for establishing your annual staffing plan and your annual budget. If an item on your budget does not support your operational plan, then it does not need to be spent or invested.

Much like the strategic plan, the operational plan asks and answers four main questions

1. What is our current status? (Situation)
2. Where do we want to be within the next 12 months? (Objective)
3. What are the best strategies to get there? (Path)
4. How will we know when we've arrived? (Operational Goals)

As you can see, operational planning is moving clearly toward more practical and measurable outcomes. It is at this point where you need to start fine tuning your activities and implementing mid-course corrections to assure that your strategic plan goals are accomplished.

It is important to remember that your operational plan is commonly used as the basis for your annual goals and objectives and is therefore subject to close scrutiny from upper management. Therefore it must maintain a careful balance between being aggressive and optimistic without being unrealistic and unachievable. It is at this level that it becomes very clear and measurable not just what you hope to accomplish but what you are really doing to achieve your goals.

Tactical Planning

Tactical planning is the down-in-the-trenches planning that maps out very specific actions and activities to assure that all of the goals that you've set become a reality. Using a military metaphor, while strategic planning may be the objective of winning the war and operational planning the plan of which battles you need to fight, tactical planning is the specific and detailed troop movements and daily battle plans that will win the battles and, in the long run, the war.

Tactical Planning
The process of mapping out very specific and short-term actions and activities to support the operational and strategic plans.

Operational planning allows for a much greater degree of mid-course corrections to assure success of the strategic plan than the other planning modes. Tactical planning, then, as the day-to-day short-term planning for allocating and reallocating resources, is the constant and dynamic tweaking of your specific actions. How do you know how to make the decisions of what and when to tweak the system?

In order to make effective tactical decisions you must have data. This data is drawn from your operational and strategic planning. Now you must constantly review and use that data to look for telltale signs of the areas that are doing well and those that are missing the mark. By these measures you then can take action to get back on track and stay there.

A common example of a tactical planning initiative would be the manager's response to a report indicating that sales of oil and filter changes were well below forecast. After evaluating the data and taking a look at the immediate market conditions the manager can decide to reallocate resources to make a very specific push to try to bring this up to standards. In this case, a special ad, some in-house merchandising, or even a short-term drop in price might be utilized to stimulate the market and get the performance back on track.

The manager's ability to be aware of the current situation and to rapidly and appropriately respond will significantly increase the chances of success and attainment of short- and long-term goals. Effective tactical planning assures that the company and the department can be responsive to unexpected changes in the market and successfully deal with them. Without an intentional focus on making these types of daily evaluations and short-term adjustments, any surprise changes in the marketplace would have major effects (likely very negative ones) on the success and profitability of the department with little hope of correcting them.

Real World Application

As a result of tracking monthly sales data the service manager has recognized that overall customer labor and parts sales are lagging about 10 percent behind his forecast (operational goals) for the year. Upon further review of the information available he determines that although the total sales are down, the total number of customers who have come in for service are actually a bit ahead of his forecast. Based on this information he decides that running ads in the newspaper is probably not his best strategy. After all, he has enough customers, but the numbers indicate that they're not selling enough service per visit to those customers who are coming in. Therefore, he decides that rather than running an ad that he will put together an internal program of incentives for his service employees. He will give them bonuses for each additional maintenance or service item that service advisors identify and successfully sell for every car that comes into the shop. His data indicates clearly that he does not need more customers; he needs higher sales per customer.

However, after two weeks he finds that the results are not enough to raise the sales up to the intended goals. Therefore, he decides to add a drawing for prizes for his technicians for every additional service item that they sell as a result of doing a free vehicle inspection. This action, combined with the initial one, results in sales that now exceed the departmental goals.

Through the use of these two tactics the manager was able to take effective short-term actions that addressed shortfalls in department performance. One objective of these short-term efforts was to get the shop energized and to get the sales up to par. However, a greater expectation was that even when the incentives were gone that the service employees had learned better how to maintain this momentum and, therefore, would continue to meet or exceed the annual and strategic sales goals.

SUMMARY

Building upon the long-range planning that was discussed in Chapter 9, in this chapter we discussed the importance of planning in a three- to five-year timeframe (strategic planning) as well as planning every year (operational planning). However, even with all of this longer-range planning in place being able to plan in one- to three-month periods (tactical planning) remains essential to ultimate success.

In addition to exploring the planning models we also identified some tools and techniques that assist in the planning process. The most notable of these is the SWOT Analysis, which helps us to identify and build upon those Strengths, Weaknesses, Opportunities, and Threats that we see both in the marketplace and within the organization.

PRACTICING THE PRINCIPLES

1. Two types of scans should be done before strategic planning. They are
   a. external and advisory group scans.
   b. political environment and market scans.
   c. internal and external environmental scans.
   d. virus and junk mail scans.
2. Medium-range planning typically done for three to five years is called
   a. a total waste of everyone's time and effort.
   b. operational planning.
   c. tactical planning.
   d. strategic planning.
3. Which of the following statements is incorrect?
   a. Tactical planning is commonly the source for your annual goals and objectives.
   b. Strategic planning is based on long-term organizational goals.
   c. You should always consider your core competencies when planning.
   d. Short-range planning helps you to adjust when unexpected events occur.

In Questions 4–10 match the definition with the term. Indicate your letter choice on the space to the left of the definition

	Definition	Term
____	4. Competition or other negative factors	a. path
____	5. what you do better than the competition	b. objective
____	6. Things that you don't do very well	c. weaknesses
____	7. Chances to do something special or better	d. opportunities
____	8. A roadmap to success	e. situation
____	9. your ultimate goal	f. threats
____	10. the current state of business	g. strengths

CHAPTER

11

Decision Making

CHAPTER OBJECTIVES

- To recognize the common tools and methods used to make consistent decisions
- To assess how to make decisions based on evaluating benefits and drawbacks
- To identify the different operating levels within an organization and how it affects decision making
- To formulate decision-making efforts at the appropriate organizational level that will result in lasting change

KEY TERMS

return on investment—ROI
Franklin decision model
reward
risk
three realms
span of control
sphere of influence
locus of control
organization level
process level
job/performer level

Introduction

Whether you look at the service operations from the standpoint of the owner, manager, or technician there are some concerns that they all share. A primary question that must be answered is what return they will realize on the investment that they have made. A fundamental way of measuring is based on the financial results, profit or loss. Many sound business, as well as personal, decisions have further reaching implications and consequences.

In this section we begin with a brief example of how this decision-making process applies to all individuals, no matter what their position. Since these issues apply to you as well as to your supervisors and your employees, you must become very familiar with methods that can help you to make consistent, sound decisions. Several methods and principles are described in the following chapter that should help you to make these decisions.

Is It Worth It to Me?

From the viewpoint of the owner, who can be anything from a third-party investor to a graduate technician who wants to go out on his or her own, the concern in making any decision is, What's in it for me? Simply, if I put all of my time, energy, and financial resources into this service shop and then risk my future by borrowing a substantial amount of money to rent and purchase the equipment and facilities, will it all be worth it? Will I get enough back to make it financially rewarding? Could I have made just as much or more as an individual without taking all of these risks? Why does doing this make sense?

From the viewpoint of the manager who is primarily responsible for the day-to-day decisions of the operation the risks and rewards are similar but different. The manager is not generally going to be the one producing the work in the shop. He has to leave that up to his technicians. However, his financial success or failure and even his job security lie in the hands of the performance of those technicians. The pay plan for a manager is often based to some degree on the performance of the shop. This can range from a salary plus performance bonus on up to being strictly paid a percentage of the net profits. Like the owner, he, too, has to assess the situation to determine whether he is taking a good risk by taking this job. He needs to decide, Is it worth it to me?

The technician is the productive member of the repair shop team. He is the one who ultimately produces the primary product that the shop sells, labor. Even though his view of the question, Is it worth it to me? looks different to him than it does to the manager or owner, he has to answer the question to decide whether this is the right job to take or the right one to stay in. The technician's decision is a bit more clearly defined since it primarily focuses on his own individual ability, motivation, and drive to succeed. Although his success or failure may be affected by some outside conditions (weather, the economy, and the location of the shop) he has the greatest degree of control over his success or failure. After all, he is the productive member of the shop and his pay is based on his own performance. Nevertheless, he is risking his financial welfare and that of his family with this decision. Therefore, it is not a decision that should be taken lightly.

We have briefly explored the importance of this question to all involved in the shop. Now that we understand the question (Is it worth it to me?), we need to explore methods that will help us to accurately and consistently answer it. Time and time again you will find that some form of the answer to this question is the primary motivation behind most, if not all, of the business decisions that are made within any organization, from the mom and pop gas station up to the mega-conglomerate dealer group. Let's explore some tools and methods to help us make more effective and consistent business decisions.

Return on Investment (ROI)

The process of deciding whether any investment is worthwhile is essential in helping the investor make the decision to buy or sell. This is true, as discussed earlier, regardless of the size of the company or your place within it. We all go through a similar decision-making process to determine what to do, why, and the implications of that decision. One of the simplest and most commonly used tools used to help make this decision is to answer the following questions:

- What is my investment in this activity (cost)?
- What will I get (return) if I participate?
- Will I get enough back to make it worthwhile (**return on investment—ROI**)?

Return on Investment (ROI)

A common financial management measurement that is determined by comparing the amount of benefits that you receive from any action to the amount that you initially invested.

You can put these questions into a formula to help you calculate ROI. There are many formulas for return on investment. In the simplest form the formula is:

$$\begin{array}{ccc} R - C & = & \text{ROI} \\ \text{(return)} - \text{(cost)} & = & \text{(return on investment)} \end{array}$$

This formula provides a quick reference that answers the question: How much do I get back beyond my original investment to justify the risk? A slightly more complex formula of ROI is broadly applied in the business world to measure the worth of investing in everything from savings accounts to large corporate mergers and acquisitions. Rather than resulting in an answer in dollars it finds the percentage of return that is generated by the investment. This ROI Percentage formula is:

$$\begin{array}{ccc} (R/C) \times 100 & = & \text{ROI\%} \\ (\text{return}/\text{cost}) \times 100 & = & \text{Return On Investment percentage} \end{array}$$

It is important to realize that there are situations where all of the factors involved in calculating return on investment are easily measured in dollars and cents. That certainly makes the calculations easy and, therefore, the decision very clear cut. Let's look at a simple example and use the ROI formulas to address it. You are considering whether or not to purchase a new transmission flushing machine that costs \$2,000. You are sure that and you will be able to sell 100 transmission flushes per year for \$70 labor apiece as a result of having this new capability. Using the first ROI formula your justification for purchasing the equipment is:

$$\begin{array}{ccc} R - C & = & \text{ROI} \\ \$70 \times 100 = \$7{,}000 - \$2{,}000 & = & \$5{,}000 \\ \text{(return)} - \text{(cost)} & = & \text{(return on investment)} \end{array}$$

Using the ROI % formula your justification would be:

$$\begin{array}{c} (R/C) \times 100 = \text{ROI\%} \\ ((\$70 \times 100 = \$7{,}000)/\$2{,}000) \times 100 = \text{ROI\%} \end{array}$$

Or

$$(\$5{,}000/\$2{,}000) \times 100 \quad = \text{ROI\%}$$

Therefore

$$\begin{array}{ccccc} 2.5 & \times & 100 & = & 250\% \\ \text{(return)} & \times & \text{(cost)} & = & \text{(return on investment)} \end{array}$$

In this example for an initial investment of $2,000 you would receive a $5,000 profit which is a 250% return on your initial investment.

One important factor to consider in using this as the sole method for decision making is that not all costs or all benefits can be simply reduced to monetary terms. This does not make them any less important, it just makes them harder to calculate. It is essential when determining the true ROI that all factors, monetary or non-monetary, are taken into account so that the best long-term decision is reached while taking into account the overall impact of that decision.

THEORY INTO PRACTICE 11-1

CASE

Ralph is currently working as manager at Silver Service. He feels that he is treated well there as an employee and is well respected by both his supervisors and his employees. He has been there now for five years. Business at the shop is very steady because the shop has a very solid reputation and it is expected to stay strong through the coming years.

Although there is no reason why Ralph needs to consider a change, he has always wondered what it would be like to be on his own. He recently heard about a shop about three miles away that is up for sale. It is in the same community and is very similar in many ways to the shop that he currently works in. Ralph wonders if this might be the chance of a lifetime.

You decide

As Ralph's best friend, he comes to you and relays the story about this great opportunity. What advice do you give him?

THEORY INTO PRACTICE 11-2

CASE

After your talk Ralph does some thinking and calculates the benefits of his current position and the potential income if he opens the shop. He knows that his total earnings for the past three years (salary + benefits) have averaged $100,000 per year and have remained steady. He has done his homework about the costs and benefits of being a shop owner and has found out that the owner of the shop where he is currently employed has earned a net profit of $150,000 each of the past three years. Further, he has found out that the shop that is up for sale, although not as successful as Silver Service, has had a net profit of $90,000 per year over the past three years. After speaking with a financial advisor and a banker Ralph knows that in order to open the shop he'll have to take out a $100,000 business loan to get the new company started.

You decide

What would Ralph's ROI be over five years by taking this opportunity based on the information that we currently have in dollars? What is the ROI percentage? Based on this information, what would you recommend Ralph do? Why?

The Ben Franklin Decision Model

It has been said that Benjamin Franklin, one of the founding fathers of our nation, was a very intelligent, thoughtful, and logical man. Along with his involvement in the American Revolution and the formation of the United States of America he was also a very prolific inventor and scientist. He had a burning desire to understand how and why things worked the way that they did. Because of this curiosity he was also acknowledged as being a very logical and dependable decision maker. When confronted with difficult decisions, it is said that Franklin had a very simple, yet useful, approach to determining the best choice that he used. This has become known as the **Franklin decision model.**

Franklin Decision Model

A simple tool to assist in decision making that is done by creating two lists, one of benefits (pros) and one of drawbacks (cons) of a particular course of action. Used in its simplest form, the final decision can be made by adding up the lists and choosing the one with more entries.

In his decision-making model, Benjamin Franklin took a blank sheet of paper and drew a straight line down the center of the paper from top to bottom. On the left side he wrote down every reason that he could think of why he should take the action that he was considering. On the right side of the page he listed all of the reasons why he should not take the action. Being a very thoughtful and thorough man, he would list as many positives and negatives as possible. Even though he might be leaning toward the pros or cons he would make a conscious effort to try to come up with as many arguments for the other side of the ledger as he could. When he finally ran out of items for his two lists he would take the last, and most important, step: he would simply add up the number of items listed on the left side and then do the same for the items on the right. Whichever list had the most items was the choice that he would make. Figure 11-1 illustrates the Franklin decision model.

Possible factors to consider:	
In Favor (pros)	Against (cons)
1.	1.
2.	2.
3.	3.
4.	4.
5.	5.
6.	6.
.	.
.	.
.	.

Figure 11-1 Franklin decision model

The true value of this model, although simple in design, is not just one to help you decide by counting up the votes for or against any decision. Rather, the essence of the model is to force you to thoughtfully and thoroughly consider both sides of an issue. You must earnestly struggle to identify both the pros and the cons to help you uncover the underlying impact that the decision will have no matter which decision you ultimately decide to make.

Using the Franklin decision model often helps you to realize that you didn't fully consider the other side of the argument. Therefore, it helps you to see that you may be entering into a decision on a more emotional than logical basis without having fully weighed the options. It is not uncommon that after sincerely exploring this simple approach that the resulting decision is either altered or, at least, tempered because you can now enter into that decision with a more complete understanding of all of the possible results.

THEORY INTO PRACTICE 11-3

CASE

Ralph's decision to start his own shop has been further complicated. A good customer who considers Ralph as his mechanic has heard through the grapevine that Ralph is considering leaving Silver Service to start his own shop. He has offered to put up all of the funds to back Ralph's new shop as a silent partner in return for one-third of the net profits of the new venture.

You decide

Ralph has decided he wants to make his move now. He asks your advice in helping him to decide whether to go out 100 percent on his own or to do it with the silent partner.. Build a Ben Franklin decision model listing all of the factors in favor of the two choices. Which did you recommend to Ralph? Why?

Risk versus Reward

As you have probably noticed from the previous section on ROI, there is a lot at stake in making a decision. In most cases, however, the decision is not quite as simple as the one listed above for Ralph where it can be made based strictly on dollars and cents. Along with the money that can be gained or lost there are often many other factors that need to be weighed to make an informed decision. Evaluating this information to come up with the best decision for you should be based on weighing the potential rewards compared with the potential risks.

Reward is what you stand to gain by taking a particular action. **Risk** is what you potentially stand to lose if the action does not work out as planned. Although it is not a clear-cut scientific method, looking at decisions by weighing risk against reward helps to make sure that you take into account the entire situation and can then make the decision that is best for you. Whereas the approach of ROI is more focused on the direct rewards, benefits, and costs the concept of risk versus reward asks you to consider a bit further those intangible results that aren't easily directly measured. You might not see the impact of those risks for some time. However, they are no less real and can have a greater long-term effect on your success than the short-term ROI costs.

Reward
What you stand to gain by taking a particular action.

Risk
What you potentially stand to lose if a particular action does not work out as planned.

It takes time and some real thought to identify all of the things that might be changed, to the good or to the bad, by an action that you take. But it is a necessity for you to make good decisions. Many times the indirect consequences of a hastily executed decision can have extreme costs. Many of these risks may not immediate financial ones, but what is the real risk to the organization if you alienate your steady customers, reduce employee loyalty, possibly lose some long-standing employees, or negatively affect a long-standing relationship with a supplier, your banker, or your manufacturer? All of these risks should be carefully weighed before making decisions.

REAL WORLD APPLICATION

University Imports, a local large automotive dealership operation, has had a stellar long-term reputation as a service shop and has one of the most decorated and stable service workforces in the entire region.

(Continued)

Because their work continues to grow, Brad, their general manager, is concerned that they might not be able to keep up with the fast pace of incoming requests for service work. After attending a recent dealer convention he returns with the idea of switching all of his appointment and service scheduling over to an online self-paced system where the customers can go online and schedule their own appointments 24/7. The cost for the new system is significant, but he reasons that it will make the operation so much more efficient that he can reduce the number of service advisors by two, which will save more than the cost of the new equipment. Brad's proposal to the owner is a simple one as he states, "Boss, this is a no-brainer. The cost of the system will be $50, 000 per year and the resulting savings in salaries and benefits by laying off two of our existing service advisors will be $75,000 per year. The Return on Investment will be $25,000 per year plus the ability to expand without adding more personnel—it's a clear winner. Can I have your OK to order the equipment today?"

To his surprise, Brad's dealer principal is scowling. He responds, "Brad, it sounds to me like you haven't done all of your homework here. Yes, I agree that on the surface the cost of the system and the savings on personnel costs appear, at first blush, to be a major savings. Tell me, how is this layoff going to affect morale? You know that we're like a big family around here. Have you taken into consideration the fact the effect that it may have on our remaining employees? . . . and another thing while we're at it . . . what about those old-time customers of ours who aren't comfortable with "those new-fangled computer systems"? Will we lose some customers if we switch to a fully computerized system? Sounds like you need to do more research on the true costs and benefits and then get back to me."

THEORY INTO PRACTICE 11-4

CASE

You promised your friend that you would meet him for lunch in the middle of your work day at Master Motors. You are given an hour for lunch every day and your boss is 'a stickler' for being on time. As you are finishing lunch with your friend you just realized that you have to be back to work in 10 minutes, and you are have a 15-minute drive to get back to work.

You decide

If you decide to drive over the speed limit to get there on time there is a chance that you'll get a ticket or, even worse, get in an accident. Is it a good risk to speed so that you can make it there on time and avoid the risk of being reprimanded by the boss? What do you stand to lose by speeding? What are the benefits of getting there on time? What would you do?

THEORY INTO PRACTICE 11-5

CASE

Ralph is still trying to decide whether or not he should leave his job at Silver Service and open his own shop. He is 35 years old and in good health. He has a wife and three small children (ages 1, 3, and 8). Ralph and his family just moved a year ago into a larger home in the suburbs that would fit his growing family. Because of the children he and his wife, Peggy, have decided that it is best for her to stay at home to raise the children. They have a large mortgage on their home ($150,000). Although their finances are tight they have been able to make ends meet based on his current income.

You decide

What risks does Ralph need to consider if he decides to follow his dream and take this opportunity to open his own shop? What are the rewards? What would you do?

Control, Influence, and Frustration

One of the most frustrating situations you encounter in your personal or professional life is that feeling of helplessness when something bad happens and you can't do anything to stop it. As a manager, you will often find yourself in this situation. The wise manager, however, learns over time how to conserve his energy and direct his attention toward those things that he can change.

Steven Covey, author of *The Seven Habits of Highly Effective People* (Covey, 1989), has effectively summarized and provided guidance on dealing with this abstract concept. He notes that everything that you try to manage or control falls into one of **three realms:** those that are within your *span of control*, those that are within your *sphere of influence*, and those that are out of your *locus of control*. Let us explore these concepts. Understanding them will help you to decide where to put your efforts and energies to have maximum impact.

Three Realms
The three major categories that everything you try to manage or control falls within: span of control, sphere of influence, and locus of control.

As a manager you do not have the time to do everything. Therefore, you must become effective in directing your attention and energy toward those activities that will most likely produce the maximum results. It is important, then, to develop an understanding of what business factors you can control, which ones you can affect (influence), and which are immovable objects. Then, and only then, can you direct the maximum amount of your energy toward actions that will yield results.

Things that are within your **span of control** are things you can change. Whether this change happens by changing yourself or doing it yourself, they do not require you to engage external forces. Deciding to make a daily to-do list is clearly within your span of control. It does not take anyone else to do this. You can make the decision and implement it, plain and simple. This principle could also be true within the work group that you supervise. You can make a decision on which car is to be worked on next, and the decision is implemented without hesitation. We all face many situations in our personal and professional lives where we make minute-to-minute decisions and take actions that are clearly within our span of control.

Span of Control
Those situations, events, or plans that you can control or change through your own direct efforts.

Things that are within your **sphere of influence** are a bit more complex. Once something requires external resources, it starts to move from the realm of span of control to sphere of influence. After all, you do not have control over other people, over other activities, or over other resources. You have to depend upon them to act as you want them to act. Therefore, in exercising management in this realm, you are likely to need to influence and/or persuade people. As a result, although you can affect the result, you cannot produce the result yourself. This is the realm that managers spend most of their time and effort living in. Therefore, it is essential that they clearly understand it and can function smoothly in this realm.

Sphere of Influence
Situations, events, or plans whose direction you cannot change alone but only through the assistance or cooperation of others.

Let's explore the idea of span of control and sphere of influence in a little more depth. A very simple example is being able to get to work on time. There are some things that you have full control over that affect your ability to achieve this goal. These factors are within your span of control. Getting to bed early enough to get sufficient rest, setting your alarm clock to wake you up, leaving for work early enough to provide sufficient drive time are all factors that are within your span of control. They are things that you can do yourself that will directly contribute to your success in achieving your goal.

In this same example there are many factors that, although you do not directly control, you can affect. These are those things that are within your sphere of influence. An example of this would be coordinating your wakeup time with the others in your household so that you are sure that you will not be waiting long for your turn to take a shower. Another factor that you can influence is reminding your son not to park in the driveway behind your car so he doesn't block your car and prevent you from heading out to work on time.

Locus of Control
Situations, events, or plans for which you can alter the results through control or influence.

The last, yet extremely important, group is those things that are beyond your **locus of control.** These are things that you cannot do yourself and upon which you can have little or no effect. The 10-ton boulder that just fell into the road in front of your car is a good example. There it is and it is blocking your way. You did not put it there and even though you might try, you very likely cannot move it or significantly change it. So what are you to do? The best choice is to recognize the immovable obstacle, acknowledge it, and devise a plan to work around it. Just as the physical boulder, you are bound to face many obstacles in your quest to get your way as a manager. Learning to identify the roadblocks early and often is a key to success.

Two common examples of events that fall in this realm are an unexpected power outage and an overnight snowstorm. Even though you set your alarm (span of control), you could not have known that the power would go out and, as a result, that your alarm would not wake you up. You provided for reasonable drive time to work (span of control) and made sure your son did not park behind you (sphere of influence) but could not have expected a snowstorm that even the 11–P.M. weather forecast on the news did not predict!

It is important to recognize that those things beyond your control will happen. That doesn't change the fact that you are ultimately responsible for achieving your goals, however. It is essential that you consider the possibilities and, when possible, take proactive measures to minimize their effect.

The discussion of the three realms is intended to help you to direct your energies where they will provide the maximum return on your efforts. As we have already discussed, you cannot possibly do everything. Thus, the better you are able to plan ahead and decide where the best place is for you to put your efforts, the more likely you will be to succeed. Accepting that there will always be some things that you cannot change and that you are better off identifying them early and navigating around them is a far better use of your energy than trying to move that boulder in the middle-of-the road.

Real World Application

Phoebe's automotive service department has been inconsistent in reaching its sales goals. However, she has taken a new approach and has committed to her boss to do everything that she can to influence to assure that they make their goals this month. In order to do this she has a plan. The major components of her plan are to

Check out prices of local competitors to make sure that her prices are a good value

Advertise in the local paper and on the radio to make sure that potential customers are aware that their service is a good value

Make sure that she has enough people on staff to produce enough work to exceed the monthly goals

Make sure her employees are all aware of the new push to meet or exceed the goal

Provide the technicians and service advisors new incentives for up selling service

Schedule enough work into the shop so there is enough work to reach or exceed the goal.

All of the activities listed are reasonable ones for Phoebe to pursue. By doing so she is creating an environment where they can succeed. Further, she is focusing her efforts on factors that are within her span of control and sphere of influence. In fact, it appears that she has tried to over-plan, that is, to plan for more than she needs just in case. By doing so she is providing a cushion that will assure that she succeeds even if something that is beyond her control or influence happens to occur . . . such as a few customers canceling their appointments the last minute! That is a good use of Phoebe's time, her resources, and her efforts.

THEORY INTO PRACTICE 11-6

CASE

Ralph is still trying to decide whether or not to change jobs. He learns that Max Mechanix has one technician who is producing 70 hours per week. He reasons that if this tech can turn that many hours the potential must be there for him to do so, too.

You decide

Is Ralph's ability to produce more flat-rate hours within his control? How would knowing this help him to make a decision to accept or reject the job at Max Mechanix?

THEORY INTO PRACTICE 11-7

CASE

Ralph has settled in at his new job at Max Mechanix. He's a bit frustrated, however, after four weeks of work that his paychecks aren't quite up to his old standard. He sits down and analyzes his situation and identifies three things that concern him.

1. He seems to be having a hard time getting to work on time and he knows that he is losing out on some great jobs first thing in the morning.
2. The service advisor that he is working with is unfamiliar with Ralph's capabilities and therefore is somewhat timid about selling some services that Ralph is capable of performing.
3. Because it is back to school time business at the shop, and elsewhere around town, has been slower than usual for the past month.

You decide

Please categorize the three issues (span of control/sphere of influence/out of control). If you were Ralph, which item would you work on first? Second? Last? Why?

The Three Levels of Performance

There is one more important factor that you must consider in effective decision making if you want your decisions to be lasting. When you see a problem occur you need to evaluate: is that really the problem that you see; or is it simply a symptom? What is the difference?

Poor performance, difficulties, failures are most often not isolated incidents. The 'root cause' is often something beyond the incident that we initially observe. If you want to keep the same incident from occurring again and again, it is very likely that you will have to identify the root cause and make changes to resolve the root cause. Without doing so the problem is bound to occur again at that level. You may have to make decisions that cause changes at the appropriate level within the organization.

Let us briefly look at the organization and the three major levels of performance within it. An organization's structure can be illustrated as shown in Figure 11-2.

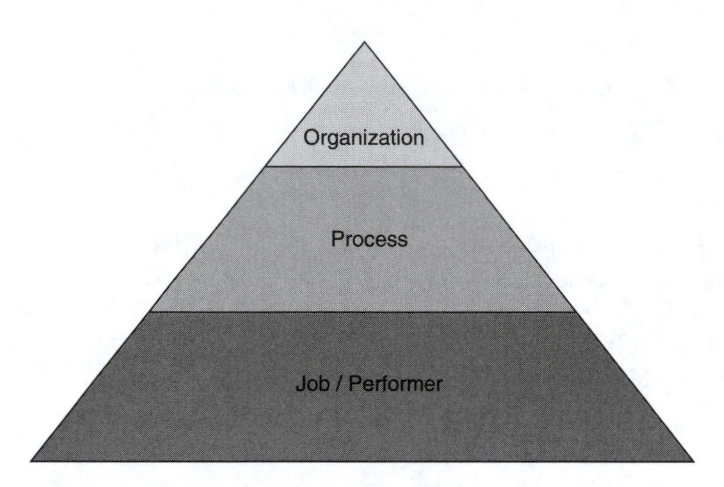

Figure 11-2 The three levels of performance

Organization Level

Organization Level
The upper management of a company or department that is responsible for setting broad mission and goals.

The **organization level** of any company typically is removed from the day-to-day operations. This is the executive level where the big-picture decisions are made that determine the direction of the organization. Regardless of what is happening on the front lines daily, the business's long-term direction is driven by top management's mission, goals, strategies, and expectations. The way resources are allocated, whether it is the assignment of personnel, space, or money, are all a result of the big-picture goals and aspirations for the company.

It is important that operations from top to bottom are aligned with the goals and strategies coming from the organizational level. If they are not, there will be confusion and a great deal of energy and resources may be misdirected. If the entire operation is not trying to pull together with the same goal in mind, inefficiency is the best result that can be expected. Many companies with great potential fail in the marketplace due to poor communication of goals and the confusion and wasted efforts that result.

Process

Process Level
The level within an organization or department where systems and workflows are determined and resources are allocated.

The **process level** of the organization is where the resources are aligned to create an efficient and effective system that gets the greatest results for the investment made (in manpower, space, andresources). The process level is where the systems and workflows are set up and the resources allocated to assure that all processes can effectively operate.

The process of producing the goods and/or services that are in demand by customers is where value is created. Value is what the customer purchases. The perceived value of your product or service makes the difference between a satisfied repeat customer and one that is lost forever to the competition. You might want to glance back at systems theory as described in Chapter 4 to review this concept again.

The effectiveness and efficiency of the processes and workflow will determine the ultimate success of any organization. If a company is to maximize its resources, its processes must be aligned with and clearly support the organization's goals. Efficient processes provide an environment where employees can succeed, and thrive, and consistently produce a quality product. Inefficiency results in waste, poor quality, dissatisfied employees, high turnover, and, in the end, loss of revenues and repeat business.

Job/Performer

The **job/performer level** is where the work is actually done. For example, in an automotive service department the job/performer level *is* the service technician repairing cars. It is where the productive employees function every day. Who are the productive employees? They are those employees who produce the products or services of the company. In an automotive service operation, the productive employees in the shop are the technicians.

Job/Performer Level
The level within an organization or department where the primary production or work of the company is done.

Nonproductive employees are not to be confused with non-essential or unimportant employees. All of the support personnel in an automotive repair shop are essential. As we saw in Chapter 3, it takes many people with a wide range of skills and abilities to staff an efficient and profitable automotive service operation.

The job/performer level is where the issues directly related to the frontline employees occur. These issues range from establishing and maintaining acceptable salary and benefits to providing a suitable working environment. All of these issues assure satisfied and stable employees, and stable employees are more productive employees. Providing clear direction, guidance, and feedback to frontline employees is also important. After all, if the employees don't know what top management wants, it is highly unlikely that the employees will produce it consistently. That is true in an assembly plant, a service shop, or a grocery store.

Changing Performance

Where is this all going, you ask? You understand that there are three levels in the organization. Each of them serves a different function within the organization and they are all essential. The key to understanding the function and value of each of the three levels occurs when you make decisions. Knowing the unique traits of each level will aid you to direct your efforts at the level necessary to make the most lasting changes to the organization. The guiding principle for changing performance is:

> First rule for changing performance: In order to effectively change performance, it is necessary to approach the problem at least one level above where the problem is observed.

The point here is that you can learn all of the techniques to make decisions, but if you keep on addressing the symptom rather than the problem it will keep cropping up continuously. When you realize fully that these three levels are interdependent and that what happens on the front lines (job/performer) is influenced by systems (processes) and priorities (organization), you be able to make effective decisions for lasting improvements. Keeping this principle in mind and directing your efforts accordingly will have a significant impact on the ultimate success of your operation.

Practical Principles

Whatever the situation that you find yourself in there are some overarching principles that will help you to improve your decision-making process. Whether you are making a life-changing decision or a routine daily one, use these principles as a checklist to confirm that you are on the right track.

- **Start with an open mind.** There is a big difference between having an opinion and having a closed mind. You need to be able to consider all of the possibilities, consider them seriously, and discuss them openly.
- **Don't take sides.** Sound management decisions are those that choose the principle or practice that will best serve the organization. In order to do this it is critical to be able to separate ideas from individuals.
- **Acknowledge your bias.** It is important for you to start by doing some soul-searching so that you can acknowledge where you stand and make sure that you don't try to force fit your idea as the only viable solution.
- **Make decisions based on facts, not politics.** Effective decision-making is not based on personalities or politics. Letting those issues cloud the process can lead to unfair decisions.
- **Consider all options.** Full and frank discussion is necessary to uncover all of the possibilities and work toward the best one. Often the best solution is not obvious. Be patient; don't try to jump to an immediate solution.
- **Consider short- and long-term effects.** Many options offer a quick fix yet leave lasting damage. Take the time to consider the implications in both the immediate and the long-term future so that you make the choice that yields the best results.
- **Don't be *too* hard line or too wishy-washy.** The role of a manager in decision making is as a facilitator, not a dictator. Although you may be ultimately charged with making the final call, it is essential that you get as much input and involvement from your employees as possible to inform that decision. You must create an atmosphere where your employees are willing to share and in turn feel that their opinions are valued and taken seriously.

Real World Application

It is all too common for management to address disappointing results by firing the person in charge. We see it happen every day in pro sports. The team flounders, and the coach gets fired. Unfortunately, similar situations are all too common in business. Take, for example, the automotive service department that has had a track record for dismal customer satisfaction over the past five years. In an effort to fix this problem they have gone through seven service managers. Every six to nine months when the quarterly customer satisfaction results come back from the manufacturer and the shop still is the lowest in the region, the owner calls the service manager to his office and fires him, and a new one hired in his place.

This happens commonly in organizations where upper management has little knowledge of the inner workings of the service operation. It is a classic case where the processes (one level above the job/performer level) or even possibly the organization (two levels above the job/performer level) are creating an environment where whoever takes on the title as service manager is doomed to failure. Doomed to failure, that is, until someone in the organization identifies the true root cause and makes the changes necessary to fix the problem.

SUMMARY

Although you can find many tools to help you in making sound decisions, there is no one easy answer. We are all different and have different personalities, needs, and tolerances for pressure and risk. This is why a universal right answer does not exist. Even with reams of evidence to the contrary you'll find someone who will intentionally make what appears to be a bad choice. How otherwise could you explain someone purchasing a brand new lime green Porsche Carrera or a loud plaid suit?

The best defense against making poor decisions is careful analysis. This is best done by using multiple methods to analyze the facts. You would also use this method when you are faced with major surgery. Getting a second opinion from another expert doctor is a reasonable approach before you take serious risks with your health and well-being. In like manner, confirming your business decisions by using multiple analysis methods increases the likelihood that any decision you make will be a sound one.

Making decisions, though, is not enough. It is essential that decisions are well-thought-out, well planned, and properly directed. Properly directed means that those decisions need to be focused at the organizational level, where they will remedy the root cause of performance problems and ensure the potential for success in the future. This is most likely to have lasting impact and to create an environment where employees have the opportunity to do their jobs and be successful. In the long run, this assures mutual success.

PRACTICING THE PRINCIPLES

1. ROI is a common decision-making tool that measures
   a. reasonable on interest.
   b. realistic options for investment.
   c. return of interest.
   d. return on investment.
2. A simple process in which you develop two lists, one of the pros and one listing all of the cons to help you make a decision is called
   a. the Ben Fuller approach.
   b. risk versus reward.
   c. ROI.
   d. none of the above.
3. If you want to change the root cause of a performance problem you must do so
   a. at least three levels above where the symptom is observed.
   b. with a sterilized, very sharp scalpel.
   c. one or two levels below where the symptom is observed.
   d. none of the above.
4. The level within the organization where the systems of operation occur is the
   a. job/performer level.
   b. process level.
   c. organization level.
   d. all of the above.
5. An effective manager directs his efforts toward those things that are
   a. within his sphere of influence.
   b. beyond his control.
   c. within his span of control.
   d. more than one of the above answers is correct.
6. Technician A says that he is always late because traffic is so heavy on the freeway. The heavy traffic is
   a. a valid excuse for him being late every day.
   b. within his span of control.
   c. beyond his control or influence.
   d. within his sphere of influence.

7. Factors like low pay and a poor benefits package
   a. must be addressed at the organization level of the company.
   b. affect the job performance of the employees.
   c. will negatively affect employee morale.
   d. all of the above.
8. If I wanted to weigh all of the possible consequences for a proposed decision, whether long-term or short-term, financial or otherwise, I'd be trying to evaluate
   a. Franklin decision model.
   b. risk versus reward.
   c. ROI.
   d. all of the above.
9. Joe has located a supplier where he can purchase brand new AM/FM/CD radio units for $50. He knows that he can easily sell them for $125 each plus installation cost. What is Joe's ROI per radio?
   a. $175.
   b. $75.
   c. $50.
   d. $125.
10. Horace has been told by his general manager that he needs to paint the shop. He has the painter lined up to do the job. He only has one more decision to make. What color? Which of these decision tools would be best suited to help him with this decision?
    a. Franklin decision model.
    b. risk versus reward.
    c. ROI.
    d. all of the above.

REFERENCE

Covey, S., *The Seven Habits of Highly Effective People* (New York: Free Press, 1989).

CHAPTER

12

Quality and Continuous Improvement

CHAPTER OBJECTIVES

- To explore the history of the quality movement
- To recognize key figures and key principles underlying quality management philosophies
- To apply principles of quality and continuous improvement
- To evaluate the cost of quality and the cost of poor quality
- To choose the appropriate actions and activities needed to maintain an environment of continuous improvement

KEY TERMS

quality
quality assurance
continuous improvement
W. Edwards Deming
J. M. Juran
statistical process control
80/20 principle
Philip B. Crosby
zero defects concept
conformance to requirements
prevention
cost of quality

Introduction

Since the end of WWII in the mid-1940s, the underlying philosophy that guides business operations has evolved dramatically. This is especially evident in manufacturing but has reached into everything we do from building to sales, service, and education. The traditional management theories that had been developed after the Industrial Revolution and were still widely practiced up to that time taught managers how to organize employees and ensure consistent performance through dividing job tasks down into their smallest, simplest components. As we discussed in depth in Chapter 5, they used these management philosophies based on directing the efforts of employees while maintaining full control and responsibility. In the post–World War II era the rebuilding of many of the world's economies also spawned the birth of new philosophies of work and management. Of these new philosophies the one that has had the most far-reaching impact has been the quality movement, often referred to also as the continuous improvement movement.

The quality movement of W. Edwards Deming and those that have followed after him has changed that the way that work is done and managed in very profound ways. In today's work environment everyone is responsible for the end product and ensuring that it is done right the first time, every time. In this chapter we will examine the philosophies and practices underlying this important backbone of the world economic engine.

Quality

Quality
A product or service that meets or exceeds the customer's requirements or expectations.

The **quality** movement is not just a set of management principles but a different philosophy of looking at how and why a business operates and, therefore, the way operations must be managed. The dramatic change in philosophy from that of traditional management theory can best be summarized by the way that managers and employees would see their role in addressing the following issues:

1. What is quality?
2. How do you know when you have achieved quality?
3. Once you have achieved quality what do you do next?
4. Who is responsible for the quality of the product and/or service that you provide?

Quality Assurance
A proactive approach to obtaining results that meet or exceed expectations through involving all employees rather than through post-production inspection.

Until all employees can answer these four questions, see that they play an essential role in assuring quality, and assume responsibility for their part in **quality assurance**, this philosophy has not taken hold. This is a dramatically different way of looking at doing business than in a traditional management philosophy in which most employees had no role in quality. This was reserved as the right and responsibility of management. inspectors and management were the only ones responsible for the end product.

The first step in changing the work process requires considering the question, Who is really responsible for turning out a quality product or delivering a quality service? The simple answer can be determined by looking at it from the end (the output in a system) back to the inputs and resulting process (for a refresher on systems theory you may want to refer back to Chapter 4). Who will be affected by poor quality?

It is not difficult to see that everyone in the business organization will be affected by poor quality. Customers whose expectations are not fully met will quickly turn away and shop elsewhere. Therefore, everyone is affected by poor quality (lack of business) and by good quality (high profits, plenty of work, job security). Thus, it is logical that efforts should be made to assure that everyone can see the part he or she plays in producing quality and, as a result of this new awareness, has the opportunity to become actively involved in assuring that quality occurs?

However, to *assure* quality it is necessary to go one step further. Because the product or service is good today does not mean that it will be good enough tomorrow. Others are out there trying to win over your customers. They are constantly doing this by lowering prices, improving the quality of their products, and, in effect, trying to show customers that they will get more value for their investment from dealing with the competition. If you do not continue to monitor and improve your business practices the day will come when the competition will slowly take away your business. You must produce a quality product or service at a reasonable price and daily strive to make it better and better value to the customer. That is the true meaning of **continuous improvement**.

Continuous Improvement

The management concept that states that quality is not a static target but must be constantly improved.

The Gurus of Quality

Three of the most influential men in the quality and continuous improvement movement, are W. Edwards Deming, J. M. Juran, and Philip B. Crosby. To best understand the dramatic difference between this philosophy and that of traditional management we need to look at the contribution of each of these management theorists to the development of the quality movement.

W. Edwards Deming

W. Edwards Deming is credited as being the father of the quality movement. An engineer and statistician by trade, Deming openly espoused his theories about how to consistently improve business operations in the United States. He was initially ignored by U.S. businessmen. During the rebuilding of Japan after World War II the Japanese became enamored with Deming's theories on statistical process control and recognized that he had developed a unique way of assuring consistent quality. They invited him to their country and openly embraced his new vision of quality improvement. The impact of his teachings on Japanese business was profound. Deming's management philosophies have been credited as the key factor in moving Japan from that of a producer of low-cost, low-quality products to the higher status that it enjoys today. One of his books, *Elementary Principles of the Statistical Control of Quality* (Deming, 1950), published in Tokyo, has been credited as the foundation of the management philosophy that helped to propel Japanese manufacturing to becoming a leader in producing world-class quality products.

W. Edwards Deming

The primary theorist responsible for the foundational theories of quality and continuous improvement, commonly credited as being the father of the quality movement.

Deming's philosophy of management is far more than a new method for counting defects and calculating statistics. Along with providing the technical tools to help track quality and performance Deming provides an innovative and far-reaching philosophy of management. He provides a school of thought that continues to change the way people look at quality: what it is, how to measure it, who is responsible for it, and its ultimate impact on business survival and success.

Deming begins by demanding that quality should occur by prevention rather than by inspection. What he really means is that it is no longer acceptable for any worker to say, It's not my job. It is everyone's job to make sure that a quality product or service is produced consistently. He goes on to propose that if a company is to succeed in the long run that good enough is not acceptable. For long-range success businesses needed to adopt a philosophy in which they commit to improve their processes, services, and products consistently and continuously. This philosophy of continuous improvement is often cited as the guiding principle of the modern day quality movement.

Constantly improving products and services is not enough for Deming. He stresses that to achieve true quality it is essential that the organization constantly strive to improve their systems of operation. This assures the business constant growth and improvement. In order to foster a climate where all employees are responsible for and involved in continuous improvement it is necessary that employees have access to additional knowledge to feed this cycle of innovation. Therefore, Deming asserts that constant training and retraining is essential.

The role of management changed dramatically in Deming's philosophy of management. In the traditional model, the boss is the brains and the workers are extra sets of hands that will do exactly what the boss has directed them to do. In the quality model, everyone is expected to be involved and to engage their brains, as well as their hands, in the process of delivering high-quality services and products.

Deming's way of operating is a learning model. Everyone is involved in monitoring and reporting and improving, but in order to do this they need to know what the standards are and must to keep track of their performance. In doing this they learn what works best. They also learn about what doesn't work, and they have the data to back up their decisions. This concept is an important one that Deming calls profound knowledge. He explained that whether the results are what we expect or not does not really matter as much as we are able to measure and document the results and to learn from them. Therefore, even a failure becomes a source of growth because, if measured and recorded, a failure helps guide our future actions and increases the chances of continuous and consistent improvement.

Finally, Deming's philosophy is a major breakthrough in the overall theory of how organizations work. As the principles and examples listed above indicate, traditional management was a function of the boss giving orders and the employees simply following those orders like drone bees. Deming involves everyone in taking responsibility for the end result, so everyone has a role and some responsibility in directing (or managing) the outcome.

What, then, is the role of the manager in this setting? The role of the manager becomes one of providing leadership and direction. The manager helps to facilitate the improvement process and leads by example. Deming's philosophy is one of the first to propose the concept of leadership as the role of the supervisor.

Deming's overall management philosophy can be summed up by the list of key principles shown in Figure 12-1.

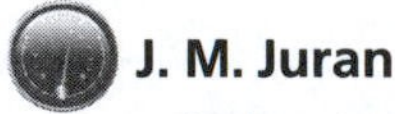

J. M. Juran
An early theorist who is credited with adding statistical foundations and the human dimension to the quality and continuous improvement movement.

J. M. Juran

J. M. Juran was a contemporary of Deming. He has been credited with adding to the statistical foundations of quality and adding the human dimension. His work

Deming's 14 Principles

1) Constancy of purpose towards improvement of product and service.
2) Adopt the new philosophy.
3) Cease dependence on inspection to achieve quality.
4) End the practice of awarding business based on price.
5) Improve constantly and forever the system of production and service.
6) Institute training on the job.
7) Institute leadership.
8) Drive out fear so that everyone may work effectively for the company.
9) Break down barriers between departments.
10) Eliminate slogans, exhortations, and targets.
11) Eliminate work standards and substitute leadership.
12) Remove barriers that rob the worker of his right to pride of workmanship.
13) Institute a vigorous program of education and self-improvement.
14) Put everybody in the company to work to accomplish the transformation.

Figure 12-1 Deming's 14 Principles

was critical to helping the broader society understand the quality concept. This greatly helped the spread of the quality management philosophy in the West.

Juran promotes three key dimensions of quality: quality planning, quality control, and quality improvement. He impresses upon others the fact that quality must be planned into the production of a product and/or service. Customer needs must be included in the planning process, resulting in the right products and processes to meet customer's needs. Once those needs and requirements are clearly understood and taken into account in the planning process, quality control then takes over. Evaluating actual performance, comparing to goals, and resolving the differences ensures that the final product consistently meets customer needs. Through using principles of quality improvement a business can continue to improve to unprecedented levels.

Even though Juran did try to expand the quality movement beyond mere statistical analysis, the measurement of performance still remains as a key underlying principle. As such, he strongly promotes **Statistical Process Control (SPC)**, a mathematical method of tracking variation of actual performance from expected outcome. This key measurement tool provides a practical method for any organization to track the actual performance of a process, whether it is production of a product or providing a service. Three critical pieces of information are required.

1. What is the optimum result?
2. What is the acceptable variance from the desired outcome?
3. What is the actual result?

Statistical Process Control (SPC)

A mathematical method of tracking and charting variations in actual performance from expected outcomes.

Real World Application

A very important part of any automotive service business is customer satisfaction. Any shop that is unable to maintain a high level of satisfied customers is bound to lose them and will, eventually, find it difficult to stay in business. For that reason the major manufacturers regularly conduct customer satisfaction surveys of customers who have had warranty repairs performed. Dealers are held accountable to maintain a specific level of performance on the customer surveys. The following is an example of how the dealer's response to their customer satisfaction performance would differ between a dealership using traditional management techniques and one that had embraced Juran's quality philosophy.

The manufacturer's customer survey scores for January have just been received for both dealerships. Although the manufacturer would like to achieve 100 percent customer satisfaction, they require that dealers maintain 90 percent customer satisfaction to qualify for their Standards of Excellence Program, a recognition that all dealers actively strive to achieve and maintain.

Customer Number		Dealer A	Dealer B
1		100	94
2		79	84
3		84	84
4		93	88
5		94	100
Total		**450**	**450**
Average		**90.00**	**90.00**

This month Dealership A and Dealership B both received customer survey results from five customers as follows.

As the data indicates, although Dealer A and Dealer B got different results from each customer, on average they have received identical customer satisfaction scores and both have been able to (just barely) qualify for Standards of Excellence.

However, because of differences in their management philosophies what Dealer A and Dealer B do with this information differs dramatically. Dealer A is a traditionally operated store. Therefore, when the dealer reviews the results and meets with his general manager the conversation goes something like this:

Dealer A: I just got our customer satisfaction results for January. Congratulations! We've qualified for Standards of Excellence with a 90 percent average. Keep up the good work but, you know, you sort of scared me by just barely making the grade. Let's try a little harder next month to move up the scores and give ourselves a little breathing room. OK?

Dealer B is committed to quality improvement and has become heavily involved in recent months in implementing Juran's quality measurement tools to help them assure that they will consistently meet or exceed their quality targets. He also meets with his general manager, but the conversation is quite different:

Dealer B: I just received the customer satisfaction results for January. The good news is that we've again qualified for Standards of Excellence with a 90 percent average. Keep up the good work, but let's take a look at our performance chart to see where we need to improve.

Dealer B continues, Even though we were able to reach the Standards of Excellence benchmark, since we consistently track our own customer satisfaction scores the chart shows us the areas where we need to concentrate to help make sure that we continue to reach the benchmark. It looks like three of our five customers gave us ratings that were below the benchmark. We need to contact each of those customers, find out what went wrong, and make the necessary changes to improve our systems so that it doesn't happen again. OK?

Only by tracking actual performance against desired performance and then by analyzing and taking corrective action to eliminate the cause of *every variation* from the desired outcome can quality be achieved.

In the preceding example, which dealership do you think is most likely to consistently meet or exceed the Standards of Excellence? Why? Because they track the data, have a standard, and take corrective action every time their performance falls below the standards they are much more likely to consistently reach the goal. On the other hand, using the traditional approach the other dealership will simply try to improve with no information to help them know what they're doing wrong or what really needs to change so that they can achieve their goal. This is a classic use of Juran's SPC process and, despite the criticisms that quality procedures only work in a manufacturing plant, these principles work quite well in this service setting.

One of J. M. Juran's principles that has found lasting value is the Pareto principle which was first introduced in his book *The Quality Control Handbook* (Juran, 1950). This is often referred to as the **80/20 principle.** This principle is based on what Juran calls the vital few and the trivial many. It states that in most cases when you analyze a situation you'll find that only 20 percent of the people do 80 percent of the work. Further, he states that 20 percent of the people influence the actions of the remaining 80 percent. The practical application of this theory is that by identifying those people, those incidents, and those systems that comprise the vital few (20%), you can target your efforts to have the maximum impact. Therefore, it is the best use of your time and resources to identify and target your efforts to where they will produce the greatest desirable results.

80/20 principle
The theory in quality assurance that indicates that 20 percent of the people or processes are responsible for influencing the remaining 80 percent.

A critical application of Juran's 80/20 principle is in its usefulness to guide efforts to correct poor performance within an organization. Most traditional organizations view performance as the sole responsibility of the employees and, therefore, they are the ones to be held accountable, blamed, and replaced to correct poor performance.

Juran views performance problems in a wholly different way. He states that organizations are complex systems and that their performance is bound by the 80/20 rule. He goes on to propose that 80 percent of performance problems are the result of poorly designed or operated systems and only 20 percent of performance problems are people problems. (Please refer back to Chapter 4 where we discussed systems theory in greater detail.) He theorizes that most people sincerely desire to succeed and produce a quality result. Therefore, he proposes that if organizations design systems more effectively and provide people with the processes and tools necessary to succeed that most performance problems will be eliminated.

One of Juran's later and most comprehensive works, *Managerial Breakthrough (Juran, 1964)*, is acknowledged as his best presentation of his overall theories of quality management. It describes in detail his step-by-step sequence for achieving breakthrough performance and has been credited as the source from which the widely accepted Six Sigma quality process was born. Six Sigma continues to be one of the most common quality benchmarking systems used by world-leading companies in all business sectors.

Philip B. Crosby
The quality theorist responsible for developing and promoting the zero defect concept.

There are three major principles upon which Juran's overall theory of quality and continuous improvement are based. These three key principles listed in Figure 12-2 are commonly referred to as Juran's Trilogy.

Juran's Trilogy
Systems Thinking
Management by data
System improvement

Figure 12-2 Juran's Trilogy

Philip B. Crosby

Zero Defects Concept

The quality theory that states that any variation from the expected is unacceptable and that each instance must be investigated, addressed, and resolved.

Conformance to Requirements

Quality principle that states that quality is not relative but is absolute and can be measured by whether or not the products, processes, or services meet requirements.

Philip B. Crosby's major contribution to quality management is his **zero defects concept.** Having worked as an inspector and then as a quality engineer in the 1950s, Crosby was familiar with the measurement of performance and the use of statistical process control to measure quality developed by Deming and Juran. Companies used these tools to track how closely their actual output matched their standards and tried to minimize errors. However, in a 'mission critical area such as the aerospace industry where he was employed, the stakes were very high and the prevailing principles didn't seem to go quite far enough to assure quality. He realized that if every part that went into a rocket varied just a little bit from its intended specifications that the resulting rocket would vary by a total of all of those variations (the total variance = the sum of all of the individual variances)—and that sum was just unacceptable. He determined that there had to be something more. There had to be a way to assure that the end product was more consistent, more reliable. Close was just simply not good enough!

Crosby's Zero Defects concept is his answer to how to resolve the dilemma of controlling quality variance. Crosby determined that close is not good enough. He developed his Zero Defects principle that redefines quality as more than performing within tolerances. It is simply and absolutely defined as **conformance to requirements.** He strongly asserts that this must be the guiding principle of quality management.

— Real World Application

The way that minute variations can all add up to create a huge performance problem is something that is experienced on a regular basis in the automotive service business. Since the typical automobile is a combination of over 22,000 parts produced by over 2,000 suppliers it is easy to see how it can happen. All 22,000 parts do not directly affect all of the others but many of them do work as part of a system. Each of these systems is susceptible to problems because of what is called tolerance stack up. Tolerance stack up is exactly the problem that Philip Crosby tried to resolve.

In the automotive service industry the value of this principle can be illustrated by the cause of a very simply front end vibration. It feels like a wheel/tire imbalance so you decide to balance the tires. After balancing the tires the problem is somewhat improved, but it still hasn't gone away. Why? The reason is that there are other components that also rotate as part of the complete assembly that is attached to the wheel and tire. The brake rotor, the CV joint, the driveshaft assembly all rotate to turn the wheel and tire. If each of them is a little bit out of balance—along with the tire and wheel being a little bit out of balance—it can result in a system imbalance due to tolerance stack up (the sum of each of the individual imbalances) and result in a lot of vibration.

As had happened in the first wave of the quality movement, American industry initially wanted to dismiss Crosby's theory of absolute quality. It was not until 1964, when an executive from the Japanese company NEC sought out Crosby to better understand his philosophy of quality that his principles began to gain acceptance. Shortly afterward Crosby was hired by ITT to install his quality system and was able to raise their products and services to become the standard of quality in their industry based on the use of his approach to quality.

Crosby went on to become one of the second-generation gurus of quality. To date, Crosby's organization continues to advise corporate giants in the aerospace, automotive, computer, and electronics industries to help them to improve the level and consistency of the quality of their products and services. In his book *Quality Is Free* (Crosby, 1979) he introduced three other quality rules to complement his zero defects principle. Together they make up the core of his philosophy on quality. Crosby's four key quality principles are shown in Figure 12-3.

Crosby's Quality Principles

The definition of quality is conformance to requirements.

The system of quality is prevention.

The performance standard is zero defects.

The measurement of quality is the price of non-conformance.

Figure 12-3 Crosby's Quality Principles

Crosby's principles are straightforward and easy to understand. Unlike the statistics-based theories of the earlier quality gurus, Crosby's principles are easier to explain and, easy for the rank-and-file employees to understand and use. We will now briefly review each of these principles.

The Definition of Quality Is Conformance to Requirements Quality is a very specific goal. In order for us achieve quality we need to be very specific in defining exactly what it is so that we will know it when we see it. Goals must be specific. Not only do managers need to know what quality is, they need to go the extra step of making sure that their quality goals are communicated to everyone in the operation. Not until everyone clearly knows what the goal is and is committed to playing his or her part in assuring that it happens will consistent quality occur.

It is very frustrating working under vague guidance. In producing a quality service or product it is essential that the goals be clearly stated and that they are measurable. Finally, it is essential that those goals be attainable. Lofty goals are important to make us all stretch ourselves, but unrealistic goals are more likely than not to make us just give up.

The System of Quality Is Prevention Consistent quality services and products are achieved when quality is built into the product. This principle addresses the change in philosophy from the old method of management where production was the job of the employees and quality was the job of the inspector and manager. In the quality philosophy, assuring that it is done correctly is everyone's job. Errors are prevented rather than found after the fact. **Prevention** is an integral part of the process of work. Therefore quality is continuous, not just an afterthought.

Prevention
The conscious act of taking active steps to ensure that desired results occur and that undesired ones do not occur.

The Performance Standard Is Zero Defects With this principle in mind, everyone needs to realize that close is not good enough. Every product or service that you deliver must meet or exceed the quality standard. More important, in order to ensure consistency in delivering this level of performance it is necessary that every time that the performance fails to meet the standard that it is dealt with. Only by investigating every failure to meet standards and using the information obtained to make improvements in the system can the performance consistently exceed the quality standard.

The Measurement of Quality Is the Price of Nonconformance Quality is not an absolute. Some say the only way to have quality would be to make everything perfect and people aren't perfect. We can't afford perfection and our customers aren't willing to pay for it. Fortunately, we aren't striving for the unattainable. We are trying to achieve and maintain performance that meets or exceeds our standards. In order to do this we need to determine the **cost of quality**. We need to know how much it will cost to do it right and, conversely, how much it will cost if we do it wrong!

Cost of Quality
The total investment required to ensure that the product or service meets or exceeds customer expectations.

Crosby has developed a very simple formula to analyze the true cost of quality. It goes like this—the measurement of quality is the Price of Non-Conformance. As such, we can determine what it costs to do it right. This is called the Price of Conformance (POC). We can also determine what it costs to repair it or do it over. This is called the Price of Nonconformance (PONC). With this information the true Cost of Quality (COQ) for any situation can be figured by using the following formula:

COST OF QUALITY

POC + PONC = COQ

You've probably heard the old adages that anything worth doing is worth doing well and probably even more often that if you can't afford to do it right, you can't afford to do it twice. The cost of quality formula is a way to identify the cost in doing poor work. As such, even though it may cost a little more to do it right the first time, in the long run it is less costly, both financially and in terms of customer satisfaction.

THEORY INTO PRACTICE 12-1

CASE

Ralph has worked as a manager for Herman, the General Manager, in a traditionally managed shop for 15 years. As such, he is accustomed to things not going as planned but he has, in general, had a solid reputation for turning out good work and has maintained an acceptable level of satisfied customers.

However, Ralph and his General Manager have just returned from training at the Crosby Quality College. It is their dealer's intention that they install Crosby's quality system in their shop to improve their work, their operation, and their customer satisfaction.

You decide

In the past, when Ralph's boss, Herman, received the daily quality scores he filed them away, waiting for the monthly report. As long as the monthly average met the company standards he was satisfied. How do you think that that will change now that this new philosophy has been adopted? What should they do the next time they get a low score from one of their customers? Why?

Practical Approach to Achieving Consistent Quality

Now that we have established a background on the history of the quality management movement and have a basic understanding of the quality principles we will take a look at how we can practically apply them in our operations. In the following section we'll explore how we can put them to use.

How do You Know When You Have Achieved Quality?

Even if you understand the philosophy behind continuous improvement and everyone commits to being involved in producing the best product for the best price do you know where you really stand? How would you know quality if you saw it? How would you define it? Take a minute before you read on and write down your definition of quality.

Definition: ____

Now, looking at your definition try to answer the following questions:

1. Am I sure that I'd know it if I saw it?
2. Can I clearly define what quality is?
3. Can I measure the degree of quality?

— Real World Application

Success in the auto repair business always involved maintaining the delicate balance between providing quality service and keeping costs under control so that you can stay in business. Many times quality and cost control appear to be warring factions. If you do one then the other suffers. For example, if you are trying to decide which 'quality level' of brake pad to use on your brake jobs you can choose between the one that costs the least but that is more susceptible to premature failure and a shop comeback (low cost but low quality) or the one that is the highest quality and least likely to give problems (high quality and high cost). How do you decide which is the best choice for your shop in the long run? One method is to use Crosby's Cost of Quality formula as your measure. To do so you need to:

1. Determine the Price of Conformance—What is the cost to do the job right?
   a. Parts cost? The cost of the brake pads
   b. Labor cost? The time needed to install them
   c. Value of a satisfied customer? The good PR and repeat business
2. Determine the Cost of Nonconformance—What is the cost if the car is a comeback and has to be redone?
   a. Parts cost? The supplier provides a replacement set at no cost, but you have to send your parts runner to pick them up, so there is time and gas involved.
   b. Labor cost? The cost to redo the job is at no charge and that takes your top tech off-line so that he is not making money for you or himself. The cost of you having to soothe the angry customer and reassure him that this will never happen again and that you'll have your porter drive him to work and pick him up when the car is done.
   c. Value of a satisfied customer? The customer may have his car fixed . . . but is a lot less likely to unreservedly recommend the quality of your work.

Now, use the formula: COQ = POC + PONC

This may be a difficult decision but you have to determine if the consequences for failures cost you enough in repeat sales, lost time, aggravation, etc. to justify using premium pads on every job and giving up a little bit of your original profit margin. It is a tough decision, but by using this method of analysis you can consider all of the facts and consistently make the best business decision.

4. Can I achieve the standard for quality that I've set?
5. Is it reasonably affordable?

The key principles to making quality consistently achievable in any organization are to make it *definable, measurable, achievable, and affordable*. Without being able to meet those four tests it is very likely just a dream that few understand, even fewer are committed to making a reality, and almost none ever achieve in their lifetime!

Definable Earlier we talked about trying to define quality and the concern that many people have trouble describing it clearly. However, if you don't know what quality looks like how will you ever know when you've reached it? How will you know when your product or service has declined in quality?

If any individual, department, or organization intends to consistently produce high-quality products or services they must first sit down and have a clear shared vision of what quality is. Until you are able to pinpoint a clear definition that everyone can understand, accept, and be involved in consistently producing, the likelihood of achieving consistent quality is nil. You must be able to define quality as a set of very concrete requirements. This directly relates to Philip Crosby's principle of conformance to requirements.

Measurable If you have to consistently achieve or conform to a well-defined set of requirements it is essential that they be set up so they are measurable. Objective measurement is the best way to be sure that you are at or above the required standard. This is true whether you are measuring the physical dimensions of a part, the percentage of customers who are satisfied, or the return on investment that the shareholders receive. Failure to meet those requirements creates poor quality.

Achievable In order to have any real meaning it is important that the quality standard be achievable. Why? Why couldn't we just aim for perfection? Perfection is not a realistic quality goal. After all, we are not perfect, our materials are not perfect, the conditions of the world around us are not totally under our control. Therefore, we need to aim a little bit lower than perfection. We need to aim for a reasonable and achievable goal.

There is one practical reason for setting a conservative quality goal rather than an idealistic one. We want all of our employees to be committed to achieving or exceeding our goal. We want the goal to be something they strive for and reach for, not something that weighs them down. One of the worst management strategies is to set goals that are so idealistic that they are clearly unattainable. The results are that the goals act as a tool to make people give up. Therefore, not only do goals need to be measurable, they also must be realistic enough that everyone involved can visualize and achieve them.

Affordable Some idealists would argue that you should never put a limit or a price on quality. You either have it or you don't. However, is that really what our customers really expect us to do? If the cost of making the improvement increases the price of our product or service so much that no one is willing to purchase it, did we achieve quality?

This characteristic of quality is a balancing factor that keeps us from overreacting. We need to be competitive, we need to meet or exceed the value that our competitors produce and our customers expect to be successful in the market. We need to consistently deliver goods and services that meet or exceed the needs of our customers, but we need to counterbalance that with keeping these improvements affordable enough so that we can still make a profit and stay in business!

Real World Application

An example of a physical standard in automotive repair would be the thickness of a brake rotor. Each rotor has a minimum thickness that must be maintained so that it can properly dissipate heat and produce the required braking force to stop the car. This minimum requirement is stamped right on the rotor.

Therefore, if a car comes into our shop for a front brake job and we measure the thickness of the front rotors and they are already below the minimum specification we know that we must replace the rotors. Why? We need to replace them because they will not conform to minimum requirements. If we let the car go out of our shop having done a brake job without replacing the rotor we will be sending out a potentially unsafe vehicle.

Is that standard measurable? *yes*: definable? *Yes*. Therefore, failure to replace the brake rotor in this case is a lack of conformance to requirements and clearly results in a lack of quality.

THEORY INTO PRACTICE 12-2

CASE

John, the top service advisor at JAX Techs, has just been promoted to service manager because of his enthusiasm and consistent success in being the top service salesman. His boss has told him that he is giving John this chance to show what he can do. He decides to have a service meeting of all of his techs and advisors and come up with a contest to help improve the shop's sagging customer satisfaction scores.

John has formulated two possible incentive plans and is trying to decide which one he should unveil at Monday's meeting. The plans are

Plan A: Provide the service advisor whose group gets the biggest improvement in their customer satisfaction scores for the next month a $100 bonus. Their score must, however, be at least a 5 percent improvement over above last month's very disappointing score of 82 percent.

Plan B: Offer an all-expense paid trip for two to the Daytona 500 for the service advisor that can achieve a perfect (100 percent) customer satisfaction score for the month.

You decide

Which plan would you advise John to choose? Why?

THEORY INTO PRACTICE 12-3

CASE

Abdul has been a service manager for ten years and knows very keenly that the key to consistent long-term success of his service business at Al's Service lies in the goodwill of past and current customers. In order to continue to build business he needs to build his base of satisfied customers. Currently his shop is receiving an 80 percent customer satisfaction rating, which ranks right in the middle of shops in the local Shop Owners Association (SOA). After a little bit of investigation he finds out that the highest score achieved is 88 percent.

Abdul sits down with his employees to voice his concerns and they brainstorm to decide what they should do.

(*Continued*)

THEORY INTO PRACTICE 12-3 (*Continued*)

You decide

Which is the best idea? Why? Why not?

1. Nancy indicates that she knows that they are capable of producing work that is as high in quality as the others. "Let's become Number 1." She further says, "If we don't aim for the stars we'll never succeed at all—let's make our goal 100 percent customer satisfaction!"
2. Floyd, who has been there for 26 years speaks up, saying, "We've got a good, loyal group of customers, why mess up a good thing? I don't think that we need to go off and do some extra special stuff and spend more money. We should just stay the way we are."
3. Chris then adds his opinion, "We know that we can be Number 1, we're not that far off! Let's set our goal of 90 percent customer satisfaction. That won't cost us too much and we can still achieve our goal!"

THEORY INTO PRACTICE 12-4

CASE

Hector is the service manager at a small local independent repair shop. His shop concentrates on doing brake jobs, exhaust system work, and general maintenance. The shop stakes its reputation on providing high-quality repairs locally and affordably. Their customer satisfaction goal has always been 85 percent satisfied customers and the shop has missed this target for the past three months. After doing some research, they have identified one recurring problem. The rebuilt brake rotors that they have been buying from AJB Brakes have been failing at an alarming rate of two out of every five jobs (40 percent).

You decide

After checking with several local parts suppliers Hector has three alternatives.

1. Stay with AJB Brakes rebuilt brakes because switching to other brands would drive up his price by $10 per brake job and he fears that he may lose some business to his competition
2. Switch to purchasing slightly higher priced remanufactured brake rotors ($20 more per job) from another supplier that come with a full 100 percent lifetime warranty.
3. Switch to purchasing only new brake rotors from area new car dealers at a cost of $50 more per job knowing that by doing so their price will be higher than the local dealers, and expect their shop reputation to keep those customers coming to them.

What would you do? Please discuss your reasoning on each of the three choices.

SUMMARY

Once we have determined what quality is, how to define it, how to measure it, how to make our goals realistic and attainable whose job is it, really? The underlying principle of continuous improvement is that quality is everybody's job. It is not an afterthought. The old days of turning out a product and then determining after it was completed whether or not it was acceptable as judged by an inspector at the end of the assembly line simply will not work any more.

It is critical to engage everyone in the process so that they understand the role they play in achieving or failing to reach acceptable quality. They must see that it is their responsibility to do their part to assure that quality happens. It is essential that we instill in them the sense of importance in the process that leads them to accept responsibility for quality and the ultimate success of the product and the company.

The quality movement and the principles of Deming, Juran, and Crosby provide a rich resource to evaluating and improving performance. These continuous improvement principles are essential guidelines that every business must adopt if they plan to be competitive in our highly competitive marketplace. Moreover, they provide the foundation to change the mindset of managers and all employees so that they embrace the process of continuous improvement.

PRACTICING THE PRINCIPLES

In Questions 1–5 match the key quality management principle with the proper individual.

_____ 1. Zero defects	a. J. M. Juran
_____ 2. Institute leadership	b. Philip B. Crosby
_____ 3. Statistical process control	c. W. Edwards Deming
_____ 4. 80/20 rule	d. Henry Ford
_____ 5. Cease dependence on inspection	e. Frederick Taylor

6. A key factor in achieving quality goals is that they must be
   a. reasonable.
   b. communicated to everyone.
   c. achievable.
   d. all of the above.
7. The cost of quality is defined as
   a. what it costs to do it right.
   b. what it costs to fix the comeback.
   c. the price of conformance − the cost of nonconformance.
   d. the price of conformance + the cost of nonconformance.
8. Joe is planning on offering an incentive. He needs to
   a. set the goal high enough to make employees strive for excellence.
   b. be very vague in how he defines the goal.
   c. make it easy for everybody to win.
   d. keep it a secret.
9. In a shop that has embraced Juran's 80/20 principle they know that
   a. only 20 percent of all problems are caused by people.
   b. we can expect 80 percent of the systems to fail.
   c. we should strive to improve our performance to 80 percent and the other 20 percent will take care of itself.
   d. people are directly responsible for 80 percent of the quality problems.
10. When you've reached your quality goals you need to
    a. set higher goals so that you can continuously improve.
    b. celebrate the achievement with all of the employees.
    c. keep it quiet so that it doesn't cost you any money.
    d. both a and b are correct.

REFERENCES

Crosby, P. B., *Quality Is Free: The Art of Making Quality Certain* (New York: McGraw-Hill, 1979).

Deming, W. E., *Elementary Principles of the Statistical Control of Quality* (Tokyo: Nippon Kagaku Gijutzu Remmei, 1950).

Juran, J. M., *The Quality Control Handbook* (New York: McGraw-Hill, 1951).

Juran, J. M., *Managerial Breakthrough* (New York: McGraw-Hill, 1964).

SECTION

4

FINANCIAL MEASUREMENT

One language common to all supervisors in a service operation, from the owner to the sales manager, the business manager to the service director, is profit and loss. Profit and loss is the barometer of success or failure. It is essential that all managers be fluent in the terminology and understand the numbers as a guideline for directing current and future decisions and actions. In this section we will discuss the major financial measurements used to evaluate performance and look closely at several major areas where a manager can affect profitability, compensation, and production planning. We will then discuss how to analyze this data and how the resulting information can be used to improve shop profitability.

CHAPTER

13

Income and Expenses

CHAPTER OBJECTIVES

- To examine income and expenses as financial measurements
- To explore the various types of expenses, how they are defined, how they differ, and how they can be controlled
- To evaluate profit and the various ways that profit is measured
- To apply the principles of income and expenses to generate and maintain profitability

KEY TERMS

income
expenses
direct expenses
indirect expenses
fixed expenses
overhead
variable expenses
profit
profit margin
gross profit
net profit
profit center

Introduction

In this chapter we will explore the basic measurements that are used to track and measure financial success in an automotive service department. The fundamental measurements are income, expense, and profit. In the following sections an explanation and overview of these three critical financial measurements will illustrate how they apply in the repair shop.

Profit is not a four-letter word. It is the lifeblood of an open-market economy and the fundamental factor that, alone, can assure that a company can continue to survive and thrive. In this chapter, we will work together to understand how to retain the largest possible portion of sales on a consistent basis and improve profitability of the service operation.

Income

Income
Something of value that you receive in return for services or products that you deliver.

Income is the most basic of all financial measurements. We all have a clear understanding of the concept of income. Income is something of value that you receive in return for the services and products that you deliver. In the setting of an automotive repair shop or dealership service department the primary item of value that the company has to sell is labor. The service repair shop generates income when a customer is billed for a satisfactorily completed repair.

Income is not only money received for services rendered but can also include services or items of value that you receive in exchange for the service that you provided. Although in the past barter was a common method of purchasing, it has become rather rare to expect a barter of the family cow in payment for repairs done to the family's SUV. There are situations where individuals still trade services rather than pay in cash. Therefore, it is important to remember that all items of value received in return for a service provided are a part of the total income.

THEORY INTO PRACTICE 13-1

CASE 1

When Harvey comes to pay for the tune-up that Phil has just done on his car the bill is $156. Harvey is pleased that he can count on Phil as being his mechanic. Harvey gladly pays the bill and leaves the shop, a satisfied Silver Service customer.

You decide

What was the total income on this transaction? How do you know?

THEORY INTO PRACTICE 13-2

CASE 2

After double-checking the recently completed repairs Harvey has second thoughts and when he sees the owner of Silver Service in the parking lot on his way out he stops and hands her a $20 tip for a job well done.

You decide

What is the total income on this transaction? How do you know?

Expenses

The costs or financial outlay involved in doing business are called **expenses.** Expenses come from a variety of different sources. They may be directly related to a specific transaction. An example would be what the local parts store charged for the new brake pads that you needed to do a brake job on Mr. Smith's Toyota. Other expenses, although just as real, are not quite so directly related to your sales. Expenses are generally divided into three major categories. These categories are direct expenses, indirect expenses, and overhead expenses.

Expenses
The costs or financial outlay involved in doing business.

Direct Expense

Costs of items or services that are directly related to a specific transaction are called **direct expenses.** They are often also referred to in some business models as the cost of goods sold. They include all costs that are specific to this transaction and do not include the rest of the business or operational costs of the company. An example of a direct expense, mentioned previously, is the cost to purchase the brake pads for Mr. Smith's Toyota so that we can do a front brake job on his car. These expenses are necessary since we cannot do the brake job without the parts. They are direct expenses because all of the costs go 100 percent toward Mr. Smith's brake job.

Direct Expenses
The cost of an item or service that is used solely for a specific transaction.

Can you think of another possible direct expense that might be related to the brake job on Mr. Smith's car? There is one that occurs with every automotive repair. It is the cost of labor. Phil's time (whether he works for himself or for the owner of Silver Service) is the primary item of value that he, or his boss, has to sell to the customer. Whether Phil is paid by the hour, by flat rate, or by some other method, he has used up 100 percent of the 1.2 hours that he spent fixing Mr. Smith's car. He charges Mr. Smith for that time. Since all of the expense for that time is only related directly to that transaction, Phil's time is a direct expense.

A test of whether or not an expense is a direct expense is to simply ask the question, Does any part of what we received affect anything else in our operation besides this specific transaction? If the answer is no, then it is a direct expense. However, a further test must also be applied. That is to ask the question, Is all of it completely used only for this transaction? If there is some value remaining that can be used for other transactions you should not bill the entire item as a direct expense to this repair. Only the part of its total cost that was used would be an appropriate billable direct expense. You have to be careful as you decide whether or not an expense is a direct or an indirect expense as you work toward understanding the financial basics of business operations.

THEORY INTO PRACTICE 13-3

CASE 1

Phil is trying to analyze his income and expenses for the past week. He comes across an invoice from the local parts store for a water pump for a 2001 Volvo. He knows that he needed that water pump and used it to fix Mr. Jones' car last Tuesday. He's sure that he charged Mr. Jones for the water pump when he picked up his car Thursday night.

You decide

Is the water pump a direct expense? How do you know?

THEORY INTO PRACTICE 13-4

CASE 2

In the process of replacing the water pump on Mr. Jones' Volvo he found that he had run out of gasket sealant. Fortunately he caught this in time and had the parts store send him a can of sealant along with the water pump that he had ordered.

You decide

Is the gasket sealant a direct expense? How do you decide?

Indirect Expenses

Indirect Expenses Costs that are used across a number of transactions or projects.

Unlike the water pump (a direct expense) and the labor to install it (a direct expense) there are many costs associated with doing business that aren't quite so neatly accounted for in daily business. Expenses that are used across a number of transactions or projects are called **indirect expenses.** These expenses may be variable or fixed expenses.

An example of this would be the special tools that Silver Service needs to own so that Phil can remove and reinstall the pulley that is pressed onto the shaft of the water pump of many different vehicles. What are the questions that you need to ask to determine whether or not the special tools are a direct expense or an indirect expense?

The puller described above is directly used in the repair. However, it is not directly used only on this one repair. It does not pass the second test of being a direct expense because it is not used up and still has substantial value that can be applied toward future repairs on many other vehicles. Therefore, the special puller tool that Phil used in the water pump replacement qualifies as an indirect expense.

Another good example of an indirect expense is an important part of Phil's compensation for working as a technician, his benefits package. Along with offering competitive wages to all of her employees, the owner of Silver Service provides every employee with two weeks of paid vacation every year. Although the cost for these two weeks is just as real an expense to the company and to the owner as the weekly payroll cost for Phil while he is fixing cars, the vacation expense cannot be directly connected to any specific transactions. Therefore, it is by definition an indirect expense.

THEORY INTO PRACTICE 13-5

CASE

In the water pump replacement repair described earlier in this chapter Phil purchased a water pump and some gasket sealant that needed to do this repair.

You decide

Were either of these items indirect expenses? Were the special tools that he used direct expenses? How do you know?

Fixed Expenses

Fixed expenses are those that are related to the existence of the company. They do not change in direct relationship to individual transactions. They continue to occur even if little or no production is occurring. Fixed expenses are often referred to as **overhead.** They are given this name because they are costs that arise from the overall operation of the business. They are not directly related directly to any specific part of producing or selling the products of the company. They are, however, essential to the successful operation of the company.

Fixed Expenses

General costs that occur as a condition of being in business.

Overhead

An expense that arises from overall business operations that is not related to any specific transaction.

A good example of overhead expenses at Silver Service is the costs for the physical facilities. The building rental and utility bills for heat, lights, and power are all overhead expenses.

Another fixed expense is the costs related to the business office. For example, Silver Service has a centralized business office staff that handles all accounting and business documentation needs for both of their retail operations, their service shop and their collision repair shop. Even though these two departments operate independently on a day-to-day basis, the business office is responsible for handling payroll, taxes, accounting, and recordkeeping for the entire company.

Because fixed expenses do not change in relationship to the work being performed or products being produced they are the most difficult to control. The best method for reducing the effect of fixed expenses on net profit is to maximize the amount of products or services that can be produced. This spreads out the cost. A simplified example follows.

If a shop has an overhead of $5,000 per month and generates a gross profit of 50 percent on sales the owners need to sell $10,000 of products or services in order to break even.

$10,000 ×	50%	=	$5,000	−	$5,000	=	$0
Sales	× Gross profit %	=	Gross profit	−	Overhead	=	Net profit

If they want to generate a profit and know that their overhead will remain steady their best plan to become profitable is to increase sales.

$10,002 ×	50%	=	$5,001	−	$5,000	=	$2
Sales	× Gross profit %	=	Gross profit	−	Overhead	=	Net profit

or even

$10,002 ×	50%	=	$5,001	−	$5,000	=	$10,000
Sales	× Gross profit %	=	Gross profit	−	Overhead	=	Net profit

As you can see, overhead (fixed expenses) does not change. The best way to reduce its effect on net profit is to distribute it (spread it out) over as large a volume of sales and gross profit as possible.

Conversely, if you discover that the fixed expenses are so high that it is impossible to sell enough services or products to cover those expenses your choices are limited and difficult. You can begin negotiations with your landlord to obtain lower rent for the next year or you can find another building and move your entire operation to another location. Neither of these changes can made easily or quickly. By their very nature these expenses are virtually immovable, or fixed.

THEORY INTO PRACTICE 13-6

CASE 1

Johnny is a recently hired service advisor at Silver Service. He has been assigned to Phil's team of five technicians at Silver's service shop. Johnny gets paid a weekly salary plus a bonus based on the total service and parts sales of his five-person team.

You decide

Is Johnny's payroll expense a direct expense, an indirect expense, or an overhead expense? How do you know?

THEORY INTO PRACTICE 13-7

CASE 2

Due to increased work volume at both the Silver Service repair shop and the body shop the owner has decided that she needs to add another payroll clerk to assist in calculating the payroll and getting it out on time every week.

You decide

Is the new payroll clerk's salary a direct expense, an indirect expense, or an overhead expense? How do you know?

Variable and Fixed Expenses

Sound management requires that you constantly watch expenses, analyze them, find ways to keep them under control, and reduce them when and wherever possible without sacrificing quality. Since we know that fixed expenses are a condition of being in business and are incurred whether or not any business is being conducted, we realize that fixed expenses are very difficult to reduce. Fortunately, there is another broad category of expenses that we can more effectively control, variable expenses.

Variable Expenses
Expenses that rise or fall in direct relationship to business that is being conducted.

Variable expenses are those expenses directly related to the performance of work. Therefore, they rise or fall in direct relationship to the volume of work completed and sold. A good example of a variable expense would be the pay for Phil, the technician, at Silver Service if he is being paid on a commission or flat-rate system. If Phil does not perform any repairs he does not earn any pay. Therefore, the cost to the company for Phil's services is directly related to what work he produces and varies directly with the amount of work produced.

If Silver Service realizes that it is losing money on every oil change that Phil performs they have several choices. They can reduce their variable expense in two ways: reduce Phil's pay, or have a lower-skilled (and lower-paid) technician perform the job. As you can see, controlling variable expenses is easier within the department than reducing fixed expenses. Therefore, as a manager, variable expenses are the ones you should become very familiar with. They can have a major impact on the company's (and your) success.

THEORY INTO PRACTICE 13-8

CASE

The owner of Silver Service's biggest competitor, Max Mechanix, has found that his shop is losing money and he is in jeopardy of going out of business. He has tried everything to increase his sales but they remain constant. Now he is looking at ways to cut expenses so that he can afford to stay in business.

You decide

If you were Max, the owner of Max Mechanix, what type of expenses would you try to reduce, variable or fixed? Which ones? Why?

Profit

Profit

The remainder of what you received once all expenses have been subtracted.

Profit is the difference between the amount that you receive for your services or products (income) and the cost of doing business (expenses). The simple formula for profit is:

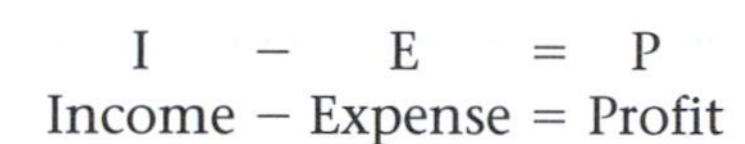

$$\begin{array}{ccc} I - E = P \\ \text{Income} - \text{Expense} = \text{Profit} \end{array}$$

As you can see from the formula, increasing your profit is possible by changing either of the factors in the formula that result in profit. You can increase profit by either increasing your income or reducing your expenses. You can also increase profit by doing both at the same time.

For example, earlier we discussed how Silver Service was losing money on oil changes that Phil did. In the profit formula if we only could change expense we would have to reduce Phil's pay or find a lower priced technician in order to make a profit. But what if we could change the other factors? What else could you change to make a profit? That's right, you could increase the income. Making more seems simple. If you want to make more money you only have three choices

1. Sell more (income)
2. Reduce costs (expense)
3. Do both a *and* b

Which would you choose?

In an effort to increase profitability the first thing that a business will try is to increase sales. Unfortunately, profitability is not often quite that easy to change. You have to consider that in order to increase income (sales) you are probably going to incur additional expenses. Therefore, you are going to have to reduce your **profit margin** and take less profit per transaction to increase your business. Here is an example of how this might work.

Profit Margin

The percentage of profit that you generate from every dollar of sales.

You decide to run an oil change special to attract new customers. You are going to run an ad in the local newspaper or send out mailers to the local residents. Both of these advertising methods are going to cost you money (expense). Unless you already have the lowest price in town you are probably going to have to reduce your price to help interest people in giving your service shop a try. When you discount the price for this service, you reduce the amount of money (income) that you receive from the customer for the oil change. However, the cost of the oil and filters (expense) and the pay to the technician (expense) stays the same. You may increase your sales (income) but because the profit margin per sale is reduced you'll have to generate a significant increase in sales in order to realize an increase in profits.

Real World Application

Although it is always important to have a quality product and to advertise, generating all of the sales in the world makes little difference if you are unable to take any of it home at the end of the day. Taking a reasonable amount home as a result of your work is why you work. Making sure that a fair share of your income becomes profit is the key to long-term success. Therefore, it is essential that from the outset you learn how to understand, measure, and control expenses wherever possible. This control is the only insurance that you will generate a profit. Once you learn the principles of expense monitoring and control, as your business grows your profits will also grow—and your business will not only be bigger, it will be more profitable.

Another important term to understand is profit margin. Profit margin is another way of measuring profit. It is the percentage of profit you generate for each dollar of sales. The formula looks like this

$$\text{Profit margin } (M) = \frac{\text{Profit } (P)}{\text{Sales } (S)}$$

THEORY INTO PRACTICE 13-9

CASE 1

Silver Service sells an oil change for $23. The company has expenses of $10 for Phil's labor and $8 for parts (oil and filter).

You decide

What is the company's profit on an oil change? What is their profit margin?

THEORY INTO PRACTICE 13-10

CASE 2

Your business is very good and your shop is normally 90 percent full each day. You decide that you'd like to really like to move up from number 3 in service sales to number 2. You are sure that if you could just attract that 10 percent of additional business that your shop can handle you it would be enough to reach the number 2 spot. However, in order to do so you feel that the best method is to lower your prices 10% on all maintenance and repair items in your shop.

You decide

Is your strategy for becoming number 2 a good one? How would you know?

Gross Profit

Gross profit is amount left after subtracting direct costs (cost of sales) from the sale amount.

Gross Profit

A common measure that service managers deal with is **gross profit.** Gross profit is the sale amount minus the direct costs.

$$\begin{array}{ccc} S - D & = & GP \\ \text{Sales} - \text{Direct cost} & = & \text{Gross profit} \end{array}$$

If you were rotating a set of tires (a simple, labor-only operation), another way to write this formula is

$$\text{Labor sales} - \text{Technician pay} = \text{Gross profit}$$
$$\text{Direct income} - \text{Direct expense}$$

Because the price charged for the sale (price of labor and parts) and the direct costs (cost of labor and parts) are those that are most directly within the control of the department manager, they are typically the ones the manager is held most accountable for. Gross profit only takes into account the income and expenses that are directly involved with individual transactions. No support staff or other indirect expenses are included. Gross profit is typically reported on the financial statement of the repair shop or dealership and is a key indicator of the manager's performance.

Since gross profit is clearly the most direct relationship of factors that are under the manager's control it is often a key element in a service manager's pay plan. The pay plan of many service managers is based all or in part on gross profit. He may be paid a salary plus a bonus for reaching a certain gross profit level or percentage. He may be paid a salary plus a percentage of the total gross profit.

The ratio between sales and gross profit, called gross profit percentage, is a widely used performance indicator that shows if the shop is keeping their costs in control in relationship to their sales. Gross profit percentage is calculated as follows:

$$\text{Gross profit } \% = \frac{\text{Gross profit } (GP)}{\text{Sales } (S)}$$

Gross profit and gross profit percentage are two performance indicators that you should know well as a manager. The expected gross profit percentage will vary from company to company ranging from as low as fifty percent to over eighty percent depending on the conditions and the goals of top management. Gross profit and gross profit percentage are, however, measures that you must be very familiar with because they are primary measures by which your performance as a service manager will be judged.

In some companies where the parts and service operations are operated as separate departments (typical of new car dealerships) the service department only gets credit for the one item that it can directly sell (labor) and the only true direct cost that can be attributed to a specific repair (direct costs). In those instances the monthly financial statement will indicate gross sales for the month (income), direct costs (direct expense) and gross profit (income – direct expense).

THEORY INTO PRACTICE 13-11

CASE

Mr. Jackson just came into Silver Service today to have the rearview mirror that fell off of his windshield replaced. George looked up the repair price for replacing that part and it is $10. Phil does the repair and earns $4 for the repair.

You decide

What is the gross profit that Silver Service earned on this repair? What is their gross profit percentage?

Net Profit

Whereas gross profit only takes into account those expenses that are directly related to the sale of the product or service (direct expenses), net profit takes into account all expenses of the company. These indirect expenses include all of the variable and fixed expenses of the company that are not directly associated with individual service transactions. **Net profit,** then, is figured by subtracting all of the company's expenses from the total amount of sales. However, since net profit is commonly shown on a financial statement below the gross profit calculation, the net profit is calculated by starting with gross profit and then subtracting indirect costs to yield net profit. The calculation should looks like this:

$$GP - I = NP$$

$$\text{Gross profit} - \text{Indirect expense} = \text{Net profit}$$

As discussed earlier in this section, indirect costs include such items as the rent for the facilities and equipment, utilities, taxes, payroll for the owner and the business office. These expenses are substantial in most organizations. For the organization to survive and thrive it is necessary that the total income exceeds the total amount of expenses so that the owner or owners are able to pay their bills and receive some sort of a return on their investment. Without a return on investment they will not be able to justify the risk that they have undertaken by being in business. You may want to refresh your memory on how ROI is calculated by referring back to Chapter 11.

In an attempt to involve all managers in seeing the big picture of the organization and be involved in working together to achieve a net profit, many companies look at an organization's individual departments as profit centers. Under this **profit center** concept they view and evaluate each department as a company within the company that is responsible for generating sales, a gross profit, and a net profit. In order to do this fairly the company must divide up indirect costs between the profit centers (departments). Dividing the indirect costs between departments is called apportionment. By dividing up the indirect costs, top management can hold the individual departments responsible for generating sufficient income to cover their direct costs (achieve a reasonable gross profit) and their portion of indirect expenses as if their department was an independent company. The cost center approach to financial management makes all of the departments keenly aware and intimately involved in working to keep the company profitable.

Profit Center

A management approach in which all costs are allocated to departments and each department is responsible for covering a fair share of indirect expenses to help the company achieve a net profit.

THEORY INTO PRACTICE 13-12

CASE 1

The service department at Silver Service sold $45,000 in service last month. The total cost to pay their technicians was $15,000. They were not given credit for any parts sales or expenses because that was the responsibility of their separate parts department. They were, however, allocated $25,500 in indirect expenses (such as rent and utilities).

You decide

What is the gross profit that Silver Service earned last month? What was their net profit?

THEORY INTO PRACTICE 13-13

CASE 2

Fred has done everything that he can do to increase sales at his shop and he has reduced employee pay rates to the point where he is concerned that further cuts may cause a mutiny. However, he is still not consistently making any net profit.

You decide

Considering the actions that he has already taken, what would you suggest that Fred look at next to help his shop become profitable? Why?

SUMMARY

In this chapter we introduced the fundamental measures of financial health, which are income, expenses, and profit. These measures are the indicators that must be understood, reviewed, and addressed to assure financial health. After looking at this evaluation of finances we honed in on the various types of expenses that regularly occur in service operations. Understanding and controlling these expenses is the key to making sure that adequate funds reach the bottom line and create a profit.

Gross profit is the most common financial measure by which the performance of service managers is measured. This is because gross profit is directly tied to those items that the manager can most directly control, labor sales and direct labor expense. Sufficient gross profit must be generated to be able to cover all of the overhead expenses necessary to operate the service shop and leave enough so that the owners earn a net profit. Net profit is the amount remaining after all expenses are subtracted from the income generated.

PRACTICING THE PRINCIPLES

Herman brings his car into Century Service for a tire rotation. The repairs cost $20. The shop pays Hector, their lead technician, one-half hour of flat-rate time to perform the repairs. Hector is paid $20 per flat-rate hour. Based on this information, please answer the following questions:

1. What is the total **income** for Century Service?
2. What is their **expense** for this repair?
3. What is their **gross profit** on the repair?

Mr. Burns brings his car in for repairs to Geoff's Garage. The repair shop finds out that they need to purchase a new brake rotor and brake pads from the local parts store to complete the repairs on Mr. Burns' car. The total bill that Mr. Burns pays for the repairs is $380. This includes charges for four hours of labor at $50 per hour and $180 for parts. Heidi, the technician, is paid $20 per flat-rate hour to perform the repairs. Based on this information, please answer the following questions:

4. What is the total **income** that Geoff's Garage realizes for this transaction?
5. What is the total **expense** for this transaction?
6. What is their **gross profit** on the parts that they used?
7. What is the **gross profit** on labor sales?
8. What is the total **gross profit** that the shop earns?
9. What is their overall **gross profit percentage** on this transaction?
10. What is the shop's **net profit?** How do you arrive at this answer?

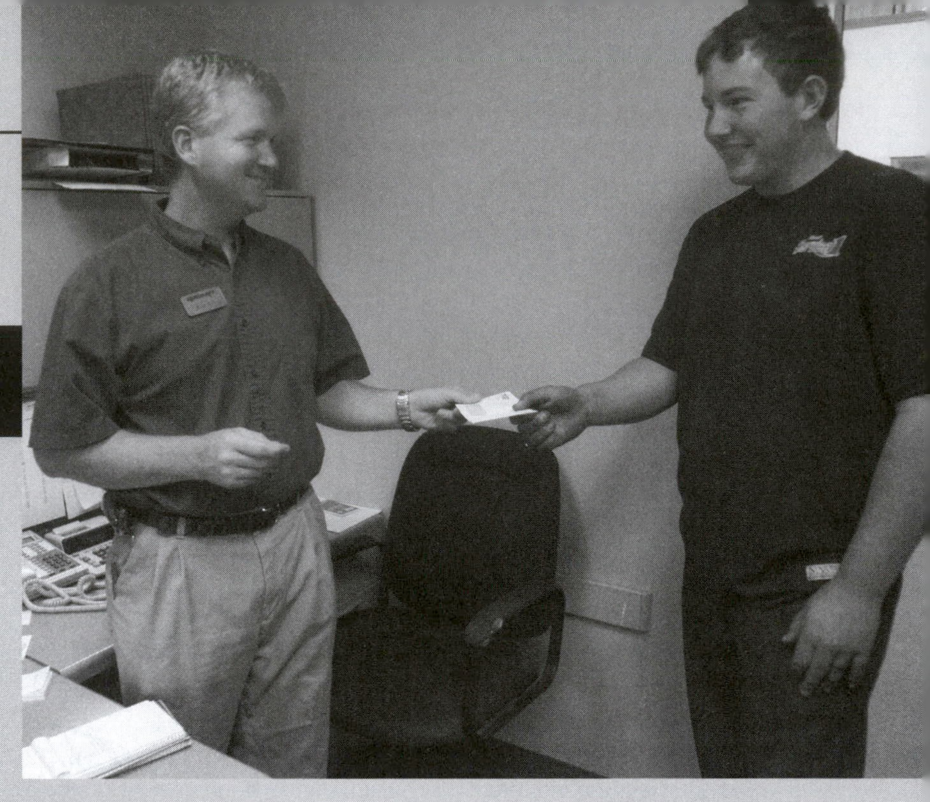

14

Compensation Plans

CHAPTER OBJECTIVES

- To explain the origins and principles of the flat-rate labor pricing system
- To distinguish the most common methods of technician pay
- To examine fringe benefits and employee compensation packages
- To calculate the overall effective rate of a repair shop
- To compare common labor pricing strategies

KEY TERMS

flat-rate pricing
time study
hourly rate pricing
variable rate pricing
technician levels
flat-rate pay
effective rate
flat rate with guarantee
hourly rate
hourly rate with bonus
fringe benefits

Introduction

In Chapter 13 we learned that controlling expenses is an essential skill required of an effective service manager. The expenses that are most within the manager's control are variable expenses, those that are directly related to service sales.

Because the major cost related to selling labor is the payroll costs of the technicians, we will focus on understanding how technicians are paid. We will begin by looking at the system that dominates both the pricing of labor and the pay of technicians in the repair industry, flat rate. We will then look at common variations of technician pay plans and the effect that they can have on expense and profitability.

There are multiple methods for establishing the labor charges that the customer pays for a specific repair. The two most common systems are the flat rate and hourly rate systems. The most common method for billing labor is to charge repairs based on a pre-established number of hours assigned for common repairs. This system is called the flat-rate system. The next most popular system for compensation is based on charging customers the actual clock hours that it takes to complete a repair. This is the hourly rate system. Each of these systems has unique benefits and drawbacks for the shop owner, the technician, and the customer. It is important to understand these systems as they have a very important impact on the profitability of the service shop.

The Flat-Rate System

In the **flat-rate pricing** system all customers are charged a predetermined number of hours for a repair. This ensures that all customers pay the same price for the same repair. For instance, if the established flat rate for replacing the alternator on a particular vehicle is 1.5 hours, then everyone will be billed and pay 1.5 hours for that repair *regardless of how long it actually takes the technician to perform the repair.* Whether it takes Joe 4 hours or 45 minutes to replace the alternator he still gets paid the same amount. More important, the customer is charged 1.5 hours regardless of how long it takes Joe to complete the repairs.

Flat-Rate Pricing
A labor pricing system based on a fixed rate for the amount of time that it takes the average experienced technician to perform a specific repair.

Using the flat-rate system allows the shop to provide accurate and consistent estimates for the actual repair cost before work is started. It allows the customer to make a better decision based on knowledge, up front, of exactly what the repair will cost. It guarantees the technician what he will be paid for doing this job. We will now discuss the concept of the flat-rate system, its origin, and its benefits.

The History of the Flat-Rate System

The flat-rate system was originally developed over 60 years ago. The origins of the system are the result of a depleted workforce in the United States during World War II. While almost all of America's young men (the typical mechanics of the day) were off fighting the war, there was a severe shortage of skilled workers. This was true in all technical professions from construction workers to auto mechanics. This labor shortage was filled by those men and women who, although they lacked previous experience or training, were willing and able to perform these needed services to those who needed them. As a result of the efforts of these home-front heroes, tanks and torpedoes, cars and trucks, and boats and bullets were manufactured to supply the needs of the war effort abroad. At the same time their efforts provided the essential services, such as automotive repair, to keep the American economy moving and its remaining workforce rolling to and from work.

The flat-rate system was developed to assure equity in these times of uncertainty. Since there were few highly trained experienced technicians available there was little consistency in performing repairs. It might take four hours for a novice to replace a water pump at one shop and three hours at another shop, whereas in the past an experienced mechanic could have made the repair in one hour. Flat rate established a set of standards that defined the amount of time that it takes the average experienced technician to perform a specific repair.

By establishing labor charges based on this flat rate, customers were assured of consistent pricing no matter who did the work and no matter how long it took. It was an ideal system for making an unstable system fair and equitable for all. The system worked so well that it became, and still remains, the general standard of how auto repair pricing is established. How do they come up with those standard times? Let's take a look at this very important question.

Establishing Flat-Rate Standards

The consistency in pricing for common repairs of the flat-rate system is based on the establishment of a flat-rate manual. A flat-rate manual is a comprehensive listing of the predetermined labor times for performing most common repairs. Every new vehicle manufacturer publishes its own flat-rate manual to cover all of its models. These factory flat-rate manuals are used primarily only to establish the labor times that the manufacturer will reimburse their dealers for repairs done under warranty. Several independent companies produce flat-rate manuals more general in scope that cover repairs for just about every make and model on the road. The most common of these flat-rate guides are the *Chilton Labor Guide Manual, Motor Labor Guide Manual, and Mitchell Mechanical Labor Estimating Guide*. These publishers now also offer this information in CD/DVD format and through online subscription services. These manuals are used by all independent repair shops and dealerships for repairs done to used cars and those that are beyond manufacturer warranty. Although these two major sources for flat-rate manuals share the concept of arriving at fixed, predetermined labor times for common repairs, their approach for arriving at these rates is quite different.

There are two methods used to establish the times published in flat-rate manuals. The rates published in aftermarket manuals are established based on national surveys conducted by the publishers. They randomly select and survey repair shops nationwide, typically by telephone, asking, How much time does it take to perform this repair? The responses that they receive to their surveys are averaged and become the published flat-rate labor time for that operation. It is important to understand that the time estimates for these repairs are established independently for each make and model, body type, and equipment configuration to assure that the flat rate is a reasonable average. Further, these rates are revised and updated at least annually to include new makes and models and to address changes to existing ones.

The second method for establishing flat-rate times is a live **time study.** Major automotive manufacturers use this method. The system they have established is much more scientific than the aftermarket method because they do not rely on second-hand information, they find out for themselves first-hand. The purpose of a time study is to clearly answer the question how much time does it take the average experienced auto technician to do this specific repair? In order to collect data, the manufacturers hire technicians to perform the repairs under controlled conditions. They typically will have three to five technicians perform a particular repair. Once all of the technicians have completed the repair they average the resulting repair times to arrive at the published flat-rate time.

Time Study

A method for establishing the average time to perform a common repair by observing the results of a number of experienced technicians performing that task.

The establishment of a factory flat-rate manual based on time studies is a very expensive and painstaking process. Every year manufacturers are required to re-study repairs to assure that the published times remain accurate for the new or updated models. More important, however, is that they have a large financial risk since they are responsible for reimbursing all of their dealers across North America for doing these repairs during their new vehicle warranty period.

Hourly Rate Pricing

The other commonly used system for determining labor charges is by charging an **hourly rate.** This hourly rate is established based on the actual time spent on the repair. In a shop that uses this system as their labor pricing standard it is common for technicians to punch a time clock so the actual amount of time spent doing repairs can be documented and accounted for.

Hourly Rate Pricing

A labor pricing system based on the actual amount of time that it takes the technician to perform a specific repair.

Very few shops use the hourly rate method to establish charges for common or competitive repairs. To ensure that they are pricing their repairs fairly in comparison to their competition most shops price all common repairs based on one of the recognized flat-rate standards. However, it is widely accepted for shops to charge customers using hourly rate pricing for uncommon or very complex repairs. Because this type of repair is very difficult to estimate before repairs begin, the only reasonable way to charge (for the technician, the shop, and the customer) is by the hour.

As a result, almost all dealership and independent repair shops use a combination of these two labor pricing methods to establish repair prices. Use of the flat-rate system helps shops ensure that their pricing is competitive. It also provides them with the ability to rapidly develop estimates of repair costs for customers. The use of hourly pricing for uncommon jobs, however, allows them a way to have some assurance of being paid a reasonable fee for those repairs that are more challenging. This combination of pricing schemes provides a reasonable level of consistency in pricing to protect the shop owner, the technician, and the customer. In today's consumer market, this ability to guarantee fair pricing is expected and required by law. We will address the legal implications of labor pricing later in this text. Now we will move on to discussing how the pricing models affect technician pay and, in turn, the service shop's direct labor expenses.

THEORY INTO PRACTICE 14-1

CASE 1

Brenda needs to have an oil leak repaired on her car. She takes her car to Silver Service and they indicate to her that the problem is just a leaking valve cover gasket, which is a common repair. They tell Brenda that the total cost of the repair will be 1.0 hours labor ($75) + the cost of the gasket ($15) for a total of $90 plus tax. They tell her that the car should be done by noon.

You decide

Do you think that Silver Service uses the flat-rate system or hourly rate system to price this repair to customers? How do you know? What should Brenda expect to pay for the repairs if it takes longer than originally expected? Why?

THEORY INTO PRACTICE 14-2

CASE 2

Herman has a very similar oil leak problem on his car to the one that Brenda experienced. However, he has chosen to take his car to Max Mechanix. The service advisor looks under the hood and tells Herman that he'll need an approval to start on the work and that they're really not sure how long it will take . . . but to just relax he will only be charged for the actual time that it takes.

You decide

What labor system is Max Mechanix using? How would this make you feel if you were Herman? How much is Herman's bill going to be?

Variable Rate Pricing

Historically, both dealership and independent repair shops have operated with a simple one-rate pricing system. That is, they have one established labor rate that is used for all repairs that they perform. Under a one-rate system the only variable in determining the total cost of repairs for the customer is how many hours of labor the job pays in the flat-rate book.

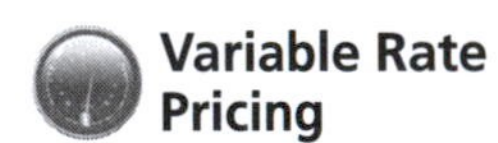

Variable Rate Pricing

A labor pricing system that uses multiple hourly labor rates based on the difficulty of the repair.

A recent pricing system that has emerged is **variable rate pricing.** This system has grown in its acceptance and usage over time and is now commonly found in larger shops across North America.

In a shop using a variable rate system, the hourly labor rate charged for a repair depends on the difficulty of the repair. Shops using this system classify repairs based on the skills required to perform them and, therefore, the expertise of the technician that is required. Technicians are often classified at different levels based on their skills. This closely parallels the reasoning for a variable rate pricing system.

A shop using variable rate pricing will normally price basic maintenance and repair services at their lowest hourly rate. A good example of this would be a tire rotation. A tire rotation is a common repair that can be performed by a wide range of technicians and shops. It does not require a technician with high skills. It does not require a shop with highly specialized equipment, tools, or training. Customers can find ads in the local paper every day listing special prices for this type of service. In order to attract customers to these highly competitive and widely available services and to keep customers from going elsewhere for service, shops must price their repairs accordingly. Using a reduced hourly rate that a variable pricing system allows can help them to do this.

At the other end of the spectrum are very difficult repairs that require specially trained technicians, special equipment, or proprietary technical information. Few shops have the expertise to perform these repairs and the repairs typically require the attention of the most experienced and highest paid technicians. Therefore, a shop using a variable pricing system would normally charge a much higher hourly rate for these repairs.

We have discussed the two extremes of the variable pricing system spectrum, the highly competitive yet simple maintenance service and the highly complex and very difficult diagnostic repair. What about the rest of the work? How do we price it? The simple answer is that it depends. It depends on how complex a system of labor rates the shop chooses to use. In the very simplest system they may have three or four labor rates (for example, A, B, C, and D rates) or they may have as many as 10 to 12 different rates.

THEORY INTO PRACTICE 14-3

CASE 3

Mystery Motors has been in business for years and has always operated on a simple one-rate flat-rate system for pricing their repairs. Based on the advice of a consultant, they have just switched over to a 4-tiered pricing system. Their old labor rate was $60 for all repairs. Their new labor rates are $75, $65, $55, and $45 per flat-rate hour. Joe, their service manager, needs to come up with pricing for a variety of different repairs under this new pricing system.

You decide

What rate should Joe assign for the following repairs . . . and why?

a. Oil and filter change?
b. Valve cover gasket replacement?
c. Diagnosis and repair of an intermittent engine miss?
d. Replacement of an engine rear main oil seal?

Technician Skill Levels

Before we look at how individual technicians are paid, we need to understand some underlying principles about staffing a repair shop. Technicians, like any other type of workers, range widely in their technical expertise, productivity, and ability to produce quality repairs. Due to these differences technicians are often categorized into **technician levels** based on these factors.

Technician Levels
Technicians are often classified into four levels, A, B, C, and D based on their technical expertise, productivity, and ability to produce quality repairs.

Those who are highly experienced, highly capable, highly productive, and produce great quality repairs on a consistent basis are the highest in demand and, therefore, command the highest pay. They are the ones who can fix anything and upon whom the shop depends to repair the really difficult and complex problem cars. They are often referred to as A techs.

A secondary, and larger, level of experienced technicians exists that aren't quite at the level of the A techs. They are experienced with a wide range of skills. They are able to fix most problems across a wide range of automotive systems. However, they aren't quite up to the technical level of A techs. They are still valuable to their shops but are paid at a lower rate than the A techs.

Based on how close their skills, productivity, and quality are to the A techs they may be considered to be B or C techs.

The third group of technicians is made up of those who are only able to perform the most basic repairs. Whether it is due to lack of experience, confidence, or knowledge and skills, the work that they can be assigned and expected to perform correctly is limited. They are normally those technicians who perform oil changes and basic repairs such as brake jobs, minor electrical repairs, and preventative maintenance. Some companies call them maintenance and light repair technicians. In the shop's classification system they are D techs.

Both the volume of work that exists in the automotive repair industry and the difficulty of those individual repairs support a need for a very large number of technicians with wide-ranging skills. Therefore, there continues to be a high and constantly growing demand for A, B, C, and D technicians.

The mix of employees that fall into these four classes differs from company to company. In a shop that is required to provide full service from the most complex diagnosis to simple maintenance services they are likely to employ technicians from all four classifications. On the other hand, shops that focus on light repairs and maintenance would tend to employ more of the C and D technicians and may have only one A or B technician to handle the occasional complex diagnostic problems that might arise.

As a manager it is important to realize that as the skill level of the technician rises, so does the cost of labor. Conversely, as the skill level drops the cost of labor also drops. Because most service shops use a single hourly labor rate to establish repair pricing, the gross profit on one hour of labor will decrease as the shop uses more highly skilled, and higher-paid, technicians to do the work and will decrease as they use a lower-skilled technician. Management's job in trying to control costs while maintaining high productivity and quality is to employ the right mix of technician classes that allows for maximum profitability.

THEORY INTO PRACTICE 14-4

CASE

Joe, service manager at Mystery Motors, has an unexpected visitor. It is Terri, one of the top diagnostic technicians in the region. She has been unhappy with her current pay and is shopping around to move to a new shop. She has heard about recent changes at Mystery Motors including Mystery's new labor rates. She is inquiring to see if they can make her a better offer.

You decide

As Joe's consultant, and based on what you've just learned about Terri's skills, what level of technician do you believe that she is (A, B, C, or D)? Why?

How would the new variable labor rate help you to be able to attract new talent like Terri?

What type of work would you be most likely to give Terri if you were able to hire her? What type of work would not be given to Terri? Why?

Technician Pay Plans

We have just completed discussing the methods that shops use to determine how to price repair labor. You will see some terms reappearing again as we discuss technician pay. It is important to understand that the method used to calculate customer labor prices does not have to be the same as the method used to pay the technician. We will discuss four methods of paying technicians: flat rate, flat rate with a guarantee, hourly, and hourly plus a performance bonus.

Because technicians are the primary direct expense in the service department, the way that they are paid has a large impact on profit and the success or failure of the shop. Therefore, we need to examine and understand the most common pay plans for technicians. We need to know how they work and their benefits and drawbacks for the individual technician. Then we will explore the impact that they have on shop management.

Flat-Rate Pay

We discussed the concept of the flat-rate system previously. Paying technicians based strictly on flat rate is the most common compensation plan. The flat-rate system establishes reasonable standards, based on experience, that indicate how much time it takes the average technician to perform a specific repair. The technician is paid a predetermined amount for each repair regardless of how long it takes him to complete it.

Another important part of the flat-rate system is that technicians who work on flat rate are paid only for the flat-rate hours that they produce. They do not receive any pay beyond what they produce in flat-rate hours. They are working on a straight commission. That is, they only get paid for the jobs that they complete, not for the time that they are at work. If there is no work, they earn no pay.

Flat rate has a large potential benefit to the highly skilled and motivated technician. If the technician is able to properly perform repairs in less time than the time that it takes the average experienced technician then he is still paid the full time listed in the flat-rate manual. For example, Phil is able to replace the valve cover gasket that pays a flat rate of 1.0 hours in 0.5 hour. Phil gets paid 1.0 hours, not 0.5 hour. If Phil's normal hourly flat-rate pay is $20 per hour he has now earned $20 in one-half hour. His effective rate for that repair is $40 per hour. Here is that calculation in detail

$20	×	1.0	=	$20	÷	0.5	=	$40
Hourly rate	×	Flat rate for repair	=	Total paid	÷	Actual repair time	=	Effective rate

Conversely, a drawback of the **flat-rate pay** system to the technician is the fact that he gets paid the flat rate of 1.0 hour to replace the valve cover gasket even if it takes him 1.5 hours to do the job. In this instance, Phil would have earned $20 but it would have taken him 1.5 hours. Therefore, his **effective rate** that he earned for the repair would be only $13.33.

Flat-Rate Pay

Technicians are paid a fixed amount of hours for a job based on an established average time to perform the repair.

$20	×	1.0	=	$20	÷	1.5	=	$13.33
Hourly rate	×	Flat rate for repair	=	Total paid	÷	Actual repair time	=	Effective rate

As you can plainly see, the flat-rate system has its own built in system of rewards and consequences. Technicians paid by the flat-rate system can be richly rewarded when they perform above and beyond average. At the same time, they are penalized each time their performance falls below average.

Effective Rate

The actual hourly rate a technician earns, which is calculated by taking actual pay and dividing it by the actual repair time.

Highly skilled, motivated, and committed technicians welcome the challenge of being on flat rate. Even though they all occasionally are penalized for exceeding flat-rate time they are able to equal or beat the flat-rate book time more often than not. As such, they are able to earn the reward of an increased effective rate of pay. They earn an instant raise each time they are able to do this. Under the flat-rate system, it is common for an experienced technician to be able to earn 50 to 60 hours pay weekly while working a 40-hour work week.

Inexperienced technicians, on the other hand, typically pay a severe penalty for being paid on the flat-rate system. Since they lack the knowledge, skills, and work habits to work up to the standard of the average experienced technician it will commonly take them longer to perform a repair than the flat-rate book allows. As such, they will be penalized for their slowness and often will produce only 20 to 30 flat-rate hours in a 40-hour week. This reduces their effective rate by 25 to 50 percent below their stated rate. It is for this reason that many employers will start new or inexperienced employees on a pay plan that provides a guaranteed minimum weekly pay. This helps to keep them motivated as they progress through the learning process so that they can work their way up to being capable of consistently producing high numbers of flat-rate hours.

There is one last very important characteristic of flat rate that should never be overlooked. Because flat rate depends on work performed, in order for a technician to earn a good wage he must be capable of meeting or beating flat-rate times AND the shop has to have enough work to keep him busy. Lack of available work can create a problem in retaining a skilled technician because his production (and his paycheck) will be significantly reduced, by no fault of his own, if the shop can't bring in enough work to keep him busy.

THEORY INTO PRACTICE 14-5

CASE

Todd works as a technician and is paid $20 per flat-rate hour. Last week Todd worked 40 hours and produced 32 flat-rate hours.

You decide

How much did Todd earn last week? What was his effective rate?

Flat Rate with a Guarantee

Flat Rate with a Guarantee

Technicians are paid fixed flat-rate times for repairs with a fixed minimum amount of paid hours per week guaranteed.

Some automotive service shops will consider blending two pay methods resulting in paying technicians **flat rate with a guarantee.** This is generally done for one of three reasons. First, it may be done to attract a top-flight technician to a new shop or one that is in transition. This is because an experienced technician may hesitate to move from a shop where he both knows that he can produce and that there is sufficient work. In moving to a new shop he may want some assurances that his pay will not drop due to circumstances beyond his control (for example, lack of work coming into the shop).

The second reason a technician might be put on flat rate with a guarantee would be to slowly help an entry-level technician transition from a fixed paycheck to flat rate. Most entry-level technicians start out at an hourly rate. This is generally done to subsidize their orientation period. However, it is common that the manager or owner will do this for the short term with the intent to move the technician to flat rate once he gets settled. This pay plan would provide a way to gently ease the technician into a flat-rate pay plan.

Another example of an employee who might be paid using this plan would be the shop foreman. Neither the technician nor the owner would want to keep him from producing as many flat-rate hours as possible. However, the greater need of the shop is to have someone who can help out less experienced workers. Therefore, the shop, recognizing this need, may agree to pay the experienced technician a guarantee so that he can provide this service and be assured that he won't be financially penalized.

THEORY INTO PRACTICE 14-6

CASE

Daryl works as a technician and is paid $20 per flat-rate hour. Since he works at a new business and the boss can't assure Daryl that they can keep him busy, they have agreed to guarantee him a minimum of 36 hours of pay per week. Last week Daryl worked 40 hours and produced 32 flat-rate hours.

You decide

How much did Daryl get paid last week? What was his effective rate?

Hourly Rate

Paying technicians at an hourly rate regardless of the amount of work produced occurs in many shops but is most commonly used for entry-level personnel or personnel who have other responsibilities in addition to performing repairs. This fixed **hourly rate** provides the employee a great degree of stability. He earns a stable income whether or not any work comes in the shop and whether he produces 20 hours of flat-rate labor or 60 hours. The shortcoming of the hourly rate plan is that it does not provide any incentive for the technician to be more productive.

Hourly Rate

Technicians are paid the actual clock hours that they work regardless of the amount of work that they produce.

Another shortcoming of this pay plan is that the management is very unlikely to be very unsympathetic to an hourly rate employee believed to be unproductive. Whether this is due to an inability to produce or factors beyond his control such as lack of work, the employer will generally be very impatient to end a working relationship when money is being lost. Hourly rate technicians are, for this reason, typically the first ones to be cut during a shop cutback and the first layoff during the slow seasons of the year. This pay plan offers the technician stability, but the potential risks to the shop can be severe.

THEORY INTO PRACTICE 14-7

CASE

Germaine works as a technician and is paid $20 per clock hour. He worked 40 hours and produced 32 flat-rate hours.

You decide

How much did Germaine earn last week? What was his effective rate?

REAL WORLD APPLICATION

It is essential that you understand that establishing technician pay plans and technician pay rates is a complex endeavor. Paying a technician based on his clock hours or paying that same technician based on flat rate can have a dramatically different impact on the shop's profitability. You must take into account not only the hourly rate but, more important, who is bearing the risk. In the flat-rate system you and the technician share the risks that there will be enough business and that he will produce enough hours. If there is no business or he simply does not produce enough hours, you both earn

(Continued)

less. In the hourly rate system you bear all of the risks because he gets the same pay whether or not the shop is busy and whether or not he produces enough hours.

Therefore, you should take risk into account when determining the rate to pay a technician. If you are bearing all of the risk by guaranteeing a fixed hourly rate then you should be more conservative and pay a lower rate. That way you can hold back a little more money just in case business or performance does not meet your expectations. This is your hedge against the risk in this type of investment. On the other hand, if the technician is willing to share the risk by working flat rate then it is reasonable to give him a greater share of the rewards by paying him a higher hourly rate.

Hourly Rate with Bonus

Technicians are paid the actual clock hours that it takes them to perform a specific repair with additional incentives for reaching a preset number of hours.

Hourly Rate with Bonus

The **hourly rate with bonus** pay plan provides the stability of income of the hourly rate plan. It also carries the potential risks of the hourly rate plan. One of the criticism of hourly rate pay plans is that employees are not motivated to produce. Adding a bonus feature to this plan provides employees with an incentive to produce more. As we have learned previously, the only major product that the shop has to sell is labor, anything that will stimulate an increase in labor hours produced is to the company's benefit.

THEORY INTO PRACTICE 14-8

CASE 1

Irving works as a technician and is paid $20 per clock hour plus he receives a performance bonus of $20 if he produces over 30 flat-rate hours. He worked 40 hours and produced 32 flat-rate hours.

You decide

How much did Irving earn last week? What was his effective rate?

THEORY INTO PRACTICE 14-9

CASE 2

Jack is an experienced automotive technician. He has just been recruited by a large local dealership and they want to sit down with him to negotiate his pay plan. Jack has been productive at his current shop to be able to produce an average of 50 flat-rate hours per week at his pay rate of $20 over the past year. As he speaks to his potential new boss, the boss tells Jack "Don't you worry, you won't have to be concerned about the pressures of flat rate anymore. Everyone in our shop works a 40-hour week and gets paid strictly by the hour. We'll be glad to give you a $3 raise from your current rate to $23 per hour."

You decide

At which shop will Jack make more money based on this offer? What are the benefits of staying on his current pay plan? What are the benefits of the new one offered to him? If you were Jack, what would you do? Why?.

THEORY INTO PRACTICE 14-10

CASE 3

Jack thinks that he'd be better off getting the benefits of flat rate but the security of a steady paycheck that he would receive if he was paid by the hour does sound interesting. He hates the pressure of being 100 percent on commission, as he is in when working under the flat-rate system.

You decide

Which pay plan could give Jack the benefits of both systems? Please explain.

Pay Plans for other Service Employees

In an earlier chapter we discussed the staffing needs of a service shop. In addition to the owner, the manager, and a host of technicians, the typical shop will have service advisors, cashiers, porters, parts personnel and business office personnel. Most of the staff are paid hourly or are on a fixed salary.

The most common exception to this fixed pay is for those employees in the shop whose jobs are directly linked to the shop's productivity (sales of labor and parts). Even though service advisors, the parts personnel (if the shop has an internal parts department), and the service manager don't actually produce the flat-rate hours, they have an affect on the labor sales. Therefore, their pay plan is commonly tied to production.

The service advisor is the link between the customers and the company. In some organizations the advisor may be called a service salesman. As discussed in an earlier chapter, the primary responsibilities of the service advisor are to recommend services to the customer, explain the repairs needed to resolve the customer's concerns, prepare an accurate estimate for the total cost of these services, and then gain the customer's approval to proceed with the needed repairs. The advisor's ability to explain the needed repairs properly, to be knowledgeable about the regular recommended services, and to be able to explain this information to the customer in a way that will encourage the customer to approve the repairs is critical to the success of the shop. In a nutshell, whatever the service advisor can't sell, the technician can't produce, no matter how skilled he is.

Because of their importance in generating opportunities for technicians to produce labor sales, service advisors are generally paid a base salary plus a performance incentive. This incentive may be based on total flat-rate hours produced on the repair orders that he has written. An alternate plan is to pay the advisor a bonus for reaching or exceeding specific sales goals. The general goal is to tie the service advisor's pay to his performance thus providing a positive incentive for him to excel.

The service manager's pay plan is almost always tied directly to overall shop production. A small number of managers are paid flat salaries and some are paid totally based on incentives but the most common pay plans are a blend of the two. Since the main factors that the manager can control are labor sales and labor expense (technician pay), manager pay plans routinely include a base salary along with a performance incentive. This performance incentive may be a percentage of the gross profit of the shop. Managers may also be paid incentives based on net profit. The percentage of the manager's pay that is based on incentives varies from shop to shop.

Real World Application

Tying an employee's pay plan to their performance is common. If done properly it encourages him to excel. If done improperly it causes him to become discouraged and results in employee dissatisfaction, low morale, and high employee turnover. For a pay plan to be effective it should be address these principles

—Only tie the incentives to those things that the employee can control or directly influence.

—Set the objectives high so that employees will have to stretch, but never make them unattainable

—Do not make incentives all or none. Allow the employees to attain small rewards for small increases and large ones for major increases.

—*Always* be willing to live with the rewards you have offered—even if the performance far exceeds your expectations and costs you more than you had planned.

THEORY INTO PRACTICE 14-11

CASE 1

Herman is the service manager at Most Motors. However, his department has not been very profitable lately since they lost their top service advisor. He has just received a call from Jacques, one of the best advisors in the Midwest, who is shopping around for a 'better work situation'. Herman begins to think that his prayers are answered. When Herman asks Jacques what type of salary he is looking for to make the move, Jacques says, "You won't have to worry about that! I'll come to work for you on straight commission. That's right. I don't want any salary, just pay me 40 percent of the total labor sales that I sell and we can both make a lot of money."

You decide

Herman is very quiet. He tells Jacques that he needs some time to think about it and that he will get back to him by tomorrow. What do you think Herman's concerns are? Do you think that he'll be willing and able to hire Jacques? Why or why not?

Fringe Benefits

Fringe Benefits
Items of value (such as a pension or paid vacation) that are given to employees in addition to their pay to ensure their welfare and security.

Most employees receive a **fringe benefits** package in addition to their weekly or monthly pay. Benefits are an important part of the total compensation package that employees receive. Although most employees judge their pay plan on their hourly rate or salary, benefits provide a great deal of security to an employee. They also come at a significant cost to the employer.

Some of the most common benefits paid for in part or in total by the employer are: social security, Medicare, health insurance, prescription insurance, dental insurance, disability insurance, retirement programs, paid vacations, holidays, and sick days. Benefits like social security and Medicare are mandated by the federal government. They are long-term benefits that are paid for jointly by the employee and the employer. Medical insurance plans (health, dental, eye care, disability) and retirement accounts are optional plans for which the shares paid by the employee and employer may vary greatly. Paid vacations, holidays, and sick days may appear to be no-cost options to the employee; however, the cost to the employer is substantial since he pays for a day's wages and at the same time loses sales and profits due to the absence of an employee for that day.

Many fringe benefits serve as a buffer against unexpected costs (health care benefits or disability insurance) or long-range costs (retirement benefits/social security). Their purpose is to create an environment where the employee is unlikely to encounter any unexpected costs that will create a hardship. Providing this security, it is hoped, will make it easier for the employee to avoid those financial and emotional stresses and encourage him or her to be a long-term employee.

Whenever comparing different employment opportunities it is best to compare the entire compensation package, not just the rate of pay. Although some employees may not feel like the benefits are as important today, they may make a big difference in the future. Most employers who value long-term employment relationships with their staff provide very rich benefits programs. The employee should realize that the value the employer is placing on him relates to the total amount of money that he is willing to invest to attract him and this total cost includes pay rate *and* fringe benefits.

As a manager, you must consider that when you determine the total cost of an employee, you must include the entire compensation package, not just the employee's pay rate. The benefits cost for many companies ranges from 20 to 30 percent of the employee's hourly rate. This varies depending on how many benefits the company offers. Therefore, when hiring a technician that the company agrees to pay $20 per flat-rate hour, the actual total costs for that employee are much higher. His actual cost to the company will be $4 to $6 (20 to 30 percent) per hour higher to pay for his benefits package.

THEORY INTO PRACTICE 14-12

CASE 2

Herman's goal is to keep his total personnel costs no higher than 40 percent of sales. His current labor rate is $50 per flat-rate hour and the benefits package that the company provides for all employees is equal to 25 percent of their hourly rate.

You decide

What is the average hourly rate that Herman must try to maintain if he wants to keep his costs at or below 40 percent?

SUMMARY

In this chapter we began by exploring the different methods that a shop can use to calculate their labor charges. We reviewed the history and benefits of the most common of these methods, flat rate and hourly rate. We then discussed the benefits of the multiple labor rate systems that have grown in popularity in the auto repair business in recent years.

The second major topic that we discussed was technician pay plans. We learned that what affects the final pay for the technician is not simply the rate that he is paid, but also the way that the rate is calculated. We explored the multiple affects on both the technician and the shop of the various major pay plans: flat rate, flat rate with guarantee, hourly rate, and hourly rate with bonus.

We concluded by briefly discussing some of the more common pay plans used for service advisors and service management personnel. We looked at the benefits of incentives, bonuses, and commissions as motivational tools. We closed by reviewing the importance of fringe benefits and the effect that they have on the total compensation plans for employees.

PRACTICING THE PRINCIPLES

1. A time study is
   a. a method for preparing for your ASE exams.
   b. a method for establishing the actual time it takes to perform a repair.
   c. a common method for equalizing the time each technician gets paid.
   d. all of the above.

2. The item in the following list that would not be a fringe benefit is
   a. health insurance.
   b. paid vacation.
   c. retirement plan.
   d. hourly pay.
3. Technician levels are
   a. ways to identify their various levels of skill and experience.
   b. ways to make all of the technicians perform the same.
   c. tools used to check the surface of cylinder heads.
   d. ways to penalize technicians by reducing their pay.
4. In a shop that uses variable rate pricing
   a. the labor rate for common repairs is the lowest.
   b. the labor rate for highly specialized repairs is the highest.
   c. several labor rates are used based on difficulty of repair and skills required.
   d. all of the above.
5. The most common method for establishing customer labor rates in shops is
   a. variable rate pricing.
   b. flat-rate pricing.
   c. hourly rate pricing.
   d. flat rate with a guarantee.

In Questions 6–8, Rogue Repairs is a new shop in town. They're trying to hire two new technicians to start immediately. The top three candidates are

Rowdy—21 years experience, ASE Master Certified, has worked in six different shops in the last three years. He demands that with his experience and certifications he will only work if paid flat rate with a guarantee of 40 hours pay per week. Rowdy drops a strong hint that it will take $20 per flat-rate hour to get him to come to work at a new shop.

Ginger—A recent graduate of the local college automotive program with an Associate Degree, she has worked for three years full-time and has earned her ASE Master Certification and completed 14 industry training courses. She insists on being paid flat rate but says that it will take $22 per hour to get her to move from her current position.

Gomer—A journeyman technician with 10 years' experience. Gomer has little formal training and, by his own admission, is not great at engine performance and heavy diagnostics. However, he has several strong recommendations of his ability to perform all maintenance and common repairs and services from his past two employers. He's a bit shy but finally indicates that he isn't willing to take the risk of working on flat rate and his past two jobs ended with him earning $15 per hour.

Based on the information provided above please choose the best answer for the following questions:

6. I would considering Gomer and Cindy because
   a. Rowdy sounds like a troublemaker.
   b. my average cost of sales would be the lowest of the possible choices.
   c. Cindy appears to be the most qualified and motivated and Gomer can do the simple jobs.
   d. I can't afford to take the risk of having two employees that have guaranteed pay plans in a new shop.
   e. all of the above.
7. If you decided to hire Gomer what pay plan would you offer him?
   a. hourly rate starting at $15.50 per hour.
   b. hourly rate + bonus at $10 per hour.
   c. flat rate at $17 per hour.
   d. none of the above.
8. Rowdy's extensive experience makes him a very appealing choice to hire. What concerns might you have based on the facts provided?
   a. He is pretty demanding and is demanding too high of a pay rate.
   b. For some unknown reason he has a hard time keeping a stable job.
   c. He may not be willing to work very hard since he wants a guarantee.
   d. All of the above.

You decided to hire all three technicians and you were able to successfully hire Rowdy @ $21 per flat-rate hour, Ginger @ $19 per flat-rate hour, and Gomer @ $16 per clock hour. Knowing this please answer the following.

9. The first week they all produced exactly 40 hours. What would be their effective labor rates for that week?
10. The second week Gomer only turned 30 hours and all three techs worked a full 40 hour week. What is his effective labor rate for week 2?

REFERENCES

Chilton Labor Guide Manual (Clifton Park, NY: Delmar Publishers).

Motor Labor Guide Manual (Troy, MI: MOTOR Information Systems).

Mitchell Mechanical Labor Estimating Guide (Poway, CA: Mitchell 1).

CHAPTER

15

Production Plans

CHAPTER OBJECTIVES

- To identify the three most common methods of organizing technicians in a repair shop: individual plan, team system, and support group
- To compare and contrast the benefits and limitations of individual plan, team system, and support group strategies
- To describe the various methods used to increase the productive capacity of a repair shop
- To identify the benefits and limitations of increasing physical facilities to increase capacity
- To compare and contrast the benefits and limitations of using extended hours, two shifts, or six-day rotation to increase production capacity

KEY TERMS

individual plan
team system
support group
expanding facilities
extended hours
second shift
six-day rotation

Introduction

A solid understanding of financial principles and major cost factors in a repair shop can help you as a manager to understand the current status of your operation. However, it often takes a bit more creativity than simply keeping technician pay in the proper range to be successful. In this chapter we will explore two major ways where you can substantially change the sales and profit outlook, by the way that you organize the technicians in the shop and by changing the production capacity of the shop.

All of the compensation plans discussed earlier are based on a traditionally organized shop. However, over the past 15 to 20 years there has been an emergence of several other ways to organize the technicians and other shop employees to maximize efficiencies and, thereby, reduce total shop costs. You are more likely to find these types of organizational plans in dealerships and most typically in medium to large-sized ones that employ 10 or more technicians. In this chapter we will explore the three main shop organizational schemes: traditional, team system, and support group and will focus on the central theme of these schemes, how they affect technician pay, and shop labor costs.

After looking at the major technician organizational plans we will then explore another method for increasing production while controlling expenses, expanding the production capacity of the shop. This can be done by increasing physical capacity or available work hours, or both. It is important to realize that while expanding capacity does not change gross profit percentage it helps to generate more sales while holding the gross profit percentage constant, and results in a greater bottom line.

Technician Organizational Plans

Individual Plan

Individual Plan
A system in which a technician's pay is based solely on his or her own production.

The **individual plan** is the traditional system used since service shops first began repairing vehicles. The vast majority of automotive service shops still subscribe to this method of organizing their shop and paying their employees. In a shop using this type of organization, employees are paid on their individual initiative. That is, they are paid for what they produce. Their individual pay may be based on any of the four pay plans discussed earlier (flat rate, flat rate with a guarantee, hourly, and hourly plus a performance bonus). The distinguishing feature of this system is that the technician's pay is not in any way affected by others in the shop nor is it shared with others.

Experienced, productive technicians generally prefer to be paid by this method. The reason is that they worked their way up through the system the hard way, starting at the bottom with the lowest pay and the lowest production level. Now that they have learned and earned their way to the top of the scale they don't want to share it with anyone else.

From a shop management standpoint, the strength in maintaining the individual pay plan system is that experienced technicians prefer this system, and so it is easier to attract them to a shop with this pay system and keep them satisfied enough to stay. Shops need expert technicians (and, therefore high-priced ones) to fix the more difficult vehicle problems. They also need technicians who have the ability to fix a wide range of different problems with different systems (again, higher-priced ones). In order to maximize their ability to meet these two needs service shops that operate with a traditional staffing plan tend to hire a high percentage of these A, B, and C techs to staff their shops. As a result, they have a high degree of expertise available. The only drawback is that this results in a high cost of sales and reduced gross profit.

THEORY INTO PRACTICE 15-1

CASE

Slick Service Center currently employs six technicians. The entire shop is organized to pay the technicians purely based on the flat-rate hours that they produce. During the past week all six technicians worked 40 hours each and produced the following number of flat-rate hours at their individual pay rates:

Bob—42 hrs. @ $18; Chuck—38 hrs. @ $18; Rod—32 hrs. @ $12

Chet—54 hrs. @ $24; Jan—60 hrs. @ $20; Terri—56 hrs. @ $22

You decide

a) What did each of the six technicians earn last week?

b) How many flat-rate hours did the entire shop produce last week?

c) If Slick Service Center charges $60 per flat-rate hour for all of their work, what was their gross labor sales for last week?

d) What was Slick Service Center's gross profit for last week?

e) What was their gross profit percentage for last week?

Team System

Team System
A system in which technicians are organized into a group of four to seven members and are paid based on the total amount of hours produced by the team.

The **team system** is most often found in larger shops. Rather than working individually the technicians in a team shop are organized into groups. They work together and are paid together. For example, instead of a shop with 18 individual technicians each working separately and with three service advisors that schedule, write up, and sell work for all of them, the team shop is subdivided into three teams. Each team of six technicians is assigned their own service advisor. They become a shop within the shop. In order to do this efficiently, the technicians on each team represent a good cross-section of experience and skill levels. This allows the team to be able to handle any type of repair that may come into the shop. The team's service advisor works only for his team, but the difference doesn't end there.

In a team system shop technicians do not work individually and they are not paid individually. As work comes into the shop the repairs are assigned to the team, not to a specific technician. The team leader, typically the senior and most experienced technician, then divides the work among the team members. The work on a particular vehicle may be assigned to just one team member but more often is assigned to several of the technicians. The group of technicians (typically four to seven technicians) on the team is expected to work as a unit. The lead technician's responsibility is to help in diagnosis difficult repairs and to otherwise maximize the productivity of the group. He does this by keeping each of the technicians doing what he does best. A key thought behind this method is that if they are able to keep everyone doing what they do best most of the time the quality of repairs as well as the production of the group will be maximized.

Finally, and probably most important, the team technicians are not paid as individuals for the amount of work that they do. They are paid a share of the total hours produced by the team. This is done by tracking and adding up all of the hours produced by the team over a pay period (typically a week), then dividing the total hours by the number of technicians on the team. They are then paid their hourly rate times that number of hours. Please note that this does not mean that all technicians, regardless of expertise, earn equal pay. Their pay rate is based on skill level. Therefore, although the higher-skilled technicians are paid the same number of hours as the rest of the team they are paid a higher hourly rate and therefore earn a higher weekly income than the inexperienced technicians.

One of the reasons why team systems were developed and have found favor in many larger shops is their ability to reduce the overall cost of labor. In shops where technicians work independently it is common that 25 to 40 percent of the technicians in the shop that are hired are A technicians. This ensures that the service shop has enough technicians available to fix even the most difficult problems that come into the shop. Although this is good to assure fast high-quality repairs it does not come without a price. A-level technicians are the highest paid and, therefore, increase the shop's cost of labor and reduce its gross profit. A traditionally organized shop would also staff the majority of the remaining positions with B or C technicians. They would normally have one or two D technicians on staff because of their limited skills for performing other than the simplest maintenance. For example, in a traditionally organized shop it would be typical that out of every 6 technicians you would find two to three A techs, two to three B or C techs, and only one D tech. With this high number of mid- to high pay range employees the cost of labor sales is higher and gross profit is reduced.

In a team shop the team leader is normally the only A technician on the team. The team depends on him to guide and direct the team and to handle all of the difficult diagnoses and repairs. In a team of six, for example, there would be 1 A tech (high pay), two or three out of six that are B or C techs (mid-range pay), and two or three out of six that are D techs (low pay). This reduction in highly paid, highly skilled technicians could lead to concerns that the overall repair capabilities and quality generated by the shop would be reduced. However, by sharing the team leader's expertise with his group members the goal is for him to provide input so that the entire team can produce high-quality results. He also becomes an in-house trainer for the team, helping to increase the knowledge and skill levels of all team members at a very affordable price.

From a management perspective, being able to reduce the percentage of highly paid technicians reduces labor costs and increases gross profit. However, if reducing the number of highly skilled technicians reduces repair quality it is probably not worth the savings. In service shops and markets where this method is an accepted way of doing business the team system has been a major contributor to increasing profitability.

Unfortunately, the team system has not been widely accepted in many markets. This is due to the reluctance of many highly skilled technicians to work under this system. Many A technicians do not want to share the wealth. They are confident of their ability to meet or exceed flat-rate times for most repairs and earn premium wages. They do not want to share this with others. Further, they do not want their pay to be dependent on the consistent performance of others. They know that they can make it on their own and would prefer to work that way.

In markets where technicians can choose to work in a traditional shop or a team shows most A techs often choose traditional shops. This is a major obstacle to the widespread acceptance of the team system within that city or town. The resulting move of A techs from team shops to traditional shops reduces the effectiveness of team systems because shops without a true A tech do not have the top-notch problem solver and mentor that is needed for an effective team. This reduces the shop's technical capabilities as well as its long-term ability to develop future technicians.

THEORY INTO PRACTICE 15-2

CASE

MaxiMizer Garage currently employs six technicians. The shop is organized using the team system approach. During the past week all six technicians on the Gold Team worked 40 hours and the team produced a total of 282 flat-rate hours.

The flat-rate pay rates for the team members are

Jamal—$16; Mel—$18; Hal—$12

Betti—$24; Heidi—$17; Tony—$13

You decide

a) What did each of the six technicians earn last week?

b) How many flat-rate hours did the entire shop produce last week?

c) If MaxiMizer Garage charges $60 per flat-rate hour for all of their work, what was their gross labor sales for last week?

d) What was MaxiMizer Garage's gross profit for last week?

e) What was their gross profit percentage for last week?

Support Group

A third way to organize shop production is by using the **support group** system. This is a hybrid of the individual and team system approaches. In a support group shop the technicians and service advisors are split into support groups which look exactly like a team. There are four to seven technicians grouped with a service advisor. The technicians on a team are grouped together so that they represent all areas of technical knowledge and experience. Much like the team shop there is normally one A tech per group who is the team leader. This team leader is responsible for assigning work, assisting and training the less-experienced group members and doing the very difficult diagnostic work. There are, however, several operational differences that set support groups apart from team systems.

Support Group
A system in which technicians are organized into a small group and work together but are paid based on their individual production.

In a support group the technicians are not paid based on their share of the total team's production. The technicians each earn the individual hours that they produce. They may work together on a single vehicle at times but they are paid for the specific repair that they have completed. For example, if a customer brings in a vehicle and requests an oil change and a transmission service two group technicians may be assigned. However, unlike in the team system, they will each perform one of the tasks and will be paid only for the task that they have completed.

In a support group system the group leader is also paid on his individual production. However, he also receives additional pay for his group supervisory responsibilities. In addition to his individual pay he receives an override (a specified amount per hour for each hour produced by the rest of the team) to reward him for performing those tasks.

The support group system has benefits similar to the team system. It provides a solution for reducing the overall cost of sales in the shop. Even after paying the lead tech the override on the rest of the team's hours the overall cost of labor is still normally lower than in a traditionally organized shop.

One of the most unique benefits of the support group system is its ability to reduce labor costs while maintaining employee satisfaction and stability. This system rewards senior technicians for their own production and they earn extra compensation for sharing their expertise with others. This extra benefit increases the likelihood that A technicians will not only stay at a support group shop, they often elect to work in them over any other type of shop. Because of this, the support group system continues to gain support in a wide number of markets where team systems are not well accepted.

Real World Application

Each of the production systems has unique benefits and drawbacks. The team system is clearly the most innovative and most likely to help you reduce your cost of sales and increase your gross profit. Applied in the wrong situation or without adequate care it is also most likely to drive you out of business as you experience a mass exodus of your long-term highly skilled technicians.

Your ability to successfully implement unique and innovative strategies is dependent on several important factors, and trust of management among your employees is the most critical of these. Unless you have established a high level of trust from your employees, making radical changes will often be perceived as gambling with your employee's pay and is likely to lead to a mutiny. You must have a sound logic behind your plans and be able to clearly demonstrate that you have considered the interests of your employees.

Whenever possible, the best strategy is to consult with one of your top employees in confidence to review the proposed strategy. He can help you identify the strengths and possible weaknesses of your strategy and give you clear guidance about the key issues that you must address to overcome the objections of the other employees. Further, once he has embraced the change he can be a valuable ally in helping to sell the concept to the rest of the shop.

THEORY INTO PRACTICE 15-3

CASE 1

CostLo Motors' service department is organized using the support group approach. During the past week all six technicians in the group worked 40 hours. Because they are on a support group pay plan, Carly, the team leader, is paid an extra $1 for every flat-rate hour produced by the entire team for her efforts on guiding and directing them.

The flat-rate hours and flat-rate pay for the technicians are

Al—42 hrs. @ $16; Edgar—38 hrs. @ $18; Ricky—32 hrs. @ $12

Carl—54 hrs. @ $24; Joe—60 hrs. @ $17; Damian—56 hrs. @ $13

You decide

a) What did each of the six technicians earn last week?

b) How many flat-rate hours did the entire shop produce last week?

c) If CostLo Motors charges $60 per flat-rate hour for all of their work, what was their gross labor sales for last week?

d) What was CostLo Motors' gross profit for last week?

e) What was their gross profit percentage for last week?

THEORY INTO PRACTICE 15-4

CASE 2

Please take a look at the three different production schemes and last week's results for Slick Service Center, MaxiMizer Garage, and CostLo Motors in exercises 15-1, 15-2, and 15-3 above. Now let's compare the results of the three companies.

You decide

a) What was the total technician pay last week for each shop?

b) How many flat-rate hours did each shop produce last week?

c) At $60 per flat-rate hour what was their gross labor sales last week?

d) What was the gross profit of each shop last week?

e) What was the gross profit percentage of each shop last week?

THEORY INTO PRACTICE 15-5

CASE 3

You are the service manager of a new shop in Pleasantville, StarService. Your three main competitors are Slick Service Center, MaxiMizer Garage, and CostLo Motors. Using the information that you learned from exercises 15-1, 15-2, 15-3, and 15-4 and expecting business to stay the same as in these exercises, please answer the following.

You decide

a) Given free choice to organize your shop however you wanted to, which production scheme would you choose for your shop: individual pay, team system, or support group? Why?

b) What are the strengths and weaknesses of the plan you chose, considering that there are three other strong competitors in your market who will constantly try to steal your technicians and outperform you?

Increasing Capacity

Many successful shops eventually reach the point where they are simply too busy to handle all of the work that is coming their way. When this situation arises they have to make some very difficult choices. Businesses work too long and hard to build up a clientele and certainly do not want to lose those customers because they cannot provide them the services that they have requested in a timely manner. So, what are they to do?

In this section we will explore several alternatives that can help a company address this situation. In order to decide what actions are the best choice you must first must be able to answer two questions: 1) is the increased demand temporary or sustained? And, 2) what is the appropriate action to take?

If the increase in demand is temporary then making major changes in facilities or staffing are most often unwarranted. An example of this would be a sudden increase in business just before a holiday. Even though everyone wants to get their car serviced just before taking the long drive to grandma's house for Thanksgiving it is a very short-lived increase in demand. Sound management principles indicate that making a major change in operations (for example hiring more technicians or adding on to the shop) just to meet a temporary (one week per year) increase in business is a poor management decision. Although this example is extreme there are often fluctuations in business because of a variety of external factors that must not be misinterpreted for a long-term increase. Misinterpreting these signs could easily lead to making a poor investment in additional capacity.

However, if the increase in demand appears to be long term the manager must consider what reasonable actions he can take to meet this increased demand. There are several actions that the shop can take to address a long-term increase in demand. These alternatives range from those that are quickly implemented and can be temporary to those that require a significant investment. Below we will briefly review four of the most common choices: expanding facilities, extended hours, two shifts, and going to a six-day rotation.

Expanding Facilities

Expanding Facilities
Adding physical space (additional stalls and or additional buildings).

When long-term demand exceeds capacity one approach to addressing this concern is to increase capacity by **expanding facilities.** Adding on to the shop, installing more lifts, leasing out another building, or moving to larger quarters are all ways that you can increase your capacity. However, all of these alternatives come at a price.

If you reflect back to some of the basic economic principles that we learned in Chapter 13 a very important lesson in understanding expenses is that overhead is the most difficult expense to control. All of the alternatives listed earlier to increase capacity increase overhead. This is because when you add facilities or purchase equipment they will continue to exist and cost you money whether or not they are needed and fully utilized.

If you decided to add six service stalls to your building to meet a recent increase in business you need to remember that the extra six service stalls that you have added will still be there if business slows down. You will have to pay for the cost of the addition, for the additional utilities, and other related expenses. Certainly, you can't unbuild the addition. If things change and you wish you hadn't added on you can't make the costs go away. You're going to have to live with them. For this reason, you should approach adding physical space to your shop very cautiously and only after serious consideration. The following are three capacity-building alternatives that should be considered because they will help you to increase capacity without adding overhead.

THEORY INTO PRACTICE 15-6

CASE

As the service manager at Quest Motor Sales you have noticed that for the past three years you have had to turn away business during the busy summer months (June–August). Your records indicate that you have been operating at 90 percent of capacity the remainder of the year and have strong evidence that there is current demand for 125 percent of current capacity during the peak months.

You decide

Should you seriously consider adding on four additional stalls to your current 16-bay facility? Please explain the reasons for your decision.

Extended Hours

The traditional automotive service shop hours of operation are from 8 A.M. to 5 P.M. Mondays through Fridays. Weekend and evening service hours were very rare. However, in today's consumer-driven marketplace, customers demand convenience. As a result, most shops now offer some form of **extended hours.**

Extended Hours
Increasing the number of hours that the shop is open to produce repairs beyond the traditional 40-hour work week.

When demand exceeds capacity one of the alternative methods for increasing capacity is to increase available service hours. This will increase some costs. Among these are increased pay for the extra hours worked by personnel and increases in utilities costs.

For example, in a shop that has traditionally worked a Monday through Friday 8 to 5 work week the shop is producing 40 hours per week. By staying open until 9 P.M. two nights per week (eight additional hours) the shop has effectively increased its capacity by 20 percent without adding any physical space. Although there are some additional costs and scheduling becomes a bit more complicated this is an economical method for increasing capacity.

Because of the complexity of staffing the additional hours many shops will extend the work weeks of their existing employees on a rotating basis rather than adding more staff. It must be realized, however, that if the shop chooses this method to extend service hours and has, for example, all employees work late every other week the increased shop capacity of the extended hours is cut in half.

The major additional benefit of extending service hours is the flexibility of this approach. You can make this change and implement it very quickly because it does not require any long-term investment. Further, if the demand drops it is possible to revert back to the previous work schedule with few residual effects. For this reason, extended hours should be considered as one of the first alternatives to implement. Even if it is done as a temporary fix while you are working on a more permanent solution, it allows you to respond to your customers needs very quickly and this method is very cost effectively.

Benefits that shops realize from extended service hours are

- The ability to increase hours of operation two to three days per week.
- Increased shop capacity without any additional facilities, equipment, or tools.
- It is the most flexible alternative to increase capacity without making any long-term commitments.

THEORY INTO PRACTICE 15-7

CASE

At Quest Motor Sales your service business continues to be brisk. Your boss is stalling you on your request to add more stalls to your shop . . . and, besides, even if he finally approves it you won't see the facility built and opened for at least 18 months.

You decide

Should you consider extended service hours? As a temporary fix or as a long-term strategy? Why?

Second Shift

Second Shift
Operation of a second eight-hour shift of employees daily to double production capacity.

A second alternative to increase capacity without increasing overhead is to put on a **second shift**. Having two crews working five 40-hour work weeks effectively doubles the capacity of the shop (100 percent increase) without the costs and permanent consequences of adding on to the facilities.

The potential increase in capacity by going to a two-shift system is much greater than can be achieved through extended service hours. However, along with the capacity comes increased complexity in managing the department. Having two shifts is much like running two totally separate shops within the same company. From a staffing standpoint you have to have an entire second crew, from technicians to service advisors to managers, to staff the second shift. However, there are also some complications that go above and beyond those experienced in two separate facilities.

Even though the two-shift approach provides the largest benefit in increased capacity it also has substantial limitations. From the viewpoint of the customer, the shop running two shifts is not at all like two shops, it is one company with longer hours. Customer expectations are that regardless what time of day they call or stop, they expect to receive consistent service. This requires a great deal of coordination and intercommunication between the employees and supervisors working on the two distinct shifts. Finally, since many of the suppliers that the shop depends on for parts and supplies do not work a full 16-hour day there are often severe limitations with regard to availability of parts and supplies. Delays in obtaining these materials can delay completion of repairs and lower overall productivity. It is also generally much more difficult to recruit and retain qualified technicians who are willing to work from 5 P.M. to 2 A.M., especially if that schedule includes Friday nights.

Benefits that shops realize from the second shift are

- The ability to double their hours of operation five days a week
- Doubling their shop capacity (100% increase) without any additional facilities, equipment, or tools

THEORY INTO PRACTICE 15-8

CASE

Business has been really great at your dealership, Millenium Motorcars, and your business has been growing at a 15 percent rate for the past three years and you have reached 100 percent of full capacity. Your boss has just returned from a national dealer meeting and tells you about a fellow dealer who has doubled his labor sales almost overnight without adding on to his facilities by going to a two-shift operation.

You decide

What information do you need to gather to decide if this is a good strategy for your shop? What concerns about two-shift operations should you bring up to the boss?

Six-Day Rotation

Just as the team system and support group were developed to address the need for a creative approach to a staffing concern the development of the

Six-Day Rotation

A method of expanding available hours by working all technicians 4–10 hour days per week and rotating three crews Monday through Saturday.

six-day rotation was developed to provide a suitable alternative to the problem of limited capacity. The concept of the six-day rotation falls between that of extended service hours and a full two-shift operation. Like those strategies it provides for increased capacity without requiring additional facilities, tools, and equipment.

The six-day rotation approach provides a shop that has traditionally worked a five-day 40-hour week to increase their overall production capacity by 50 percent by working one day longer and increasing the work day. At the same time, it does so without increasing the average work week of the individual employee. Here's how it works:

- Instead of working 8 hours per day × 5 days per week (40 hours) all shop employees move to working 4 10-hour days per week.
- The shop's hours of operation change from being open 8 hours per day Monday through Friday to being open 10 hours per day Monday through Saturday.
- In order to coordinate staffing and allow for having 40 hour per week employees scheduled evenly to cover 60 available hours the shop is generally organized into three work groups.
- The three work groups work a three-week rotating schedule.

An example of a three-work group schedule is presented in Figure 15-1.

Week 1	Monday	Tuesday	Wednesday	Thursday	Friday	Saturday
Group A	x	x	x	x		
Group B			x	x	x	x
Group C	x	x			x	x

Week 2	Monday	Tuesday	Wednesday	Thursday	Friday	Saturday
Group A			x	x	x	x
Group B	x	x			x	x
Group C	x	x	x	x		

Week 3	Monday	Tuesday	Wednesday	Thursday	Friday	Saturday
Group A	x	x			x	x
Group B	x	x	x	x		
Group C			x	x	x	x

Figure 15-1 Six-day work week rotating schedule

Moving to the six-day rotating schedule shares some of the challenges with the two-shift schedule. The most common one is that the schedule requires a greater deal of intercommunication between the work groups. However, since this schedule does not require that the shop stay open late into the evening, delays in obtaining parts and supplies are substantially reduced.

Although there is generally an initial reluctance to work a six-day rotating shift it is not as difficult as finding employees to work a second shift. Even though there are drawbacks in that all employees have irregular schedules (not the same every week) and they are required to work Saturdays two out of every three weeks. This system also provides some benefits that will attract highly qualified employees.

Employees who work on a six-day rotation only work a four-day work week. Although they do work two Saturdays per rotation they have the added benefit of having a mini-vacation built into their schedule. Referring back to Figure 15-1 you can see that, for example, between weeks 1 and 2 of the schedule Group A gets five full days off in a row. This happens for all three work groups every three weeks. It has actually been observed that in many service shops that use a six-day rotation, employees ask to work their normally scheduled vacations in exchange for the extra pay since they're already getting a vacation every three weeks.

Benefits that shops realize from the six-day work week are

- The ability to provide extended hours of operation five days a week
- The ability to provide a full day of Saturday service
- A 50 percent increase in shop capacity without any additional facilities, equipment, or tools
- Increased employee satisfaction at working a four-day work week

THEORY INTO PRACTICE 15-9

CASE

After evaluating the situation at Millenium Motorcars more carefully, you acknowledge that your shop is booked beyond capacity right now and due to a huge boom in the local economy you can easily grow your business by 20 to 40 percent in the next two years, and expect to be able to double it in five years.

You decide

Under these circumstances, what are your short-term and long-term strategies to prepare your company to capture this market? Please justify your plan and/or plans.

Real World Application

One of the keys to getting on top and staying on top is constant vigilance and creativity. It is not enough to be above average, you must constantly be ahead of the crowd in leading the innovation. To do this you have to be willing to take risks. However, those risks should be carefully calculated and, whenever possible, leave a reasonable fall-back position in case they don't succeed so losses and future damage to operations are limited.

The production expansion plans that we've discussed (expanded hours, two shifts, and six-day rotation), although creative, can be reversed, leaving little permanent after-effects to the shop. Unfortunately, it is not as easy to reverse a physical expansion. Once the investment has been made the increased overhead costs remain. This type of strategy limits its fall-back position. As such, the adage that "brick and mortar is the last resort" holds true. Therefore, whether you're dealing with expanding capacity or any other major investment in the organization, you need to be extra careful before you act . . . and make sure that there isn't some other more flexible alternative that you can try first!

SUMMARY

In this chapter we have explored two widely used methods for changing the complexion of the service shop to increase sales, reduce costs, and help us to attain our overall goal: increased profit. These methods are technician organizational plans and expanded shop capacity.

The three different methods of organizing technicians (individual pay, team system, and support group) demonstrate that there are several ways to obtain the most out of your human resources while controlling cost of sales. Each of these systems has unique benefits and drawbacks. Therefore, the organizational plan that will work best in your shop in your market should be seriously considered.

When you have increased the efficiency of your facilities and your personnel to their absolute maximum and are still striving to keep the momentum moving forward, expansion of shop capacity is necessary. The two ways that you can accomplish this is through physical expansion of facilities or expansion of available hours. The three most common methods to expand available hours are: extended hours, two shift operation, and the six-day rotating work week. When trying to decide whether to add on to a facility or to expand available hours it is important to remember that each of these alternatives has unique benefits that should be carefully considered.

PRACTICING THE PRINCIPLES

In Questions 1–5, match the terms with their definitions:

____ 1) Team system	a) increasing the size of the building
____ 2) Individual plan	b) paying technicians for what they produce
____ 3) Extended hours	c) paying technicians as a group
____ 4) Expanded facilities	d) increasing the hours of operation
____ 5) Support group	e) having technicians work in a small group

6. All of the following are benefits of expanding the size of your shop except
   a. increases number of technicians you can have in the shop.
   b. increases the available labor hours you can sell.
   c. increases the overhead of the shop.
   d. gives the shop room to expand into as business increases.

7. All of the following are benefits of the team system except
   a. reduces average cost of labor.
   b. reduces the control that top tech's have on their own pay.
   c. reduces overall shop payroll.
   d. provides more technical assistance for new technicians.

8. Many technicians love the six-day rotation because
   a. they have a long weekend every three weeks.
   b. they only work 40 hours per week.
   c. they only have to work four days per week.
   d. all of the above.

9. Which of the following technician organization plans groups the technicians together rather than having them work individually?
   a. team system.
   b. individual plan.
   c. support group.
   d. a and c.

10. Fred Hammer has just changed jobs and is looking at his pay from the past two weeks to see if he made a wise decision. He worked at Melody Motors last week where he was paid on an individual plan. He produced 50 hours at an hourly rate of $20 per flat rate hour. This week was Fred's first week at Mac's Muffler Service where they work on a team system. He was hired at a rate of $22. He was excited because his six person team produced 288 hours this week. What is the difference between what Fred earned last week and this week? Based solely on these results do you think that Fred made a wise decision to change jobs?

CHAPTER 16

Analysis and Action

CHAPTER OBJECTIVES

- To identify the major ways to affect profitability
- To analyze the impact of various methods of increasing sales and capacity
- To analyze the impact of various methods of controlling variable costs
- To analyze the impact of various methods of controlling overall costs
- To determine the best course of action to increase production and/or reduce expenses, taking into account the benefits and drawbacks of the available choices

KEY TERMS

bottom line
net loss
break even point
average cost of sales

Introduction

By this point you should have a basic working knowledge of sales, gross profit, and net profit. In order to be able to effectively manage an automotive service operation an understanding of these concepts is essential. We have taken some time to explain the major factors that you, as a manager, can control and change in your effort to generate an acceptable profit. Now we can begin to use this information to understand how the decisions that you make can significantly alter the profit of your shop, your paycheck, and, ultimately, your job security as a service manager.

Achieving a Net Profit

Companies must earn a profit to survive. If they did not consistently do this they would quickly be unable to pay their bills and go out of business. As presented earlier, net profit is the amount that is left after all expenses are deducted from the total amount of income as follows

$$\text{Income} - \text{Expenses} = \text{Net profit}$$

It is important to remember that the two ingredients of net profit (income and expense) are not always separate. As you make extra efforts to increase income, you may incur additional costs for those efforts (increased expenses). Likewise, as you try to curtail expenses you need to be careful that you do not trim services or quality that will result in fewer people choosing to purchase your service (reduced income).

If you want to maintain or increase net profit there are only two factors that you can change, leaving you with the following three choices:

1. Increase income (sell more).
2. Decrease expenses (lower cost).
3. Do both.

Increasing Income

A great way to increase profitability that should always be strongly considered is through consistently increasing sales. In Chapters 25 through 28 we will discuss some of the tools that you can use to stimulate sales, such as advertising, marketing, and merchandising. Stimulating sales is the best way to make sure that you are maximizing your use of the resources that you have at your disposal. However, if increasing sales is the sole focus of your business planning, it is likely to produce very disappointing results. Without considering both of the ingredients of profitability, income and expense, you are likely to work harder, sell more, and file bankruptcy.

Let us explore a bit little further the contribution that increased sales can have to achieving and maintaining profitability. Increased sales contribute directly to the **bottom line** (net profit). This is especially true if increased sales can be achieved while holding expenses constant. Figure 16-1 demonstrates this principle. In this example, the shop starts in January with total monthly expenses that are constant but exceed total income.

A common business term meaning net gain or profit.

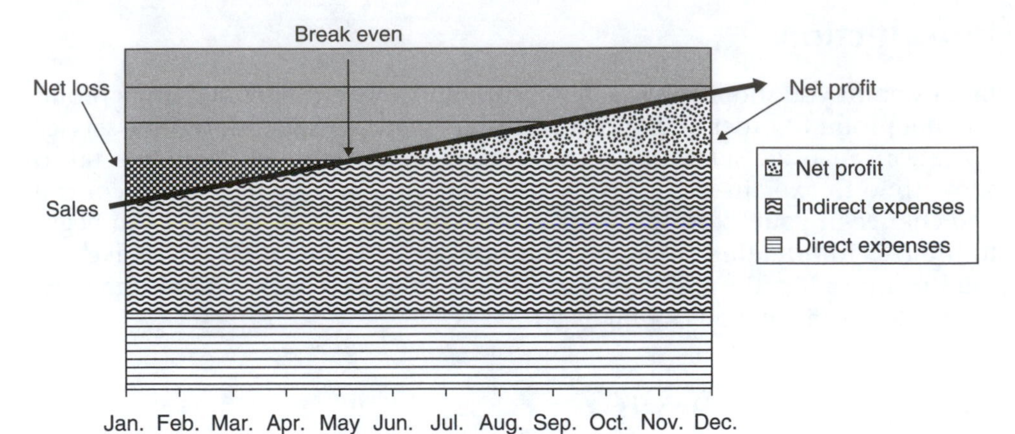

Figure 16-1 Increasing sales with constant expenses

Net Loss

A common term used to describe a negative net profit.

Break Even Point

The point at which income equals expenses.

The shop is losing money (**net loss**). The shop increases sales 5 percent monthly while holding expenses constant. You can see how this increase in sales helps them to move from a monthly net loss to a monthly net profit.

In this example you can clearly see that with constant expenses and steadily increasing sales the shop's financial picture begins to change as the year progresses. They begin the year where the expenses exceed the sales and they are generating a monthly net loss (income < expenses). This is true for the first four months of the year. However, with the steady increases in sales the loss continues to diminish. In May, they reach the point where income equals expenses. This is called the **break even point**. Finally, in June they achieve their first net profit (income > expenses). Then, as the sales continue to increase, the monthly net profit grows.

If it were always possible to hold all of the factors constant while changing only one, management would be a much simpler job. However, sales and income do not typically increase without any increased costs. For example, if technicians are paid flat rate, an increase in flat-rate hours (sales) also results in an increase in technician pay (direct expense). Although the profit does increase, you can see in Figure 16-2 that it takes a little bit longer for the shop to move from a net loss to a net profit.

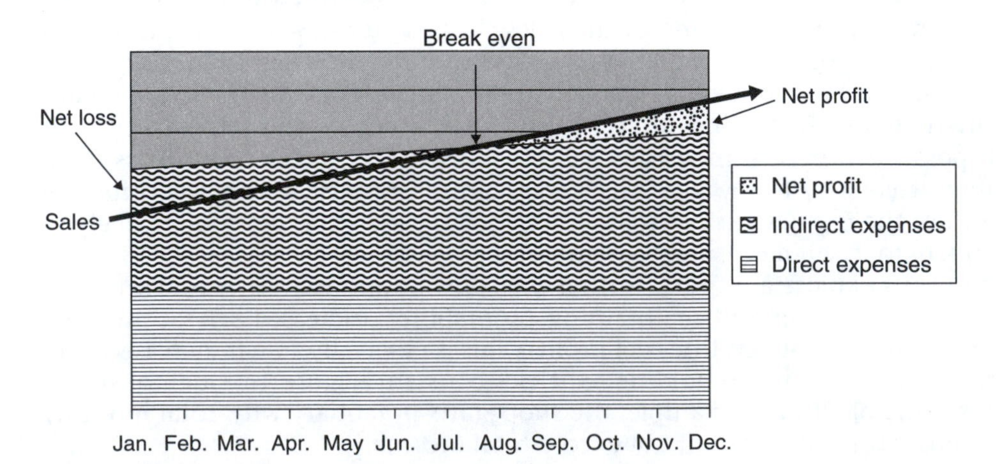

Figure 16-2 Increasing sales with increasing direct expenses

A third possibility is that when you increase sales you are going to increase both direct expenses (technician pay) and indirect expenses. Here are two examples of how that might occur. If you aggressively focus on increased sales as the only means to increase profit you might consider advertising to a wider audience to bring people into your shop from far away. Unfortunately, in order to do that you will have to spend more money to advertise (increase expenses) to let those people outside of your local area know about your services and to give them a good reason to travel further to see you, and advertising is not cheap. Your indirect costs will be increased. So, just as in the previous example where increased sales have increased direct expenses, in this situation both your direct and indirect expenses increase. The resulting profit chart will look something like Figure 16-3.

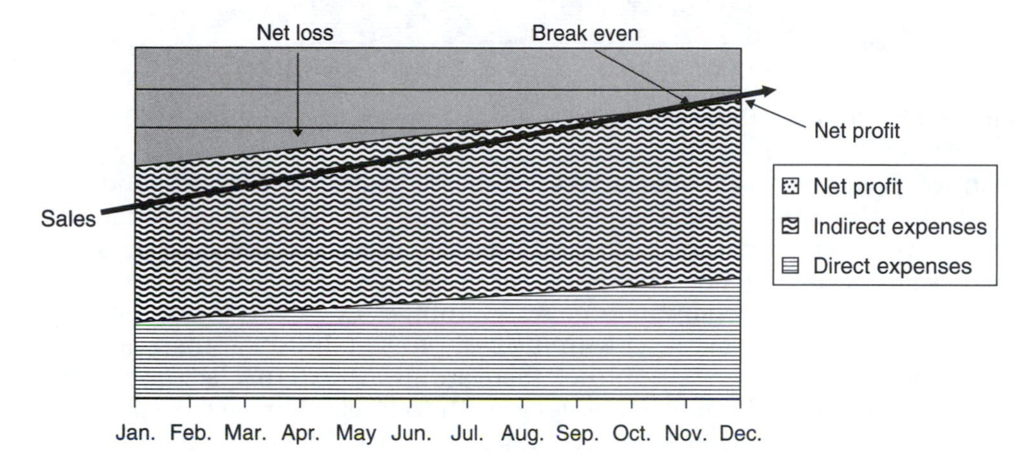

Figure 16-3 Increasing sales with increasing direct and indirect expenses

As you can see in this example, sales have continued to increase at a constant rate. Direct expenses have continued to slowly increase in direct relationship to the increased sales. Now, when we add a small monthly increase in indirect expenses to account for a small increase in advertising, the profit picture has changed again. The break even point is not reached until November and the shop achieves a net profit for only one month, December, and it is small.

If you are able to attract people from farther away to come to your service shop, you will reach a point where your shop is too busy to handle all of the work. Then what will you do? Will you stay open later? You would have to hire more technicians and more support personnel to staff your shop (increased expenses). For each small increase to expenses the break even point moves further and further into the future.

A final example of the possible results of increasing sales would be when you reach the point where you have to consider moving or adding on to the facilities just to keep up with the increase in business. When this happens you will be increasing indirect expenses by a significant amount. You need to remember also that the expenses for the facility (building costs plus utilities) are overhead expenses and, by their very nature, the most difficult to control. Once you have built an addition you cannot easily make it go away. Therefore, the added indirect expenses will continue no matter what happens to your sales. This significant and constant increase in indirect expenses is represented in Figure 16-4.

The example shown above demonstrates the effect of a 25 percent increase in overhead such as one that would occur with a building expansion. As you

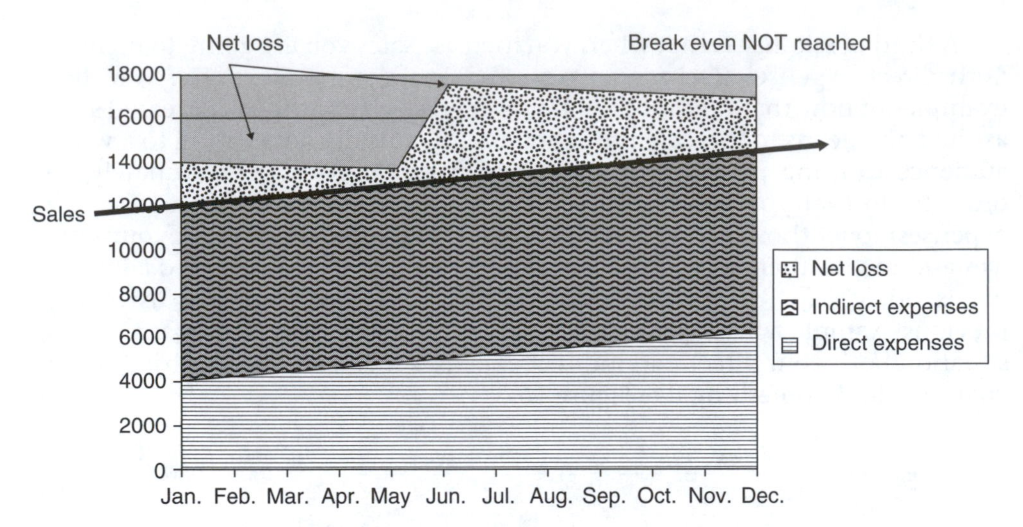

Figure 16-4 Increasing sales with a 25% increase in overhead

can see, even though all other factors remain the same, the increase in indirect costs is both significant and immediate. The impact of the change is that the break even point is pushed further off into the future and the shop does not achieve its break even point by the end of the year.

Although it is a good way to increase profit, sales growth is not the only answer. Even the best marketer with the best product finds that there are limits on how much he can sell. Further, there are always external factors beyond your control that will cause your sales growth to level off or even decline. For example, if you are selling service in a small town and you have the best service available it is still very unlikely that you will sell more oil changes than there are cars in the county this month. There is a limited market and, therefore, a limit to the amount that you can sell.

I hope you have noticed that there is a recurring theme in the four examples presented. It seems that every time you try to increase sales you have to do something that is going to cost you more money. These examples are typical and help to explain the reason why focusing on increased sales alone is not a long-term solution to making a profit. Consistent profitability is achieved through a combination of increasing income and controlling costs. Let us talk more about how to control costs.

THEORY INTO PRACTICE 16-1

CASE 1

Congratulations, due to your marketing efforts your shop business has grown by 40 percent. Unfortunately, you are now experiencing a shortage of space and are starting to lose customers because they have to wait so long to get an appointment to have you work on their car.

You decide

What do you do?

a. Raise your prices?
b. Hire more technicians and start extended service hours?
c. Buy a bigger building and move into it?
d. All of the above.

Please explain the reason behind your choice

THEORY INTO PRACTICE 16-2

CASE 2

Your business has been slowly declining over the past two years. You know that you still have a good reputation in the local community, but things have been tough in your town due to them closing down two local manufacturing plants. You are faced with making some tough decisions to keep your shop profitable.

You decide

What do you do?

a. Lower your labor rate?

b. Advertise more outside of the local area?

c. Hire lower cost technicians?

d. All of the above.

Please explain the reason behind your choice.

Controlling Expenses

In the automotive service shop there are two main areas where expenses can be controlled. The expenses that are most clearly under the control of the service manager are the direct expenses. The main source of these expenses is technician payroll expense. In Chapter 14 we discussed the different methods for paying technicians. It is suggested that you consider going back to review this information if you are unclear about the differences between these pay plans.

Since flat rate continues to be the most common pay plan for technicians, we need to take a look at how this method of pay affects gross profit. The chart in Figure 16-5 shows the relationship between technicians' pay and the gross profit when the technicians are being paid solely on flat rate.

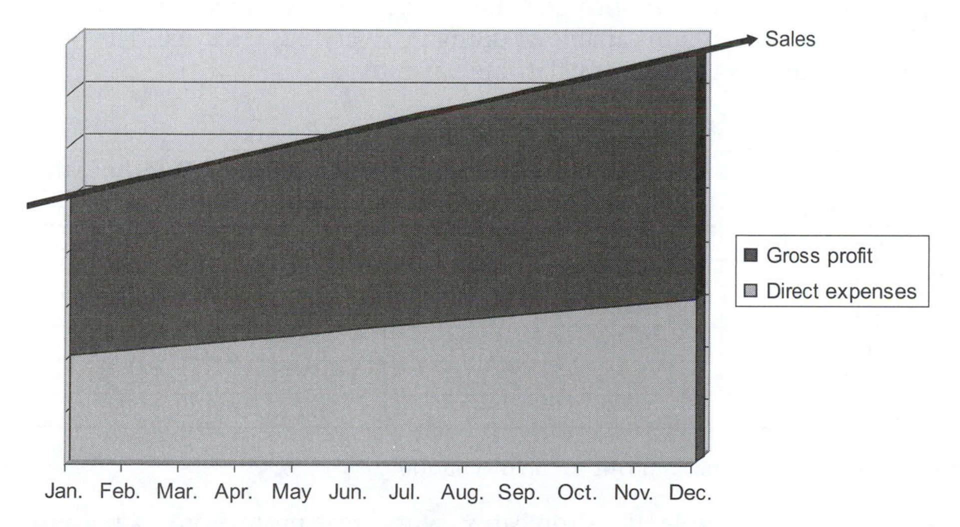

Figure 16-5 Relationship of flat-rate pay to gross profit

There is a direct relationship between technician pay and gross profit in the flat-rate system. This means that if the sales increase, so do the direct expenses. If the direct expenses are too high, there is only one way to reduce them—reduce technician pay. This may sound simple but it is definitely not. Due to the consistently high demand for technicians and the need for qualified technicians to do quality work, it is difficult to recruit and retain technicians. You certainly cannot expect to recruit and retain qualified technicians by underpaying them.

You cannot afford the consequences of underpaying a highly skilled and experienced technician. Fortunately, not all work that comes into your shop requires a high level of skill and experience. The typical repair shop performs a wide range of maintenance and repair services which require lower levels of skill and experience. Therefore, it is possible to control the overall direct expenses by altering the 'mix' of technicians. That is, changing the combination of A, B, C, and D technicians that you have in the shop changes your average technician pay and your direct expenses. Maintaining the proper balance of technicians within the shop to meet the needs of the customers is the solution to controlling direct expenses.

Although it would seem ideal to have a shop full of the top technicians in the world this would pose more of a problem than it would be a benefit. Top technicians demand top pay. However, asking a $26 per hour master certified technician performing $22.95 oil changes is a waste of talent. It is also a waste of money. It is likely to create employee dissatisfaction by making the technician feel like he is wasting his skills doing menial tasks. The way to resolve this problem is to hire personnel with the right skill levels to do the job.

Here is a simple example of how choosing the right technician for the job can influence the cost of sales and gross profit. A very common service provided by every service shop is an oil change. It is common to see these repairs advertised at the price of $22.95. If the shop intends to sell the oil change for that price and has a total cost for the oil and filter of $5.95, they are earning $16.00 per oil change in labor. All technicians are paid 0.3 hours to perform this service. Although the labor sale amount will be the same on every oil change that they do, the gross profit will change dramatically depending on which of their four levels of technicians performs the work. Figure 16-6 shows the gross profit and gross profit percentage generated by these four different technicians, who are all are capable of doing this very basic service. The only factor that changes is their hourly flat-rate pay rate.

	A Technician	B Technician	C Technician	D Technician
Tech Flate Rate	$26.00	$20.00	$14.00	$8.00
Customer Labor Rate	$60.00	$60.00	$60.00	$60.00
Labor for Oil Chg.	0.3	0.3	0.3	0.3
Labor Sale	$18.00	$18.00	$18.00	$18.00
Cost of Labor	$7.80	$6.00	$4.20	$2.40
Gross Profit	$10.20	$12.00	$13.80	$15.60
Gross Profit %	57	67	77	87

Figure 16-6 Labor and gross profit for an oil change

Based on this example, the shop can vary its gross profit from 57 percent up to 87 percent solely based on who does the oil change. Having the proper mix of different skill levels of technicians is the key. This will allow supervisors to assign work to capable technicians without overpaying an expert to performing routine work.

Average Cost of Sales

The average labor cost for all repairs performed in the shop.

Achieving the proper **average cost of sales** in a shop so that you can maintain the proper gross profit percentages is essential to achieve profitability. You cannot afford to have costs so high that you constantly lose money.

Conversely, you have to spend enough money to retain technicians with the right combination of skills and experience to fix cars right the first time. It is the delicate balance of these two factors, cost versus expertise, which makes staffing a repair shop such a difficult challenge.

In Chapter 15 we discussed alternative production plans that can be considered to deal with the problem of staffing costs, teams, and support groups. They were created to try to reduce average cost of labor while not sacrificing overall quality of repairs. Taking into account the possibility that we might be able to use production plans as a tool to control cost, let's revisit a scenario similar to the ones that we have just discussed to consider alternative methods to address the question of controlling average cost of sales.

Average cost of sales is a very important measurement tool in trying to control costs. You can calculate average cost of sales by doing the following three simple steps:

1. Calculate total hours produced by each technician multiplied by their hourly rate.
2. Add the totals of all technicians together.
3. Divide the total by the number of technicians.

This will give you the actual average cost of sales for the entire shop during a specific period of time. This average will change as business goes up and down and as individual technician productivity varies. Therefore, it is an important measurement to track on a regular basis so that you can monitor your current cost and gross profit.

It would be easy to manage and control the cost of sales and gross profit if business was stable. Unfortunately, business never remains constant. As a manager you cannot assume that the type of work that you are getting in your shop will be exactly the same every day. Finally, the productivity of your technicians is dependent on a variety of factors including the type of work that they get, their level of motivation, their health, and so on. This makes the decision-making process for properly staffing your shop and maintaining the required profit margins quite a bit more complex.

As a final exercise in this chapter, we will take another look at a situation similar to the ones that we have addressed in the previous exercises. However, this time we are going to add in the fact that not all of your technicians produce exactly the same amount of work every week, a variable that is a reality in most shops.

THEORY INTO PRACTICE 16-3

CASE 1

Your goal is to staff your shop with four technicians and maintain an average cost of sales that allows you to earn a gross profit of 72 percent. You run a full-service shop and need technicians that can do everything from oil changes to electronic diagnosis.

You decide

Using Figure 16-6 as your guide and assuming that all of the technicians produce exactly the same number of flat-rate hours per week, how many combinations of technicians out of the four categories can you arrive at that will give you a 72 percent gross profit? Which of these combinations would *you* choose if it was your shop? Why?

THEORY INTO PRACTICE 16-4

CASE 2

You are managing a four-bay shop that is a franchise of one of the large tire companies. In addition to selling and installing tires your shop specializes in front-end alignments, brake jobs, and preventative maintenance services. You do not do any heavy repairs or electronics diagnostics. You send those back to the dealers.

You decide

Using Figure 16-6 as your guide and assuming that all of the technicians produce exactly the same number of flat-rate hours per week, what combination of four technicians would you select to staff your shop? What would be your average cost of sales? Average gross profit percentage? Why did you select this mix of technicians?

THEORY INTO PRACTICE 16-5

CASE 1

You are trying to track the actual average cost of sales for your service department. You currently have four technicians working for you. Their information is as follows:

	Lisa	Fred	Omar	Horace
Technician Flat Rate	$26.00	$20.00	$14.00	$8.00

You decide

Using this information, please calculate the average cost of labor if

a. Lisa, Fred, Omar, and Horace all produced 40 hours last week.
b. Lisa produced 50 hours, Fred produced 40 hours, Omar produced 40 hours, and Horace produced 30 hours last week.
c. Lisa produced 60 hours, Fred produced 40 hours, Omar produced 36 hours, and Horace produced 24 hours last week.

THEORY INTO PRACTICE 16-6

CASE 2

Your goal is to staff your shop with six technicians and maintain an average cost of sales that allows you to earn a gross profit of 72 percent. You run a full-service shop and need technicians that can do everything from oil changes to electronic diagnosis.

You decide

Using the chart as your guide and assuming that all of the technicians produce exactly the same number of flat-rate hours per week, what combination of technicians from the four classifications would you choose to achieve an average gross profit of 72 percent or more using a traditionally organized shop? Please explain why you chose this combination of technicians.

	A Technician	B Technician	C Technician	D Technician
Technician Flat Rate	$26.00	$20.00	$14.00	$8.00
Weekly Hours Produced	56	48	32	24
Customer Labor Rate	$60.00	$60.00	$60.00	$60.00
Gross Profit	$34.00	$40.00	$46.00	$52.00
Gross Profit %	57	67	77	87

THEORY INTO PRACTICE 16-7

CASE 3

You achieved your goal of a 72% gross profit in the last exercise. Your owner has just returned from a national conference and tells you that 72% isn't good enough. He wants you to explore alternative production plans.

You decide

What would be your technician staffing choices if you were using the team system production plan? What gross profit percentage would you achieve using this choice? Which technicians would you choose if you were using a support group? What gross profit percentage would you achieve using this choice?

REAL WORLD APPLICATION

It is important as a manager that you achieve a sense of balance in your actions. Just because you are successful today it is usually a bad strategy to let things run the way that they have. You should constantly analyze your performance and look for ways to consistently improve your operation and increase your profitability.

On the other hand, you cannot afford to make sweeping changes daily. Implementing change haphazardly without a great deal of thought and consideration will create a great deal of unrest among your employees and is likely to cost you a great deal through employee dissatisfaction and a dramatic increase in employee turnover.

You need to strike a balance and carefully keep track of the data. You need to track it, analyze it, and then when you are sure that it is not just a short-term issue you will be prepared to *cautiously* and thoughtfully take appropriate action.

THEORY INTO PRACTICE 16-8

CASE

Your goal remains to produce a gross profit of 72 percent or higher in a shop of six technicians.

You decide

Using the chart provided, how would the gross profit results change for the staffing choices that you made in the previous exercise where you selected your technicians for the three production types (traditional/team/support group) if you learned that the four technicians consistently produced the number of hours listed in this chart?

	A Technician	B Technician	C Technician	D Technician
Technician Flat Rate	$26.00	$20.00	$14.00	$8.00
Customer Labor Rate	$60.00	$60.00	$60.00	$60.00
Gross Profit	$34.00	$40.00	$46.00	$52.00
Gross Profit %	57	67	77	87

SUMMARY

In this chapter we have explored a variety of scenarios to help you deepen your understanding of the importance of sound financial management. Through the use of these examples we investigated the potential benefits and drawbacks of a variety of different actions that have an impact on your bottom line.

We discussed how increasing income serves as a primary method for increasing net profit. We then discussed how increasing income is rarely done without any effect on costs. We looked at several common situations where increasing income is the cause of increased costs.

We then spent the remainder of the chapter looking at a variety of different ways that you can bring cost of sales under control and keep it under control. We applied some of the concepts that we learned in previous chapters to help us reduce fixed expenses and, thus, increase gross profit. We then worked through several exercises that demonstrated how changing the mix of technicians in the shop and alternative production plans can help you to increase your gross profit percentage.

PRACTICING THE PRINCIPLES

1. By reducing the average cost of sales the service manager can
   a. increase labor hours.
   b. increase gross profit.
   c. reduce the overhead.
   d. reduce overall sales.
2. A service manager can reduce cost of sales by
   a. replacing his top technician with a lower paid one.
   b. hiring more entry level technicians at a lower rate.
   c. cutting every current technician's pay.
   d. all of the above, although I would not recommend it.
3. The term *average cost of sales* refers to
   a. the total hours produced divided by the number of technicians.
   b. the normal amount of hours that John turns weekly every year.
   c. the average pay rate of your technicians divided by forty.
   d. none of the above.
4. A shop achieves the break even point when
   a. it finally makes a net profit.
   b. gross profit – all other expenses = 0.
   c. income – expenses = 0.
   d. more than one choice is correct.
5. If you want to increase your shop's gross profit you can
   a. reduce your overhead expenses.
   b. increase cost of sales.
   c. increase fixed expenses.
   d. increase labor sales.
6. If you want to increase your shop's net profit you can
   a. reduce your overhead expenses.
   b. increase cost of sales.
   c. increase fixed expenses.
   d. reduce labor sales.
7. If you want to increase your shop's gross profit percentage you can
   a. increase your total labor sales.
   b. increase cost of labor sales.
   c. decrease your fixed expenses.
   d. decrease average cost of sales.

In Questions 8–10 you have two technicians working for you. Your shop labor rate is $50 per flat-rate hour. Jeremy, who is paid $20 per flat-rate hour, turns 60 hours this week and Alfred, who is paid $10 per flat rate per hour, produces only 30 hours.

8. What is your average cost of sales for the week?
9. What is your total gross profit for the week?
10. What is your gross profit percentage for the week?

SECTION

5

Organizing and Managing Your Efforts

Multitasking is not a new concept. Multitasking continues to be the norm for managers in the automotive repair industry. Automotive managers are expected to possess a wide array of skills and to be able to use them on a moment's notice. None of us has an unlimited amount of time. There are many situations that are beyond our control. Organizing yourself and prioritizing your efforts to get the most use of your time and energy plays an important role in determining your success as a manager.

CHAPTER

17

Managing Yourself and Your Time

CHAPTER OBJECTIVES

- To identify what your strengths are and how to use them to your advantage
- To examine basic principles of how to prioritize efforts to get maximum results
- To recognize the importance of organization and time management in improving productivity

KEY TERMS

strengths
weaknesses
prioritizing
multitasking
procrastination

Introduction

We live in a world where there is abundance. There are so many places to go, people to see, things to do. There is so much work to get done and so little time. How do you decide what to do? What to do first? When to say no? Overwhelmed by the choices and the pressures of today's world, many people say that they feel as if their life is out of control. They feel like they are constantly pushed and pulled in so many directions that they do not feel like they are really making the decisions.

In the ever-accelerating pace of change, technology, and life the demands placed on each of us continue to expand. There is little you can do to reduce the demands. Fortunately, there is something that you can do to help manage those demands. You must become better at getting the best use out of the most precious commodity that you have, your time. Most people would be willing to pay a high price for just a little more time to . . . So, the big question is can you be different? Can you get control of your time?

In Chapter 18 we will spend some time helping you improve your organization skills. However, and more important, in this chapter we will discuss the most important part of getting really organized, deciding what your priorities are so that you will have a foundation on which to organize your life.

What Do You Do Best?

Most people are multi-talented. We have the ability to do a wide variety of tasks; we can master and pass courses in a wide range of subjects; do work from cutting down trees to repairing wiring to writing articles to running. These things have little in common but they demonstrate the versatility and the wide range of potential of the human body and spirit. Do you know what you are good at? Have you ever made a concerted effort to identify what skills and abilities you really have? If you really tried to make an exhaustive list of all of the things that you know that you *can* do it would wear you out. Not what you want to do, not what you choose to do, not what you prefer to do . . . what you *can* do.

THEORY INTO PRACTICE 17-1

CASE

Take a blank sheet of paper and for the next three minutes write down as many different things as you can that you have done in your life. Do not stop and think too much about it. It does not matter if they were simple, complex, important, or silly, 20 years ago or yesterday, just write as many down as fast as you can.

You decide

Now that you have completed your list, stop and take a look at the wide range of things that you have done. It is quite astounding . . . and if you did not get too exhausted from writing you could continue coming up with more and more things that you have done. That list represents only a small fraction of the vast array of things that you, as the unique human being that you are, are capable of doing.

Even though we each have a very wide range of knowledge and skills no one (that I know of) has been able to be a master of everything possible in our world.

So here is one of the first secrets to success: *The better that you are able to identify your talents and abilities, the more likely you are to succeed.* It's almost too simple. We can't all do it all. Each of us can do some things better than others and they, in turn, can do some things better than us. Therefore, it is to our advantage to take the time to figure out what we do best and work to our **strengths**.

Strengths
The areas of your knowledge, abilities, or capacity.

You can work harder, practice more, and study longer to try to compensate for your **weaknesses**. In many cases in your personal or professional life you will be faced with challenges that draw upon your strengths. However you will also be expected to do things that you are not so good at doing. In those cases you clearly have to work to minimize or overcome your weaknesses.

Weaknesses
The areas of your least knowledge, abilities, or capacity.

You need to realize that it will take greater effort to overcome your weaknesses than doing those things that you naturally do easily and well. For that reason, it just makes good sense that the better you are able to identify your strengths and put yourself in a position where you can draw upon them the more likely you will be at the top of your game. Whether it is in your personal life or your career the better you are able to consistently identify your strengths, acknowledge them, and direct your efforts to find the niche where your unique qualities are valued, appreciated, and rewarded the more likely you will be successful.

THEORY INTO PRACTICE 17-2

CASE

A new manager is hired into an existing import dealership service department. The shop has been around for many years and has a very loyal customer following. Like many small import shops all of the technicians are full-service technicians. The problem that has resulted in your hire is that the shop has been showing a constant decline in productivity and repair quality. This has reached the point where customer complaints have been increasing and even some of the most loyal customers are starting to go elsewhere for their repairs.

After analyzing the situation it becomes apparent that these problems have been growing as the vehicles have become more complicated and complex. The great news about the shop is that the workforce is very stable. Unfortunately, not all of the technicians have been able to keep up with the changes in technology. As a result, some of them really struggle when they run into complex electrical and electronic problems. Others have difficulty with the very complicated new dual overhead-cam 12-cylinder engines or the electronically actuated transmissions. Unfortunately the more computer savvy technicians in the shop may be busy doing oil changes, replacing brake pads, and doing simple maintenance services.

You decide

Faced with this situation what solution or possible solutions would you consider? Why?

Doing What Makes You Feel Fulfilled

Identifying your strengths and working to them is a very important ingredient in making you productive and successful. However, it is not a guarantee that you'll be satisfied and happy. Productivity and success are measures of how much you produce in comparison to others, whereas satisfaction and happiness are measures of something far more intangible—and ultimately far more important—how it makes you feel about yourself and your self-worth! Can you be both good at what you do and happy?

Real World Application

I was faced with a situation very much like the one in the case that you just completed. In that instance I found that what worked was to identify what each technician did best and to set up a system with the simple goal of having everyone what they do best most of the time. After evaluating productivity and training records over time it was easy to determine what the technical strengths and weaknesses each of the shop technicians were. Once this was done, a plan was devised to change the method of work distribution from the service desk. No longer would a technician be assigned a car and be expected to do everything, no matter what it needed, to that vehicle. Instead, the dispatcher was expected to assign only specific repair items to individual technicians. As a result, a car might require two or three technicians to work on it to resolve all of the concerns, but all of the concerns were addressed by the technician most likely to repair it right the first time and in the least amount of time.

This major philosophical change in the shop was at first accepted with reservations by the technicians. I met with the technicians prior to the rollout and maintained an open-door policy to discuss any concerns that they had. I asked them to give me the benefit of the doubt and to trust me and to try it for 30 days. The end result was better quality of repairs, more shop productivity, and bigger paychecks and higher job satisfaction for the technicians.

Most of us have come home from work after a long day and as we sunk into the couch we were greeted by the question: How was your day? Some days you felt totally drained, totally exhausted, you likely reported that you didn't feel like you really accomplished much. It was just draining. However, after working just as hard—and possibly even harder—after another long day you've come home and rather than feeling drained, exhausted, overwhelmed, you're energized, happy, upbeat, enthusiastic, and looking forward to someone asking how your day was. What was the difference between these two days?

Was the difference that you got more sleep the night before? Were you in better health? Was the weather better? Was it sunny outside? Although these external factors may have had some effect, it is likely that they were minimal. You can probably easily think of both good and bad days that happen regardless of your state of sleep, health, or other external factors. So what was it, really? Here's a brief exercise that may help you to understand the difference.

The short exercise that you just completed is not that scientific, not that complicated, but is intended to point out to you two different things about what you do every day in your personal life and in your professional life. It comes as no surprise to you, I'm sure, that there are many things that you spend your time and energy doing that you don't feel particularly skilled at doing!

However, even more important, once you have been able to eliminate those things that you're not good at, the remaining list still typically contains a variety of activities that don't make you feel good. Why not? You have the knowledge. You have the skills. Yet they don't satisfy you. Again, why not?

The simple answer to why not is that although we all possess a wide range of skills and abilities, just because *we can* do something does not mean that *we want to* do it. In that subtle difference lies the answer to personal and job satisfaction. The better you are able to make the distinction between what you are capable of doing and what you are motivated and driven to do the more often you will experience the situation presented earlier where after a hard day you come home energized, happy, upbeat, enthusiastic. The simple difference is learning what makes you feel fulfilled and then directing as much of your efforts as possible at aligning your activities with those tasks.

Certainly, all of us are required to do many things that we do not choose to do. We are not in total control of our time and our energies. However, the more often we are able to get our head, our heart, and our energies going in the same direction, the more likely we are to feel like a success in our work and in our lives.

THEORY INTO PRACTICE 17-3

CASE

Take a blank sheet of paper and prepare two lists. Please spend no more than two minutes quickly writing as many things down as you can think of that answer the following questions. Don't take the time to get into detail. Provide quick information off of the top of your head

You Decide

1. List as many tasks/jobs/events/responsibilities that you have done at work any time over the past two weeks.
2. List as many things as you can that you have done in your personal time in the past two weeks.

Remember there is a 2-minute time limit. Once you've completed your list please do the following:

Please go down the list and cross off all of the things that you had to do but you don't feel you're good at doing. That narrows the list down to just your strengths and interests. Now, count up the short list of your strengths and interests. Then number each of the items that make you feel the best, starting with your top choice as number 1, your second choice as number 2, and so on.

3. Look at your lists. Based on this information what are your strengths?

Establishing Your Priorities

It is obvious that no one has time to do everything. We constantly face points where we have to decide which things get done and which ones we have to put aside for later. Therefore, if you want to be satisfied, productive, and successful, **prioritizing** your activities helps you determine what matters most to you and allows you to focus your efforts on those items. The exercises in the previous two sections should help open your eyes to how to begin that process. That major decision process will help you to organize and prioritize your efforts so that you put your time and your effort where it will be most valuable to help you reach your goals.

Prioritizing
Arranging events or activities in order of importance.

Now that you have a better idea of what your skills and abilities are and what makes you feel self-fulfilled, you can begin the process of translating this knowledge into a broad roadmap for action. This roadmap can be built by establishing a set of personal and professional vision, mission, and goals statements. You may want to refer back to Chapter 9 if you're not clear on these three items and how to develop them.

On a personal basis, establishing a vision, mission, and goals does not need to be a long, involved formal process. One of the easiest ways to begin the process is to ask yourself three of the most common questions asked in job interviews. They are

- What do you want to be doing and where do you want to be in the next 5 years?
- What do you expect to be doing in 10 years?
- How about in 20 years?

Interviewers ask you these questions to see if your professional goals and that of the current position and the company are aligned. They realize that both you and they are much more likely to succeed and thrive if you have mutual interests and goals. You owe it to yourself to know the answers to these questions. Armed with this knowledge you can build a vision, mission, and goals so that you can achieve your aspirations for the future.

THEORY INTO PRACTICE 17-4

CASE

Take a few minutes right now and write down the answers to the following three questions.

You decide

Close your eyes for a moment and dream about what your work life will look like in the future if everything turns out the way that you want it to be. Then, answer the following:

1. What do you see yourself doing (where you will you be working, job title) five years from now?
2. What will your work life be like 10 years from now?
3. 20 years from now?

Now that you've answered the last three questions take a few minutes to reflect and make a brief list of the things that you need to do to *make sure* that you are ready to take advantage of opportunities that will help you to achieve these goals.

Once you have clarified your aspirations for the future the next step is to write them down and keep them handy. In this way you can constantly remind yourself of your intended goal. That will help to assure that you stay on that path. Remember, you need to be careful: If you don't know where you're headed you just might get there. However, the more clearly you keep on the path to your intended target the more likely you will be to reach it faster and with less frustration and lost effort.

Now that you're clear about your goals and ambitions you need to take the time to brainstorm about what things you can do to help further your goals. Do you need to take a class? Attend a seminar? Start associating with different people? Join a club? Change jobs? You need to answer to the best of your ability the question: What do I need to know and be able to do if I want to be best prepared to achieve my goal? Although no one can guarantee you that just because you are prepared the world will fall at your feet, please be assured that your best chance for success is to be prepared, ready, and anxiously waiting when the door of opportunity opens.

You Choose: Fireman or Fire Prevention Specialist?

You are not a fireman and you do not plan to volunteer to race into a burning building so, you ask: What does this have to do with me? Everything! Allow me to explain. In the complex world of work and, especially, in the complex and high-pressure world of automotive customer service it is essential that you consider how you would answer this important question. If you are currently working in the service business I'm sure that you know what I'm speaking about. It goes something like the scenario that follows.

> You go to work all pumped up and excited about what you hope to accomplish only to find out that by the end of the day you've never had the time to get around to your priorities. Instead, you've spent your day answering other people's questions, solving their problems, being distracted by this and that and you end the day feeling worn out, exhausted, and disappointed. When asked how your day went your answer is likely to sound something like this: "I'm exhausted, but I don't feel like I really accomplished anything important today. It seems that I've spent the entire time putting out other people's fires."

Without a clear vision of your goals and, therefore, your priorities *before* you start your day you are likely to get hopelessly sidetracked by the needs or wants of someone or something else. Without something to help you to refocus your efforts you are likely to give up your quest to complete your goals and fall into a constant pattern of putting out fires. This is a very common yet crucial difference between those that are successful and those that just put in their time. It is one of the critical differences between working smart and working hard.

The highly motivated, dedicated, and directed individual needs to realize that if he allows himself to slip into the role of spending too much time putting out fires that he is never going to have enough time to change things. It is not until he can fight against this tendency that he will be able to make changes so that fewer emergencies occur. Ultimately, it is the ability to fight against the urge to put out fires and to make changes to prevent fires that will make you successful.

The purpose of this analogy is to help you see that with the limited time and resources that all of us are faced with you can't do it all. Therefore, you need to make conscious decisions as to how to best use your limited resources. Do you want to leave things as they are and deal with the symptoms of the problems in the current system? Or, would it be better to redirect at least some of your time to improving the system so that you've reduced or eliminated the likelihood of the symptoms occurring? In the final analysis, your choice in this matter should be a well thought out and intentional one, not something left to chance.

Focusing Your Efforts and Taking Control of Your Time

We've talked about defining what matters to you personally and professionally. Once you know the reason why, you can tap into that for internal energy and motivation to keep you moving ahead even during the toughest times.

However, even with a large amount of internal drive it is common to find yourself in situations where you feel things have simply gotten out of control. With a lack of self-awareness and self-motivation you'd have major difficulties mustering up the energy to keep on pushing. But even with the highest degree of motivation, persistence, and the best motives it is impossible to do it all. Therefore, it is necessary to look at the more practical aspects of getting organized to help you with the nuts and bolts of your daily existence. Here is a simple three-step process that can help you organize anything and everything that you do.

Getting Organized: The Three-Step Process

No matter what types of tools and techniques you use to help you to get organized, the fundamentals underlying the process are the same. It is a simple three-step process. The first step is to identify all of those activities and responsibilities that you need to deal with. Once you have identified them all you need to quickly and efficiently prioritize them. That is, to determine which ones are *really* the most important to deal with right now. Finally, you need to organize them so that you can intentionally and consistently do them in order of importance and urgency.

Identifying

This first, and most basic step is the one that is often missed. In the process of being busy, hurried, and stressed it is difficult to stop for a moment to see what is really going on. In order to correctly identify all the activities and responsibilities that you need to deal with you must at some point do something very difficult—stop. That's right, you have to stop *doing* so that you can pull back from the situation and take a look at the big picture.

The idea here is to sit down and think about all of the tasks, jobs, and responsibilities that you have to deal with. The purpose is to help you to gain a better sense of the overall picture of all of the directions you are pulled in every day. The ultimate goal here is for you to improve your decision-making skills on what to do next and why. How can you possibly do that without taking the time to step back and know what you are really spending your time doing and why?

One of the simplest, yet effective, techniques for doing this is to sit down with a simple sheet (or pad) of paper and make a list. The goal is to list all of the things that you are supposed to do tomorrow. Not what you want to do tomorrow, but what you feel that you are expected to do tomorrow. This can be focused specifically on just those activities, job responsibilities, and deadlines that you know that you'll have to deal with at work.

THEORY INTO PRACTICE 17-5

CASE

Before you can effectively organize and prioritize what you do, you need to begin with a basic understanding of the activities and responsibilities that you have to deal with on a regular basis. An easy way to begin a personal planning process is to practice by looking at just one typical day in your busy life.

You decide

Take five to ten minutes and make an exhaustive list of all of the things that you will be doing tomorrow. This list should include several groups of items. It will surely include the basics like waking up, eating breakfast, showering, and so forth. It will include those things that others, your teachers, your parents, and/or your bosses expect you to do tomorrow. It will also hopefully allow for time for you to do the things that you personally want to do. Take the full time to push yourself to write down as many items as you possibly can to build the list. When it is completed review your list one more time to and add anything that you think you'll do tomorrow and making sure that you've addressed it in your list.

Stepping back and taking a really hard look at the variety of activities, deadlines, and other demands that are put on you in just one day should begin to give you some perspective of why you feel so tired and overwhelmed. As you look at your list are you surprised by how many things are on it? Are they all things that you expected? Are there some items on the list that you wish you could avoid or eliminate?

Taking a look at your days and, in the bigger sense, at your overall job and your life is an uncommon activity for most people. Yet, without consciously knowing what you're doing and why how is it possible to take control of your life? And, if you can't take control of your life, how can you expect to ever be happy during your life's unique journey? For this reason, this is the first and most important step in helping you to get control of your life and how you spend your most precious commodity, your time.

Prioritizing

Once you have some sense of what you are doing today, tomorrow, and beyond you need to think about what you are going to do with this new-found knowledge. It is not time, quite yet, to spring into action. There are a few more steps that you need to take first.

Before you begin to arm yourself with tools and techniques that will help you to manage all of the duties, assignments, and responsibilities that are thrown your way it is essential that you answer one simple question: Why am I here? This may sound too simple, but try it. The point in this simple exercise, whether it is related to your overall existence or to your responsibilities and goals at work, is critical to your ultimate success.

Until you know the answer to the why question you can't possibly be able to sort out what. That is, until you know what is important to you it will not be able to sort through the many things that come your way to determine which ones are priorities. Not until you are clear on your priorities will you be able to focus your best efforts on making sure that they always stay first and foremost in your mind, in your attention, and in your efforts. Finally, not until you make those issues and items foremost in your efforts will you be able to be sure that you are putting your best foot forward toward getting them done.

THEORY INTO PRACTICE 17-6

CASE

Before you can decide what to do you need to prioritize. The key question that you must answer to be able to prioritize is: What is most important? Please answer the following few questions based on your understanding of the way that your boss or your teacher would want you to answer.

You decide

Please answer the following:

1. What are the top three responsibilities that you have as an employee/student?
2. What are the three most important things that I am expected to do tomorrow in my job/class?
3. What are the top three factors upon which my success as an employee/student will be measured?
4. The answers that you have provided are from the perspective of your employer or teacher. Now please answer these same three questions again from your own personal perspective based on who you are and what you want to become.

Once you can see how you would identify what the most important items are and why they are important you now have the basic knowledge to prioritize your activities for an hour, a day, a career, and a lifetime. It is simply a matter of using this same simple concept and expanding its use in these other longer-term settings.

In our ever-accelerating world working faster just will not cut it. You need to be able to prioritize, to work smarter, if you want to succeed. Clearly identifying what is most important to you and to others is the only way to be sure that you put your best effort into what really matters.

Even if you had the luxury of an unlimited supply of time, you'd feel much better if you got the important things done and could sit back and be satisfied with your accomplishments. It is also likely that those who depend upon you (your boss, your teacher, your family, and friends) would express their pleasure that you had made it a priority in your life to meet their needs.

With our limitations of time, energy, and effort understanding how to prioritize is essential. No matter how hard you work you simply can't do it all. If you allow that to drag you down it can lead to frustration and disappointment. However, what you can do is focus your efforts into what is most important and, in doing so, accomplish most, if not all, of what is really essential. Your skill in prioritizing provides you the ability to manage your time and your efforts to your best advantage.

Organizing

It has become very common that we do not live, work, or think about one thing at a time. In our world it is so common that they (whoever they are) have invented a new word to describe dealing with this phenomenon. Do you know what it is? That's right—multitasking. Believe it or not, as common as this word is, it is a fairly recent addition to our language and our lives. However, it is, without a doubt, the way of today and the demand of the future.

Because we are constantly bombarded with input, questions, tasks, and concerns it is essential that we be able to keep track of all of them. At some point in our daily routine the combination of multiple ideas bouncing around in our heads along with those that we see and hear in the world around us make us reach the point where we can't absorb it all. Our brains help us to naturally filter out some of the inputs. It is our job, however, if we are intent on keeping our priorities in order and in mind to make sure that we don't forget about those things that are important to us.

We need to find tools to help us to develop a system for us to keep track of important ideas, important items, and important responsibilities. By tools I don't mean that you should go out and purchase the latest PDA, tablet PC, or other gadget. Although those appliances can be useful they are not, in and of themselves, the tools that we need to think about. The methods for keeping track can range from scraps of paper to sticky notes to pages from a legal tablet to a tablet PC—the most important thing to remember is that the recording tool is not what is important—the act of recording it so that we don't forget it is.

Multitasking
The ability to perform multiple activities at the same time.

Multitasking

Earlier in this chapter I introduced the work world that we live in as the age of **multitasking.** Very simply put, in today's world we cannot expect that we will be left alone to do one thing at a time in a calm, orderly, and totally focused fashion. In the automotive service business this is especially true. We can expect to be interrupted by phone, e-mail, and unplanned visitors that demand that we stop what we're doing and address their demands immediately. How can we do it all effectively? How can we get our priorities accomplished yet meet their demands? The answer is: we need to learn how to juggle.

Juggling is a great example of what we need to do every single day. We must keep our eye on multiple tasks and priorities (just like the 3, 4, or even 5 balls that the juggler keeps in the air at one time) if we want to be effective. We can't afford to focus on only one thing at a time and totally block out the others. If we do, the others are going to fall. When they fall everything else is out of balance and we're likely to drop them all. So, what are we to do? We must learn to multitask effectively. That is, we need to learn to be able to keep multiple projects and activities going simultaneously without losing sight of any one of them.

Chances are good that you already multitask very successfully. Do you watch TV while you're looking up things on your PC? Talk on your cell phone while you are listening to music? Carry on a conversation while you're walking down the hallway? How many of these are you able to do at one time? All of these are examples of your brain's ability to allow you to multitask. The key to success in multitasking is your ability to keep everything in focus, not forgetting about any of the balls that you have in the air. Using organizational tools like reminder notes, your trusty to-do list, or even a bookmark can help you to remember what you were doing, where you left off, and where you need to restart once this diversion is addressed so that you minimize lost time and effort when you are sidetracked by other priorities.

Procrastinating

Making the conscious decision to put something off until a later time is important in keeping your priorities in order. However, making decisions to put things off is very closely related to its very negative and productivity-killing cousin, **procrastination.** If you are to be effective in getting your work accomplished you need to carefully guard against procrastinating.

Procrastination
A consistent behavior of postponing or putting off tasks, activities, or responsibilities until a later time.

There is a subtle and very important difference between delaying action and procrastinating. You can delay action on an item due to a conscious decision that something else is a higher priority. However, procrastination is the act of putting things off habitually. That means time and time again you are faced with this task, objective, or goal and you decide to put it aside. Why? Is it because you don't want to do it, because you don't understand it, because it is unpleasant? Whichever of these is the case it is essential that you take the time to make sure that when you put something aside to deal with it later that you are doing it for the right reasons. The right reasons are only because you have something that is more important and more urgent to do first. Any other excuse is a justification to procrastinate.

Procrastinating takes time. Every time you go through your to-do list and decide not to deal with an item it takes time and energy. This little time robber may easily have taken you several times the total investment of time and energy that it would have taken to resolve the issue in wasted time thinking about how to justifying putting it off. That does not mean that you need to go to the other extreme and feel the need to deal with each item on your list one after another in exact order so that you don't waste time. You still have to prioritize your efforts and do what matters most first. This is simply a warning of the trap that you may catch yourself in if you're not totally honest with yourself.

SUMMARY

In this chapter we have discussed the importance of taking the time to stop and decide what is important before you act. Identifying your priorities both personally and professionally will help you be more efficient with your time. It will help you to be able to achieve the old adage work smarter, not harder and feel much more satisfied that you've accomplished things that you value.

Once you've had a chance to sit back to recognize and set your priorities, it is important to start working on the practical side of getting better organized to squeeze the most productive use out of your efforts. We have discussed some general principles and practices that will help you get started in thinking about how to set up a system that works for you to get better organized and get better control of your environment.

In the Chapter 18 we will take this process a step further. We hope that you now have a better idea of what you want to do and why it is important to become more organized. With all of that clear direction, organization, and drive we now need to figure out how to help you get the most out of your most precious commodity—your time!

PRACTICING THE PRINCIPLES

1. When there is simply too much to do and you're won't be able to get everything done you should
   a. find a new job.
   b. prioritize your actions.
   c. complain to your boss.
   d. work longer and harder.
2. You will feel more satisfied with the work that you do if you learn to
   a. identify and work to your strengths.
   b. learn to hide your weaknesses.
   c. work harder and longer.
   d. make believable excuses for your poor productivity.
3. Effectively multitasking means that you are able to
   a. do several things one thing at a time.
   b. do everything at once.
   c. work on several activities and keep them all straight.
   d. get several people to do your work for you.
4. If you want to be highly productive it is strongly suggested that you are able to
   a. identify and work to your strengths.
   b. get everything done immediately.
   c. be able to find others to do the things you don't want to do.
   d. prioritize and disorganize your efforts.
5. You'll feel much worse after a hard day's work if you've been
   a. working to your strengths and interests.
   b. working in a group that really cares.
   c. working in areas that are your weakest.
   d. given a promotion at the end of the day.
6. When trying to organize your activities you need to remember that
   a. there is only one best way to organize your activities.
   b. you need to find tools and methods that work best for you.
   c. it is important that you find tools that you will keep up to date.
   d. all of the above.
7. The three-step process to getting organized requires that you
   a. organize, prioritize, produce.
   b. identify, organize, list.
   c. identify, prioritize, organize.
   d. prioritize, chart, track progress.
8. Prioritizing is valuable because it helps you to
   a. put out more fires.
   b. go with the flow.
   c. do everybody else's work first.
   d. None of the above.
9. A common occurrence in today's world is the need to juggle more tasks, assignments, and responsibilities at the same time. The ability to do this effectively is called
   a. working smarter.
   b. multitasking.
   c. working harder.
   d. being overworked.
10. One important fact that you need to realize about your job and your life, and a major reason why you need to prioritize your actions, is
    a. you have to do it all.
    b. you'd better do it all.
    c. you can't do it all.
    d. none of the above.

CHAPTER 18

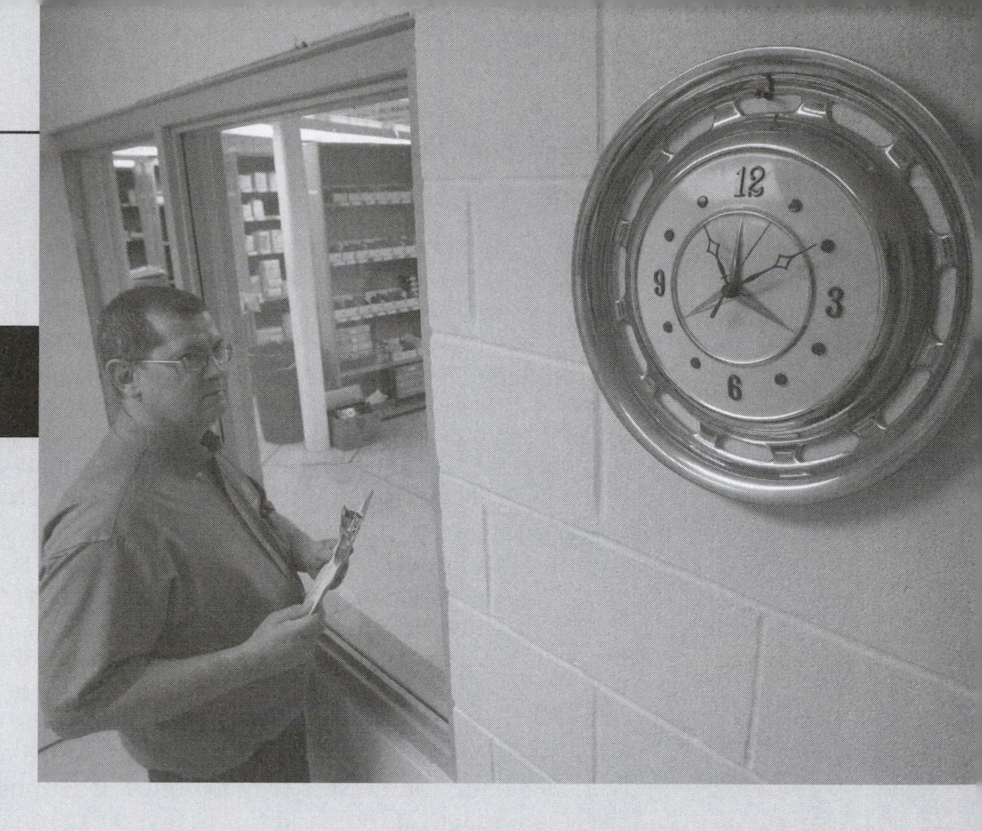

Organizing Tips and Tools

CHAPTER OBJECTIVES

- To identify techniques and tools that can help you to get organized
- To examine the importance of developing useful tools to track projects and performance
- To develop basic methods to consistently keep track of communications
- To organize the multiple activities that are a part of management

KEY TERMS

timeline
tracking
to-do list
archiving e-mail
phone log

Introduction

In this chapter we will discuss several important tips and techniques that enable you to become better at keeping track of all of the many tasks and responsibilities that you face every day as a manager. The ultimate goal is to become more efficient, more effective, and more satisfied with the results that you are able to consistently produce and the success you achieve as a result.

Is there anyone out there who really feels that life is easier, slower, more relaxed today than it was yesterday? Three months ago? Three years ago? Do you feel frazzled by all of the things that keep coming at you moment to moment? Do you see any end in sight? If you don't feel that the end of this hectic existence is in sight you are in good company—all managers deal with these same issues every day.

In recent years, as the pace of daily life and the responsibilities that go with it have continued to multiply there have been hundreds of articles, chapters, and self-help books written on the topic of organization and time management. When people are questioned about the thing in their life that they lack the most it is not money, it is time. In this chapter you will find some practical tools and tips that you can use daily to get the most out of your most precious commodity—time.

Sorting Your Workload

A very simple technique for organizing your activities, whether it is something as simple as today's mail or e-mail or as complicated as the many projects that you have been given is to develop a consistent practice of assigning them a value right away. At first glance you know whether a letter or a project is critically important or not worth your time. However, it is common practice to put off making the key decision to assign everything a priority. An easy way to do this is to organize your work into four piles, or lists. You can choose which works better for you in your work environment, but the key part is to do it, do it now, and commit to do it always.

All of your work fits into four categories: (1) items of top importance and urgency, (2) routine items of importance, (3) low priority assignments/tasks, (4) trash. The key is to quickly identify each item at first contact and then deal with it accordingly. You need to become disciplined enough to act just like an umpire in baseball. You cannot afford to hesitate—it's taking up your valuable time and energy. Now that you have started to categorize things at first sight let us briefly review how you will deal with your newly organized workload.

If you have any aspirations for a long and successful career you can't afford to ignore the group 1 items for very long. The group 2 items, although they will not have as rapid an effect on your career, are a foundational part of your job responsibilities and probably are those items that you will spend most of your day working with and on.

Group 3 items are those that you have decided: I will get around to it if time permits. They do not command your immediate attention or resources because they are of low value. However, they should be put somewhere where you can easily access them as their priority could change at any time. For example, if the boss receives a call from a colleague who is upset about that group 3 e-mail that you have not replied to it will likely make the leap to today's group 1 list.

Finally, there is the fourth group—items that should go directly to the trash and not be considered any further. This is the daily spam, junk mail, and other clutter that gets in the way of your ability to be productive and successful. Your best strategy is to identify it quickly and deal with it once and forever by getting it out of sight and out of mind.

Dealing with Routine Tasks

One way that you can reduce lost time is to handle routine tasks, like paperwork, only once. When you open the mail or receive an internal notice or phone call that requires your thoughts and your attention be sure to ask yourself: How long will it take to handle this now and forever? If it is something that you can quickly handle now why put it aside to have to deal with it again at a later date? Which choice is the best use of your time, spending five minutes now or spending a minute or two now to decide that you will deal with it later and then an additional five minutes to re-familiarize yourself with the issue later and finally address it?

You can save yourself time by realizing that as soon as you pick up those small tasks, assignments, or decisions that it is probably best not to procrastinate but rather to get closure on them right now, once and forever. In his book *How to Get Control of Your Time and Your Life* Alan Lakein strongly urges that whenever possible you handle paperwork only once (Lakein, 1973). However, as with everything else we have discussed, you must maintain a balanced approach to what you do. If you allow yourself to get distracted from your priorities doing this busy work too much of the time the end result will be that you will be busy, get much done, but fail to get the important work accomplished. Failure to get to and accomplish the true priorities is a recipe for disaster.

Dealing with the Big One

Although I am not sure who the original author was of this great piece of philosophy and management wisdom, I believe that at one time or another we have all heard the following riddle:

Q.: How do you eat an elephant?
A.: Simple. You eat an elephant the same way that you eat a hamburger, one bite at a time!

This simple piece of wisdom is the key to accomplishing those overwhelmingly large, complex, and time-consuming assignments that we all encounter regularly. Simply put, we need to learn to break them down into bite size chunks that we can deal with within the time available in our days and weeks. In this way we can make slow but steady progress toward ultimate, and timely, completion of the overall task.

The advice above makes it all sound simple. But it isn't. It requires careful planning, organizing, and the skill to keep this task somewhere on your radar so that working on it is not postponed and/or forgotten. One of the most common reasons why the big ones do not get accomplished on time is that those involved waited too long to get started. The excuse is that they simply did not have a big enough block of time to dig into something so complex.

There are several key components to attacking and completing these large tasks in a timely and efficient manner. You must have an organized plan to

Timeline

A list of important events and tasks of a large project or process organized in chronological order.

analyze the whole project and break it down into reasonably sized chunks. Once you have identified the pieces, you must develop a **timeline** that prioritizes those chunks. Then you must be sure to prioritize doing those tasks within the project that require more lead time or need to be done prior to other steps. Otherwise further progress down the line will come to a halt. Finally, you must take great care to identify those tasks that require the help of people or other resources outside of your area and, as a result, allow more lead time in your timeline so they can be completed.

Generally the best way to make a working plan to address major assignments is to do a timeline first. The project timeline in Figure 18-1 can be as simple as putting a list of the smaller tasks on a to-do list with deadline dates for each one. The task could also be more complex, requiring you to chart the project and/or even use computer-based project planning software to keep track of events, deadlines, and overall progress.

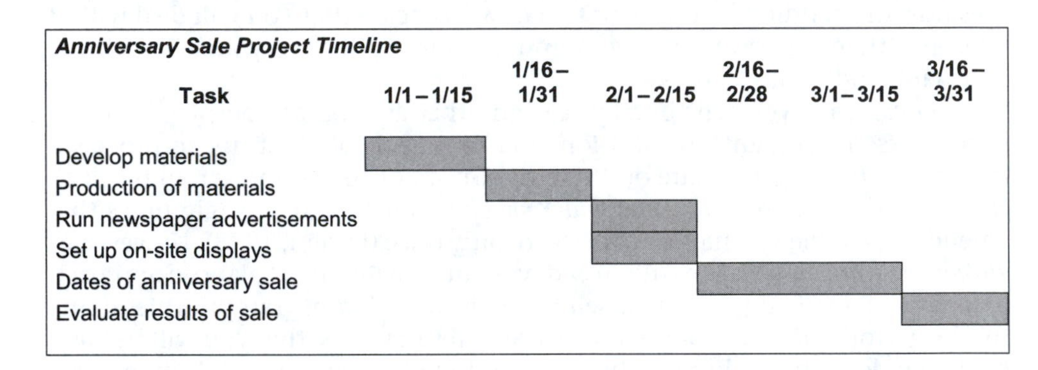

Figure 18-1 Project timeline

As situations arise that require a timeline for large and complex activities you need to make sure that you have it available and access it regularly to track your progress. This may require that you provide a visible spot in your office area that you reserve to place your chart (on the wall?) and your to-do list (right next to your computer on your desk?) so that you cannot forget about them and overlook them. Make access to them convenient and inescapable.

As is the case with any tools, they need to be ones that you feel comfortable with and, therefore, you are willing and likely to use on a regular basis. Failure to use some tools or methods to break down the biggest tasks into manageable parts is not a viable option. Time and again it has been proven in a variety of settings that failure to break down complex and time-consuming projects and develop a detailed plan of action results in missed deadlines and severe consequences.

Tracking Tools

The world that you live in requires you to multitask. Especially in the work world, you can expect to be doing one thing, thinking about the other five you need to do, and then get interrupted 10 times by phone calls, questions, or other distractions. How can you keep all of this in your head? Should you be able to?

While you are thinking about organizing why not give your brain a break? It is totally unreasonable—and unnecessary—for you to be expected to keep juggling all of your ideas, tasks, deadlines, and so on in your head and keep them all straight! When was the last time that you honestly felt that saying "I forgot" was enough reason for your boss or a loved one? Therefore, the best rule of thumb for your actions should be: *If you cannot afford to forget it, you cannot afford not to write it down!*

There is a wide range of tools that are readily available to help you with **tracking** minor events that you cannot afford to forget. Everything from shreds of notebook paper to more formal tools like notepads, microcassette recorders, PDAs, and PCs. Jotting things down is essential for ensuring that important information is not lost. However, just as in the case with all of the other tools and tips we have talked about, you have to remember that they are just tools. You do not want to become the person who walks in the door at night and empties out his pockets full of wadded up notes, cards, shreds of paper, and a PDA. You need to develop a system that works for you and you need to try to keep it simple and consistent.

Tracking
Maintaining a constant and consistent record of events/activities and progress toward their completion.

Tracking Communications

The majority of communication today is done via e-mail and telephone. If you are to be effective in keeping track of where you stand on your numerous assignments it is essential that you able to maintain a simple and easy history of the communications with others that affect those projects.

The To-Do List The simplest form for keeping all of your activities and priorities in front of you is to build and maintain a **to-do list.** It does not really matter whether you keep this on your PC, your PDA, or in a notebook. Again, what matters is *that* you keep track of everything, not *what* you keep track on!

To-Do List
A record of all outstanding tasks and responsibilities.

One of the most important factors in deciding on how you are going to set up your to-do list is easy access. The list needs to be somewhere that is convenient and readily available to you at all, or almost all, times. It is intended to be your steady reminder to keep you from forgetting any of the many responsibilities, assignments, and deadlines that you have. If it is to serve this function it must, first and foremost, be available.

A word of caution is important here. There are people who can progress from being disorganized and unable to complete tasks on time to becoming so well organized that they do not have time to complete tasks. That is, they become so involved in making and maintaining lists that they do not have any time left to do productive work. This can often happen when they use the newest, best, and greatest tool to keep track—and have to spend great amounts of their time becoming good at using the appliance. Others run into this same problem because, in their desire to always have the list available, they decide to maintain multiple lists—one on the office computer, one on the PDA, one in the planner, one on the home PC, one on the cell phone, and so on. By doing this the result is that they have four or five lists that never agree. Thus, they spend huge amounts of time trying to update the other four lists every time they change the fifth one.

With these warnings in mind, there is no one magic bullet to keeping a to-do list that works for everybody. You need to find and build a system that works best for you with these things in mind. My suggestion is that you keep it as simple as you can so that you do not spend any more time building it and maintaining it than is required but that you spend enough time to make sure that it is complete and current and works for you.

The essential characteristics of a to-do list are simple. Along with being user friendly, the list needs to be a complete, listing of all of the tasks, responsibilities, and deadlines that you need to accomplish. The list needs to not only indicate what needs to be done; it also needs to indicate when it should be finished. In its simplest form it can be a page or two of one-line entries on a yellow pad that have the following headings: date assigned, assignment, due date (Figure 18-2). An effective to-do list should be able to quickly remind you of the answers to the question: What do I need to do and by when to accomplish my goal and/or meet my deadline? All of the details surrounding who assigned it to you, the complexity of the task, and other supporting information can and may be recorded as a part of your efforts to accomplish your goal, but that is too much information to include on the to-do list.

To do list for: ________		*Week of:* ________	
Date Assigned	**Task**	**Deadline**	**Date Completed**

Figure 18-2 To-do list

Some to-do items may be very long, involved, and complex activities or projects. Because of their complexity you might not feel comfortable with listing them as a one-line entry on your list. You may be concerned that you will have trouble keeping track of exactly where you stand on an important and complex assignment. When you find this to be the case, and in an effort to break those overwhelming tasks down into smaller bits, you may find that subdividing the single big assignment down into smaller sub goals and sub to-do items works better for you. This technique is commonly used to help keep a better handle on these assignments. However, remember to keep in mind that if you start to spend more time breaking down your to-do list into smaller and smaller items that you will be spending increased time babysitting your to-do list and less time getting your work done—so be careful. The purpose of the to-do list is to be a simple, usable reminder tool that keeps you on track.

Now that you have determined a simple but usable format that works for you, the last and most important rule is that you need to review your list on a regular basis and update it. No to-do list is effective if you never use it! It is recommended that you review your to-do list daily and revise it at least once per week. Many who use this important organizational tool make sure that it is easily within sight and reach and will start each day by glancing down and reviewing their to-do list. This can be valuable as a means of keeping priorities straight before heading into the day's activities.

Another useful suggestion for maximizing the value of the to-do list is to consider setting aside a small amount of time at the end of each week, just before you leave for the weekend to review and rewrite your to-do list. This can become a powerful tool in reviewing what you have accomplished during the past week as you can eliminate those tasks and goals that you have completed. In addition, by writing down all of your open items (or at least reading them all) it helps to remind you about those items that may have slipped your mind during the past week and to which you need to recommit your time and efforts to make sure that they get done correctly and on time.

Here are a few final suggestions on the use of your to-do list. I highly suggest that you follow these four simple rules in working with your list, at least from the start if you are new at it. Once you get comfortable with your list you can establish your own rhythm, but these pointers should help you to get off to a good start

1. Always keep your to-do list *within reach.*
2. *Update* your to-do list *constantly*—whenever you have things to add, to modify, or to mark as completed.
3. Review your to-do list *every* day, preferably first thing at the start of your work day.
4. Rewrite or revise your to-do list at least *once a week*, preferably as your last act as you close down for the weekend or first thing Monday morning.

Theory into Practice 18-1

CASE

We have discussed the importance of the to-do list as a tool for organizing your efforts. Your assignment is going to be to make a personal to-do list.

You decide

Take out a blank sheet of paper and create a to-do list form. Remember that the way that you set up and structure your to-do list (layout, number of headings, and so on) is totally up to you. It can be as detailed or as simple as fits your needs. What is important is that will be able to understand and use it on a regular basis. Now finish the assignment by listing the ten most important items that you need to accomplish this week on your new to-do list form.

Tracking and Archiving E-Mail E-mail has become the most widely used method for quick communication and so tracking and **archiving e-mail** communications is an absolute necessity. Fortunately, most e-mail host programs provide a method for organizing and storing e-mails. If you do not take the time to organize your e-mails you will pay dearly with lost e-mails and lost time trying to find them when you need them. Failure to take the time to do so is one of those gifts that keeps on giving as time and again you frantically search for that essential message that you know is there . . . somewhere.

Archiving E-Mail
Storing past e-mails as permanent records so that they can be recalled.

Organizing e-mails into subfolders requires the same logic and skills that you've used before organizing your drawers and file cabinets. In effect, it is a digital filing cabinet system that is modeled after the file folders in a physical file cabinet. Even though this is a simple and familiar task, just like organizing physical file cabinets, it requires that you take the time to set up a logical set of file folders that you can use to organize and retrieve all of your important messages.

Phone Log

A basic organizational tool that lists all incoming or outgoing phone calls to maintain a constant record and enables tracking of those conversations and their content.

Phone Log Tracking telephone conversations is just as important. This, however, requires that you develop and maintain some sort of logging method of your own. For tracking important phone calls I suggest that writing it down on a scrap of paper or keeping it in your head may just not be consistent enough. For that reason, and especially if you are in a situation where you receive a volume of phone calls daily from a variety of people you may consider the idea of building and maintaining a **phone log.** A phone log is a list in which you immediately record the basic information of every phone contact. Information such as date, time, name and number of caller, brief description of message, and then a block to record your comments or resolution of the request is detailed enough. By maintaining them in a notebook it will allow you, in similar fashion to your e-mail folder system, to go back and reconstruct the history of communications that have occurred in an important situation.

My suggestion is that you keep the log as simple as possible, but that you seriously consider keeping one. Figure 18-3 shows a sample of a basic format that you might consider in setting up your own phone log.

PHONE LOG FOR **Name** ____________________

Date	Time	Caller Name	Phone Number	Message	Notes
3/4/06	8:30	Roger Edwards	(888)254-1234	Would like to schedule appt. for 30K	C/B 9:20 Scheduled

Figure 18-3 Phone log

Organizing Your Surroundings

We have discussed organizing your efforts, but what about your surroundings? Even though it is not necessary to be a neat freak to be successful it is far less likely that you will be able to produce consistent results amidst disorganization and chaos. We have all experienced the co-worker who has piles and piles everywhere. Obviously he is very busy. But as you think about it further, is this person busier getting work done, or finding where he left things among those piles? He has lots of information, yet if you try to ask for a simple answer in most cases you will probably get an answer such as "I will have to get back to you on that. I have a file on it somewhere. I will just have to find it first." That is called lost effort. Lost effort saps our time for productive effort. It makes us work harder, rather than smarter.

Organization, like a to-do list, is a personal thing. It is just as important that it works for you as it is that things are organized. The fact remains, however, that without some consistent organization and maintenance of your work area you are likely to fall into the same trap as the folks mentioned earlier. Do not let it happen.

Determine what the right or best place is for all of the tools that you use regularly. This will reduce lost time because you know where they are and that they are accessible to you at a moment's notice. This is one of the best time savers that you can ever find—and it's free.

Just as important as getting things in their right place is developing the habit of keeping them there. It will save you having to look for it when it is not where you thought you put it. This is simply a matter of having a plan and sticking to it so that looking for it does not waste your most precious and scarce commodity, your time.

Finally, you need to remember that organizational tools are simply tools. They are not the reason why you work or the goal of your job. Therefore, you need to keep them in perspective and not get obsessed with organization. Yet, if you take a reasonable amount of care to get organized, stay organized, and operate in this mode for a while you will see that you reduce lost effort and frustration. You will find that you have recovered a significant amount of your previously non-productive time.

SUMMARY

Planning in its essence is an intentional and consistent effort to identify, prioritize, and organize those things that you do to maximize your results. It is through this simple process of taking a step back and looking at the big picture and then consciously determining what you need to do and in what order that you can improve your productivity. You need to develop a plan of action and consistently work that plan.

You need to find the methods that are comfortable to you so that you are willing and able to commit to using them on a regular basis. One of the simplest, yet most effective, organizational tools is the to-do list. Regular use of this tool can ensure that you keep on track and are better able to remember your many activities.

A basic rule that can help you to be more productive is to handle paperwork and small projects only one time whenever possible. This saves time. On the other end of the spectrum, dealing with the big ones, the really large and complex projects, requires a completely different strategy. They should be broken down into smaller bite size chunks and then set up on a timeline to move from activity to activity through the project in an organized fashion that will assure timely completion.

A word of warning. Although organizing your activities and reviewing your lists regularly are important to improving your productivity, becoming obsessed with the lists can become counterproductive. The lists and charts are not your goal. Your goal is to regularly and consistently get your work done well and on time. The lists and charts are simply organizing tools. Like any other tools you use them when you need them. Don't play with them. By that, I mean that if you get caught up in writing, and rewriting, and revising your to-do list daily just because it looks a bit messy, you may be using up time that you could be using for better value—making progress in completing items on the list!

PRACTICING THE PRINCIPLES

1. One of the most effective ways to handle small tasks like mail is to
   a. handle it and deal with it only once.
   b. ignore it until it is too late.
   c. read it, log it in, and then deal with it later.
   d. none of the above.
2. A common basic tool to organize your activities is a
   a. flowchart.
   b. timeline.
   c. to-do list.
   d. all of the above.
3. One of the biggest reasons why big projects don't get done on time is
   a. starting on them too early
   b. notifying outside partners far in advance
   c. not breaking the project down into small parts
   d. they are impossible to get done
4. A to-do list
   a. must be in a specific format.
   b. has to have at least 8 columns and be on special forms.
   c. needs to list every single thing that you do.
   d. none of the above.
5. The most basic form of a to-do list should include what information?
   a. date assigned, task, date due.
   b. date assigned, priority, task, due date, completion date, comments.
   c. whatever information you want it to have.
   d. time, date, location, task.
6. A useful tool to help you to keep track of a string of phone conversations and messages is a
   a. road map.
   b. phone log.
   c. to-do list.
   d. project tracking report.
7. A simple tool for keeping track of all of your activities and deadlines is a
   a. calendar.
   b. to-do list.
   c. critical path timeline.
   d. detailed financial analysis.
8. Date, time, name, phone number, and brief message are the basic pieces of information that can be found on a
   a. telephone information system.
   b. to-do list.
   c. project tracking timeline.
   d. phone log.
9. The basic information on an effective to-do list
   a. should be rewritten daily.
   b. should be reviewed quarterly
   c. should be written down and then forgotten.
   d. should be reviewed daily.
10. Sitting down and simply listing all of the things you have to do helps you to
    a. make a grocery list.
    b. procrastinate from having to do them.
    c. have a false sense of accomplishment.
    d. identify what you need to do.

REFERENCE

Lakein, A., *How to Get Control of Your Time and Your Life* (New York: David McKay Co., 1973)

SECTION

6

CUSTOMER RELATIONS

Even if an organization has the best location, the best price, and the best product it is doomed to failure in the long term if it doesn't understand and respect the value of its customers. The number-one responsibility of any automotive service operation is not fixing cars, it is fixing the customers. Building and maintaining a strong base of customers is one of the best ways to assure the long-term success of any company. Developing these positive relationships so customers become vocal advocates and your best advertisements in the community is one of the best strategies for any service organization.

CHAPTER

19

The Value of Satisfied Customers

CHAPTER OBJECTIVES

- To appraise the effect that satisfied and dissatisfied customers have on business success
- To examine the high cost of attracting new customers
- To assess the benefits of return and repeat customers on business
- To identify some of the fundamental traits of human behavior

KEY TERMS

customer satisfaction
opportunist
silent majority
11/4 rule
C.S.I.
word-of-mouth advertising

Introduction

Each of us is bombarded every day in every direction that we look by ads, promotions, commercials, and billboards. Why? The reason is clear. No company, even with the best product or service, can survive without enough customers. Those companies that have the longest and most consistent track record of performance have learned that this must be taken one step further; no company can survive without enough loyal customers. They all know that even if they have the best product that people have to know about it before they will buy it. Even when customers know about a great product they must feel good about the company that provides it. Thus, smart business people know that their survival hinges on their ability to attract and retain customers.

This chapter is a brief overview of the importance of satisfied customers to the health of any organization. Further, in it we will discuss some general principles that you should keep in mind to guide your efforts to build and maintain a growing base of your most valued commodity, return customers.

Customer Orientation

Customer Satisfaction

The intentional practice of meeting or exceeding customer expectations.

Opportunist

A person who intentionally takes advantage of a situation.

Very simply put, **customer satisfaction** is the key to repeat sales. This seems obvious. None of us chooses to do business with a company that we do not trust, that we believe has tried to take advantage of us, or has taken the opportunity to gouge us when they could by charging too much. Yet, each of us continues to experience situations like this in our daily lives. Why?

Whether it is intentional or due to ignorance, there will always be companies that are blinded by the opportunity to take advantage of a situation for immediate gain. These companies are called **opportunists.** After all, they are in business to make a profit. The short-term benefits of being an opportunist go right to the company's bottom line. Who can blame them? The answer to that question is: you can, we can, and, ultimately, we do. Any of us may be guilty of dealing with a particular company in spite of these bad business practices but that only holds true when we feel that we have no other choice.

When a vendor is the only source of a product or service that we strongly desire we will go counter to our best judgment and deal with them in spite of their practices. We will pay the higher price and/or forego the security that they will treat us fairly if a problem occurs. We are willing to take the risk. However, as soon as we find ourselves in the position of having a choice to deal with a more reputable vendor that we feel will treat us fairly we will switch. That is the ultimate consequence that the opportunistic company will eventually pay.

It is for this reason that you can easily name several companies that have risen meteorically to great fame and fortune and then, just as quickly, plunged into non-existence. They took advantage of the situation on the short term and then paid the ultimate price in the long term. That is certainly the last business practice anyone should follow.

It is a far better long-term investment to be very aware and sensitive to customer perceptions so as not to, even unintentionally, build the reputation as an opportunist. The way to steady, long-term success is through striving intentionally in everything that you do to build and maintain customer trust, customer satisfaction, and, thus, customer loyalty. It is the repeat customers and the personal testimonies and free word-of-mouth advertising that they will provide for you every day that will be the biggest boon to your ultimate success.

The Silent Majority and the 11/4 Rule

There have been numerous studies done, reports generated, and articles printed that report a variety of data about the importance of satisfied customers. Although the numbers cited vary, a common thread in all of them is that dissatisfied customers are much more outspoken about talking about their bad experience than satisfied customers are about doing the same. As a result, one unhappy customer has a much greater affect on your company than one satisfied customer does. How does this affect me? Why does this matter? Let us take a closer look.

In the quest to continue to build a greater and greater body of satisfied customers conventional logic indicates that if your company has 25 percent customer complaints that they are doing a good job. After all, that means that they are satisfying 75 percent of the customers and, therefore, as long as they can get three out of four coming back and telling all of their friends to do the same the company will continue strong growth. Or will it? Unfortunately this logic is a bit too simplistic and fails to take into account two big common principles of customer behavior: the silent majority and the 11/4 rule.

Silent Majority

A title given to the large group that, although they are the largest in number, often do not openly and actively express their opinion.

First of all, let us talk about the impact of the **silent majority**. Just because only one out of four customers complains does not indicate that three out of four are satisfied. It only indicates that only one out of four is angry enough to take direct action and complain. Where do the other three really stand? Are they very satisfied, satisfied, somewhat dissatisfied, or just too busy or angry to even bother to complain? The problem is that you really do not know the answer. Therefore, it is important that you not assume too much simply from the level of vocal complaints from customers. It is typically true that the majority of dissatisfied customers do not complain, they simply vote with their feet. That is, they choose to say nothing but decide then and there to do all future business elsewhere. In addition they are likely to tell their friends why they changed to another service shop—and encourage them to do likewise. You may wonder what you can do about this situation. We will look at ways to obtain that information in the section on Measuring Customer Satisfaction C.S.I. (Customer Satisfaction Index).

11/4 Rule

Dissatisfied customers will tell 11 others about their bad experience, whereas satisfied customers will only tell four others about their good experience.

The second important principle that you need to keep in mind is the **11/4 rule.** The 11/4 rule of customer satisfaction is

> A dissatisfied customer will tell 11 others about their bad experience while a satisfied customer will tell four others about their good experience.

Using the 11/4 rule the impact of just one dissatisfied customer is amplified. A dissatisfied customer is much more likely to speak out and tell more people about his bad experience than a happy customer will do regarding her good experience. As a result, it only takes a very small percentage of vocal, dissatisfied customers to have a major negative impact on your public image and on the overall perception of your organization.

Taking both of these principles into account let us take a look at a scenario that demonstrates how these two principles work and why you need to take them into account when you try to assess where you stand with customer satisfaction.

> A&B Service does not have any formal process in place to measure their customer attitudes but has depended for years on their informal measurement of the number of complaint calls that they have received during a month to indicate how they are really doing. Based on their last three months business

and the number of complaint calls that they have received they feel confident that they are satisfying 80 percent of their customers. Here is the data for the past 3 months

Automobiles serviced = 100
Customer complaints/returns to shop = 20
Satisfied customers = 80 (80%)

In addition to that information, they have received five letters or calls from customers thanking them for their great service. Based on this information they believe that they are doing a great job by satisfying 80 percent of their customers. Or are they?

The logic that A&B is using is based on some assumptions. These assumptions are very likely to be faulty. Since they have not directly asked all of their customers how they really feel they are assuming that if customers did not complain that they are happy. This is not a valid assumption. Based on the principle of the silent majority we know that most dissatisfied customers will not do anything except quietly go away and never come back. Therefore, how many out of those 80 percent who did not complain are really happy? Somewhat happy? Somewhat dissatisfied? Or, just too angry and/or too busy to complain but planning to go elsewhere? The answer is that we do not know.

Taking into consideration the rule of the silent majority A&B Service may have some serious customer relations problems to worry about. Based on the limited information that is available A&B Service believes that they are satisfying 80 percent of their customers. However, since they have not asked each of the 80 customers that did not complain whether or not they are really satisfied. Therefore, they really can not be sure that their estimates are accurate. All that they are really sure of is that at least 5 percent of their customers are very satisfied (the ones who wrote letters). Therefore, their true customer satisfaction percentage could range anywhere from 5 percent to 80 percent. That is a very wide range of uncertainty. Without better information A&B Service may be losing a great number of customers each month and by the time that they figure it out they may be out of business.

Let us now explore some of the effects that the 11/4 rule can have on the overall customer satisfaction of A&B service in this case. They are fortunate that they know that at least five of their customers are vocal advocates (the letter writers). Based on the 11/4 rule they know that those five customers will each tell four friends about their satisfaction with A&B Service and encourage them to go there for service. That accounts for twenty new potential customers for A&B Service. On the surface, it would sound like they just found a source to replace the twenty dissatisfied customers that they lost last month. Unfortunately, that is only half of the 11/4 rule. Let us look at the other half.

A&B Service has twenty customers that are dissatisfied. It is possible that if they do nothing to follow-up with those dissatisfied customers and make their best effort to turn most of them into satisfied customers they can have a major negative impact on the company's future business. Using the 11/4 rule, if all twenty of those customers are very dissatisfied and they each tell eleven friends about their poor service experience they will have told two hundred and twenty customers (more than two times A&B's monthly total customer base) about their problems and encouraged them to shop elsewhere for service work.

A&B Service believes that they are satisfying 80 percent of their customers, a sound foundation for the future of their business operations. However, when you consider the full impact of the 11/4 rule in the above example, in the worst case scenario A&B Service may have gained twenty new customers through positive word-of-mouth and then lost two hundred and twenty potential customers due to negative word-of-mouth. A net loss of two times their total monthly customer base (−200 customers) in one month's time.

The potential impact of A&B Service's uncertainty about their true customer satisfaction rate may be the cause of some serious future problems. Their lack of certainty about how many of the 80 percent that did not complain has left them with a false sense of security. Further, the potential negative affect that the 20 percent that complained may have on future business is far greater than A&B has ever considered.

Measuring Customer Satisfaction

As the previous section clearly indicates, unless you actively seek out the information to be sure how your customers feel you will have to manage by best guesses. This is especially important in trying to get a true pulse on the silent majority, who are most likely to neither praise or complain but, since they are such a large group, will have a significant impact on your long-term success or failure. So, what should you do?

In today's competitive marketplace and with stakes this high you must ask the question. Satisfied customers are the lifeblood of your organization and you need to *know* that they are satisfied. Further, you need to know if and when they are even mildly dissatisfied. You need to have this data to inform your future decisions so that you can be sure you are satisfying as many customers as possible. You need to know your true Customer Satisfaction Index (**C.S.I.**).

C.S.I.
Customer Satisfaction Index is a formal measure of the percentage of customers that are satisfied with their service or sales experience.

Whether you are in a dealership, a chain store, or a small local repair shop, C.S.I. is a common measure that just about every company with an eye for the future is concerned about, measures, and uses as a key performance indicator. Although there are many ways to collect and measure this data the results gained from obtaining customer feedback are a valuable management tool. The key is to intentionally and consistently ask all of your customers about their service experience.

C.S.I. surveying is commonly done via a paper and pencil survey or an online survey to all service customers. This may vary from a survey handed to the customer at the time of pickup from service, left in the car for them to mail back in, or a survey mailed to (or e-mailed to) all owners several days after service. Although the information obtained is valuable, one shortcoming of the mail or e-mail method is that many customers fail to take the time to respond. This still allows for a silent group that may be either satisfied or dissatisfied.

In an attempt to reduce this non-response group, some organizations have made the additional commitment to conducting live telephone surveys of their customers. Using this method has several benefits. It not only reduces the number of non-respondents, it also provides immediate feedback to the organization about any problems or questions. This immediate feedback gives the company the opportunity to respond immediately and resolve the problem. A quick and decisive response from the company is far more likely to turn a negative situation into a positive one. The ability and willingness to fix a problem quickly can turn a potential vocal critic into a strong advocate.

Real World Application

One of the most telling experiences that I have had in my industry experience was the positive impact of actively striving for satisfied customers. As the service director in a large metropolitan dealership I was charged with the long-term and sustained growth of the operation. When our manufacturer came out with a program that rewarded and acknowledged dealership service excellence, a key required component of that award was our performance on the monthly C.S.I. (customer satisfaction) surveys.

Trying to stay one step ahead of the competition we decided that rather than being reactive and responding to the customer survey results we would make an investment in an early detection system by hiring a customer relations specialist. The idea was to have this person call 100 percent of all customers three days after their cars left our service department. Her mission was to find out if they were satisfied. If they had a problem or a question she was to immediately notify me so that we were able to immediately make arrangements to resolve their concerns.

Our new customer relations specialist, Audrey, was a retiree who had a great bedside manner and was very satisfied to be able to do this part-time work from the dealership and even from her home. As such, we expected good results. However, the results of this initiative far exceeded our wildest dreams. Not only were we able to identify and resolve complaints more effectively, we actually created a new customer climate.

As a result of this personal touch, our customers no longer had any concerns about whether or not we really cared. They knew that we cared. They knew that we were going to be calling. They looked forward to the regular call from Audrey to check up on them. This was clearly demonstrated when she was unexpectedly off ill for a week and I started receiving customer calls asking if she was OK. We had raised the level of our organization in the eyes of our customers from simply being a company that fixed cars to one that cared about their needs.

Prior to this initiative we had always been an above-average dealership in the market. In fact, we had finished second in the previous year's district rankings in customer satisfaction. The ultimate result of this was that the dealership was able to set new standards as the highest in C.S.I. rating in the district, in the entire zone, and we were nationally recognized as having one of the highest C.S.I. ratings for large dealerships in the nation. I firmly believe that this one activity was instrumental in helping us to earn the corporate service excellence award six years in a row.

The results went far beyond simply receiving a plaque. We saw a substantial positive affect on our bottom line as a result of our customer satisfaction work. We experienced significant and sustained growth of the sales and profitability of the service department. As the word spread, vehicle sales increased based on our reputation. Finally, we had a noticeable increase in employees from our competition actively seeking to come and work for us.

Not every company has the resources to invest in expensive customer surveying activities. The most important factor, however, is that no company can afford to ignore the importance of doing what they can to obtain this rich and essential information. If you want to be successful you need to actively solicit responses from every customer, to obtain specific data on every service transaction, and to provide the company an opportunity to take immediate corrective actions. The data itself is valuable as a management tool to help you know, for sure, what your true percentage of satisfied customers is.

The satisfaction statistics, although important, are not the most important benefit. The greatest long-term benefit is providing you the opportunity to make a rapid response in identifying and addressing the problems of the few dissatisfied customers that you have. It is through this proactive approach that you are most likely to be able to save those customers and turn them into satisfied customers rather than quietly allowing them to become part of the group that tell 11 friends about their bad service experience.

The High Cost of Cultivating New Customers

One of the reasons why taking care of your existing customers is so important is simple economics. It is very expensive to cultivate and attract new customers. In order to attract one new customer it is necessary that you take planned (and expensive) actions to go out and compete with the entire market for that customer's attention, their consideration, their business, and, most of all, their loyalty. Every customer is constantly bombarded with media trying to get his or her attention. Competing for a new customer in this open market means that you have to make a very large investment just to be recognized as one of the potential players.

Advertising costs are exceedingly high. Whether it is television, radio, newspaper, direct mailers, posters, or billboards, there is no guarantee of the return on your investment. You have no way to know how many responses you will get. Remember, that at the same time you are advertising to attract these new customers everyone else in the market is also advertising to get them. The more you advertise and start to attract new customers the more the others will advertise to try to win them back, and so forth and so on. It would be a lot simpler to invest just a few more minutes of your time and energy in taking care of the customers that you already have.

You must remember that automotive service is not high on most people's list as a fun activity. They only come to you when they have a need. Even with your extended hours, your polite employees, your exceptional service, it is at best a major inconvenience for a customer to arrange their day to bring the car in for service. As a result, just about any customer will do anything within reason to minimize this inconvenience. One of the best ways to minimize inconvenience is to go with a sure thing. Going somewhere that they know will do the job right the first time for a fair price. The best source for that is to continue to deal with people who have proven that they can consistently meet those standards. As a result, all of the advertising in the world is highly unlikely to pry away a good and very satisfied customer from you no matter what claims the competition makes.

The Low Cost of Repeat Business

Attracting new customers is an expensive proposition and there is not an unlimited supply of new customers. Remember the situation that A&B Service found themselves in earlier in this chapter? If you continue to lose current customers and, therefore, have to constantly work to attract a large number of new ones to replace them you will ultimately run out of potential new customers. No market has an unlimited number of customers.

With the high cost of attracting new customers it makes good business sense to retain all of the current customers possible. Then you will have to make a much smaller investment in advertising to attract new customers. This also makes it likely that if you are successful in your advertising you will not only replace the small number of current customers that you have lost, you will end up with a net gain in total customers.

The cost of retaining current customers is by far the lowest per customer cost that any company will encounter. After all, you know for sure that if you satisfy this customer that they will stay, and that is a 100 percent guarantee that they will remain if you treat them correctly. Conversely, if you advertise to reach 10,000 customers there is no guarantee that out of that 10,000 any of them will become your customers. Remember, you cannot be sure that those who hear your message have a need, have an interest, are not already loyal to a competitor, and/or have not been wooed away by an even stronger advertisement from a competitor! That is the reason why the odds are stacked against you to obtain major increases in new customers without constant, persistent, and expensive efforts.

Exceeding Expectations

The low cost and high value of retaining customers is good motivation to be open and willing to go above and beyond what is required to keep them. Your existing customers are a captive audience. You could ask, "Why should I give them more than I have to? They are already happy with what they are getting." However, if you are only meeting their minimum requirements so that they do business with you rather than having to go through the trouble of finding another shop you may be hanging on to them by a thread. Why not consider ways to exceed their expectations to reinforce their decision to continue to choose you?

By making a continuous effort to reinforce your current customers decision to choose you as their shop you not only are making a good investment in retaining their current business, you are actually making a strong investment in obtaining additional business. This additional business can come from two sources, increased sales from these customers and referral sales from their friends and associates.

There is clear evidence that the more that any customer deals with an organization with repeated good results the more likely they are to feel confident to spend more. A long-term repeat customer is likely to slowly transition from the customer who initially chose you to provide a service, testing you out to see if you were worthwhile, to a customer who considers you as their sole source to advise them and provide solutions for all of their automotive service needs. This type of loyalty is something that you can only wish to attain. However, even in today's highly competitive market instances of strong customer loyalty still exist.

REAL WORLD APPLICATION

Although you might believe that it is a remnant of a bygone era, in spite of all of the competition in the automotive market there are still loyal customer/shop relationships out there to be cultivated, nurtured, and enjoyed. Based on my work as a manufacturer's representative, the idea of a lifelong loyal customer was something that I saw with some regularity in the small town shops but never observed through my encounters in metro dealerships in the several large cities that I had covered.

When I took the position as service director at a metro dealership the thought never even crossed my mind that we could try to cultivate and build these types of relationships. That was until one day, while helping out at the service drive I greeted a lady at her car. She identified herself and I asked her how I could be of service. She simply said, "Tom is my mechanic. Please have him look over my car and call me later to let me know what he thinks it needs." I was absolutely floored. What? In this day and age how could this be true? It made me really rethink a lot of assumptions about customer care in the big city.

Tom was consistently our most productive technician. He had worked at this dealership for almost 20 years. That day I found out one of the keys to Tom's consistent status as the number one technician. Along with his technical expertise, his drive, and his motivation, he had become "their mechanic" in the eyes of his loyal following of customers. Through his thorough yet controlled advising of customers he had been able to, in spite of the skeptical world around him, nurture and build a loyal customer base that continued to return. Not only did they return, they completely trusted him as their technician and their expert technical advisor. They were not manufacturer-bound or dealer-bound, they were Tom's customers.

Based on the realization that this type of customer relationship is still possible in any market, it certainly changed my perspective. Further, I was able to use this as a lesson to share with service advisors and technicians alike at that dealership and also in subsequent positions to cause them to pause and rethink the potential of developing that type of loyal clientele. As a result others that I worked with began to work just a little bit harder and smarter to, hopefully, build a clientele just like Tom's some day.

Word-of-Mouth Advertising

The benefit of the loyal returning customer goes beyond their trust and their openness to spend more at your shop. Probably their best benefit to you is their willingness to provide you with the best advertising that you can get: **word-of-mouth advertising.** No other type of advertising has the credibility with the public that in any way compares to that of hearing a genuine, unsolicited testimonial from one of your current customers—and the best part is that the advertising is *free.*

Unsolicited comments that individuals share with others about their satisfaction or dissatisfaction with a product or company.

Our potential customers are very busy people. They want and need to have automotive service as a convenient, trouble-free experience. In an attempt to navigate their way through the masses of shops competing for their attention and their business, they will commonly look for any source of a referral. There is no advertising medium that can assure a potential customer that you actually meet or exceed what you promise. Yet that is the type of information that they desperately seek. The only true source of that type of information is through an unsolicited recommendation from a current customer.

Customer Loyalty

For the reasons mentioned earlier it is important to make every effort to retain your current customers. However, to be truly successful you must not stop there. You need to work to move your customers up the ladder of customer satisfaction (Figure 19-1). You need to make a concerted effort to move them from being a

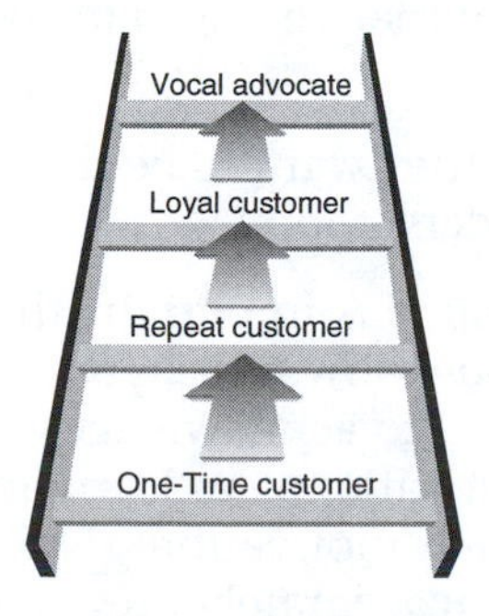

Figure 19-1 Ladder of customer satisfaction

one-time customer to being a *repeat customer*. You do this by meeting or exceeding their expectations. You do this by treating them as a valued customer.

You then need to move them from being a repeat customer to being a *loyal customer*. Your loyal customers are those who think of you first whenever they have a service question or a service need. This is because they have confidence that you will be able to address their needs in a competent, fair, and friendly manner.

Finally, you need to try to move as many of your loyal customers upward to becoming *vocal advocates* of your shop. It is when they have reached that level of positive relationship with your shop that you will begin to earn all of the long-term benefits of increased sales, trust, and word-of-mouth advertising that can really help your shop to develop a reputation as being head and shoulders above the competition.

Fundamentals of Human Behavior

Price, product, and availability are touted by marketing experts as three of the top reasons why customers choose to buy. However, when you are trying to build loyalty you need to remember that the focus of this effort is to go beyond these three reasons. They are what help you to get your foot in the door so that you have the initial opportunity to serve the customer. Although they will always remain important, it takes quite a bit more to build a positive relationship that will retain customers.

After all, your ultimate goal should be to develop the type of relationships that Tom developed with his customers in the example cited earlier. You need to constantly strive to become the single-source provider for your customers. You need to become their automotive consultant, their service expert; the first person that they think to call to ask "What do I do?" regarding anything automotive. It is through raising the level of your relationship with your customers to that of a respected consultant from that of a service writer or a mechanic that you will ultimately succeed. However, building these types of relationships requires that you are willing and able to keep up your end of the relationship.

There are three basic principles of human behavior that you need to acknowledge and heed if you want to build a respectful and trusting relationship with your customers. Remember that your goal is to build a relationship with every customer so they will trust you as their consultant. To do this you need to become very conscious and sensitive to each individual's unique needs, wants, and behaviors. It is through your ability and willingness to see them and appreciate them as unique individuals that you can build the necessary bonds of trust. The three key principles of human behavior that you need to consider are

- Respect the differences in people.
- Always treat someone the way you think they want to be treated.
- People want, first and foremost, to be understood.

In building a knowing, trusting relationship it is important that you do not jump to conclusions and assume that you know what your customers want and need. It is for this reason that you need to acknowledge and respect the differences in people. You have to have the patience to learn and understand their ways, their individual quirks, and their motivations. Not until you have reached that level of understanding can you accurately prescribe the best solutions to meet their individual needs.

Respect is something that is earned. The safest way for you to demonstrate your respect for others is to always treat someone the way you think he or she wants to be treated. There is little that can cut a relationship short faster than when an individual feels talked down to and/or for any reason disrespected. You need to make a concerted effort to be cautious in your approach to each customer to avoid offending his or her sensitivities or insecurities. One of the best ways to do this is to avoid stereotyping individuals and assuming that you can be sure what they know or do not know, need or do not need without giving them the respect of listening for clues and asking them.

In order to build a trusting relationship it is essential that customers feel that you understand where they are coming from. They simply want to be understood. You may not agree with their position, but it is, nevertheless, necessary that you take the time to hear them out so that you can gain their perspective. It is not until you understand where they are at and what they really want and need that you can begin to do your best work. You can only then begin to help move them from their condition of frustration and need to one of comfort and satisfaction—positions that will be rewarded as they become satisfied and loyal customers.

Quality Customer Service

Although we have spent an entire chapter talking about how important customer satisfaction is, providing quality service is not really that complicated. Once you have the right attitude and commitment all that is needed is persistence and a willingness to continue to keep in mind the following advice. The foundation of quality customer service can be summed up in four simple principles. They are to

- Have a positive attitude.
- Identify the needs of your customer.
- Meet or exceed the needs of your customer.
- Work to ensure that your customer returns.

Having a positive attitude is the most obvious of the four principles. Your attitude and approach to your customer demonstrates your willingness and commitment to be of service. It shows that you appreciate and value each customer. Meeting and greeting the customer with a smile, a warm handshake, and giving your undivided attention helps to communicate that he or she is important to you. This is the best first step in initiating a positive customer relationship.

There is a subtle, yet dramatic, difference between listening to what the customer says and what he means. By approaching the customer with an open mind and trying, first and foremost, to identify the customer's needs rather than trying to sell him something you are able to assure that the focus of your actions is to meet those needs. Identify the customer's core needs is the ultimate test of whether or not they will be satisfied and trust you now and in the future. That is the basis for building a positive customer relationship.

Recognizing the difficulties and inconvenience that having their car serviced poses to most customers is very important. Although price is always an issue, the biggest obstacle to satisfaction is inconvenience because we all suffer from a shortage of time in our lives. By recognizing this and providing resources to make the service experience as pleasant as possible, customer frustration can be minimized. Finally, and most important you must address their core needs by resolving their problem the first time so that you can assure them of no further inconvenience.

Even though you have been pleasant and professional, listening to understand what the customer needs, and fixed the car properly and on a timely basis this does not guarantee a lifelong customer. Considering the high value that a loyal, repeat customer brings to any organization there is one last, yet essential point in quality service that is required so that you can build a loyal following. You need to exceed the customer's needs. Some key ideas to consider that can assist you to consistently provide this superior service experience are to

Provide added value—strive to exceed customers' expectations, not just to meet minimum requirements.

Sell the benefits, not the price—work to provide value, not just a low price, and take the time to make sure the customers see what they are getting in return for their investment.

Provide more than the competition—promote and remind your customer the strong points of doing business with you and why you are the best choice.

Answer "Why would they want to do business with me?"—When trying to determine what services to provide and focus on customer needs.

Follow-up after the sale—be proactive in attempting to contact all customers after the sale to be sure that they are satisfied. Never leave this to chance.

SUMMARY

The main purpose of this chapter was to explore the value and importance of satisfied customers to the success and continued existence of your business. Two principles that highlighted the importance of being sure that you know if customers are satisfied are the silent majority principle and the 11/4 rule. They clearly illustrated the significant positive or negative impact that a handful of customers can have on overall customer satisfaction and long-term business success.

We discussed the need to make a concerted effort to build your existing customer base from being repeat customers to being vocal advocates of your organization. Several examples highlighted the need to know if your customers are truly satisfied. The use of a customer satisfaction survey and an active plan to do 100% customer follow-up was highly recommended to assist in obtaining this important information.

To accompany that newfound respect for the value of satisfied customers we concluded with some key concepts to keep in mind that will aid you in improving your interactions with customers. Long-term survival and ultimate success in any customer-based service industry requires that you are customer focused. This requires a daily focus on customer satisfaction.

PRACTICING THE PRINCIPLES

1. Which of the following is not a principle in providing quality customer service?
   a. Sell the benefits, not the price.
   b. Provide value-added.
   c. Give as little as possible.
   d. Follow up after the sale.
2. A key principle of human behavior is
   a. respect the differences in people.
   b. always treat someone the way you think they want to be treated.
   c. people want, first and foremost, to be understood.
   d. all of the above.
3. Which statement is not true regarding the value of customer satisfaction?
   a. It is easier to attract new customers than it is to keep current ones.
   b. There is a high cost in cultivating new customers.
   c. Repeat customers can be your best advertisement.
   d. The cost to keep repeat customers is relatively low.

4. Measuring C.S.I. helps you to
   a. know how popular this TV show really is.
   b. use forensic evidence to catch felons.
   c. accurately measure the number of dissatisfied customers.
   d. win dealership awards.
5. Two factors that you have to take into account to know your true customer satisfaction are
   a. the silent majority and the 11/4 rule.
   b. the 7/11 rule and the vocal minority.
   c. the color of money and the value of repeat business.
   d. the low cost of repeat customers and the cost of litigation.
6. When measuring customer satisfaction you need to be aware of the silent majority because
   a. many people that are dissatisfied will not complain.
   b. people sometimes do not complain, they just go away mad.
   c. most people are too busy to take the time to complain.
   d. all of the above.

In Questions 7–10 please number the four types of customers listed from lowest (1) to highest (4) as the rank moving up the ladder of customer satisfaction

___ 7. repeat customer.

___ 8. one-time customer.

___ 9. vocal advocate.

___ 10. loyal customer.

CHAPTER

20

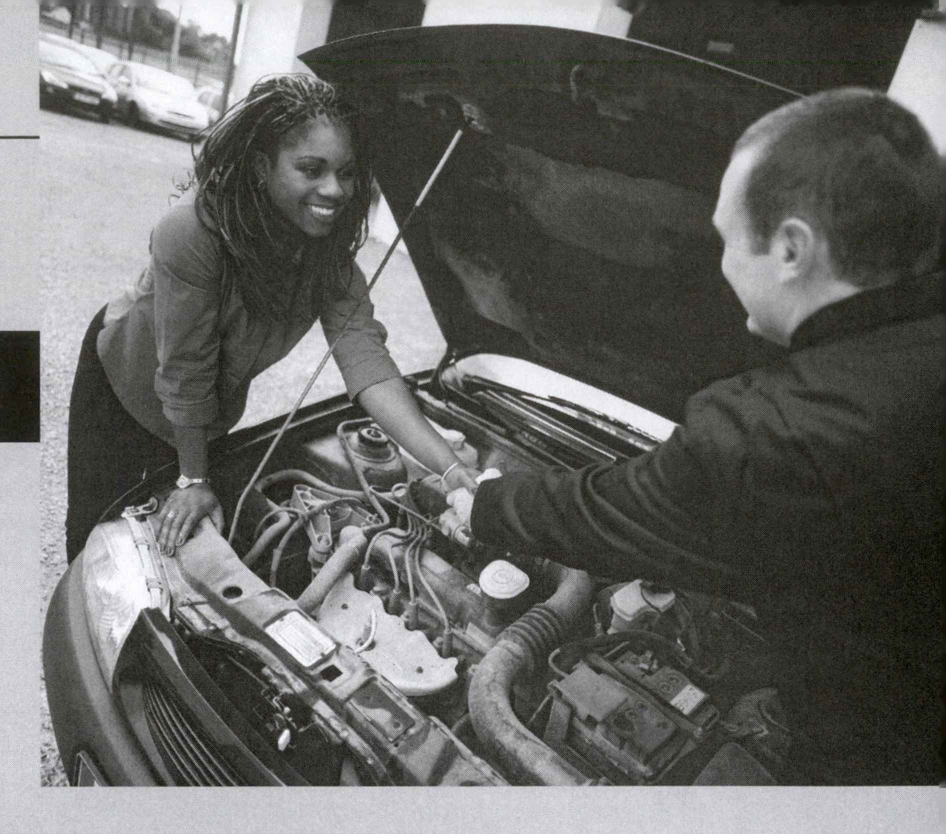

Building Basic Communication Skills

CHAPTER OBJECTIVES

- To identify fundamentals of behavior that affect communication
- To recognize the influence of nonverbal signals on the message that is received
- To examine how tone of voice alters the intent of your message
- To examine the influence of body language and gestures on communication
- To use basic questioning techniques to more effectively obtain information
- To demonstrate the value of questioning techniques in controlling difficult interactions.

KEY TERMS

tone of voice
body language
nonverbal communication
questioning techniques
open questions
closed questions

Introduction

Sound communication skills have a profound affect on all that we do in our lives. There are very few days when you are not called upon to use some portion of your skills and abilities to share information and discuss topics. Occasionally you need to draw on your higher-level communication skills when you find the need to consult with others to problem-solve difficult issues or to negotiate to overcome impasses between family, friends, or business associates. Our abilities to clearly and effectively communicate have a profound effect on our relationships, both personal and professional.

In the business world, and especially in a retail environment, a great portion of your time and a great measure of your ultimate success can be directly attributed to your ability to effectively communicate with your customers, your suppliers, and your co-workers. This is even more important as you rise through the ranks of management. You are often called on to summon your higher-level communication skills to resolve problems, clear up misunderstandings, and negotiate solutions to difficult situations.

This chapter is intended to provide you with some general insights on human behavior so you can better understand and communicate with others whether they are your bosses, your subordinates, irate customers, or your significant others. In addition we will briefly explore two sets of communication tools: nonverbal communication and basic questioning techniques. These tools, when properly applied, can increase the likelihood of successful communications. Although the examples will primarily focus on your most difficult communication situations such as those with dissatisfied and even irate customers, these tools can be applied to improve your communication at all levels and with all audiences, both personal and professional.

Basics of Communication

Before you learn about tools and techniques that you can use to become a more effective communicator it is important that we talk about some of the basics. At one point in our lives we have all been exposed to people who are very good at delivering a "canned speech." They do a great job of saying just the right things the right way so that they can try to convince those who are listening to agree with their point of view. Unfortunately, in many cases they are not able to convert many to their way of thinking. Why is this so? Why do you not trust them or want to believe them? Most often, it is because although they are good in their technique, they lack sincerity.

Because effective communication will be one of the major keys to your success or failure it is, therefore, important that you are skilled at it. You need to be sure that you are communicating with sincerity. You need to believe what you are talking about or people will be able to see right through you and doubt your intentions. More important, if you are to effectively communicate you need to know your audience. You need to have some understanding of their needs and values. The better you are able to understand your audience and acknowledge their needs the easier it will be to establish a trusting relationship. This trust is essential for both parties to really share information and openly and honestly work toward agreement.

You must realize that your values and your motives are not shared by everyone. Each of us is unique. As a result, we all come to the table with different backgrounds, different experiences, and different expectations. The starting point of any good communication is accepting and appreciating those differences rather than assuming that everyone thinks like you.

No matter what your background, the idea of treating someone the way you think they want to be treated seems to be nothing more than common sense. It even sounds quite a bit like the golden rule "Do unto others as you would have them do unto you." Unfortunately, this common sense adage is not common practice. Sensitivity, care, and consideration are all too often forgotten under the guise of the business relationship.

Just as we need to appreciate the differences in others, we need to step back and assess the other person's position if we hope to have an effective interaction. We do not need to feel sorry for them or to show sympathy, but we do need to appreciate their condition, to show empathy, and acknowledge that we understand and appreciate them. When we can acknowledge this as a starting point in our communication and they realize that we appreciate their feelings and position we can break down barriers of distrust and openly and freely work toward the best solutions.

Unless you are able to demonstrate to the other person that you understand their position you will not be able to carry on any effective communication. You can talk, they can listen, but communication will not occur. Communication indicates sharing of information and little sharing will occur while the other person is expending all of their energy hanging onto their position. Have you ever heard an argument where one of the parties involved keeps on saying "but you just do not understand" over and over again? Most of us have. This is a classic case where one party feels that he has not been able to make a point and he is unwilling and unable to move forward in any discussions until he is sure that someone understands his point.

The foundation for effective communication is your ability to acknowledge and understand others. Techniques will not resolve the problems that you seek to solve. Making a sincere effort to understand others is the best foundation for achieving open and effective communication.

Real World Application

Early on in my career as a manager, low-performing employees really got on my nerves. I was frustrated that they did not seem motivated or focused enough on getting things done on time. I was growing more and more impatient with their inability and apparent unwillingness to change.

One day while chatting with an associate he told me that it sounded like I needed to have a heart-to-heart with my problem employees and tell them about the hereafter. "What do you mean?" I said. He said that the hereafter was a short explanation that he used with his employees to get their attention. It went something like this: "Working here is like the hereafter, if you are not here after what I am here after, I will be here after you are gone." He smiled as he said that it was better than just threatening to fire them, and he had used this little talk to motivate several of his problem employees.

I was excited. I thought that was exactly what I needed. I was anxious to use this ingenious new technique the next time I got frustrated and had to deal with an underperforming employee It sounded like such a witty (sarcastic) way to deal with difficult situations in a lighthearted manner. Shortly thereafter I found just the right opportunity to use the "hereafter" speech and was very proud of myself.

But the results that I had hoped for, better performance, did not materialize. In fact, it seemed to only to make things worse. The employee's performance did not improve and his attitude got worse. Why?

I abandoned this little trick but did not immediately understand why it had been such a failure. It was not until a little bit later through reading and experience and some more failed attempts to use "canned solutions" to fix employee problems that I realized that I was the one who really did not understand the hereafter. I had to learn to understand, acknowledge, and appreciate what others were here after. That was, more often than not, different than what I (and the company) was there after. Only with that knowledge could I consistently find a way to motivate employees to improve their performance. I had to learn what they were here after, what they valued and what motivated them to action, before I had any chance of changing their performance or behavior.

Nonverbal Communication

What you communicate to others is determined by much more than just the words that you say. Your **tone of voice** definitely affects the message that the hearer receives. Beyond words and tone of voice, there is another major factor that influences the message that you communicate. It is your **body language.**

Tone of Voice

The manner in which the words are expressed including loudness, emotion, and rhythm.

The study of **nonverbal communication** and the connection between these gestures and body language to the total message conveyed are not new. Charles Darwin, the scientist most often cited for his research in genetics and natural selection, is credited as the first scientist to research and report on this topic in his book *The Expression of the Emotions in Man and Animals* (Darwin, 1899). The most often quoted contemporary research in nonverbal communications is that of Dr. Albert Mehrabian of UCLA. As a result of his research he found that nonverbal communication not only has a direct affect on the message that is received, it actually plays a more major role in the total message than either the words said or the tone of voice used.

Body Language

Body position, movements or gestures that are a part of direct communication.

Nonverbal Communication

The part of a message conveyed during a face-to-face encounter beyond the words including posture, body position, facial expressions, and voice inflection.

Mehrabian's findings are summarized in his 7%-38%-55% Rule which is shown in Figure 20-1 (Mehrabian, 1971). His findings indicate that in face-to-face communications the words that are said only contribute 7 percent to the total message that is conveyed. The tone of voice used in stating the message

The 7%-38%-55% Rule of Communication

Spoken Words	=	7%
Tone of Voice	=	38%
Body Language	=	55%
Total	=	**100%**

Figure 20-1 The 7%-38%-55% Rule of Communcation

conveys 38 percent of the message. Thus the total affect of the words spoken only account for 45 percent of the message. The key factor of these findings is that more than half of the message received by the hearer comes not from words or tone of voice, but rather from the body language demonstrated by the person sending the message.

You may think that the 7%-38%-55% Rule is a bit extreme, but there are many cases where what is said is not nearly as important as the situation and the way that is said. The key here is that you need to take seriously the influence that tone of voice and your nonverbal communications can have on the message that your hearer receives and understands.

Tone of Voice

The tone of voice plays a much larger part in the message communicated than we realize. Let us look at a few examples that we have probably all encountered in our daily lives.

While hanging out with a group of friends, one of them makes a crude comment or calls you a name. This is something that would normally cause you to want to confront the person here and now. Yet, in this case you immediately brush it off without giving it any more thought. Is it because it was your friend that said it? Or, was it the *way* that it was said? Although both factors may have been involved, it is very likely that simply by the tone of voice you were able to read into the intent of the message that it was just a joke, not a serious assault on you.

During a day at work a customer comes up to you who is really upset. After a few minutes of listening without being able to get a word in, you feel like this is a personal attack. You feel like this customer is talking down to you, accusing you, blaming you. In these situations it is likely that the words do not create the hostile environment, it is the tone of voice.

The effect of tone of voice on the message that is conveyed is not isolated only to irate customers yelling at you as a manager. Tone of voice is an important ingredient in the message that you communicate every time you interact with others. Even the calmest communication can leave a lasting, yet unintended message. Here are some examples of very negative messages that can be very clearly, yet unintentionally, communicated through tone of voice:

- Impatient—I do not really have time for this
- Unimportant—Listening but trying to break away and get back to other things
- Condescending—Making the other person feel unimportant or talked down to
- Blaming—It is all your fault
- Judgmental—You meant to do this to me

In each of these cases this message can be communicated, whether or intentional or not, to the hearer. The range of messages that are conveyed by tone of voice is broad. If you want to be an effective communicator you need to be sensitive to these unintended messages that you may be sending to others. To be an effective communicator you need to work to assure that your total message, verbal and nonverbal, matches your true intent.

THEORY INTO PRACTICE 20-1

CASE

Pair up with another student. Take turns with one of you being the service manager and the other being the customer. This is an opportunity for you demonstrate how the difference in tone of voice affects the message that it communicates and the difference in how it makes the hearer feel.

First, here are three common statements that a customer might say:

"You need to fix my problem right now."

"You are responsible for this."

"What are you going to do about this?"

Now, here are three different scenarios that describe different customers and their very different approach to this interaction with the service manager:

Very detached and intellectual . . . just reporting the facts.

Very impatient and agitated

Judgmental and blaming . . . wanting to make somebody pay for this mistake

You decide

Take turns role playing as service manager and customer saying each of these three statements as you think the customers would say them to the service manager under these circumstances.

Did the different attitudes and approaches result in you receiving a different message? How did it make you feel?

Body Language

Just as tone of voice contributes to the total message received, body language plays a major role in the complete message that the listener receives. Whether or not the body language is intentional it affects the final results. Body language includes all of the gestures, body positions, and other mannerisms that the sender exhibits during a conversation. Being able to understand and control the body language messages that you send when you are interacting with others can help you to dramatically improve your ability to communicate clearly. Just as in the case of tone of voice, the most important first step in maximizing your communication skills through intentional use of these communication methods is self-awareness. That is, you need to become very aware of the nonverbal messages that you are sending and how they may be perceived by the listener.

Figure 20-2 provides some common examples of nonverbal communication signals that can directly affect the message received. As you can see, they create an environment for the listener that conveys a strong, clear message to the listener of the speaker's intent.

Through increased awareness and intentional use of nonverbal communication tools you can dramatically improve your ability to successfully and consistently convey your intended message. Here are three tips to keep in mind that can help remind you every day to maximize the positive impact of your nonverbal communications.

1. Be vigilant not to let negative nonverbal messages creep into your conversations that might confuse the hearer or otherwise counter your intended verbal message.
2. Intentionally use nonverbal signals that support the verbal message that you are trying to send.
3. Strive to gain more consistent control of your body and your tone of voice as intentional components of your total message.

Category	Nonverbal signal	Message received
Legs	legs crossed	defensive
	legs relaxed and open	friendly, receptive
Arms	crossed over chest	argumentative
	relaxed at sides	open
Hands	Rubbing chin	thoughtful
	rubbing nose lightly	doubting
	rubbing eyes	disbelief
	hands in pockets	dejected
	clasped in lap	very defensive
Fingers	Tapping fingers	impatience
	pointing	intense/frustrated
Eyes	Darting/looking away	deception/lying
	looking down	dejected/disappointed

Figure 20-2 Nonverbal communication signals

THEORY INTO PRACTICE 20-2

CASE

Pair up with another student. Take turns with one of you playing the role of the service manager and the other as the customer. The customer arrives at the service drive and tells his story as provided below. Here is the conversation.

Customer: "I do not understand how this could have happened. I have done everything in the book to take care of this car. I have done all of the prescribed maintenance. I come in here regularly to report even the slightest symptoms. I have been a careful driver and never driven the car recklessly or beyond the speed limits—and now this. I was just driving down the freeway and all of a sudden 'clunk, bang' and the engine just stopped running."

Service Manager: "Mr. Customer, I really feel bad about your situation. I understand your concerns. I am sure that there is no way that this is your fault. I can assure you that we will do everything in our power to get your car fixed and back to you as quickly as possible."

You decide

Part A: Pull up two chairs and act out the scenario while you are seated in the service manager's office.

Part B: Re-enact the same scenario again, but this time while you are intentionally using nonverbal communications that go along with the following attitudes:

Customer—The customer is lying and has been out street racing the car every chance she gets. The engine actually started making noises two weeks ago but she was just too busy to waste her time coming in to have it checked out.

Service Manager—Although genuinely a trusting individual, the service manager is late for an important meeting with his boss and feels as though he does not really have time for this right now.

Note to both parties—Remember: use exactly the words provided here—the only changes should be in nonverbal communications.

Questioning Techniques

The ability to interact with customers is an integral and very necessary job responsibility for every service advisor and manager. These communications can be unexpected. They can be lengthy. They will be important. Your success in getting your job done depends upon your ability to make these communications effective.

One of the most valuable sets of basic tools to help you to improve the efficiency and effectiveness of your communications is your ability to use proper **questioning techniques.** Questioning techniques can help you draw out the essential information from customers so that you can provide the needed background to your technicians to aid them in their efforts to identify and resolve customer complaints. Questioning techniques also provide great benefit in helping you to guide and maintain control of difficult interactions with irate customers.

Questioning Techniques

The intentional structuring of questions that affects the type of response that they generate.

The basic premise underlying the intentional use of questioning techniques is that the way that you ask a question can have a profound impact on both the type and quality of response that you get in return. By making an effort to carefully construct the way that we ask questions, we can increase the chances of getting the right information and getting it in the way that will be of most use. Let us explore the fundamentals of questioning techniques by looking at the difference between open and closed questions, their value, and their uses. This will help us to better understand the importance of structuring our questions to gain maximum value in the minimum time.

Open Questions

Open questions are those questions that are asked in such a way that they draw out a detailed response. Open questions are the essay questions of conversation. Good examples of open questions are those that include words such as why, how, what. (For example, Why did you do that? How do you feel? What happened?) The normal response to any of these questions is a detailed explanation. This explanation will be an open-ended response in which your listener will try to provide what they believe is all of the important information regarding the subject.

Open Questions

Questions that are asked in such a way that they elicit a detailed response or answer.

Open questions can be very beneficial when you are trying to obtain a lot of information. They can be helpful when you are trying to get to know someone better. However, there are potential consequences that come with open questions. They are a call for the respondent to let out anything and everything that is on his or her mind on the subject. Although this might be interesting, it may also be more than you needed or wanted. The key is that you need to know the *type* of response that you are going to get before you ask the question. Through intentionally structuring the way that you ask the question, you can ensure that the type of response will be appropriate to meet the unique needs of the situation.

Let us talk a little about the use of open questions with one of your most difficult communication encounters, the irate service customer. When an obviously irate customer approaches you in the service drive you can be pretty sure that they want to go on and on telling you the harrowing tale of their day and their difficulties with their "piece of junk" car. As soon as you greet them and ask "How may I be of service?" (remember, *how* is an open question word) you will be greeted with an essay answer. The customer may spend the next 10 minutes telling you anything and everything that has ever gone wrong with this car.

When you encounter this situation, take notes. Somewhere within all of the information that the customer will let loose will probably be answers to some of the important questions that you need so that you can help identify and resolve his car problems. However, all of the information will come spewing out in an unstructured way and you will have to try your best to pick the treasures out from among the trash if you hope to get any useful information out of the exchange.

This might seem like a strong argument to never use an open question. It is not, however, so clear cut. There are many times when you want to and need to get the details. When those situations arise, open questions are the best method to obtain that rich information. Still another use of open questions could be when you want to intentionally allow a customer to vent. At times customers are so upset, so frustrated, so angry, that they simply need to release some steam before they can calm down, become more coherent and logical, and be able to move toward having a constructive conversation. The key here, though, is that you need to learn to form your questions, so that you intentionally use open questions. Once you have learned to use them when you need them and avoid them when they are inappropriate you will be better equipped to carry on more effective and efficient conversations.

THEORY INTO PRACTICE 20-3

CASE

There are three simple scenarios provided below. In each of these three situations you are trying to obtain some detailed information from the other person.

Scenario A: You see one of your technicians just standing sort of in a daze in the shop. You are concerned about why he is doing this.

Scenario B: A customer approaches the service desk and looks somewhat puzzled and lost.

Scenario C: A customer approaches the desk and you can see that he is very, very angry. Based on your past encounters with this customer, you realize that you need to let him vent a little bit before you will be able to make any headway in solving his problems.

You decide

You know that in each of these situations you need to draw out a detailed response from the people involved. What would be the first question that you would ask each of these three individuals to begin your conversation?

Closed Questions

Closed Questions
Questions that are structured to illicit short answers and/or very specific information.

Closed questions are questions designed to get very specific information. They are asked in such a manner that the response will typically be a short and precise answer. This can range from a yes/no response to providing a specific piece of information. Some words that are commonly used in closed questions are: when, who, and where. Closed questions are best used to get directly to the detailed information.

One benefit of closed questions is that you can focus the discussion in a structured manner rather than letting the conversation ramble.

In a service setting, some examples of closed questions that might be asked are

- What is the current mileage on your car?
- How do you spell your last name?
- When was the last time you were in for service?

When questions are presented this way they elicit an answer that is short and to the point.

THEORY INTO PRACTICE 20-4

CASE

Using the same scenarios presented in exercise 20c you are now intentionally trying to get a short and specific piece of information from each of the three individuals.

Scenario A: You see one of your technicians just standing sort of in a daze in the shop. You are concerned about why he is doing this.

Scenario B: A customer approaches the service desk and looks somewhat puzzled and lost.

Scenario C: A customer approaches the desk and you can see that he is very, very angry. Based on your past encounters with this customer, you realize that you need to let him vent a little bit before you will be able to make any headway in solving his problems.

You decide

You want to elicit a yes/no or short and specific answer. What question would you ask in these scenarios that would be an appropriate closed question?

Combined Use

Under most circumstances you will need to use both open and closed questions in combination to obtain the information and the results that you need. The important part is being able to maintain control of your speech so that you can intentionally switch back and forth as the situation demands to get the best results.

In the service write-up process you require specific information from the customer. Name, address, phone number, and vehicle mileage are all examples of specific data that is necessary to create the repair order. All of this information is best obtained by asking very pointed and direct closed questions. An example is: "Mr. Jones, what is the best phone number to reach you at between 10 A.M. and 2 P.M. today?' However, when you are trying to understand exactly how the car acts so that you can accurately and completely relay the symptoms to the technician you will probably need to use open questions. These open questions will help to draw out the details from the customer. An example of this is to ask the customer, "Mr. Jones, please explain to me exactly what the car does when it acts up."

Through a complete understanding of the benefits of each of these question types and your ability to select the proper type for every situation you can learn to effectively shape the questions based on what kind of information you need to obtain. If you come to the end of the questions listed above and still find a specific piece of important data is missing (for example, finding out if someone else has been working on the car for this problem) you can smoothly transition back to closed questions and ask "Mr. Jones, has the car been worked on recently?" Conversely, if you are still not sure that you understand the customer's explanation of the symptoms you can use an open question and ask, "Mr. Jones, so that we are better able to understand the symptoms, please tell me more about the driving conditions under which we are most likely to get the car to act up?"

Finally, there is another valuable use for open and closed questions. That use is controlling the direction and flow of the conversation. This is particularly valuable when you encounter a difficult or irate customer. As with all customers, you need to obtain several different types of information. With a very irate customer, however, you may find that communication is difficult and frustrating for both of you. This could be because the customer is so tense and so upset that until she is allowed to let it all out the likelihood of carrying on a productive conversation is nil. In this case you would use an open question to encourage the customer to speak in detail about her experience. Conversely, in a situation where the customer continues to insist on rambling on and on and you are having difficulty picking out the pertinent details you would move to the use of closed questions. These closed questions will help you to get the specifics you need and, at the same time, provide you an opportunity to regain control of the direction of the conversation.

THEORY INTO PRACTICE 20-5

CASE

In your monthly department meeting you open the floor to questions. One of your new advisors, Casey, says that there are several customers that really frustrate her. "For example," she says, "When Mr. Frederickson comes in for service he tends to always ramble on and on. Every time I ask him a question, he starts his story all over again just like a broken record. It is almost like he has rehearsed this speech before he came in and does not know how to say it any other way. What do I do?"

You decide

Based on the principles that we have learned about questioning techniques what would be your advice to Casey and your other employees about how to deal with this type of difficult situations?

SUMMARY

The focus of this chapter was improving communication. Communication skills are essential in business and this is especially true in retail trades such as automotive service. First and foremost, however, before learning techniques that will improve communication, it is necessary to start with the underlying knowledge and understanding needed to guide your communications with customers, co-workers, and friends. You need to have a sincere interest in your customers and make a concerted effort to understand them if real communication is to occur.

Nonverbal communication plays an important role in the total message that you convey to others. Research has indicated that nonverbal communication actually accounts for over one-half of the total message that your listener receives in a face-to-face interaction. Posture, body position, facial expressions, and voice inflection are all important elements of the nonverbal messages that you send to your hearer.

We closed this chapter with an introduction to the understanding and use of basic questioning techniques. Understanding how the way that you word a question can affect the resulting response plays an important role in helping you to communicate more effectively. The features and unique benefits of open and closed questions were discussed. The chapter closed with a brief discussion on how you can use these simple questioning tools to effectively address difficult face-to-face interactions.

PRACTICING THE PRINCIPLES

1. Which of the following statements is not true regarding effective communication?
   a. People need to listen to you first and foremost.
   b. Everyone has different motives.
   c. You should always communicate with sincerity.
   d. You need to treat people the way that they want to be treated.

2. If you want to be able to effectively communicate with others you need to

a. realize that they have a need to be understood.
b. make them understand your point first and foremost.
c. never attempt to identify their needs.
d. all of the above.

3. Nonverbal communication includes all of the following except
   a. body language.
   b. explanations.
   c. tone of voice.
   d. mannerisms.

In Questions 4–8 please match the nonverbal communication listed below to the best description of the message that it sends from the list on the right.

_____ 4. hands in pockets	a. lying/deception
_____ 5. legs crossed	b. dejected
_____ 6. tapping fingers	c. guarded/defensive
_____ 7. eyes darting/looking away	d. thoughtful/considering
_____ 8. rubbing chin	e. impatient

9. Please mark an X on the line before those questions that are closed questions.

   _____ What happened to your car?
   _____ When did this occur?
   _____ Why didn't you bring it in sooner?
   _____ Who is the owner of the car that ran into you?

10. Please mark an X on the line before those questions that are open questions

   _____ What is the current mileage on your car?
   _____ Did you drive the car very far after the noise started?
   _____ Why didn't you bring it in sooner?
   _____ How did you get your car stuck?

REFERENCES

Darwin, C., *The expression of the Emotions of Man and Animals* (New York: D. Appleton & Co., 1899)

Mehrabian, A., *Silent Messages* (Belmont, CA: Wadsworth, 1971).

CHAPTER

21

Resolving Customer Disputes

CHAPTER OBJECTIVES

- To examine key principles necessary to successfully resolve customer complaints
- To apply the basic principles of negotiating an agreement
- To employ a consistent procedure to assure to handle all customer complaint situations

KEY TERMS

the bucket
empathy
perspective
negotiation
value-added
win-win

Introduction

We have already discussed at some length the importance of making and retaining satisfied customers. Unfortunately, customers do not always begin and remain satisfied. Success in business is heavily dependent on your ability to satisfy customers and keep them that way. Resolving customer concerns can turn potential enemies into your strongest and most vocal advocates.

In this chapter we will address some ideas and methods that can improve your ability to deal with customer complaints and enable you to become more effective in reaching positive outcomes. These tips and techniques are designed to help you as well as provide you with some tools that you can easily share with your workers so that everyone can become more effective at resolving customer issues.

The Rules of Complaint Handling

An often ignored, yet very important, aspect of successfully dealing with customer problems is taking the time to prepare for the encounter. That is, whenever possible, it is important that you take a moment to prepare yourself mentally and emotionally for what may be a very trying experience. Therefore, the first rule of customer complaint handling is

> Rule number 1—Prepare for the encounter.

In order to prepare for the encounter successfully you need to be able to put everything else aside and plan to focus 100 percent of your time, energy, and attention solely on dealing with this situation. This is essential if you are to fully absorb all of the information coming at you. You will also need to be emotionally prepared to absorb all of the negative energy, complaints, and accusations that may be unleashed by an unhappy customer out of frustration over the situation. Therefore, the second rule of customer complaint handling is

> Rule number 2—Focus 100 percent of your energy and attention.

In addition, there is one more essential piece of vital information that you need to keep in mind to help to guide you in your pending interaction with the customer. It is not uncommon for a customer who has a complaint to be unhappy, even visibly angry. In this state of mind it is likely that he or she will lash out at anyone and everyone. However, it is critically important that you realize that rarely is that anger or frustration really aimed at you. You are the target of that anger because you are the customer's only direct contact with the company at that point in time.

It is important for you to always begin with the assumption that customers are upset over the situation. They are rarely upset with you personally. Taking this approach is valuable in helping you to keep from taking their anger as a personal attack on you. Your failure to distance yourself from this hostility may lead you to respond inappropriately to the customer, which will only result in an escalating war of words. This is not the pathway towards achieving a peaceful solution to a problem. Maintaining your self control is essential.

Your ability to detach yourself so that you do not take the attacks personally will make it much easier for you to remain calm and unaffected by the customer's anger. In order to be effective at resolving customer complaints on a consistent basis it is essential that you are able to recognize and avoid the danger of taking it personally.

Rule number 3—Don't take it personally.

We've just spent time going over three essential rules, and they don't even really deal with the actual customer interaction. They are rules to put you in the right frame of mind to be prepared for the customer encounter. Now, armed with this very essential background knowledge you are finally ready to meet and greet the customer.

The first few steps in meeting with an upset customer are very simple, yet essential to creating an environment that will yield positive results. It is highly recommended that you always begin every encounter in a customer complaint situation the same way that you should initiate every other customer interaction—begin with a smile, a warm handshake, and a positive welcome.

If you are hoping for a positive interaction and a positive result it is essential that you begin by creating a positive environment. In an already emotionally charged situation it is important that the customer sees you as someone who is willing and able to help him, not as an adversary. Based on the many horror stories that they have seen and heard in books, newspapers, and on television about service problems they are already defensive and fearful. You must realize that the general public is wary of the perils of the auto repair industry. They probably don't know much about cars and because of this lack of knowledge they feel insecure in their ability to effectively argue their point with you, the expert. You need to do all that you can to assure them that this is not a confrontation; it is an opportunity to work together to solve a mutual concern.

Few small gestures have greater impact than a smile on your face and a friendly handshake. These simple acts are symbolic of your willingness to reach out to the other person. They indicate your desire to begin from a position of trusting them and hoping that they can, in turn, trust you. The best way to build trust is to do everything that you can to begin on a positive note. Therefore, rule number four is

Rule number 4—Always start with a warm, friendly greeting.

Once you have completed the greeting it is important that you begin the dialogue by allowing the customer to speak first. He, very likely, has quite a bit on his mind and has thought and re-thought what he wants and needs to say to you. Give him the opportunity to get it off of his chest.

Even though it may seem hard to believe, the vast majority of difficult customers you encounter don't go around every day lashing out at everyone about their problems. It is much more likely that this is uncommon territory for them and they may have had to go to some lengths to get up the courage to come and confront someone about this very troubling situation. It is not uncommon that they have thought it through several times on the ride to the shop trying to script out their presentation in their head so that they get their message across to you in just the right manner to get your attention. So, let them vent.

The Bucket
An analogy that explains that all people have a limited capacity to take in and process information at any one time based on their current state of mind.

The Bucket

Although I am uncertain of its origins, the best analogy that explains why it is essential to allow the customer to speak first and vent is called **the bucket.**

Each of us has a limited capacity to take in information, process information, and communicate information. Even though those capacities may vary from person to person we each have a finite capacity. Let's call that capacity our bucket. We can only hold so much in our bucket.

Now, consider the case of the irate customer. Just like the rest of us, he may have many other things filling his bucket that are totally unrelated to the car problems. He has work, family, health, finances, and other concerns that keeps his bucket pretty full without the additional strain of this unexpected automotive service concern.

When you add the additional stress, strain, and information of the car problem to his already nearly full bucket, it is now overflowing. Anything else that we or others try to put into his bucket will just spill right back out. Sounds reasonable, doesn't it?

Therefore, in trying to allow the customer the opportunity to be in the position of listening and processing any additional information it is first important that he be given the chance to make room for the new information. An irate customer needs to be allowed to empty part of his bucket so that he has capacity to listen and take in new information. The best way to do this is to allow him to speak first, and to unburden himself of those concerns and emotions that he is holding inside.

Rule number 5—Allow the customer to empty his or her bucket.

While you are allowing the customer to tell you his story there are several important techniques that you should employ that will help you to focus and help calm the customer's fears and potential for distrust. Often the customer is busily engaged in not only recounting to you the technical difficulties that he is experiencing. He is likely to do much more, to try to tell you how it has made him feel, causing him worry and concern. He wants to be sure that you understand the full effect that this has had on him. Your ability to let the customer know that you can relate to his situation and understand how he feels goes a long way toward validating his feelings. This helps to leave him open to considering you as someone who is capable of making the right decisions to resolve the problem. Rule number 6, then, is

Rule number 6—Listen with empathy.

Empathy is an indication that you can relate to the customer's situation. Unlike sympathy, where you feel sorry for the customer, it is a situation where you indicate that you can understand how he feels. This is a very important distinction. If you show sympathy, the customer may mistake that you are feeling sorry for him or talking down to him. Empathizing with him, on the other hand, shows that you can relate to his situation and have a personal interest in wanting to find a reasonable solution.

Empathy
The ability to be aware of and relate to the position and situation of another person.

Along with empathizing with the customer it is essential that you are listening carefully and that you are making it clear to the customer that you hear and understand what he is saying. Especially in the heightened emotional state of a difficult customer complaint situation if the customer does not feel that he has your undivided attention and that you hear him, the feeling of disrespect that this will create seriously undermines any chance of a mutually satisfactory resolution.

One technique that can help is the use of active listening. Periodically asking the customer questions to verify that you understand what he has said along with feeding back brief statements of what you understand his issues and concerns are can go a long way to assuring him that you have heard and understood him. In addition, it shows that you genuinely care about his concerns and his issues. Therefore, the seventh rule of customer complaint handling is

Rule number 7—Make sure the customer knows you've heard him.

You have created an environment that is friendly and accepting. You have reassured the customer that you care and are listening. Now it is time to begin fact finding. Even armed with the most sincere intent to make the customer feel at home, little progress will be made unless you can get the facts. You must listen to all of the information presented to you, analyze it, and arrive at a complete understanding of what is wrong and what needs to be resolved to remedy the situation.

In order to arrive at the best decision it is essential that you are able to separate emotions from the facts. This is the foundation for making a decision based on sound logic. By using steps 1 through 7 you have created an environment that will allow the emotions and personal attacks to be minimized. This will open the door for you to get to the real issues at hand. Once you begin fact finding it is essential that you maintain the direction of the conversation in identifying, clarifying, and addressing the key issues. This will never happen unless and until you are able to consistently practice rule number 8

Rule number 8—Stick to the facts.

Listening for the core issues and problems is a much more difficult process than it seems. It would appear that once you are able to strip away the emotions, the anger, and all of the other conflicting motives the real answer would become apparent. That is often true from *your perspective*. However, whose problem are we trying to resolve? Yours? If not, then we need to be able to see things through the eyes of the one whose problem we are trying to resolve—the customer's.

You will not likely be able to see the problem through the eyes of the customer until you have allowed him to completely vent and tell his complete story while you sit back and reserve judgment. You want to allow the customer to tell his whole story so that you can see what he believes is important, what he wants, what he expects, what concerns him. This requires that you resist the strong urge to jump to conclusions and suggest solutions before you fully understand the customer's core concerns. It is essential that don't only fix the car. It is equally, if not more important, that you fix the customer. You will only be able to do this if you have a clear idea of what his true concerns and priorities are.

To test the effectiveness of your fact finding you need to check with the customer to verify that you have a clear understanding of his concerns. Once that has been confirmed it is important that you reach an agreement on exactly what the customer's expectations are for a satisfactory resolution. It is important not to assume that you know exactly what it takes to make the customer happy. You may know full well what it takes to fix the car. However, you can only assume that you know what is needed to fix the customer. The best way to gain an understanding of this is to ask.

It is important to realize that at this point if you've done your job you have not yet done anything to fix the problem. You have created an environment where both parties have developed a level of trust, have communicated and improved their understanding of the situation, and now are finally willing and able to try to come to a reasonably negotiated solution that will satisfy the needs of all concerned. You are nearing a conclusion, but before you can arrive at a workable solution you need to make sure that you have seen and understood the problem from the customer's perspective and, therefore, can propose alternatives that will speak to his needs. Therefore, do not jump to solutions until you are sure that you've achieved an understanding of rule number 9

Rule number 9—See and understand what is important from the customer's perspective.

THEORY INTO PRACTICE 21-1

CASE

Mr. Hammond arrives at your shop insisting that he meet with you, the service manager. He has told your service advisor that his left front wheel came off of the car one week after you did a brake job. It damaged his front fender and the wheel and tire are both destroyed. He wants you to make it right.

You decide

You are extremely busy and it sounds from what the advisor has told you that his story, although not proven, is possibly the result of your shop's work. Which of the following alternatives do you think is the best option?

Option A: Send the advisor back out, asking him to apologize to Mr. Hammond and committing to fix the car and provide him with a free rental car until it is done, no questions asked.

Option B: Meet with the customer immediately, apologizing for the type of scary situation that he has just been through. Ask him to explain all that has happened during the time following his last visit to your shop, and offer to bring the car in the shop immediately for a physical inspection, at no charge of course, where you can both look things over and be sure, and then go from there.

Option C: Meet with Mr. Hammond and explain to him that a week has passed since the repairs that you did and that, although unfortunate, there is no way that the car could have run fine for a week and then had a failure if it was really directly a result of his last repair visit. Offer to call his insurance company for him.

Please justify the reasoning behind the choice that you've made.

Armed with the facts, in an environment that is now much less emotionally charged, it is possible to work toward a negotiated settlement. Negotiated settlement? Why can't I just fix it? you might ask. The reason is clear. Think back to the beginning and the unsettled and insecure feelings about auto repair that your customer is likely to feel. With that in mind, if you chime in with "This is what we're going to do for you today!" you're likely to undo all of the good foundational work that you've done. To be successful in customer handling you need to be able to see the negotiations from the customer's **perspective**, and be especially sensitive to and avoid creating any situations that the customer might perceive as an effort to talk him or her into something.

Perspective The unique viewpoint of any individual or group based on their position in the situation.

Although situations occasionally arise where fact finding results in a clear understanding by all parties that one of them is 100 percent at fault, this is rarely the case. That would just make it too easy. Therefore, it is more common that an important step in complaint resolution is negotiating a settlement that satisfies the needs of all parties involved. This is rule number 10:

Rule number 10—Negotiate a mutually acceptable solution.

Negotiation
Working with another person or group to arrive at a mutually agreeable solution, normally requiring compromise.

Each **negotiation** will be unique, but there are several key factors to consider that you can consistently use as guidelines to help you to arrive at successfully negotiated settlements. The five key factors to negotiating an agreement are to

1. Agree upon the facts.
2. Present the alternatives and costs.
3. Discuss responsibility.
4. Propose possible solutions.
5. Negotiate to an acceptable solution.

Not until you have agreement on all of the five points are you likely to arrive at a mutually satisfying solution.

The last, and probably most important, step in the entire process is to make sure that once you've reached a solution that you follow through to make that solution a reality. Not until all parties have made good on their promises can you be assured that the problem is really resolved and that the benefits that you hope to obtain (for the customer and for the shop) will be realized. Therefore, the final and eleventh rule is

> Rule number 11—Follow through to assure that the complaint is completely resolved.

The process of complaint handling may seem lengthy and cumbersome. However, once you consider the possible costs of not arriving at an acceptable solution (lost customers, bad publicity, legal action) it is an investment of time and energy that is well worth making.

Some Additional Thoughts

In the beginning of this section we talked about the importance of good customer relations. Customer satisfaction is highly dependent on our ability to turn negative circumstances into opportunities for more satisfied customers. It has been said that the best and strongest advocate of any company is that irate customer that they were able to turn around into a satisfied one. The ability to redirect that negative energy into positive energy can turn a potential enemy into a lifelong friend and a staunch supporter and advocate. That's just the type of person that you need to provide you with your best type of advertising—word-of-mouth advertising. For now, let us discuss how taking the extra step can help you turn the potentially damaging results of a dissatisfied customer into a strong positive for you and your organization.

As we've discussed, it is very rare that a customer complaint situation ends up being a clear-cut situation of 100 percent customer responsibility or 100 percent shop responsibility. (Remove the word fault from your vocabulary if you are trying to take the right approach to satisfying customers.) However, the way that the opportunity is handled, not the situation itself, will dictate the ultimate customer satisfaction and long-term net results of the opportunity. Let us explore the results of two very different customer complaint handling scenarios.

Customer at fault The customer comes into the shop upset that he had a brake failure as a result of the recent visit to the shop where you did an oil change. The shop could easily take a hard stand that an oil change didn't cause a brake failure and summarily deny any responsibility and have a complete unwillingness to talk further about it. This is very likely within their rights. But is it the right thing to do?

If the shop takes this hard-line approach, the customer will feel publicly embarrassed and is likely to go elsewhere for service in the future. The net result is that the shop wins the battle—and loses the war (lost customer).

However, if the service shop enters the situation with an open mind and, although they are 99 percent sure that they are not at fault, offers to reach out and check the vehicle for the customer, they have the opportunity to verify beyond any shadow of a doubt their innocence, convincingly demonstrate this to the customer, and then quietly and humbly work to turn this misunderstanding into a way to earn more business (a brake job) by handling the customer in a gentle manner. They might even offer to provide the work at a discounted rate, thus exceeding the customer's expectations. Net result—both the service shop and the customer win.

Shop at fault In a similar scenario where the brake failure is the result of carelessness on the part of the shop they can either deny responsibility (result = lost customer and probably a lawsuit), assume full responsibility (result = fixed the car, but may not have fixed the customer), or go above and beyond.

In this situation the first choice obviously will have negative results. However the *way* the shop steps up to their responsibilities for the repairs will do far more to create a lasting positive result than what they do in fixing their error. If they made the error they have an obligation to make it right. However, they can do this reluctantly, or seize the opportunity to exceed expectations and try to turn an upset customer into a loyal one. This can be done by a combination of the shop's attitude (apologetic/concerned/thoughtful) and a reasonable effort to go above and beyond, providing more than the required service (free rental car/additional services at a discount, and so on) to show that they value the customer and don't want to lose him.

Both of these scenarios are absolute opposites. Yet, they both present opportunities to create satisfied customers and lasting relationships or to result in a lost customer and bad will. The difference is in the attitude in which the opportunity is approached. That's right, not the problem the opportunity. Handling each customer complaint situation presents the opportunity for positive or negative results. As is demonstrated in these two examples, the idea of reaching out and going above and beyond what is required and expected is the key to making the best out of a bad situation. Remembering that the goal is not merely putting out the fire but creating a lasting positive result I recommend an additional rule for your consideration

Rule number 12—Try to find a '**value-added**' solution.

Value-added
The result of a transaction that provides greater benefit than was originally expected or required.

Diffusing the Situation

If you have ever been in an emotionally charged situation with a customer you might ask at this point: Yes, sure I need to follow these rules, but how do I get the customer to stop screaming at me? That is a valid question and the answer is—you already have the tools that you need. Let's do a brief refresher on how you can use some of the communication tools and techniques that you learned in Chapter 20 along with some additional tips that you have picked up in this chapter to address this critically important question.

When a customer begins an encounter full of hostility, anger, and negative energy it is important to find a way to diffuse the anger, channel the energy, and calm the situation down. Failure to allow the customer to vent is certainly not the best solution because he will be unwilling and/or unable to listen to reason until he has emptied his bucket (at least to some degree). So, the first important principle is not only to allow an angry customer to empty his bucket, to encourage it to happen before you proceed.

However, as soon as the customer has had the opportunity to let off a little steam and tell his story and you are able to see that you can now start to safely redirect things in a more positive direction you can use the questioning techniques (open questions/closed questions) to help get the situation under control and begin to work toward gathering the facts. The use of closed questions, specifically, can be a powerful tool to permitting the customer to continue to provide information (so he doesn't feel ignored or disrespected) while guiding and directing the conversation so that you can obtain the important facts that you need. Closed questions, if you recall, are those that can be answered with a simple, direct, and specific answer (for example, yes/no or left or right) but do not lend themselves well to a lengthy answer. Now that you can see a reason why you need to know about open and closed questioning techniques this might be a good time to go back to the previous chapter and review them.

It is important that you realize that allowing customers to empty their buckets and to vent are, while essential, not an open ticket to allow them to be loud, abusive, and to go on forever. You need to develop the skills and abilities to allow for these essential activities while maintaining control of yourself and of the situation. The ultimate solution is working to attain a balance. This is an essential skill that requires practice and patience and, once mastered, will serve you very well in any situation where you work with other people.

The Power of Thinking Win-Win

Often a complaint is not a clear-cut either/or situation. Therefore it requires that after carefully considering all of the facts involved, consideration is given to a resolution that allows all parties involved to save face and feel that they have received reasonable value. This is where real negotiating takes place. This is where a strong manager thrives because it brings out his or her ability to work to find a **win-win** solution. Let us discuss the concept of win-win solutions a bit further.

Win-Win
A problem solving strategy that seeks to find a solution that creates positive results for all involved parties.

A customer complaint situation can be likened to a two-player game. Such a game always ends with a clear winner and a clear loser. Those are also the common rules by which many people and businesses operate. Unfortunately, with this type of win/lose mentality there will always be some damage to the relationship that results. The loser may feel embarrassed, cheated, or just simply incompetent. In any case, after several losses the loser is far less likely to want to play that game again, at least against the same opponent.

Maybe customer relations does not have to be a game. Maybe it can be raised to a new level with different outcomes. Does someone really have to lose each time? Reconsider the examples that we discussed earlier about the brake failure. In the first scenario the customer was at fault. Did the customer lose? Why not? The clear answer here is that the business owner saw a far more important objective at stake than simply winning the game. It was retaining the valued customer. The same can be said for the second example where the shop was at fault. Again, they tried to negotiate their way to some sort of a win, no matter how small, out of a situation where they were clearly the initial loser. Again they did not stop at the win/lose mentality but sought to find a better solution.

Finding win-win solutions to customer relations problems and to other business and personal problems is a means of getting the most out of any situation. It requires more time, more effort, and more thought but consistently provides new opportunities to make the best out of any situation for all parties involved.

THEORY INTO PRACTICE 21-2

CASE

Mrs. Jones comes into your shop absolutely furious that she brought her car in for a radio repair and just down the street from leaving your shop the muffler fell off. "I'm sure that you must have done something to cause that," she says. "There's no way that it is just a coincidence. I've heard about how you automotive service shops prey upon helpless consumers by bugging cars to cause further problems. So, what are you going to do about it?"

You decide

As service director at ACE Auto Service it's clear to you that the radio repair and the muffler situation must be a mere coincidence. Which of the following alternatives do you think is the best option?

Option A: Explain to the customer that you weren't even working under the back of the car and that it is not your fault. Give the customer an estimate for the full cost of a muffler replacement and leave it up to her to decide if she wants you to do the work or not.

Option B: Explain that it is not likely that the two are related, but, just to remove any doubt, offer to bring the car in the shop immediately for a physical inspection, at no charge, of course, where you can both look over the situation and be sure and then go from there.

Option C: Since customers are valuable to you and you know that the customer believes that it is your fault, just go ahead without any further discussion and replace Mrs. Jones' muffler at no cost to her.

Please justify the reasoning behind the choice that you've made.

Complaint Handling Process

We've discussed concepts and rules to keep in mind to guide all customer interactions in dealing with customer complaints. Let us now recap the entire complaint handling process and break it down into a simple step-by-step model that you and all of your employees can learn to consistently employ. By keeping this simple nine-step process in mind you can be sure that you're not missing an important step as you work toward customer satisfaction. The nine-step process for resolving customer complaints is

Prepare for the opportunity to assist—Get yourself in the correct frame of mind to be of service is essential. You must be ready to be of service and provide your undivided attention to the situation at hand.

Make a professional first impression—Your initial approach and your friendly attitude can go far at diffusing a difficult situation and turning it into one of collaboration.

Listen attentively and demonstrate empathy—Ask checking questions to assure that you clearly understand, and to make sure that the customer agrees. Extend yourself by letting the customer know that you appreciate the difficulty of the situation.

Calm the customer down—Always allow the customer to go first and share his or her story. This will often help them to release the tension and anxiety and lead to a calmer dialogue.

Stay focused on the issues—The issues at hand are the circumstances, failures—not the people. Don't allow it to get personal. Stick to the issues to avoid hurt feelings.

Fix the problem—Arrive at a clear and mutually acceptable solution to resolve the situation and make it a priority to take action immediately.

Explain the solution—Before proceeding, make sure that there is complete agreement between all parties about the proposed solution and each of their responsibilities and expectations.

Summarize and thank the customer—Once an agreement has been reached, recap one last time and thank the customer for the opportunity to be of service.

Follow-up to a conclusion—Resolve all outstanding issues as quickly as possible and follow up after actions have been taken to assure that they have achieved their intended aim.

SUMMARY

This chapter has been dedicated to providing you with a wide range of principles, practices, and techniques to handle customer complaints. Customer complaints are an unavoidable part of any customer-based industry and automotive service is one of the largest customer service industries in existence. We discussed the basic rules of customer handling, some key principles to keep in mind, and closed with a short nine-step process that is easy to remember so that you can consistently use it to handle all of your customer service opportunities with the best results.

Your ability to resolve customer disputes will have a profound impact with the ultimate success and growth of your organization. Without a solid base of satisfied repeat customers, your long-term success is in serious jeopardy. Therefore, it must be your goal and your responsibility as a manager to do more than handle customer complaints and make the complaints go away. For the successful manager this is your best opportunity to turn those negative situations into positive opportunities that will help you build a base of satisfied customers and assure your future success.

PRACTICING THE PRINCIPLES

1. In dealing with an irate customer it is essential that you keep in mind that
   a. you are the representative of the company.
   b. you should take their attacks personally.
   c. you need to block out what they say.
   d. none of the above.
2. When asked to meet with an upset customer you should remember that it is important to always
   a. be sure that your life insurance premiums are paid up.
   b. let someone else meet with the customer whenever possible.
   c. focus 100 percent of your attention on the situation.
   d. all of the above.
3. The analogy that explains why it is important to allow the customer to vent and tell their story before you do anything else is called
   a. the plate.
   b. the bucket.

c. letting off steam.
d. letting it all out.

4. A good technique to make sure that the customer realizes that you're listening and understand what they are saying is
   a. asking checking questions.
   b. active listening.
   c. empathizing with their situation.
   d. all of the above.

5. So that the customer understands that you can relate to their situation it is important that you show
   a. empathy.
   b. sympathy.
   c. inconsideration.
   d. disdain.

6. It is important that you are able to ______________ ______________, rather than quickly jumping to conclusions if you want to resolve a customer complaint
   a. avoid having a perspective.
   b. try to avoid seeing it from any perspective.
   c. see it from the customer's perspective.
   d. disregard the company's perspective.

7. Trying to find a solution that provides benefits to both parties involved is called a _________ solution.
   a. 50/50.
   b. lose win.
   c. win/lose.
   d. win-win.

8. In trying to come up with the best solution, and in an effort to make a logical decision, it is important that you stick to
   a. the prearranged timeline.
   b. the facts.
   c. your customer's feelings.
   d. your guns.

9. Finding a solution that goes beyond the minimum required is called ______________ solution.
   a. a cost-effective.
   b. seeking the best.
   c. a value-added.
   d. a long-term investment.

10. The step in the nine-step Customer Complaint Handling Process that you do not take before arriving at a possible solution is to
    a. thank the customer.
    b. begin with a friendly greeting.
    c. stick to the facts.
    d. empathize with the customer.

SECTION

7

Employee Relations

The greatest asset of every successful organization is its people. Success in building and maintaining an employee team begins with a comprehensive and well-planned recruiting and selection process. Comprehensive strategies to evaluate, motivate, and educate existing employees play an important role in long-term employee retention. The success of every business depends on its ability to motivate all employees to work together to attain organizational goals. Even the unfortunate situation of "the problem employee" can result in a loyal, productive employee if the company uses a positive approach to employee problem solving. Finally, in the rare case where chronic employee performance or behavior problems cannot be resolved it is essential for every manager to know the correct methods and processes required to properly address these situations.

CHAPTER

22

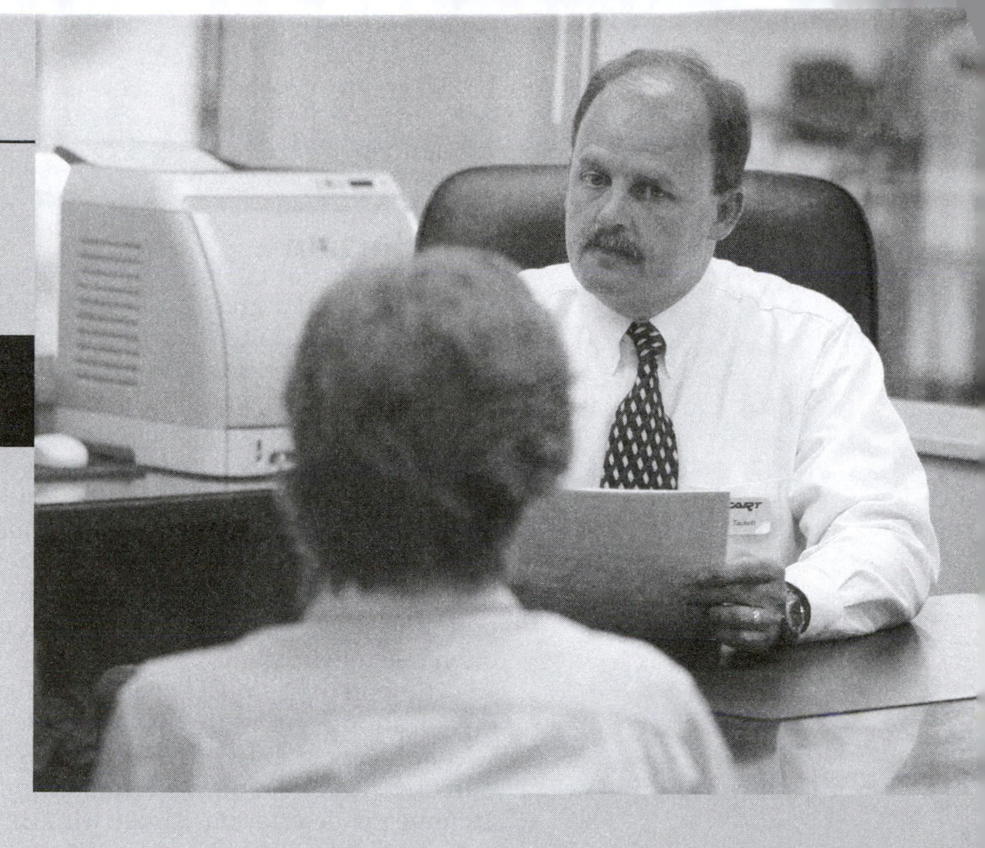

Recruiting and Selection

CHAPTER OBJECTIVES

- To identify the major steps in the recruitment and hiring process
- To identify the knowledge, skills, and abilities required to perform specific job tasks
- To develop a task analysis to determine the key responsibilities of a job
- To examine the major methods for finding qualified candidates
- To define the steps necessary to narrow down the candidate pool
- To recognize the importance of orientation and integrating a new employee into the company

KEY TERMS

job description
task analysis
KSAs
discriminatory hiring practices
rich candidate pool
headhunter
referral
screening
interview

Introduction

Managers spend a great deal of time motivating and inspiring those people under their direction. Much of the frustration that they feel is directly related to difficulty in getting the performance that they need from all of their employees. In some cases this lack of performance is due to an employee who lacks the necessary skills or abilities. Even more frustrating is the situation with an employee who has the ability but is unwilling to perform up to potential. Unfortunately, even when in the midst of these management difficulties very few managers stop to think that they may have been able to minimize or even completely avoid these situations if they had just been a bit more careful in the recruiting and selection process. The recruiting and selection process has a profound impact on the ultimate performance of the organization and is too often taken lightly.

The potential impact that individual employee performance has on the organization requires that you take the process of candidate recruitment and selection very seriously. The process begins long before you run the want ad. It starts by clearly defining job responsibilities and developing a complete and accurate job description. Armed with this information you can launch a much more focused job search to identify qualified candidates.

Once the best candidate has been chosen the process is not over; the real work is just beginning. You may have identified the candidate with the best potential to be successful, but it is what you do with that raw talent that will determine whether or not the candidate reaches full potential. Hiring is a process and not an event. The final step in the process is helping to ease the new employee's transition into the company, making him feel welcome and appreciated, and helping him to become a productive member of the team.

Defining the Job

If you ask any employee what his job is you should expect that he can easily give you an accurate description with little effort. If you ask his supervisor what the job description is for that same job the supervisor can also provide a description. Hopefully, you will find similarities between their two definitions. Unfortunately, you are just as likely to notice some significant differences between the descriptions given by these two people of the very same job. Do you find this difficult to believe? Try it yourself.

It is commonly assumed that employees and management have a common understanding and agreement of job responsibilities. They should agree on what the job responsibilities and priorities are, what the expectations of management are, and what it takes to be successful. That is true if the job description has been well thought out, well documented, and clearly agreed upon between both parties. Unfortunately, that often is not the case.

When a misunderstanding exists between an employee and management about job requirements and responsibilities this leads to inefficiency. The employee may be doing things incorrectly or not focusing on the highest priorities. It leads to important tasks being put off or not done at all. It can lead to poor work performance resulting in disciplinary action or even dismissal. It will also contribute to substandard department performance, which will jeopardize the manager's job security. These performance concerns may not be due to the employee's inability or unwillingness to do the job right. It may be solely due to a simple lack of clear and complete communication of expectations.

Lack of a clear and detailed definition of job responsibilities may result in a highly qualified candidate underperforming. It is also possible that without a clear job definition on which to base candidate selection the individual hired may start out lacking some of the skills and abilities that are essential to be successful. Neither of these problems can be fixed by motivation or discipline.

The long-term implications of a vague or poorly communicated job description are that the conditions are likely to continue to repeat. Replacing the current employee will not improve anything. Similar results will continue to repeat until the organization recognizes that the solution is to clearly define the job and the knowledge, skills, and abilities required to perform that job.

THEORY INTO PRACTICE 22-1

CASE

The purpose of this exercise is to describe one of your current positions. If you are employed you should do this with your job. If you are not working, you can do this with this course.

You decide

This exercise is meant to capture your first responses. Please do not take time to think deeply. Write down the first things that come to your mind in answer to the following requests:

1. What are your top ten responsibilities in your current job (or course)?
2. Once you have completed the list go through and prioritize the items with 1 being the most important to 10 being the least important.
3. Ask your supervisor (or professor) to do the same.
4. Compare the two lists. Place a checkmark in front of those that are the same or similar. Place a star in front of those that are different.
5. Do you have any items marked with stars? Why might the lists be different?

Job Descriptions

Development of a complete and accurate **job description** helps the organization to ensure consistency in hiring. They will also get better and more consistent performance from new employees once they are on board. The first step in developing a job description is to do a **task analysis** that defines the important responsibilities of the job. With that framework in place it is then necessary to identify the knowledge, skills, and abilities that a candidate must possess to be qualified to perform those critical tasks.

Job Description
A listing of all of the important characteristics and responsibilities of a particular position.

Task Analysis
The development of a comprehensive listing of all of the individual duties and activities that must be performed in a particular job.

Being armed with an accurate job description and a complete task list is not enough. Every supervisor's dream is to find the perfect candidate who matches the job description, has extensive related experience, possesses all of desired knowledge and skills, and is available at an affordable price. This, however, is not very likely to happen. Therefore, the best method to address this common situation is to prioritize the importance of the tasks, the knowledge, and the skills to develop a shopping list from which you can effectively select the best match out of the available candidate pool. This prioritized list will provide you with a clear idea of the investment that you need to make in the new employee to help him or her strengthen any weak areas so that he or she can grow into an ideal employee.

Task Analysis

A task analysis is the foundation of every job description. It takes into account all of the activities that an employee is required and expected to do in a particular job. By doing a little bit of research you may find that a complete and accurate task analysis already exists for a particular position. The federal government, the work of research universities, and analyses developed by other companies can provide you with a good starting point. If time and money permit, you can conduct a formal task analysis process by convening a panel of experienced individuals and enlist their help to break the job down into its component parts.

In most cases, however, you are likely to have limited time and limited funds to perform this important task. When you need to hire a new employee it is most often because of a vacancy. You cannot close down the shop for six weeks while you do the background research to develop a job description. But even though your situation may limit your options, you cannot afford to take the importance of a task analysis too lightly.

The logical solution in most cases is to do a task analysis using those resources that you have at your immediate disposal. Here are a few suggested ways that you can obtain the information that you need to develop a task list for any job.

Option 1. Based on your experience supervising people in this position, sit back and, starting from when the employee arrives at work, try to write a journal that recounts all of the events and activities that would occur in a typical day for an employee doing this job. This should be the story that describes the wide variety of tasks, both planned and unplanned, that an employee in this job is likely to experience in a complete day.

Option 2. Ask one or more employees who are currently working in this job title to keep a journal of their activities for several days. This journal should be a log, a minute-by-minute account, of all of the tasks, both planned and unplanned, that they perform each day.

Using the information gathered from these processes you can begin to develop a task list for the job. Out of the outline or journal you can then create a list of each of the unique tasks that are part of the responsibilities of this job. Once you have completed a list of tasks you can begin to group them. This should provide you with a list that indicates all of the major tasks that need to be performed and, just as important, how often each of them occurs in a typical day. From this you can develop a final list of all tasks that defines, in rank order based on the number of times that they occur, the most common tasks down to the least common ones. This provides you with a basis for developing a job description that will clearly communicate what you expect and need from an employee holding this position.

THEORY INTO PRACTICE 22-2

CASE

A task analysis is a detailed description of all of the activities that you do within a period of time. It is most commonly used to explain job requirements of a particular job but it can be used in a variety of other situations.

You decide

You are going to do a brief task analysis. Pick one hour of your day. It can be at home, at work, or at school. Write down every single thing that you do every time that you do it for that one hour. The list should include everything from the major activities down to the insignificant ones. All activities, whether planned or unplanned, should be listed. The resulting detailed chronicle is an example of a task analysis for you for that specific day and time.

Knowledge, Skills, and Abilities

Your ultimate goal is to find the best person to do the job. In an effort to do that, you have set out to develop an accurate and complete job description. First you conducted a task analysis. The information you gathered tells you what an employee in that position needs to do. However, just knowing what needs to be done is not quite enough to help you to be sure that you are finding the right candidates. You need to further analyze the activities of the task analysis.

If you are to identify a candidate who is most likely to succeed at any job you need to clearly understand the traits that a successful candidate must possess. That is, you need to have a clear and complete understanding of what knowledge and skills a person needs to make him or her capable of doing the required job. Further, you need to know what abilities that person should possess in order to be able to be successful in this position.

A candidate who is most likely to succeed at a job must possess a blend of all three of the key characteristics of knowledge, skills, and abilities (**KSAs**). One or two of the three is not enough. It is only through a balance of all three of these characteristics that you are likely to identify the right candidate.

KSAs
The knowledge, skills, and abilities that an individual must possess in order to perform a particular job or activity.

You can develop a list of KSAs by creating a list of what your ideal candidate would look like. However, you are most likely to develop a more accurate and complete list by using a task analysis as your basis. Start with a particular activity that is required as a part of the job. With a clear idea of what the task is (for example, performing an oil change), you can then break the task down into the component parts of KSAs as follows:

- What *knowledge* is required for an individual to correctly perform this task?
- What *skills* does an individual need to have to correctly perform this task?
- What *abilities* does an individual need to possess to be able to correctly perform this task?

By answering these three questions for every task listed in the job responsibilities you can develop a comprehensive KSA profile for the job. Some tasks will require significant knowledge but may not require extensive skills. Others may require specific abilities as a higher priority. For example, special abilities may be a low priority in performing a tire rotation. The ability to deal well with people in stressful situations, however, is an essential requirement to deal directly with customers.

It is most common that the extensive list of KSAs that you derive from analyzing all of the job tasks will be very long. However, you will find that there are different tasks that require the same knowledge, skill, or abilities. The number of times that a specific KSA is repeated generally indicates that the specific factor is a high priority for an individual capable of doing this job. That knowledge is essential in helping you to decide which factors are most important and, therefore, which candidates are best qualified to meet your needs.

THEORY INTO PRACTICE 22-3

CASE

You are the service manager. You have just interviewed the following two applicants for a position as engine performance/diagnostic technician:

Candidate A: This person is very interested in the job. She has provided you with proof of her knowledge having recently passed all eight of the A.S.E. Light-Duty Automotive Technician certification exams. She has provided you several references from previous employers where she worked—a major retailer and at a parts warehouse that indicate that she is intelligent, reliable, and highly motivated.

Candidate B: This candidate has provided you with references from the last three shops where he has been employed. He is A.S.E. certified in Brakes and Steering & Suspension and has worked at these shops doing preventative maintenance. All of his employers agree that he is a model employee and is very reliable and motivated.

You decide

Take just a few minutes and list the knowledge, skills, and abilities that you find in the information provided for Technician A and Technician B above. Based solely on this information would you choose Technician A or Technician B for this position? What is the basis of your decision?

THEORY INTO PRACTICE 22-4

CASE

You are the service manager. You need to hire a new service advisor. Through doing a task analysis you know that a high priority responsibility of the service advisor is scheduling customer appointments when they call the shop.

You decide

Please describe the basic knowledge, skills, and abilities that a candidate must have to be able to perform this important task.

Effective Job Descriptions

A complete and accurate job description will be a valuable tool as you attempt to identify and hire employees to fill vacancies. However, its value does not end there. An effective job description should be the foundational documentation that is used to make sure that management and the employee have a common understanding of job requirements, responsibilities, and priorities.

A well-developed job description provides an objective basis upon which all employee performance appraisals should be based. Finally, comparing employee KSAs and the job description should clearly indicate those areas that are high priority for employee training and development. By developing and implementing a plan to remedy acknowledged weak areas the employer is able to provide the new employee with tools for success. This creates a positive environment for employee and employer alike to get the job done, grow within the organization, and succeed.

Objective Criteria

There is one last thing to remember when developing a job description. It is essential that all of the criteria used to define knowledge, skills, and required abilities are job-related, essential, and unbiased. You must be careful that the criteria that you use do not discriminate against any individual or group. Every criterion must be able to pass the test that it is necessary and reasonable. Otherwise it is likely to leave you open to criticism and/or even legal action for **discriminatory hiring practices.** Here is an example of a criterion that, although well-intentioned, might cause a problem.

Discriminatory Hiring Practices

Those rules or practices that unfairly exclude groups or classes of potential employees.

> The service manager of a small tire store is setting up the criteria for a new position of assistant service manager. Every employee is expected to do a wide range of tasks in this store. Therefore, this individual will be required to occasionally handle and restock tires. In trying to be on the safe side the service manager writes into the job description the need to lift and handle 75 pounds. He knows that the only tire/wheel combinations that reach this weight are the big truck tires. He also knows that they rarely have a need to handle them because they do not stock or sell many. However, he decides that it is better to have a high weight limit rather than risking an employee getting hurt in the process.

After posting the job and hiring an employee, the shop owner is notified by several candidates that they believe that the company is discriminating against women in their hiring practices because women are less likely to be able to meet the criterion for lifting and handling 75 pounds. In this case the shop is opening itself up to bad publicity and even a discriminatory hiring practices complaint since it has unintentionally discriminated against a particular group of potential candidates by setting this requirement higher than is reasonable.

The best way to ensure that the criteria are complete, accurate, and not unreasonable is to review each of the job tasks and KSAs with the following questions in mind:

1. Is this a job requirement?
2. Is the requirement set at an appropriate level?
3. Does this requirement discriminate against any group or class?

Criteria for any job do not have to be reduced to an unreasonably low level to provide access to all potential candidates. However, they must be reasonable and based on required tasks. The knowledge, skills, and abilities required should be based on acceptable performance of the job and normal circumstances. Although you may have the best intentions in being safe, you have to balance that desire with the assurance that you are not discriminating.

Finding Candidates

Once you have developed clear criteria so that you know exactly what you are looking for in a job candidate it is time to find that candidate. If you are to get the best employee it is important that you use a variety of methods to find the largest pool of qualified candidates from which to choose your new employee. If you have followed the direction provided earlier in this chapter you have done all that you can to clearly define what it takes to do the job. As a result, you have a solid basis for identifying the right candidate. Now you need to turn your efforts to the search process.

Rich Candidate Pool

You should use a variety of resources ranging from mass media to personal referrals to reach and attract the largest and most diverse pool of qualified candidates possible. This requires using different types of communication. You must identify those that are most likely to reach different populations within the marketplace. Most mass media stations intentionally produce their material to reach a specific and narrow target market (youth, 20–35-year-olds, sports enthusiasts, women). Using a group of TV, radio, and direct mail sources that appeal to the same audience will get the attention only of that narrow segment of the population but will do nothing to reach the rest of the community. It is important to carefully target market when looking for new employees (just as you would in your sales activities). To do so you must identify a selection of media that will reach across geographic areas and groups within the community. When you do this, you will have a **rich candidate pool** to choose from.

Rich Candidate Pool
A group of applicants that is sufficiently large and diverse to be representative of the qualified talent available in the marketplace.

Your ultimate goal is getting the best candidate to fill your needs. You want to be the best. The fastest way to accomplish this is to attract and employ the best. You can be sure that you are identifying the best candidate when you start the process by inviting all qualified candidates to apply. You need to be aware if you want to be responsive to the public that should have a workforce that is representative of that population and can, therefore, best address their unique needs. Having a representative workforce is as important as having employees with the right knowledge and skills. However, only through an intentional plan for targeting diverse markets can you be sure that you will accomplish this goal.

Advertising

The typical marketing budget for employee recruitment is limited. In addition, in most cases personnel needs require a speedy resolution. Many of the mass media methods are too expensive or take too much lead time to prepare to be suitable for these situations. (*You may want to refer to the materials presented in Chapter 25 on the benefits and drawbacks of various advertising media. This information can help you get the best value for your money when you are running a help wanted ad just as it can when you are advertising for new service customers.*) The most common methods for finding job candidates are newspapers, headhunters, job boards, and referrals. Each of these has unique benefits.

Newspaper advertising has long been the most common method for running wanted ads. It enables you to get your message out very quickly, typically within a matter of two to three days, and ensures that your message reaches a broad audience. In many large communities there are several papers to choose from. The large metropolitan paper has the widest reach and can blanket the area. Suburban and special-interest newspapers should also be strongly considered as a part of your advertising strategy. These newspapers cater to smaller, more localized audiences. These audiences may be localized to a specific neighborhood, suburb, or target audience within the larger community. These newspapers can target specific populations at a reasonable cost and help ensure that you are attracting a rich cross-section of the overall population.

Headhunter

Independent recruiter whose sole job is to actively seek out qualified candidates to fill job positions for companies.

Headhunters have recently become increasingly available in the automotive service industry. Whereas previously this method for finding candidates was limited only to corporate white-collar positions, the prolonged shortage of technical workers has resulted in multiple headhunter organizations that cater to automotive service personnel needs. The explosive growth of the Internet as a primary communication source has brought with it the rapid growth of online job boards and Web-based employment agencies that can be accessed quickly to help you to expand your employee search.

Referral

Individuals who have been recommended or directed to a company as a client or potential employee.

A final, and very valuable, source for finding new employees is **referrals** from your suppliers, your customers, and your current employees. Who knows your organization better than those groups? As a result, who would be best qualified to refer candidates to you that are most likely to meet your needs and "fit in" to your organization? In a healthy organization where the employees, customers, and vendors are proud to be associated with your company, referrals are one of the most reliable sources for new employees.

Even though you may find strong candidates through referrals, this method has its own potential problems. Most of the referrals that you receive are likely to be current employees of other suppliers and/or direct competitors. Nothing can tarnish your reputation in the industry faster than developing a reputation for stealing employees from your competitors. In most businesses there is a gentleman's agreement that companies do not steal employees from each other. So, what do you do? Here is an example.

Real World Application

As a service director for more than five years in the same dealership and an active participant in the local service and parts manager's club I knew my market well and had a good working relationship with my fellow service managers. We worked well together, sharing ideas and tried to support each other's growth even though we were direct competitors. One of the things that had always bothered me was the habit of a few shops stealing employees from their competitors on a regular basis. That seemed totally wrong to me until one day when I was faced with a unique opportunity.

Totally out of the blue I was visited by one of the top technicians from another service shop down the street. He asked if I had a few moments and advised me that he was actively looking to make a job change. He said that he definitely intended to leave where he was working as soon as he could find a suitable new employer and wanted to know if we would be interested. I was immediately very excited and very concerned. Here in front of me sat one of the top three technicians in the city and he was ours if I wanted him. Yet, he was an employee of a competitor and close collaborator. Was it right? What should I do?

I asked the technician to give me a few days to get back with him. I considered the possibilities and the potential consequences. How could I pass this up? How would it affect our reputation if I did not pass

(*Continued*)

this up? After much thought I called the technician and laid out the facts to him. "I am very interested in having you come to work for us, and I would love to have you here. However, we have a very good and long-standing relationship with your current employer and I do not want to jeopardize that. I know that this might sound weird but what I would like to do, with your permission, is to call your manager and talk to him. I need to try to find a way that both saves our reputation with him and others in the city yet does not allow you to end up working for some other manufacturer or independent shop. Is that OK with you?" He agreed.

Later that day I called his service manager. I let him know about the visit. I asked him if he realized that this technician was out shopping around. I reassured him that I had not changed my position on stealing technicians from other service shops. However, if this technician had made up his mind to leave his current job I would like to have the opportunity to have him rather than seeing him go to some other competitor's shop. I closed by telling him that I was calling out of respect to him and to give him the opportunity to meet with his technician to try to iron out their difficulties. I told him that if they were unable to settle their differences that I intended to actively pursue hiring this technician. After some discussion he agreed that this was a reasonable approach.

The final result was that the technician had already made up his mind that it was time for a change and was set on leaving his current employer despite the efforts made by his boss to keep him. He called me back after having a heart-to-heart talk with his current manager. We were successful in hiring this talented technician.

After the fact, several of our fellow service managers heard about this encounter and thought that it was an odd approach. However, by taking this extra care I was able to hire a great employee while maintaining our dealership's reputation and, on the personal side, maintaining a friendship with the service manager down the street. It was an investment of time and effort well spent.

Screening and Selection

The final steps in the process of finding the right job candidate are screening, interviewing, selecting, and hiring. These are all combined into one group because they typically fall together in a rapid-fire sequence of events. Determining what you need is a long and involved process. Finding those candidates who best exemplify the knowledge, skills, and abilities that you need to fill the position takes some time. However, once you have finally pulled the candidate list together and are satisfied that you have a large enough, rich enough pool of candidates you will likely be impatient to hire someone.

Although these final four steps can be accomplished in a relatively short time do not be impatient. You need to take the time to move through each of these steps methodically to ensure that you have not wasted all of your previous efforts.

Screening

Screening
To carefully look at and separate those qualified or unqualified based on pre-established objective criteria.

Depending on the size of your company or your department the initial **screening** may be done by your human resources department or by you. However, the purpose of this step is the same whatever the setting, and that is to thoroughly review all applications and narrow down the pool of candidates based on a few very basic decisions. The first of these is: Does the candidate meet all of the requirements in the job description and job posting?

Conducting a fair and effective hiring process means it must be an objective process. Filtering the candidate pool by eliminating all candidates who do not meet the minimum requirements as stated in the job posting helps to assure the objectivity of the process.

Once you have eliminated candidates that did not meet the minimum requirements you will find that you have:

1. not enough candidates that are qualified to proceed forward,
2. a pool of candidates that, although qualified is still too large to interview, or
3. a reasonably sized yet rich pool of qualified candidates.

The appropriate action if you have pool that is too small is to re-open the search process. This may delay the hiring process, but it will improve your satisfaction in the end. If, in contrast, your remaining pool is too large you need to take additional steps to narrow it down to a reasonable number for interviews, typically six to 12 candidates. Have the selection committee evaluate and rank the candidates based on the information provided in their applications. Once you have narrowed the pool to a reasonable size it is time to proceed to interviews.

Interviewing

Interview

A formal meeting intended to identify and verify qualifications and characteristics.

In many automotive repair shops the **interview** process is the sole responsibility of the direct manager who will supervise the new hire. In some organizations the human resources department or a specially appointed selection committee conducts the initial interviews. In either case the goal is to conduct an organized process to verify, based on a face-to-face meeting, the degree to which candidates meet your job requirements.

Candidates who make it to this stage of the process have already met the scrutiny of the screening process, which means that they meet the minimum requirements. The interview process allows you to verify this information, clarify any areas in question, and gives the candidates the opportunity to make a personal appeal to convince you why they are the best candidate for the job.

There is a big difference between best qualified and best fit for the organization, though. Being successful requires a blend of both. Not only is it important that you verify that the candidate has the proper qualifications, you also have to evaluate personality, style, and attitudes to see if he or she is a good fit for your organization and its unique culture.

The interview process is a combination of objective and subjective evaluations by the interviewer(s). One of the best ways to ensure that the interviewers have a sound basis for comparison is the use of a structured interview process. This will provide you with the best opportunity for evaluating all candidates according to the same criteria. A structured interview should have a common location, time schedule, and a prepared list of questions. With these tools in place you will have a better basis for comparing all the candidates—under similar conditions based on identical criteria.

One of the potential problems with interviewing multiple candidates is the possibility of getting the candidates and/or their responses confused. One way to address this issue is to use a scoring or ranking system. By assigning a score or ranking on each of the responses from each candidate you can reduce confusion as you complete multiple interviews. This will allow you to debrief on and score each interviewee at the conclusion of the interview. Then, you can proceed to the next interviewee without needing to remember previous issues or questions.

Occasionally the interviews will result in one candidate that emerges as the clear favorite and is your first choice to hire. More often, though, the group of candidates will be closely ranked into several groups. The first group is those candidates that you do not want to consider any further. At the other end of the continuum are the clear top three or four that are all qualified and very close when compared. If you have trouble clearly separating the top candidates, a second, more in-depth interview with these finalists is highly recommended. For this second interview you may want to consider involving individuals who hold similar positions or will be working closely with this new employee. You may also want to involve your supervisor for an unbiased second opinion.

Selection

The information provided by the applications and the interviews should provide you with enough information to make your final selection. It is important that you can support your final decision as being a clear, unbiased, and objective one. In today's society it is not uncommon for a candidate who is not chosen to contest your decision. This may range from a complaint to you or your boss up to a threat to file a discrimination lawsuit. If your process was built upon a well-defined foundation of clear and complete job requirements, identified knowledge, skills, and abilities, and a rigorous and objective screening and interviewing process you will have little to worry about.

There is one last action that is a vital part of this step. It is completing the background check. You probably stated in your job criteria that all candidates must have a valid driver's license, a clear police record, and be drug free. However, because of privacy issues many states and localities limit your ability to perform these background checks until you make the job offer. Under these circumstances when you have made your final choice you offer the candidate the position contingent upon his or her ability to pass these screens. The selected candidate needs to be clearly informed that employment cannot begin until the results have been received and verified. Once this happens you can finalize the job offer and hire the individual.

Hiring

After having completed the exhaustive process that we have covered in this chapter you might believe that it is finally over. You have hired your new advisor, technician, porter, or other employee and now you can just put him or her to work and go back to the millions of other responsibilities that have stacked up on your desk while you were spending time with this. You could take that approach, but it is not recommended.

Hiring is not an event, it is a process. When a new employee shows up on the first day for work the process is not over. It is entering its last important phase. Having taken the time and effort to identify, select, and then convince the right candidate to take the job you need to be sure not to drop the ball at this point. Your new employee is a stranger in your company; he or she may know a few of your employees but is bound to be somewhat insecure and confused working with new co-workers, in a new place, with new rules and new expectations. The faster and better that you help that new employee to integrate into your organization the sooner they will feel comfortable and become a productive member of the team.

A great way to start this process of integrating a new employee into your organization is to set aside time to put him or her through a new employee orientation. This orientation should include completing all of the new employee paperwork and explaining it all. More important, however, this orientation should include introductions to co-workers in your department and to key employees in other departments within the company. Taking the time to review your company handbook and to discuss company policies and your specific expectations will further help the new employee to understand his or her responsibilities.

Taking the time to orient the new employee as the last step in the hiring process is important. It helps the new employee to feel wanted, to feel accepted, and to start out with a clearer understanding of what is expected and required. Finally, by clearly demonstrating how glad you are to have this new employee on board and how much you value him as an employee can easily make his first impression a very positive one. You needed someone, you wanted him, you selected him . . . now start off his employment by making sure that he knows it.

SUMMARY

In this chapter we discussed the entire process necessary to identify, select, and hire the best people to fill job positions within organizations. This process does not begin by advertising for new employees. Rather, it requires that significant background work is done first to clearly identify what is needed and what is required to perform the job.

The background work required begins with a task analysis. This process breaks down the job into its component activities. This helps to clarify those skill sets that a properly qualified candidate must possess. By defining the knowledge, skills, and abilities (KSAs) a candidate must possess to effectively perform the many and varied job tasks you can build a definition of what the job is and what the job requires. You can then build an accurate job description and will know what to look for to find the right candidate to fill that position.

Armed with this knowledge you can begin the recruitment process. This process starts with advertising to attract qualified candidates. Once an adequately large and diverse pool of candidates has been collected, it is necessary to screen the applicants to eliminate those who do not meet the minimum job requirements. When the candidate pool is narrowed down to only qualified candidates, the process proceeds through interviews. The interviews verify the knowledge, skills, and abilities and assess how well candidates will fit into the culture of the organization. The next step in the process is hiring. However, this is not the last step. The final step is to help to integrate the new employee into the organization through conducting a new employee orientation.

PRACTICING THE PRINCIPLES

1. The last step in the hiring process is
   a. interviewing.
   b. selecting.
   c. orientation.
   d. screening.
2. A __________________________ lists of all of the important characteristics and responsibilities of a particular position.
   a. KSAs.
   b. job description.
   c. task analysis.
   d. newspaper article.
3. If you establish job requirements that are not essential or are too difficult to match the actual needs of the position you might
   a. get sued for discrimination.
   b. get bad publicity.
   c. screen out some good candidates.
   d. all of the above.
4. The best way to obtain a rich candidate pool for a position is to
   a. only advertise in the high-income suburbs.
   b. use a variety of media and publications.
   c. target specific audiences to assure diversity.

d. a and c.
e. b and c.

5. KSAs are
   a. knowledge, skills, and abilities.
   b. knowledge, skills and aptitudes.
   c. knowing, seeing, alerting.
   d. three letters.

6. A process that can have a profound impact on the ultimate performance of the organization and is too often taken lightly is
   a. recruiting and selection.
   b. hiring and orienting.
   c. advertising and promotion.
   d. incentives and promotions.

In Questions 7–9 please fill in the blanks

7. A ________________ is an independent company that actively finds candidates to fill jobs for other companies.

8. When one of your current customers sends a potential candidate to you for a job opening this is called a ________________.

9. To develop a comprehensive listing of all of the individual duties and activities that must be performed in a particular job you should conduct a ________________.

10. Please mark the proper letter from list A that best describes each statement in list B.

List A	List B
A—Knowledge	a. outgoing and friendly _______
B—Skills	b. able to perform complex repairs _______
C—Abilities	c. able to pass ASE tests _______
	d. cooperates well with others _______
	e. types 25 words per minute _______
	f. can memorize specifications _______

CHAPTER

23

Motivating Employees

CHAPTER OBJECTIVES

- To recognize the importance of motivation as a tool for improved employee morale, retention, and productivity
- To develop and communicate clear performance goals to employees
- To discuss the importance of regular performance reviews
- To examine the relationship between compensation plans and the resulting performance

KEY TERMS

expectations
tracking performance
sub-goals
metric
comeback
redo
compensation plan
incentives

Introduction

Keeping employees motivated is a very complex endeavor. One of a manager's key responsibilities is to motivate employees, obtain consistent performance, and then help them and the department to continue to improve. Your ability to do this is based on clearly defining expectations, consistently tracking performance against those expectations, and maintaining open communication with employees to regularly advise them of their progress.

Setting Clear Expectations

Expectations
Clear and well-defined statements of responsibilities and intended outcomes.

A common cause of sub-par performance is often not an employee's unwillingness or inability to perform. The primary cause is lack of a clear understanding of management's **expectations.** With a lack of very clear and specific expectations it is quite possible for employees to have a different understanding of the goals, directions, and priorities than what management intends. Employees may be working their hardest in the direction that they believe that they are supposed to be headed. Unfortunately, without clear expectations provided by and consistently reinforced by management they can very easily be heading in a totally different direction than management intended. If that is the case they may reach a destination—but it will not be the one that management had in mind.

In today's hectic world of work it is difficult enough to finish those things that are top priority. There certainly is not enough time to be diverting any energy or resources to activities that are not as important. This loss of productivity is likely to assure your failure to meet your goals. Therefore, it is essential that you clearly and consistently define the goals, objectives, and priorities of each job and of the organization. Only with this clear and consistent communication can you be sure that everyone is exerting all of the effort that they have toward accomplishing the right results.

The key test to be sure that the goals and objectives that you set are sound is that they meet the test of the following four questions:

1. Are the goals clearly defined?
2. Is the level of expected performance reasonable?
3. Within the limits of the time and resources available, is the goal achievable?
4. Have the goals been clearly communicated to the employee(s)?

Your ability to successfully answer these questions about any goals and objectives you develop will greatly increase your employees' ability to achieve them and, thus, markedly increase your chances for ultimate success.

We have already noted the importance of clearly communicating expectations. However, if your goal is to obtain maximum performance it is not only necessary to define and communicate the goals, they must be reasonable and achievable. Why is this true?

Goals and objectives set a clear direction for action and, if properly constructed, act as incentives and motivators for performance. Anyone who enters a race has a clear idea of where the finish line is. In addition, each competitor has his sights clearly set on reaching that finish line. But what would happen if the finish line was so far in the distance or so poorly explained that the competitors might very well get lost? They also might lose their enthusiasm and motivation because the goal seems too vague, too distant, and appears unreachable in spite of their best efforts.

When goals and objectives are not clearly stated or are far too ambitious, rather than being motivators they become morale-breakers. If goals are not clearly defined and employees are unsure of exactly where they are headed, they are unlikely to fully commit their energies and resources to them. When employees feel that the goal is simply unattainable their response is most likely to dismiss it. The result is that the goal has a negative effect on productivity and morale. In order for the goals and objectives that you set to become motivators for excellent performance you need to be absolutely sure that they will be viewed by the employees as reasonable and obtainable and, therefore, goals that they can willingly accept, support, and commit to.

Tracking Performance

Once goals and objectives have been clearly communicated, it is important that you are **tracking performance** on an ongoing basis. The combination of monitoring performance and keeping employees advised of their status toward goal achievement is essential to success. It reminds employees what the goals are and that you are keeping them clearly in focus. It provides them with encouragement that you are noticing the fruits of their efforts. Finally, it gives them adequate warning when performance is lagging so that they have the opportunity to make the necessary changes to assure ultimate success. All these factors help to make the long, hard pull up the hill to reach the final goal a consistent effort. This will help reduce stress, keep employees focused and engaged, and will let them know that you see and appreciate their successes.

Tracking Performance

Consistently monitoring actual performance against measurable stated objectives.

Many major goals are not accomplished overnight. The longer it takes to achieve a goal the more essential it is to have methods in place for maintaining focus. Using performance tracking is essential as we work toward achieving the final goal one step at a time. Major goals are often long-term and complicated. You will need to be wary of your employees putting off working on the overwhelming larger goals until it is too late.

Putting these major goals off is easy. It is easy to get distracted or misdirected into working on tasks that are simpler, more easily completed, and that provide rapid rewards. Careful planning, tracking, and status reporting on progress toward the big goal will help ensure that it stays in the forefront of your employees' minds and efforts. An additional technique that you may find helpful is to break the big goal down into several smaller segments.

Breaking down big goals into **sub-goals** reduces anxiety and makes the task less overwhelming. Carefully planning each of these sub-goals allows you and your employees to make the journey toward the big goal one step at a time. Then as they accomplish each sub-goal they should be reminded how they have just finished one more step toward the big goal. This will continue to re-energize their commitment toward the ultimate objective.

Sub-Goals

Small, short-term goals that are part of a larger, more complex overarching goal.

Measuring What Is Important

Setting clear goals and expectations makes tracking and motivating employee performance much easier. Managing with data is essential so that you can be objective in your employees' evaluations. The ability to draw a clear connection between stated performance objectives and actual performance makes the process of employee evaluation more valuable to both you and the employee. Although it may be difficult for an employee to accept the fact that his performance is below par, this difficult conversation is much easier to deliver—and much easier for the employee to tolerate—when it is based on objective performance data.

Establishing measures, however, is a bit more complicated than just gathering data and running reports. It is important that the data that you report and measure is closely aligned with the core responsibilities of the job and organizational priorities. Data is a valuable tool, but you need to remember that this data reflects only a portion of an employee's overall performance.

Metric
Easily definable measurement (usually numbers) used to monitor and track performance.

An example of a very measurable performance **metric** for technicians is productivity (number of flat-rate hours produced). It is a very important factor in the ultimate success of the department and the organization. This number is commonly used to measure performance, to motivate employees, and even to reprimand employees when productivity is below expectations. The beauty of such data is that it is a clear, specific, measurable, and definable goal. However, be careful that this data does not take on more importance and weight than it deserves. Data cannot measure every important part of the total job responsibilities. Your performance evaluations must include more than just easily measurable information, they should answer the question: What are the overall goals and objectives of this position?

Care needs to be taken to look at the big picture of the total job responsibilities. Taken to an extreme, measuring and managing solely based on easily measurable data is a huge mistake. How is that possible?

Comeback
A recently repaired vehicle that returns to the shop because of customer dissatisfaction with the completeness or accuracy of the repairs.

If you measure, reward, and punish based on productivity then the only thing that your employees will really value and strive to achieve is productivity. However, productivity is not likely to be your only goal. Customer satisfaction and quality of repairs are also major goals as are several others. The point is that if you consistently measure and report productivity and stress this measurement (or any other one) too much, then regardless of what you say to the contrary employees will realize that the way to get recognition, the way to get on the boss's good side is to produce more hours (productivity). Nothing more, nothing less—despite the other things that you have said about the importance of reducing errors, **comebacks**, and complaints. Let us look at a real-world example of how overemphasis of one measurement can lead to trouble.

Real World Application

When taking on a new position as service manager in a large dealership my employer advised me that they were "looking to make a change. We need someone who knows and understands how to build satisfied and loyal customers." Upon starting the job I found out that this was no small problem. The dealership had the lowest customer satisfaction ratings in the entire region of the country—and one of the lowest in the entire United States. Why was this so?

I looked around the shop for clues on the root cause of the problem and for ideas to turn this situation around. I quickly learned that, but for a few minor exceptions, the shop was staffed with some very competent and conscientious technicians, was well equipped and in a great location. The service advisors were experienced, polite, and responsive to customer needs. They did a very good job addressing customer complaints. The telephone operator and cashier were both professional and polite. How could a problem of such magnitude exist in a shop that had the potential to be a leader in providing quality service?

Although the solution was not accomplished overnight or as the result of one simple action, the pivotal change that resulted in turning this situation around centered on identifying one very simple fact. The shop measured, rewarded, and displayed one thing, and one thing only. This was the total number of flat-rate hours produced by each team and each technician daily. Even though the dealership talked the talk that they were interested in quality, previous management had promoted and rewarded only productivity. The greatest testimony to this focus was a large whiteboard hanging on the shop wall where the daily productivity of each technician and team was posted for all to see. It was positioned so that all of the technicians walked by it every time they headed up to the service desk to get an order, get an approval, or ask a question. They prided themselves in "being on top on the board" and competed intensely among themselves to earn and maintain that status. They kidded the lower producing teams and shamed those who produced fewer hours on their own team.

In this situation, what do you suppose would help to change the attitudes and the performance? The answer was to change the board. The board was not removed or broken up and burned (although those options were considered). The board was used, but used to report and reinforce what management said was their real number-one priority, satisfied customers.

In addition to changing the board, a temporary position, of quality control technician, was created to double-check the quality of repairs. Those vehicles that were not fixed correctly were returned to the technician before the customer even picked them up and these incidents were tracked as **redo's**. Those few instances where cars were delivered to the customers and resulted in customer complaints were tracked as comebacks and given top priority when they came back into the shop.

Most important, the board was not used any longer to track hours produced. Its big numbers, still posted daily, reported the number of redo's and comebacks that each technician and team tallied. At the end of every month there was a special ceremony and lunch where the shop celebrated the team with the highest quality ratings. The team was treated to a free lunch of pizza and soda and received acknowledgement for their important achievement.

You might think that this was just a shift from overemphasizing one measure for another. However, since all of the technicians were paid based on flat rate it was already clear to me that they had internal motivation to maintain and continue to grow those numbers. The shift of the board's focus helped to add another important measurement to their thoughts and actions.

In less than two years, as a result of these efforts—and measuring and rewarding what management really valued—the shop went from last place to first place. We were visited by the regional manager from the manufacturer and acknowledged as having made the single largest improvement in customer satisfaction ratings in the entire region.

Performance Evaluations

Conducting semi-annual or annual formal evaluations of employee performance is important to ensure that all parties know where they stand. This benefits the supervisor as much as it does the employee. Therefore, this should happen regularly and be taken seriously as an important part of doing your job as a supervisor.

Redo

A repair that does not meet quality standards and must return to the shop for additional repairs before delivery to the customer.

Taking the time to sit down and prepare an annual evaluation requires that you take time to reflect on the past year. It provides for a formal mechanism to debrief on all of the events and actions, no matter how large or small, that have contributed to the year. Successes and failures both need be addressed. The overall evaluation should be balanced. It should cite positive behaviors that you want to reinforce and see occur regularly. Likewise, it needs to clearly address those unfavorable incidents or instances where performance fell short of expectations so that focus can be placed on them in the coming year to resolve and avoid them.

We have been called a critical society. As a culture we commonly fail to provide adequate reinforcement and praise for the good things that happen. Whether as children or as employees it is common to hear the question, "Why do you only say something when I mess up? What about the good things that I do?" If we are to help build the skills and morale of our employees it is essential that we acknowledge their best performances, the bright spots in their year. In fact, the best way to start off any counseling session and, especially, an annual evaluation, is to list the strong points and highlights of the year first. It gives the employee reinforcement to expand those positive areas. It makes the rest, even if it is very critical, more palatable.

Beginning with praise for the best efforts of the past year is especially important when evaluating someone who is experiencing serious performance problems. The intent here is not to sugar coat the problems. It is not to divert attention from the concerns. However, it is important to make it clear that the concerns that you are about to review do not mean that he or she is a bad person. Conversely, he or she has shown some positive traits and performance. However, there are some serious issues that need to be resolved. By approaching it in this manner the goal is to separate the behavior (lack of performance) from the person. It is much easier to change behaviors than it is to change people. Because of the importance of handling some of the more difficult employee performance situations we will dedicate significant time to covering a formal process to work with those situations in Chapter 24—Progressive Discipline.

The Evaluation Process

Evaluations should provide a review of the time period (year/six months/quarter) for each of the important performance criteria for the employee. This time period should be determined in advance, clearly stated at the time of hire, and consistently followed. Using a standard format for evaluating all employees ensures consistency. It also ensures that no important issues are unintentionally omitted.

The list of items that should be discussed at a periodic evaluation should include the job responsibilities of the employee's position and observed behavior and performance related to those responsibilities. This clear and constant alignment of responsibilities and evaluation reinforces to the employee that their stated job responsibilities and the periodic direction and guidance that you have provided are, in fact, the exact basis for evaluating their performance.

Although the annual evaluation meeting should be a comfortable situation, be certain to provide enough structure so that it does not become a conversation with no specific point or outcome. In many situations this may be the only instance where an appointed time has been set aside to discuss past performance and future expectations. Communicating this information is essential to assuring that the employee and the employer both clearly understand each other and what is expected. This is also one of the best times for providing the employee the opportunity to air any questions or ongoing concerns.

Many larger companies use a prewritten evaluation instrument that covers a broad range of general criteria to ensure that all evaluations are consistent and cover the full scope of job knowledge, skills, and abilities. Some examples of these criteria are: ability to work well with others, takes initiative with minimal supervision, and is rarely late or absent. These performance criteria help assure that the evaluation interview is a broad-based recap of performance. They help make it easier to start some of the difficult conversations about performance issues with everyone from the poor performers to the exemplary ones who, although above average in some areas, may have some issues to address.

Many companies, especially smaller ones, do not rely on a formal evaluation instrument to conduct evaluations. However, thoroughness and consistency are essential characteristics of an effective evaluation no matter what form it takes. Therefore, even in the case of locally developed criteria it is strongly recommended that the supervisor prepare a list of performance standards, expectations, and other important performance criteria against which all employees to be evaluated will be measured. By measuring all employees against the same standards of performance the supervisor is then assured of being able to conduct a thorough, meaningful, and unbiased evaluation.

Regardless of whether they are conducted in a mega-corporation or a small two-person shop, regular evaluations are essential tools for employee development. The annual evaluation is one of the most effective means to ensure that all, employees and management, are in agreement about what is expected and what has occurred during the past twelve months. More important, they leave the evaluation with clear expectations for the coming year and a better understanding of how they are going to work together to achieve them.

Employee Compensation

There is no more serious issue in dealing with any employee than their compensation plan. Any change in pay is likely to have significant impact on their performance, overall satisfaction, and willingness to stay with your company. Therefore, one of the first rules of management is *Do not mess with your employee's money!* This is more than a matter of economics. It is often a matter of great pride and is closely tied to their self-worth. Their status among fellow employees and where they see themselves being ranked as a part of that group is at stake in the minds of most employees.

Real World Application

As service director in a large metropolitan dealership I was fortunate to have a very talented and stable group of technicians. Turnover was uncharacteristically low because of a strong commitment from the entire management group to provide a comfortable and stable work environment. I thought that I really valued my employees and demonstrated that in the way that I worked with them and treated them on a daily basis. I thought that I knew how important an employee's pay was. That was not true until I learned the following lesson the hard way.

At our dealership all of the technicians got paid weekly, at the end of their normal work day every Friday at 5 P.M. One very typical Friday I very unexpectedly caught a glimpse of one of my most loyal and long-term technicians loading up his toolbox. His work area was at the other end of the shop. Nothing had been said, nothing had occurred. He was always one who was willing to help anyone at any time. He was as loyal as the day was long. He was the last technician who I would have expected this behavior from.

I approached him and cautiously asked, "What is the problem?" His reply, without hesitation, was that he did not want to work any longer at a shop where the employees were not respected. "Not respected?" I replied. "Yes," he replied. "This is the second time in a row that you have been late getting our paychecks to us. We're supposed to be paid at 5 P.M. on Fridays and it is already 5:10 and—no paycheck. I can tolerate a lot but I just cannot work for anyone who messes with my money. I am here on time every day. I am rarely late or absent."

(Continued)

I stopped him at that point, explaining that I was sorry and that I had gotten involved with a customer question and did not realize that it was so late. Besides, I thought to myself, it was only 10 minutes. It was not a matter of us not having the money to make payroll—it was not that the checks were not ready. It was simply that I had been distracted and lost sight of the time.

He had already loaded his toolbox in the back of his car. He did not appear to be mad at this point. However, he was not ready to commit to changing his mind about quitting, either. He quietly drove off. There I stood surprised, frustrated, and afraid that I had, through my ignorance and insensitivity, lost one of our best technicians!

As I went home that evening and over the course of the weekend I thought over and over about my unintentional blunder. I made several attempts to call him at home to talk further about it but was not able to reach him. Finally, on Sunday evening I was able to talk to him and, based on the otherwise solid relationship that we had along with his long-standing respect of top management and his co-workers he reluctantly agreed to give me/us one more chance.

This near catastrophe left an indelible mark in my memory about the relationship between an employee's pay and your relationship with them. To many employees their paycheck is the clearest measure of how much you value and respect them.

Compensation Plan
All of the pay and benefits that are received by an employee including regular pay, incentives, paid time off, insurance, and retirement contributions.

It is important to realize that your employees' compensation plan is more than simply his or her hourly rate. The total **compensation plan** is a combination of all of the pay and benefits that are received. In addition to direct monetary items such as hourly rate and performance bonuses other valuable benefits provided may include paid vacation and sick time, health and life insurance, and disability and retirement benefits.

It is important that you are aware of the full range of compensation benefits and that you offer and maintain a direct link between performance and compensation. Since changes in pay rates or performance bonuses are the most likely compensation items to be individually changeable, they are commonly the ones that can be closely tied to the employee evaluation process. The annual evaluation is the ideal time to sit down and reward your employee by giving him a pay increase that is directly tied to a glowing annual evaluation. To the same extent, a pay increase that is less than expected can and should be tied to a substandard evaluation. By doing this, the employees can all see a clear relationship between performance and rewards. Based on this logic, care should be taken to avoid two very common errors—positive evaluations with no reward and pay raises across the board that are unrelated to performance. Although some work environments may make these situations unavoidable, such as under a union contract, it is strongly suggested that you be vigilant and try to avoid these situations when possible. Failure to tie performance to rewards sends a dangerous mixed message to employees that can confuse them and significantly harm their morale.

Let us consider the possible implications of such situations. It is very difficult to conduct an evaluation with an employee in which you give him a glowing review filled with praises of his exemplary performance and then announce that there will be no raises this year. What message does that send to the employee? How would you feel? Even during tight financial times it is important to avoid this situation. If it is at all possible you need to work to provide some type of reward, no matter how small, that you can tie to exemplary performance and an exemplary evaluation.

If an unavoidable situation exists where you find yourself in circumstances where you have no ability to give any raises for the year, it is strongly suggested that this be announced well in advance of evaluation time. This will help to separate the individual and their performance from the compensation issue. It will help temper employee expectations.

The second pitfall of passing on raises is the across-the-board raise. This method of giving raises equally rewards all employees—and that is often cited as its benefit. However, not all employees have worked equally, performed equally, and been dedicated to the company and its success equally—so why would you reward them equally? The across-the-board raise sends a mixed message to your employees. You say that you want performance, commitment, and dedication and yet you pay for showing up. It is easy to see how employees would be confused about the message you are sending.

Even though it is clear that there are significant pitfalls to giving raises in this way there are situations where this type of pay raise strategy is mandated. What do you do then? You should do as you have with any situation that is beyond your control. You acknowledge it, understand the possible implications on morale and motivation, and move forward better armed to deal with it since you realize the potential problems that it may present in the future.

Incentives

Incentives are short-term benefits or bonuses that are tied to specific performance within a limited time period. An example of an incentive is a $5 bonus for every set of four new tires that a technician recommends and sells. Another incentive might be a month-long competition for two tickets to a local race event for the technician who sells the most additional labor and parts. Incentives are intended to provide very specific and immediate rewards for increased performance over the short term.

Incentives
Short-term benefits or bonuses that are tied to specific performance within a limited time period.

Incentives can be very beneficial. It should always be your goal that they will result in a short-term increase in performance and, more important, that they will have a lasting effect. Through encouraging employees to go 'above and beyond' what they have previously done it is hoped that they develop the self-confidence that they can and will perform at this higher level after the incentive is over. With this in mind, incentives can be an effective part of a long-term improvement strategy to stimulate and increase performance levels.

Even though incentives are short-term, it is important to remember that just like all changes to overall compensation they follow the rule stated above—Do not mess with your employee's money! As such, it is essential that incentives be structured so that all employees are confident that the incentives are fair and equitable. Failure to do this results in complaints of favoritism and cheating and can reduce employee morale rather than improve it.

Tying Performance to Compensation

The last, and most important, rule about the value of compensation as a motivator is that it is essential that you reward what you value. What does this mean? If you refer back to the story earlier in this chapter about turning around customer satisfaction in a dealership you can see how changing the focus and goals of a shop can change performance. By simply refocusing the employees' attention on quality rather than simply on production it was possible to make a dramatic improvement to the shop's customer satisfaction rating.

On a day-in day-out basis the best way to keep each individual employee focused on the right mixture of objectives and priorities is to pay careful attention to how employees are paid. Therefore, the rule of thumb in designing and maintaining a compensation plan for an employee is that it should be clearly aligned with the goals and objectives of that job. This way you will be rewarding the exact performance that you believe is the most important.

Do you value production? If so, then the compensation should be tied to producing labor hours. Do you value quality? If you do, you should make sure that you have built in some reward to the employee for customer satisfaction. Your employee compensation plan serves as a constant reminder of your goals and objectives. There is nothing that can communicate them to your employees more clearly, directly, and constantly. Since their compensation is closely tied to their self-worth and feeling of being valued, the best way to assure their success and yours is to tie their compensation plan to achievement of organizational goals and priorities.

SUMMARY

Motivating employees is one of the most basic responsibilities of a supervisor. Without proper direction and motivation, the performance levels from each employee that you expect in order to succeed will never be reached. Setting clear performance expectations that are measurable and achievable and clearly and regularly communicating them to your employees are essential steps in motivating employees. You should develop a set of metrics that can be tracked and communicated on a regular basis to provide reinforcement to every employee about progress that is being made. In addition this provides an early warning when performance is lagging and changes are needed.

Establishing and communicating clear expectations on the department or organizational level will aid all employees in directing their efforts toward company goals. However, you must remember that each employee is unique and requires individual attention if you hope to get the best performance. The regular one-on-one performance review process and establishment of personal goals helps bring your guidance and direction down to a very personal level. This allows you to praise their successes, provide guidance on areas in need of improvement, and encourage their growth during the coming year.

One of the best reinforcement mechanisms to support individual evaluations is for employees to see a direct link between company goals and the performance expectations that you have set for them. Further, there should be a clear relationship between your performance expectations and specific goals for employees and their individual compensation plans. By developing a clear link between goals, expectations, and rewards you send a clear and unwavering message of what is important.

PRACTICING THE PRINCIPLES

1. It is important that expectations be _____________.
   a. definable.
   b. reasonable.
   c. achievable.
   d. none of the above.
   e. all of the above.
2. In terms of performance measurement, metrics are
   a. based on the scale of 10.
   b. a measurement to track results.
   c. a different system than SAE.
   d. none of the above.
3. Whenever possible you should attempt to
   a. separate compensation from performance.
   b. tie performance to compensation.
   c. never give performance evaluations.
   d. reward performance and ignore lack of performance.
4. __________ are short-term benefits to help motivate specific performance.
   a. Bribes.
   b. Incentives.
   c. Penalties.
   d. Compensation plans.
5. Employees often do not do what their management wants them to do because
   a. the goals have been clearly defined.
   b. they are not getting paid enough.
   c. goals have not been clearly communicated.
   d. they just are not motivated.

6. Which method is least likely to help your department achieve major, very complex goals?
   a. Get all of the little goals out of the way first.
   b. Break the big goal down into sub-goals.
   c. Tie pay incentives to completion of the goal.
   d. Make sure everyone knows what the goal is.
7. A well-designed and prepared performance evaluation will not
   a. discuss both employee strengths and weaknesses.
   b. be conducted on a regular basis.
   c. be posted on the company bulletin board.
   d. cover a variety of skills and abilities related to the job.
8. It is important that you track and reward _______________.
   a. what is important.
   b. everything that you can.
   c. personal details about everyone.
   d. poor performance.
9. One of the pitfalls of tying an employee's pay to one factor such as flat-rate pay is

   ____

   ____

   ____
10. List four items that are part of a comprehensive compensation plan

   ____

   ____

   ____

   ____

CHAPTER

24

Progressive Discipline

CHAPTER OBJECTIVES

- To recognize the application of discipline as a positive tool for employee development
- To describe the necessary steps of the progressive discipline process
- To examine the use of counseling and advising in attempting to correct poor behavior or work performance

KEY TERMS

progressive discipline
advising
counseling
warning
punishment
reprimand
separation

Introduction

Motivating employees is very tricky and complex. Even more difficult is addressing those personnel performance problems that are not and cannot be addressed and resolved through positive motivation. What do you do about the employee who insists that she will not pick up the pace? The one who has a chronic tardiness problem? The one who always bends, spindles, and mutilates the company rules? Progressive discipline is the toolset that you need to get out and utilize to deal most effectively with all of these issues.

Progressive Discipline Process

Progressive discipline is a tool, actually a set of tools, that can help you to maintain a positive and constructive environment while doing the really tough work required to try to resolve the most difficult personnel problems. This process ensures that you have in place a systematic method for trying to resolve personnel problems for all of your employees in a positive and constructive manner and even address termination of employment when that is the last resort available.

Progressive Discipline

A structured and consistent human resource development process that works to gain the best results out of difficult employee performance situations.

It is unfair to allow someone to continue to fail and bring down the organization. It does nothing for their morale or their future to allow them to wallow in failure. It is unfair to sentence the rest of the crew to having to overwork and overproduce just to compensate for the shortcomings of one employee. It is certainly unfair to the owners and investors in the company to let one person's unwillingness to contribute their fair share undo what it has taken a lifetime to build.

Performance issues are often not a matter of blame or fault. Rarely is the employee's behavior malicious or intentional. It is not that he is a bad person who is trying to ruin things for everyone else. In the vast majority of cases performance problems fall into one of two categories: (1) the employee does not realize what he is doing wrong or doesn't know how to change things, or (2) he is in the wrong job and you owe it to him and the organization to do what you can to get him out of that bad situation.

I Did Not Realize It

Have you ever been in a situation where someone taps you on the shoulder and very politely says, "Pardon me, but you are standing in my way?" Chances are that you did not realize that you were blocking the person. It is likely that your response goes something like "Oh, excuse me. I did not realize that I was in your way." This simple, common scenario is very similar to many of the performance problems that occur in the workplace.

In this scenario, all that it took to resolve the problem was to make the offending party aware of what she was doing that was creating the situation. Once advised, she gladly and apologetically moved and, in so doing, resolved the problem. In this case merely taking the time and mustering up the courage to say something led to a speedy and complete resolution to the problem.

However, some situations are a bit more complicated than that one. If you pulled up to an intersection in your car and were blocked by the car in front of you, you might use the same technique to get the person to move. However, what would you do if you asked her to move and she said, "I would be glad to, but the car has a flat tire and I have never fixed one before."

Once notified that she is causing a problem she is, like in the first situation, very willing to move. Unfortunately, she has a problem that she cannot or at least does not know how to quickly resolve. At this point you have several options. You can: (a) change the tire for her, (b) show her how to change the tire and help her to do it, (c) wait for someone else to help her, or (d) decide that you are more willing to continue waiting than you are to get involved.

Both of the scenarios presented are very simple. However, they are simple examples that closely parallel common performance problems that we encounter at work on a regular basis. Fortunately for us, the majority of personnel problems fall into these two categories: ones that require notification and ones that require notification and temporary assistance and training.

In both of these groups of issues the first and most important ingredient to success is communication. Most often the one at the center of the problem is either not aware of the problem or is aware but unable to resolve it alone. Not until you identify the issue at hand and take the time to open a dialogue with the party involved so that she is aware of the problem and offer assistance or guidance will the problem move toward being resolved.

The progressive discipline process can be universally applied to deal consistently and effectively with these situations. It provides a consistent method for addressing issues ranging from the most simple (our first scenario) to ones that are far more complicated and intense.

In the Wrong Place

This second group of performance problems are more complicated and, therefore, difficult to resolve. Jim Collins, in his book *Good to Great* uses a powerful analogy of "getting the right people on the bus" (Collins, 2001) to provide us some direction on how to deal with these types of personnel issues. As a manager and leader it is your responsibility to the organization and to all of your co-workers to "get the right people on the bus." That is, hire and retain the people with the right knowledge, skills, abilities, and attitudes to help maximize the productivity, profitability, and overall success of the organization.

Beyond getting the right people on board, it is critical that you work to get the right people in the right seats. That is, that you know your people *and the needs of* your operations well enough to consistently match up the right people with the right jobs and responsibilities.

However, occasionally situations arise where you find that you have the wrong person in place. Then what? Is it that you misjudged him in the first place? Did you hire the wrong person? Did you put him in the wrong position? Or . . . did he change? In the final analysis it is not nearly as important what the cause is. What is most important is that you recognize that a problem exists, and do something about it.

Clearly, the hardest part is acknowledging the problem and taking action. However, once you have overcome this hurdle the problem then becomes one of determining the proper course of action. The best course of action in all personnel problem situations is to proceed through a consistent and steady process of progressive discipline to make every effort to resolve the performance issues at hand.

Discipline or Punishment?

Progressive discipline is not a pathway to punishment. It is a system that provides for and assures that a consistent and fair approach is taken to communicate with employees, identifying performance problems, and providing counseling and guidance to resolve performance problems. Finally, and only when all else fails, it provides for disciplinary action up to and including dismissal.

The goal of progressive discipline is to resolve the performance issue and save the employee. That is, by separating the performance issue from the personality, the goal of this process is to work with the employee to resolve the performance problem. As a result, the ideal ending is to reinstate the employee as a happy and productive member of the team and to eliminate *only* the substandard behavior or performance.

Steps in the Process

The main steps in the progressive discipline process are

- Advising
- Counseling
- Verbal warning
- Written warning
- Written reprimand
- Written reprimand with penalty
- Separation from employment

As the title indicates, the intent is to have a consistent and logical pathway that you can follow in resolving personnel issues. The tools and steps in the process can be used informally in the case of minor or incidental issues. However, it is important to carefully and methodically follow the procedure to deal with all important or persistent performance issues.

Just as it is essential that the process is followed every time, it is critical that it be followed as its name implies, progressively. That is, by following step by step and not by bypassing steps in any but the most extreme cases. It is important to note that there are a few severe incidents that may merit accelerating the process, but every attempt should be made to follow the process step by step as often as possible.

Finally, just as it is important that you understand the steps and the intent of the process, the same is equally true for all your employees. For the process to be most effective it is essential that all of your employees are aware of the steps and the intent of the process so that they understand what you are doing and why you are doing it when you formally enter this process. The employee must have a clear understanding of the positive and corrective intent in which you use this process. Now, let us take a little time to discuss each of the steps of the process in more detail.

Advising

Advising
Providing formal feedback or notice to an individual of their performance or behavior.

Advising is often considered as a pre-disciplinary step. Regular advising and providing consistent and positive feedback should be ongoing in your department. Your employees cannot be assured that they are doing the right things unless you provide them with regular feedback to guide them and reinforce their positive actions.

Advising is necessary to make sure that employees know when what they are doing is straying from the intended goals and directions of the company. Regular communication and advising is an important foundation to assure positive and properly directed efforts and is essential to minimize the need to move into more formal processes like the remaining steps of progressive discipline.

It is important to note that advising *is* actually the first step in discipline. It is your most common and low-key method for answering the all-important question that you as a supervisor must be able to answer: "How can I be sure that my employees know what is expected?" It is only fair to be sure that they clearly and consistently know the rules before criticizing or penalizing them for not following them. You must have clear evidence that you have exercised this step early and often before you consider moving to the next more formal step, counseling.

Counseling

As you move through the steps of progressive discipline each step builds upon the previous one and becomes a bit more formal. Counseling is very similar to advising because the message and the intent are to communicate what the required performance is and what the issues and concerns are that you have with their substandard performance.

Counseling
A formal conversation and discussion with the specific intent of making an employee aware of concerns about performance or behavior.

In **counseling**, the supervisor moves from informal conversation to a more formal and structured one. At this point we have tried to make the employee aware of the concerns but the performance has not changed, or has not changed enough. Now we need to take the time to make it explicitly clear to the employee that a performance problem exists, that it is a concern, and what the expectations are to address and resolve this issue.

Although counseling does not need to be conducted in an intimidating manner, it does require that the supervisor find an appropriate method to be certain that the employee clearly understands the importance of the discussion. This is often done by holding a special meeting or discussion with the sole purpose of covering this issue. In that way, it reduces the chances that the employee will take it lightly or dismiss the concerns that are expressed as a suggestion only. Finally, it is highly recommended that the supervisor document and retain in writing a brief accounting of the meeting as supporting documentation in the event of the need for further discipline.

Warning
A formal notification either verbally or in writing to inform an employee of unacceptable performance or behavior accompanied by a clear statement of future penalties and consequences if a substantial improvement does not occur.

It is important to point out that this process is not a one-way street. At any time where significant progress is made toward resolving the performance issue at hand the supervisor can move back up the ladder to a more informal step to ensure that the gains are maintained. After results from a counseling session prove successful the supervisor can revert to ongoing advising. However, if counseling does not yield marked improvement and additional action is required, the process then moves on to a formal verbal **warning.**

Verbal Warning

Unfortunately, attempts to advise and counsel do not always produce sufficient results. In these cases it is important to continue to move forward in the disciplinary process. It is important to remember that the intent of the process is not discipline but rather resolving performance problems. However, when sufficient progress has not occurred or there is a relapse after a brief improvement, a verbal warning is in order.

The verbal warning closely resembles the counseling session. It is an event that is intentionally arranged to focus on current specific performance issues. It is intended that the sole focus of this meeting is making the employee aware of the concerns and also of their gravity.

The difference between the counseling session and the verbal warning is the addition of two key ingredients, direct notification that this is a warning and a clear statement that continued concerns may lead to further disciplinary action. In an ideal sense you hope that the employee understands the gravity of the situation and the need for immediate action. Unfortunately, although this is most often true, there are cases where the employee is either unwilling or unable to make sufficient progress. In these cases, formalizing the disciplinary process really begins to take shape with the verbal warning.

Keeping in mind that the ultimate goal is a resolution of the issue at hand, the threat of direct consequences for continuing with the current behavior and/or lack of performance is brought clearly into the picture. It is essential that the supervisor takes the time to reassure the employee of the ultimate hope for a positive outcome so that this is not seen merely as a **punishment.** At the same time, the supervisor must be very direct in spelling out in detail the issues in question, what is expected to resolve them, and the consequences for failure to resolve them. In the event that noticeable improvement does not result it is necessary to move to the next step, a written warning.

Punishment
A penalty that is assessed in response to unacceptable performance or behavior.

Written Warning

The final step in the progressive discipline process before implementing penalties is the written warning. It is not dramatically different from the verbal warning. It is a progressive (step-by-step or gradual) increase upward from the previous step.

When a written warning is given, the employee again has a formal meeting with the supervisor with the sole intent of discussing performance issues. The past history of advising, counseling, and verbal warnings should be recounted to make it clear to the employee that this is not a new issue. The positive intent of the progressive discipline process must also be reviewed and discussed. At this point, however, the employee needs to be clearly advised that the problems, and the resulting lack of progress, have brought the situation to the point where it is now necessary to commit this to writing to be put into their personnel file. Finally, as a part of this written warning, the employee is reminded that to this point there have been no direct consequences or punishments but that if clear and substantial progress is not immediately evident that the next steps will include penalties ranging from time off up to and including dismissal.

Just as in all of the previous steps, the intention is to resolve the deficiency. Also, as in the past, the intention is to turn up the heat to, hopefully, get the employee's undivided attention to the problem and to resolving it. If this goal is not achieved, the process then proceeds on to a written reprimand.

Reprimand
A formal and typically stern warning based on unacceptable performance or behavior that includes an immediate penalty combined with a clear statement of future penalties if the situation is not resolved.

Written Reprimand

The written **reprimand** step in the process, although very similar to the written warning in content, generally will add two additional and very important characteristics. Typically the written reprimand is conducted by the direct supervisor along with his/her supervisor or a representative from the company's business office or human resources department. The inclusion of the next level supervisor demonstrates solidarity and commitment of the entire organization to this course of action and the importance of resolving it immediately.

The second additional characteristic is the inclusion of an immediate penalty. Depending on the severity of the infraction this penalty may be a fine, elimination or delay of an expected pay raise, or a suspension from work with or without pay. The clear intention of the penalty phase is to stress the importance and urgency in resolving the performance problem and the commitment of the organization to taking whatever steps are necessary to resolve it.

As with the other steps in this formal process, the written reprimand also includes a clear statement of a plan for corrective action. This plan for corrective action will provide guidance and may include some very specific and intentional assignments that are hoped will help in leading to a change in performance. The document will also very clearly state the additional steps and penalties in the process if the change does not occur.

Depending on the severity of the problem and the policies and procedures of the organization this step may be repeated several times with increasing penalties before moving forward. There is a very delicate balance that must be maintained when a problem has escalated to this high level. It is important to be consistent and persistent in continuing to move forward in the process if significant progress is not evident. At the same time, it is even more important than before to continue to reassure the employee that although the situation is serious, the ultimate hope of the supervisor and the company is that this can finally be resolved, put behind them, and that life can return to normal for all involved. For this reason, the supervisor needs to be patient and allow time between steps so that the employee that is trying hard to change has the opportunity to show progress.

Unfortunately, in a handful of cases, in spite of your best efforts to try to guide, direct, and motivate an employee and provide every resource to help them to succeed it just does not happen. This results in the progressive discipline process playing out to its final step, and certainly the last resort in any personnel issue, separation from employment.

Separation from Employment

Termination of employment as a result of severe or chronic unresolved performance or behavioral concerns of an employee.

The final step in the process is **separation** from employment. Termination of employment is rarely the wish of any employer or employee. After all, you hired this employee because you needed to get a job done. You thought right from the start that he was the best qualified for the job. You have tried to work with him, motivate him, guide him, train him. You have invested a great deal of money and time toward assuring his success and, yet, somehow you have failed.

The separation meeting is conducted just as the previous step of written reprimand. A formal meeting is arranged with the direct supervisor and other company official along with the employee. The focus of the meeting is to recount the ongoing performance problems, the repeated attempts to resolve them, and their continuation. Each of the steps moving through the progressive discipline process should be reviewed. Finally, the ultimate decision to terminate employment should be stated along with any plans and scheduling for exit activities, if needed.

It is common for a supervisor to feel a great deal of sadness and loss when faced with the unenviable task of calling in an employee to dismiss him. It is truly a lose-lose situation. The company and the department lose all of the time and energy that they have invested in trying to develop a good employee and have to start over at square one, running ads in the paper in the hope of finding someone as skilled and capable as the person they must now dismiss.

Certainly for the employee the sadness and loss is very direct and personal. He may feel that he is a failure, he may feel a loss, he may feel angry. It is hoped, however, that through the use of progressive discipline that in most cases the employee is able to see that the intention of the supervisor and the company has been a positive one and that they have tried their best to help.

Dealing with Separation

Knowing how difficult separation from employment is to any supervisor and to any employee, I would like to take just a few minutes to reflect back to our earlier discussions about "having the right people on the bus" (Collins, 2001). It is unfortunate that in spite of our best efforts that occasionally we choose the wrong employee. This is also true when some major change in the company or the individual occurs that makes a previously good match turn into a chronic problem situation—but it does happen.

Progressive discipline and separation from employment is a very intense, emotional, and time-consuming process that none of us, employers or employees, chooses to face. However, in being accountable to our organization and, ultimately, to each other, we must. It is not fair to allow an employee to drag down the ship and for everyone else to have to pay the penalty whether that is in doing extra work or in accepting lower pay because of diminished overall performance. When a situation arises that in spite of our best efforts we cannot resolve, it may seem unfair to the employee to terminate employment. But, it is even more unfair to everyone else who is doing their job to penalize them by allowing the employee to stay.

Finally, although it may not seem so in the short term, it is unfair to allow an employee to stay in a situation where he or she continues to fail. What motivation, what satisfaction, what feeling of self-worth can be gained by wallowing in a situation where one continues to underachieve? It is not personal. It is not that he or she is a bad person. It is that the employee is in the wrong seat and, quite possibly, even on the wrong bus. After all (and to take the analogy a step further), if their intended destination is Denver and you are headed to Miami, it really is better for all concerned to let them know as soon as possible so that they can get on the right bus and that you can fill that vacant seat with someone who will benefit from going where you both want to go, together.

Skipping Steps

In the intense environment that caused you to utilize progressive discipline it is common that once you have made the determination that there is no other alternative and that you need to move forward that you must strike swiftly and effectively. There is a natural tendency to postpone and avoid entering into a disciplinary situation with an employee. After all, it is an acknowledgement that all is not well and is the beginning of what may become a long, difficult, and time-consuming process. Unfortunately, most personnel problems do not go away on their own. Therefore, since it is not going to heal on its own, the longer you wait the worse it gets and the harder it will become to achieve a positive outcome.

Many managers, because of the stress and time commitment may try to delay moving into progressive discipline and then want to skip steps and get right to the penalty and/or separation steps. After all, they've already been too patient and now they have made up their mind.

Actually, when a supervisor wants to move to the end of the process what he or she has most likely done is fail to take the time and make the commitment when the problem was first identified, and now is trying to make up for lost time. The supervisor waited too long to make the difficult decision to start the process.

In all but a few cases it is the best for the supervisor, the company, and the employee to begin the process and follow the process, step by step, and allow reasonable time between steps no matter how late the process has been started. As in most processes there are exceptions to this rule based on the chronic nature of a problem or its severity. This may warrant in certain conditions to move quickly from step to step or even to skip a step. However, to provide the employee with the best opportunity to correct the problem performance or behavior (which is really the ultimate goal, right?), the thoughtful and methodical process that is progressive discipline is generally the best solution.

The Need for Consistency

Progressive discipline is a system and is more than merely a group of tools. It really is part of an organizational philosophy that supports a positive, prescriptive approach to addressing personnel problems. It is founded on the concept that the majority of these problems can be resolved amicably and to the best benefit of both the employee and the employer.

Following this procedure for all employees is a must if your organization is truly to benefit from all that it can offer. No, of course that does not mean that you are disciplining everyone. It means that you are communicating regularly with everyone. It means that you are advising and guiding everyone on a regular basis so that they know where they stand, what they are doing well, and what they need to improve—remember the first step? That is right, it was advising.

An advisory and counseling relationship should permeate your entire organization. This is the best preventative medicine to avoid personnel issues and performance problems. Only through this communication channel can the employee and the employer be confident that they know where they stand and where they are headed. Fortunately, this lends itself very well to moving into formal discipline much more easily and comfortably in the rare occurrence that a problem develops that needs a higher level of attention.

Outside Resources

Although it is suggested that all supervisors consider this system when working with all personnel issues and concerns it does not mean that you are expected to do it alone. In fact, there are cases where it is highly recommended that you involve external assistance.

Just as in the case with anything that you do, you need to recognize your strengths and your abilities as well as your weaknesses. Your desire to resolve employee problems and your commitment to progressive discipline does not make you a psychologist, a doctor, or a lawyer. Therefore, it is important that when you become involved in a situation that goes beyond your expertise you draw upon expertise that will help you in these sensitive areas.

Situations arise that are the result of causes that require skills and knowledge that you simply do not possess. Family, legal, and psychological issues are just a few general areas where your ability to fully understand and know the proper course of action may be limited by your experience and knowledge. In these cases, involving appropriate external resources must happen at the earliest stages. No matter how good your intentions, without the right skills and expert guidance in these situations you may unwittingly make the situation worse, thus reducing the likelihood of you reaching your original goal, a happy and productive employee.

Timeliness Is Essential

There is one last and very important principle that you need to follow. That is being timely with both praise and criticism. This principle can be applied to all of the relationships that you have with your employees. However, just as it is important to recognize and reward exceptional performance or exemplary behavior when you see it so that you reinforce it, it is also true that you must address negative situations in a timely manner.

If your true goal is to identify, acknowledge, and correct the behaviors or other problems you must not hesitate to take action. The closer that the corrective action follows the offense, the more likely that positive results will occur. This timeliness allows for you to discuss the issues while they are still fresh in everyone's minds. If it has risen to the level where some penalty is justified, it helps to make a clear connection between action and consequence.

Failure to act quickly confuses the situation. This delay can have a strong demoralizing effect on the employee. The employee may feel that you are opening up old wounds weeks or months after the incident. Rapid response simplifies the situation. It helps to keep the employee from feeling like he or she is a failure and limits it to "I made one mistake." Seeing a direct link between error and consequence makes taking corrective action easier for both employer and employee.

SUMMARY

One of the most misunderstood principles in personnel development is the use of progressive discipline as an approach to improve employee performance. Discipline is too often seen as a last resort method of dealing with and dismissing the employee who has gone off track and for whom there is no other reasonable alternative other than termination of employment. For this reason the process of discipline is too often delayed well beyond when it should have been initiated.

Progressive discipline is a development-oriented process of identifying and methodically defining, following up with, and addressing performance issues in the workplace. Its primary intent is that through advanced warning, appropriate guidance and counseling, and consistent follow up that many difficult situations can be resolved. Therefore, valuable employees can be retained. Punishment and separation from employment are treated as last-resort options within this process. Although it is hoped that in the vast majority of cases taking proper preemptive action will correct performance, the progressive discipline process also provides a methodical and well-documented audit trail in the unfortunate circumstances that the final inevitable result is termination of employment.

PRACTICING THE PRINCIPLES

1. The practice in progressive discipline that is considered a pre-disciplinary step is
   a. termination.
   b. counseling.
   c. written reprimand.
   d. advising.
2. When going through the disciplinary process it is important that the manager is careful not to
   a. let them see you sweat.
   b. start the disciplinary process too soon.
   c. skip any steps in the disciplinary process.
   d. all of the above.
3. As a manager you may find it very appropriate to ___________________ as a part an effective disciplinary process.
   a. skip right to termination.
   b. go it alone.
   c. seek outside assistance.
   d. skip as many steps as necessary.
4. Started early and followed step by step, _____________ _____________ can be an effective tool in employee development.
   a. progressive discipline.
   b. harsh punishment.
   c. providing unannounced bonuses.
   d. none of the above.
5. ___________ is essential in helping the employee be able to see the direct relationship between their performance problems and the consequences of their actions.
   a. Empathy.
   b. Sympathy.
   c. Inconsideration.
   d. Timeliness.
6. Once an employee has been advised and counseled about an ongoing performance problem and has had a verbal warning if the performance does not improve, the next step in progressive discipline is
   a. a written warning.
   b. immediate termination.
   c. notice of termination if not resolved.
   d. a second verbal warning.
7. The difference between a ______________________ is that one simply makes the employee aware that a problem exists while the other provides immediate negative consequences.
   a. reward and punishment.
   b. termination and a separation.
   c. day off without pay and separation.
   d. warning and a reprimand.
8. Too often managers see discipline only as a means of _____________.
   a. counseling employees.
   b. punishing employees.
   c. getting employees to quit.
   d. two or more answers are correct.
9. Effective methods used to get the employee to improve their performance are
   a. counseling and advising.
   b. threatening and docking their pay.
   c. advising and threatening termination.
   d. warning and punishing.
10. The primary goal of the Progressive Discipline Process is to
    a. fire ungrateful and unproductive employees.
    b. be a tool to help improve employee performance.
    c. protect the company from lawsuits.
    d. punish poor performance and reward good performance.

REFERENCE

Collins, J., *Good to Great: Why Some Companies Make the Leap and Others Don't* (New York: Harper Business, 2001).

SECTION

8

Marketing, Merchandising, and Selling Service

Automotive service is a very competitive business. For this reason it is essential the manager is able to clearly communicate the reasons why the public should choose their shop from the crowd. Effective marketing is essential to help them build customer awareness and a solid client base. However, the financial resources of any organization are finite. Better understanding of the benefits of each of the mass marketing mediums is important to help business to use their resources most effectively. As with any other industry, there are specific types of marketing that are most effective in reaching the target audience for automotive service. The understanding of mass marketing and point-of-purchase merchandising methods and techniques are essential in developing a successful marketing strategy. Once marketing efforts have attracted customers the automotive service employees need to be prepared to gain the maximum return on this investment by recommending and selling needed maintenance and repair services to all of their customers.

CHAPTER

25

Marketing and Mass Media

CHAPTER OBJECTIVES

- To recognize what marketing is and its importance in the success in a competitive marketplace
- To identify the basic qualities that establish value to a product or service
- To develop proper pricing to be profitable and competitive in the marketplace

KEY TERMS

marketing
value
price
performance
convenience
availability
quality
advertising
mass media

Introduction

Marketing
A complex process that lets customers know what you have to offer and what value it brings to them.

In business you may have the brightest idea and the best invention yet fail. The cause is that not enough people know about you, your business, and what it can do for them. Without this awareness you are bound to fail. **Marketing** is the complex process that lets the world know what you have to offer and what value it brings to them so that they will enthusiastically "beat a path to your door" to become your customer. Having a great product or service is an important factor in being successful in business, but if people do not know about it you will surely fail.

Marketing is not making a product or providing a service. It is not manufacturing or sales. Marketing is a process. In its most complete and thorough sense, this process should begin early in the product development process. The process of gathering information to help guide the development of a product and the initial strategy to get it to the public is market research. This research helps to assure that the product or service is targeted to meet the needs of a specific group of potential customers.

In automotive service your involvement with marketing as a manager will rarely begin until the product is developed and ready to go on sale. This more common aspect of marketing refers to the development and implementation of an intentional campaign to promote a product or service to the public. This is typical of the marketing efforts that you will be involved in planning and implementing to ensure the success of your service operations.

Marketing helps you to clearly direct your efforts by helping you answer these simple yet critical questions:

- WHO—Who has an interest in my product or service?
- WHAT—What is their specific want or need?
- WHERE—Where can I find them?
- HOW—How can I best reach them?

The answers to these four questions provide you with a solid foundation upon which you can build a plan to bring attention to and develop interest in what you have to sell. Armed with this background information, your ultimate goal is to move a group of people who do not even know that your product or service exists to becoming loyal customers and vocal advocates.

The Five Basic Goals of Marketing

One of the overarching goals of any marketing initiative is to intentionally move your target audience through the five basic goals of marketing (Figure 25-1).

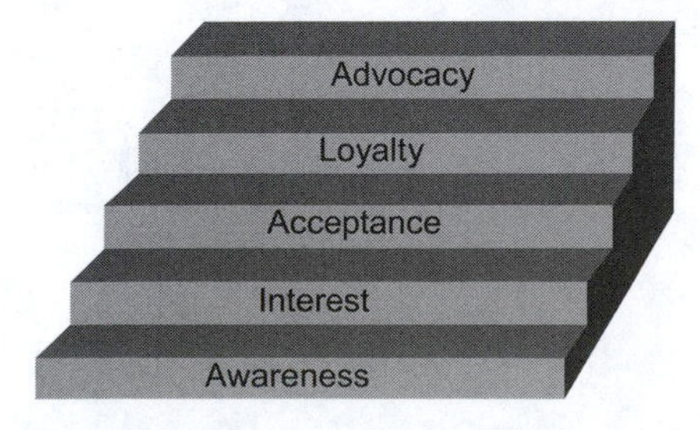

Figure 25-1 Five basic goals of marketing

The ultimate goal is to influence and move as many potential customers as far possible up those steps.

Here is how the five-step process works. If, for example, you have a new company or a new product you begin at ground zero. People do not even know that your product exists. The first step, then, is to reach out and build *awareness*. Once potential customers are aware that your product exists you need to create *interest* that will entice them to investigate your product. Once they have learned more about your product your goal is that they reach the level of *acceptance* and try it. You are now halfway up the steps and have moved these potential customers to become consumers of your product or service.

Once customers have tried your product, you need to meet or exceed their expectations so that they will be willing to come back and purchase again. Now you are moving toward the next goal of becoming their preferred vendor for this product, *loyalty*. The last, and final, step is by far the hardest to reach. It should be your ultimate goal that through your efforts and the excellence of your products and services that your customers not only become loyal and return as regulars, they are so pleased that they openly recommend you as the best source for this product. When you have reached this plateau you have achieved the ultimate goal of *advocacy*.

It is important to note that although these five goals appear simple, they are a simple roadmap to a long and difficult journey. There is intense competition in the marketplace and while you are striving to build a base of loyal customers your competitors are trying equally as hard to take them away. It is for that reason that your plans to develop and market your products must be based on sound principles that guide customer buying decisions. Most customer buying decisions are based on logic and that logic is one of making a purchase that provides them with the greatest value. Let us discuss the factors that make up value in the mind of the typical customer.

Establishing Value

Potential customers are not likely to do business with you unless you are able to clearly communicate what sets your product or service apart from the competition. You must demonstrate the unique **value** of your product. With that in mind let us take a few minutes to talk about some universal characteristics that customers value.

Value
The relative worth and usefulness of a product or service.

Characteristics of Value

There are five common characteristics that potential customers consistently use to guide their purchase decisions in the very confusing, crowded, and highly competitive marketplace of today. These major characteristics are

1. Price
2. Performance
3. Convenience
4. Availability
5. Quality

Whether someone is looking to purchase an exotic sports car or a 10-year-old pickup truck, a home in the city or a room to rent for the night, they are likely to find that they have several choices. The decision process used to make that choice takes into account the five major factors. Together they are the major part of the value of that product or service to the potential customer.

Different people may value some characteristics more than others. Their immediate priorities may even cause them to shift their opinion of what is of the greatest value to them at any one time. However, no matter how much this may differ from person to person and from time to time people will continue to make their purchase decisions based on value. Therefore, you need to clearly understand these factors and the impact that they have on the final buying decisions if you hope to succeed in business.

Real World Application

Having delayed the start of a 700+ mile drive home after a week of vacation and knowing full well that I needed to be home the next day I set out for the trip. In addition to the late start, construction on the freeway further delayed my progress in getting home at a reasonable hour. At 2 A.M., still several hundred miles from my ultimate destination, I felt myself getting so tired that I simply could not go on. I had reached the point where I was not only falling asleep at the wheel; I was starting to see things.

The only two reasonable and safe choices were to sleep in the car or to get a hotel room to get a few hours' sleep before I headed on the last leg of my journey. I quickly decided against sleeping in the car. I needed to get a few hours of good rest. I decided that a hotel was the only solution.

I began looking for road signs along the side of the freeway and at the exits that indicated what hotels were available. I needed to find a room fast. I did not really need a place with a pool and a restaurant, just a place that was clean with a good bed. My priorities at that point were availability number 1, performance number 2, and price number 3. I simply wanted somewhere I could find right away that was reasonably clean and comfortable and would not cost me a small fortune.

In normal circumstances, given the time to shop around and without the urgency of being exhausted and in danger of falling asleep at the wheel and crashing, my priorities and decision process would be very different. However, under these particular circumstances that is what mattered most to me, and those are the priorities that guided my purchase decision.

Perceived value is a combination of all benefits received (such as quality, convenience, features, reliability, and so on). It is a complex and sometimes unpredictable calculation that customers make in factoring in what is important to them at that time and then making the decision that best meets those immediate criteria for perceived value. As in the example of getting the hotel room, the perceived value for a customer can and will change based on the particular circumstances when they determine that it is time to buy.

Even after considering the purchase of a big-ticket item (new car) for months and doing all of the research a customer's priorities may change. The importance that the buyer places on vehicle reliability, resale value, price and quality may change as the buyer's priorities change and affect the resulting final purchase decision.

Price
The amount of goods or money exchanged to receive a product or service in return.

Price

The importance of price is often overstated. **Price** is an important factor in purchase decisions. Yes, you can price yourself out of the market. However, market research consistently demonstrates that price is not the number 1 factor in establishing value. More often it is rated number 3 or number 4 in customer surveys. Price alone is not the answer to marketing success. Customers make their final purchase decision based on the total perceived value of the product or service, not solely on price. However, price cannot be ignored, it must be seriously considered along with all of the other factors.

If you fail to pay adequate attention to pricing you may price yourself right out of the market. This is a warning that we have all heard from time to time. An important characteristic of pricing is that it is very likely to be the easiest and most common factor for making side-by-side comparisons. With many choices savvy consumers will use price as one of the first criteria to narrow their search. They can do this from the comfort of their home whether in the newspaper, on the phone, or over the Internet.

There are two major groups of factors to consider in establishing your price: internal factors and market factors. The internal factors are those that determine what price must be charged in order to make a reasonable profit and, therefore, make providing the product or service a good business decision. The external factors are those that dictate the current rate in the marketplace. That "going rate" is the range of prices that the competition is currently charging for comparable goods or services.

Internal Factors It is essential to clearly define the physical costs of bringing a product to market. The direct costs are the cost of materials and the cost of labor. In addition to these raw materials it is important that you also include a third, and more often neglected cost, the cost of support services. Without factoring in these costs in you are likely to receive a far lower net profit than you originally expected.

Support services takes into consideration all of those other expenses that, although they are not directly related to this specific product, are required in order for the product to be produced. These include the facilities, equipment, utilities, and other staff (accounting/sales/etc.) that are not a part of the product. However, without them the product would never have been made. These support services are generally referred to as overhead or indirect expenses.

The last internal factor is profit margin. Even having accurately and thoroughly accounted for all direct and indirect expenses that are part of the product, unless the activity can provide a reasonable return on investment it is not a good business decision. It is essential that you are able to include within the final retail price a return on your investment that justifies your commitment of time, energy, and capital. Armed with a thorough knowledge of what it costs to make the product and what pricing levels you must achieve to make this a good business decision you can then look at the marketplace to determine what price the market will bear.

External Factors The common phrase "what the market will bear" describes what the perceived value is to your target audience. It is the worth of a product to potential customers taking into consideration your product and all others out there that can meet their needs. After all, it is not reasonable to expect that customers will pay more than they have to for any goods or services. The information obtained by doing a price survey of the competition should give you a range of prices that can guide you in establishing your price. Remember that you do not have to be the cheapest—just the best value—to be the most successful.

We have spent quite a bit of time talking about pricing because it is important. Remember that it is not the only factor nor is it the most important factor. It is, however, a factor that must not be ignored since it is one of the easiest factors for customers to use to rule you out as a potential vendor.

Performance

Performance
The ability to meet or exceed expectations to carry out an expected function.

A very important factor in establishing the overall value of your product or service is the **performance** of that product. Clearly identifying the performance characteristics of your product is essential in differentiating your product from the competition in the marketplace. A key question in defining your performance is: What makes my product unique? That is, what does my product do or do significantly better than the rest of the products available to consumers?

In order to compete effectively and market the performance of your product it is also essential to clearly understand the features and benefits that your competition has to offer. What are the features and benefits that your competition heavily promotes to distinguish them from the rest of the competition? Once you know what the competition's direction is in establishing their competitive advantage based on performance you will be able to counter that strategy with one of your own. You can determine that their key characteristic is not important, you can choose to compete head-to-head, or you can differentiate yourself as having greater value based on your unique solution to the customer's needs.

In the final analysis, you must remember that unless you are willing to bet your future at being chosen at random among your competitors, you must clearly differentiate yourself from them in the marketplace. You must give the customers a reason to choose your solution because it has a higher perceived value in their minds.

Convenience

Unless you have a product or service that is so unique or such a great deal that customers will drive past hundreds of competitors just to get to your door and do business with you, you will have to consider the benefit of being convenient as part of your marketing strategy. The local exotic sports car dealer is probably a good example of someone who does not have to worry too much about convenience. They are the only game in town and people will travel great distances to get to their site. That is not likely to be so, however, if you are selling or servicing mainstream vehicles. You are faced with hundreds of competitors in your marketplace, many of whom are located closer to parts of your target market. So you need to factor **convenience** into your marketing plan if you want to succeed.

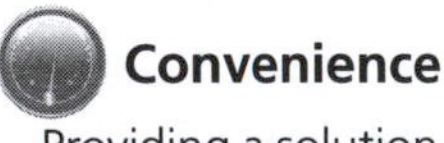

Convenience
Providing a solution that is comfortable or easy.

Convenience is a highly variable factor. Although customers would like to be able to get service done right here, right now, 24/7/365, they are not very likely to value that convenience so much that they would pay a very high premium in price to get it. The amount of convenience that you can and should look to provide is based on a combination, just like price, of how much it costs you to provide it and its added value to customers.

The most common convenience factors are location, hours of operation, and payment methods. The relevance and importance of these factors varies from industry to industry and from market to market. Although service facilities do not necessarily need to be located on prime real estate they generally need to be conveniently located to provide service to their target audience. Unfortunately, no matter where you locate your business you will always find a competitor who is closer to some of your market and every bit of inconvenience that you cause is just one more opportunity for the competition. It creates one more reason for some of your clients to choose to conduct their business elsewhere. However, if the perceived value that you provide is greater than that of your competitors, your clientele is likely to go 'a little bit out of their way' to seek you out.

Hours of operation is one of the most often-cited convenience factors in the minds of service customers. However, the value of evening and weekend service hours may vary greatly in different markets. For example, in an area populated by young working couples the value of evening or weekend service hours is very high. The ability to get maintenance or service performed without having to take a day off from work may be a significant factor in the customer choosing a repair shop. In contrast, in a South Florida suburb that is heavily populated by retirees the importance of evening and weekend service hours is significantly less. The perceived value definitely changes based on the specific target audience.

The importance of convenience is also measured in comparison to the competition in the marketplace. If several of your major competitors offer this benefit then it is worth considering just to prevent them from using this against you. On the other hand, if none or few of the competitors offer this service it might be a benefit to explore to provide your shop with a unique feature that will set you apart from the competition.

Willingness to accept a variety of payment methods is a convenience benefit that is expected by many consumers in today's marketplace. Customers expect every business to accept a wide variety of debit and credit cards along with cash and possibly personal checks. Even though providing access to these payment methods adds to the cost of doing business this flexibility is an expectation. Failure to meet this expectation may be the deciding factor that sends customers to your competition who provide this basic service.

THEORY INTO PRACTICE 25-1

CASE

You are the owner of a local three-bay quick oil change location. Your normal hours of operation are 10 A.M.–6 P.M. Monday to Friday and 8 A.M.–4 P.M. Saturdays. In your most recent batch of customer satisfaction surveys you have seen several comments requesting that you stay open until 10 P.M. during the week.

You decide

Do you extend your hours? What information would you need to consider to help you to decide if it is a good business decision?

Availability

Availability is the capacity to deliver your product and/or service in a timely manner. Common examples of this characteristic in the automotive service business would be how far in advance it is necessary to schedule an appointment to get service work done or how likely it is for your shop to have the needed parts in stock or locally available so that work can be completed the same day.

Availability

The capacity to deliver a product and/or service in a timely manner.

Lack of capacity to meet customer demands in a timely manner can create a problem for the shop with the best reputation and most affordable service in town. After all, customers also expect convenience. Significant industry research has examined the negative impact of having to schedule service too far in advance. Results indicate that once the wait time exceeds three to four days even the best shops begin to lose repeat business because of inconvenience.

This is an important issue that requires serious thought and careful planning. All of the efforts that you make to provide quality service, maintain a competitive price, and offer competitive service hours can go for naught if you are so successful that you become backlogged with appointments 10 days in advance. Unfortunately, this type of backlog not only costs you immediate business; it can also turn the word-of-mouth testimonials of your most loyal customers against you, thus hampering future business.

When capacity is overwhelmed by demand it is time for the company to make some difficult decisions. As we just discussed, allowing the situation to remain that way will undo the goodwill and good reputation that you have in the community. Something has to be done, whether that is increasing staffing, adding on to your facility, or extending service hours. If nothing is done the negative consequences are inevitable.

THEORY INTO PRACTICE 25-2

CASE

You are the service manager at a very popular yet small fast-service shop in town that is located on a crowded corner in an old two-bay service station. You have developed such a good reputation for providing high value with a competitive price, convenient hours, and friendly and professional personnel that you are swamped with work. You have so much work that you've had to go to an appointment system and are currently booking appointments for oil changes and tire rotations two weeks in advance. As a result of this you have had several customers confront you and threaten to change shops even though they love the quality of your work.

You Decide

What would you do? Which of the following options would you consider to improve the convenience of your shop?

a. Go to a complete second shift to double shop capacity?
b. Add on two more stalls in the parking area and purchase nearby land to park the cars?
c. Raise prices to slightly slow down runaway demand?
d. Consider all of the above suggestions after carefully reviewing them?

The example provided above is intended to bring to bear several principles that we have talked about in this chapter as well as in ones presented earlier in this text. When demand exceeds supply you need to make some important business decisions. As noted in the first option you can expand service hours and thus increase capacity without enlarging the building or noticeably increasing overhead. The second option offers a plan to expand physical capacity. The third option deals with something that we have discussed briefly in this chapter, pricing. In the final analysis you can address problems of this type by using any one of these strategies or more likely by employing a combination of several of them.

Before we leave this topic, there is one more situation to consider. What do you do if you have excess availability? That is, you have significant unused capacity or supply? The same principles that we have already talked about apply. In this situation, however, you would consider reducing the workforce, reducing the facility space (sell it/sublet it/use it for a different purpose), and consider lowering price to get demand and supply more closely aligned.

Quality

Quality is an attribute of any product or service that is a powerful combination of perception and reality. People perceive quality when what they receive performs meets or exceeds their expectations. This can be absolute or relative. The ability to meet the intended use would be a minimum expectation and, therefore, an absolute criterion. In comparison, the ability to do a better job than the competition would be a relative criterion for evaluating a product or service as being high quality.

Quality
Excellence or superiority as a result of continuous improvement of process and product.

Quality should always be measurable and definable. However, quality in the mind of the consumer is not a static objective. It varies based on the customer's expectations and needs. In many cases it is part of an evaluation based on multiple measurements (such as the highest quality for the price). For more in-depth background on quality please refer to Chapter 12 where we address the underlying philosophies of quality and continuous improvement in greater depth.

The quality of your product is one of the attributes that will set you apart from the competition and give you a competitive advantage. However, it is important that you do not go overboard. You need to meet or exceed customer expectations while not overbuilding your product. That is, you need to be good enough but know when additional improvements are not noticeable or have little increased value to the customer. Failure to realize this important distinction can lead you to providing something that goes far beyond customer expectations and, in the process, has become so expensive that you have priced yourself right out of the market!

How Much Is Too Much?

When considering and addressing any of the five major characteristics it is important that you keep moderation and balance in mind. That is, you need to clearly understand how important each issue is to your target market. You need to appropriately respond to their needs. Not overreact or underreact. You may need to extend your service hours but the cost of 24/7 service may be too high. A compromise of service until midnight may be the best solution in this situation. Going to an extreme will cause you to make an investment beyond what is needed, and you will be wasting your money. Another example would be an obsession with quality. When your focus on making the best product goes beyond what the customer needs or is willing to pay the benefit will become a deterrent that will chase customers away.

What is needed is an appropriate and balanced response to addressing all five characteristics in the combination that best suits the wants and needs of your target market. This requires that you have clearly defined and intimately know the wants and needs of this target audience. If you do not do your homework in defining and understanding your potential customers you are likely to make careless investments of your time and resources where they will not have maximum impact. If, however, you keenly understand the needs and motivations of your market you will be able to get the maximum benefit in improving your perceived value in their minds with the minimum amount of time, effort, and cost.

Advertising
The communication of a marketing message to gain attention and encourage the purchase of a product or service that you have to offer.

Mass Media
Mediums of communication (TV, newspapers, Internet, and so on) that are designed to reach large audiences of people.

Advertising

At the start of this chapter we defined marketing as the complex process that is involved in letting the world know what you have to offer. **Advertising** is a major component of any marketing plan. It is one of the biggest action steps in the process. After you have identified what you have to sell, its features and benefits, and how you want to promote it to the public the next step is to advertise it. **Mass media** is the most common method of advertising your message to the public. The most commonly used mass media vehicles are Internet, e-mail, television, newspapers, magazines, direct mailing, radio, and billboards and signage. Each of these media has unique strengths and weaknesses. A brief overview of some of the strengths and weaknesses of each of the mass mediums is provided in Figure 25-2.

Benefits of mass media types					
Mass Medium	**Total Cost of Usage**	**Ability to Reach Audience**	**Access to Target Market**	**Ability to Target Specific Audience**	**Ability to Personalize**
Internet	Low	High	Mid	Low	Low
E-mail	Low	High	Mid	High	High
Television	High	High	High	Mid	Low
Radio	Mid	High	High	Mid	Low
Magazines	High	Mid	Mid	Mid	Mid
Newspapers	Mid	Mid	Mid	Low	Low
Direct Mail	High	High	Mid	High	High
Signage	Mid	Mid	Low	Low	Low

Figure 25-2 Benefits of mass media types

Web-Based Media

The Internet has grown to be the most widely used medium for sharing information worldwide. It has the potential to reach the entire world in a matter of milliseconds after you post the information on the Web. The cost to post a message on the Web is the cost of having a Web portal and is the least expensive of any mass communication medium. The primary methods of using the Web for advertising are through Internet postings, Web ads, and through the use of e-mail. With this great power for instantaneous and low cost communication via the Web why is it not the best and only method to spread your message?

The strength of the Web is that it reaches a large market quickly. However, what it possesses in wide reach and low cost it lacks in discrimination. That is, developing a company Web site and posting announcements and advertisements on it does little to target the message so that it reaches the specific audience that we want it to reach. Therefore, it reaches most people but may not get the message to those that you want it to reach in a manner that will assure that they will see it, read it, understand it, and be likely to respond to it.

Those of us who regularly surf the Web fail to realize that even with the explosive growth of the Web that there still remains a significant portion of the public who may not have convenient access to the Internet or may not access it on a regular basis. Therefore, although it has the potential to reach everyone in the world it may not be effective in reaching people right in our neighborhood and, most important, in our target market.

Web-based advertising is a much more costly alternative than general Internet postings but is much more likely to be found by potential customers. Web advertising requires that you link to a Web service (search engine or a buying service site) that will post your ads as pop-ups or inserts on their pages as people use these commonly used sites. Both of these methods are very poor for providing the information to your specific, local target market. Another alternative, however, is the use of Web directories. These directories provide information about businesses, similar to a phone book, which may be worthwhile in helping potential customers to find you in time of need.

The last Web-based advertising medium, e-mail, is a direct targeted person-to-person communication on the Internet. It is an electronic version of direct mail marketing. Since it is addressed to specific individuals it can overcome the ambiguity of Internet postings. It makes sure that it reaches specific individuals. It also has the benefit of speed since it travels in milliseconds from the sender to the receiver.

The strengths of e-mail are low cost and high speed. The drawbacks are limitations of the receiving audience. This first limitation is that you can only send a direct e-mail to those individuals who have provided you with their e-mail addresses. Those communications are limited to those of your current customers or customer contacts who are willing to provide you with this private information. This means that those who you can reach are a subset of those that you already know. This makes this approach suitable for customer retention activities but of minimal value for attracting new customers.

Unfortunately, the convenience of being able to reach everyone via e-mail so quickly and affordably has created its own set of problems. We as consumers have been so inundated with volumes of unwanted e-mails that we have created a whole new category of communication to describe them—spam. The rapid expansion of the amount of unwanted e-mails has resulted in most individuals having to use spam-blocking software to manage the great volumes of unwanted and unsolicited e-mails they receive daily so that they can keep their important e-mail traffic down to a manageable level. As a result, most of the e-mails that you send out with the intent of reaching a potential market will never be seen or read by their intended receiver. They will be caught, quarantined, and deleted electronically by spam-blocker software and, therefore, never reach your target audience.

Broadcast Media

Prior to the explosive growth of the Internet, television was the medium of choice to reach the largest audience in the least amount of time. Like the Internet, television and radio have the ability to reach a wide audience. However, the need to develop and produce a commercial is expensive and requires lead-time before it can be aired. In spite of these high costs to produce and air a commercial it remains one of the best ways to reach an entire market because more people have access to TV and radio broadcasts than they do to the Internet.

Automotive service is generally a localized activity. That is, the target market lives within a small geographic area that is close to your shop. Definite drawbacks of TV advertising are high cost and its minimal ability to reach a narrow market. As an advertiser you want to reach your target audience but do not want to waste your time or money reaching those who have no interest in your product or service. TV advertising can be targeted choosing the placement of the ad in relationship to programs that the target audience is most likely to watch. This does not, however, assure that any one ad placement will be viewed by the target audience. Further, within the broad group who watch a particular show you are likely to be paying to advertise to a much larger group who are not part of your target market.

Radio provides a lower cost broadcast alternative to television. Radio has much in common with TV advertising. It, too, reaches a broad geographic area and reaches many people that are not your target market. It does not have the staying power of a print medium where it can easily be saved. However, its ability to reach a wide audience quickly makes it worthy of consideration to help to build awareness of a new company, a major change, or a major marketing push.

Print Media

One benefit of newspapers and any other print medium is staying power. With live mediums like TV you have 15, 30, or 60 seconds to get your message across and then it is gone. With print mediums like newspapers, magazines, and direct mail the customer has the ability to take his time reading your message and to keep it for future use if it appeals to him. This staying power is a substantial benefit to print media. This means that the number of possible exposures that you get out of one ad is much more than just the initial posting.

Newspaper advertising is one of the largest and most common forms of print media used in automotive service advertising. Automotive service advertising can be found every day of the week in large metropolitan daily papers and in local neighborhood weekly papers. Advertising in the metropolitan paper is a much higher-priced option than the local papers. It provides broad reach to an entire metropolitan area. However, with this wide coverage come increased cost and the likelihood that much of the exposure is going to be wasted on people who are not your primary target market. Local community newspapers are a much lower-cost alternative. They allow you to reach a much more narrow geographic territory.

Magazines have a longer shelf life than newspapers and the average reader will see your ad several times. However, much like TV advertising, they reach a very broad market. Although automobile manufacturers may advertise in magazines to build public awareness this medium is cost prohibitive for service advertising. There is, however, one exception. It is the local shopper magazines that are delivered in the mail or inserted into newspapers. These publications are a hybrid of a mailer and magazine. Although they are printed in a booklet form, they have no articles and are simply a compilation of advertisements from a variety of local businesses. They provide a mid-priced option to reach your target market with print advertising.

The most common form of print advertising used to promote automotive service is direct mail. By designing a very specific advertisement and then mailing it only to those who are in your target audience this medium can be highly efficient. The cost for production and mailing per piece is much higher than for newspaper ads but the amount of waste (those ads that are going to people who are not your potential customers) is much lower. Two major types of direct mail are commonly used to promote automotive service. They are those that are sent to a predetermined customer base or those that are sent to a specific geographic area. The predetermined customer base mailing addresses can be targeted to an audience that meets specific criteria such as location, household income, type of car owned, or other characteristics. There are market research companies that specialize in developing and selling targeted database mailing lists in most major markets.

Billboards and Signage

Billboards and signage are a unique part of mass media. They do not have the benefits of speech and motion, they cannot be saved for the future, and in most cases they cannot be changed rapidly to address an immediate need. However, they are a constant silent salesman to keep reminding customers that you are there and that you are interested in their business. They keep you in potential customer's minds as someone to consider when the need arises. People commonly think of billboard media as the gigantic fixed signs along the freeway or above the roadways at major intersections. However, this same medium can also be found at bus stops, on park benches, and even on a movie screen as you walk in prior to the start of the movie previews.

Onsite exterior advertising signage is an effective use of this medium on your property. In addition to the signage telling customers that this is your location, advertising billboards onsite can be a silent salesman that will remind people that you are right here, right now and are ready and willing to serve their needs. The recent expansion of electronic billboards has resulted in shops being able to present colorful, attention-grabbing messages to attract business much like a TV ad but targeted to the local audience.

THEORY INTO PRACTICE 25-3

CASE

Your assignment is to find an automotive service ad in some form of local print media (newspaper/flyer/magazine). The purpose of this exercise is to see how many of the different marketing principles you can see applied in the ad.

You Decide

Review the ad and circle and mark those items in the ad in which the company has used any and/or all of the following marketing principles:

—Price

—Performance

—Convenience

—Availability

—Quality

SUMMARY

In the world of business it is not enough to have the best product in the world if no one knows about it and therefore does not buy it. Identifying a target market or audience for your product or service is the first essential step in developing a marketing strategy. To do this you must answer four simple questions: Who has an interest in my product or service? What is their specific want or need? Where can I find them? and, How can I best reach them?

Marketing is the process of letting potential customers know what you have to offer and its importance to them. The goals of marketing are to influence customer behavior so that they become aware of your product, develop an interest in it, purchase it, become regular customers, and become vocal advocates of its benefits.

Effective marketing of any product or service is based on understanding and communicating the important attributes that build the value of your product or service in the mind of potential consumers. The five major factors that determine that value in the mind of a customer are: price, performance, convenience, availability, and quality. Although price is an important factor and is often used to narrow down a customer's choices it is rarely the most important factor in a customer's ultimate buying decision. The importance of these five factors on any specific purchase decision can vary from customer to customer and situation to situation. Therefore, the importance of all five factors should be seriously considered.

Effectively advertising and promoting your product or service is critical to your success. There are several mass-communication mediums that can be used to get the word out about you and what you provide. Primarily due to their high cost TV, radio, and magazines are rarely a good choice for promoting automotive service. The most common advertising in the automotive service industry is direct mail and newspaper advertising.

PRACTICING THE PRINCIPLES

1. _______________ is communicating of a message to gain attention of a product or service.
   a. Mass media.
   b. Advertising.
   c. Television.
   d. Politicking.
2. The most important factor upon which customers decide which one to purchase is ____________________.
   a. Lowest price.
   b. Perceived value.
   c. Lack of availability.
   d. Random choice.
3. __________, although not the top factor in determining the customer's final choice to purchase is often used to help them narrow down their choices.
   a. A dartboard.
   b. Price.
   c. Value.
   d. Gold plating.

In Questions 4–7 please match the terms with the best definition.

_____ 4. Quality — a. meets or exceeds expectations.
_____ 5. Availability — b. excellence or superiority.
_____ 6. Convenience — c. delivered in a timely manner.
_____ 7. Performance — d. comfortable or easy.

In Questions 8–10 please fill in the blanks to complete the following statements.

Television, radio, the Internet, and newspapers are all examples of (8) ____________.

The most commonly used methods for advertising automotive service are (9)____________________ and (10)____________________.

CHAPTER 26

Target Marketing and Building an Identity

CHAPTER OBJECTIVES

- To examine who your market is, along with their unique needs and wants
- To identify the features that differentiate you from the competition
- To demonstrate how to formulate a unique market identity
- To apply general marketing principles to your product or service

KEY TERMS

target market
market research
wants
needs
awareness
identity
logo
tag line
image
personal media

Introduction

Target Market
The group of people who have a want or need that may be satisfied by a specific product or service.

Target marketing is the application of marketing principles to efficiently and effectively direct your message to your potential customers. To do this it is first important to clearly define your potential **target market.** Once you have done this you can determine the most efficient means to communicate with those individuals so that they know that you exist (awareness), know who you are (identity), and know what sets you apart from the competition (image). These factors will enable you to establish your competitive edge in the marketplace that will attract customers and help them to become loyal customers and advocates of your company.

Whether you are starting with just an idea or have an existing product or service, if you are planning to effectively market it you must begin by defining your target market. There are few products that have universal appeal and are needed by everyone. Further, advertising and promotion are very expensive. To maximize the results you need to take steps to clearly define who your potential customers are and how you can best communicate with them. Your target market is the "who" that you are looking for.

If you have done a thorough job of defining your market you should be well on your way toward reaching your target audience to let them know that you have a product or service that will meet their needs. The important question then becomes "What do I tell them?" Reaching them is important. More important, however, is to know what to say. Your goal is to get their attention and convince them to buy from you. To do this you need to know what your target market values and what motivates them to make a purchase decision. Armed with this information you can focus your message to make it clear to them that you have what they need.

Defining Your Market

Before you can effectively market your product or service to the right audience it is essential that you sit back and reflect on your goals. If you do not know who you are and where you are going it is going to be impossible to effectively communicate to the public. So you must first define your vision, mission, and goals. We spoke about this at an organizational level back in Chapter 9. These principles and techniques can be universally applied and should be used not only in organizational planning but also in activity planning.

In general, to effectively reach your target market you need to identify the who, where, how, and what of your potential buyers. The following questions will help to break this thought process down in more detail. When you can clearly and definitively answer all of these questions you can be assured that you know your target market and are ready to begin your marketing initiative, assured that your investment is well directed toward reaching your ultimate goal. The questions are

- What is the specific customer want or need that this product or service will address?
- How large is the market for this product or service?
- Is there a sufficient demand to make this effort worthwhile?
- Who is my competition and what do they have to offer?
- What is unique about the way that I am addressing the need?

- Who are the potential customers that will value this most?
- Where are they?
- How do I reach them?

Every manager should be able to sit down and answer all of the questions listed above before making the investment of time and energy to set out in a new direction or begin a new initiative. If you do not know the answers to all of these questions it is probably time for you to do some research before you proceed.

Market Research

Doing **market research** before you act will help you to define the demand that you are looking to satisfy. A clear example of this is the need to define how big the potential market really is and if there is sufficient demand to support your efforts. These are questions that are too often ignored. In their enthusiasm to launch a new product or service many companies have failed because they did not do the research to verify that the market was able to support their plans. Their initiatives were doomed from the outset.

The study of the marketplace that helps to determine the exact size and nature of the market.

Because of the constraints within your small business it will rarely be possible to hire an outside marketing consultant every time you have a new idea or consider a new product. Fortunately, a great deal of market research data already exists in the city or county where you do business. Good sources of this data are the local chamber of commerce or small business administration in your area. In most cases is not necessary that you do a high-level (and high-priced) study to answer the questions about the size and nature of your target audience. What is necessary, however, is that you take a step back and ask the people that you currently serve and those that you hope to serve: Am I on the right track? Do you want or need this?

Beyond defining who you will be soliciting as customers you must also have a clear picture of your competition. You need to identify the current pricing and value of products provided by them. This is essential to make sure that there is enough demand in the marketplace so that you can stake out enough territory to make it worthwhile for you to expend the effort and investment. Effective methods to quickly identify target audience and competitor information are through the use of surveys, media audits, and shopping the competition.

Surveying the marketplace can take many forms. However, the simplest and quickest is done by telephone or via the Web. If you know your market you should know your competition. If you know your competition then you should easily be able to survey your most direct competitors to obtain this information. For example, if you were interested in finding out what price your competition is charging for an oil change this week how would you find out? The easiest way is to ask them! Pick up the phone and call them posing as a potential customer. This is a low-cost, quick, and effective method of obtaining this essential information.

A second method for doing market research is through checking the media. In the automotive repair industry the most common methods of media used are newspapers, flyers, and direct mail. Careful review of all of the publications in your market can provide you with a rich resource for identifying what value the competition offers and what features and benefits they are promoting as the reason to buy from them. Careful review of their ads should help you determine what value they are providing. (Remember the five key characteristics of price, performance, convenience, availability, and quality?) Print advertising will be valuable in identifying the features and benefits that they are promoting and the overall public image that they are trying to build. Checking your competition's advertisements is something that you should use to your advantage to help you to identify and stake out your unique market niche in the marketplace.

A final method that is more involved and time consuming than the survey or media research is "shopping your competition." Shopping the competition requires that you, or someone on your behalf, visits the competition posing as a potential customer. By doing this you will obtain firsthand detailed information about the entire experience of dealing with this competitor. Telephone surveys will provide you with a brief overview, media research will provide you with information about how the company wants you to perceive them; however, shopping the competition provides you with the richest input about the competition based on firsthand experience.

Shopping the competition can provide the added input of what the physical environment of the competition is really like. Here are some of the important market research questions that you will be able to answer as a result of shopping the competition that you would not be able to answer by using the other methods

- Was the shop clean and professional?
- Were the people friendly?
- Did they seem like they cared, or did they just ignore me?
- Did they try to high pressure me to buy or were they more interested in finding out my needs and addressing them?
- Was the business the same as what I had expected based on what I have learned about them in their advertising?
- Is there something that they are doing that I should consider?
- What shortcomings do they have that I can capitalize on in trying to attract their customers?

The best way for you to differentiate and distinguish yourself from the competition is by knowing the competition's capabilities and the needs of your target market. Market research is an essential tool that must be used to properly position yourself in your market.

Wants versus Needs

Wants
Things of interest; desires.

Needs
Specific items or issues that must be addressed with some degree of urgency or risk negative consequences.

What is the difference between **wants** and **needs**? And why should you care? There is a significant difference between what people want and what they need. It is important to understand the difference if you want to effectively market any product or service and make a profit.

Needs are very specific items or issues that must be addressed with some degree of urgency or you run the risk of negative consequences. Wants, on the other hand, go beyond needs and although they seem important, do not carry the same risk. They are often more accurately described as desires. Here is an example. I am going to go out to buy a brand new sports car because I need reliable transportation to commute to and from work daily. Out of that past phrase we can separate the needs and wants. I *need* reliable transportation to get to and from work. However, I *want* a new sports car. A reliable vehicle and/or a bus pass or carpool would probably be adequate solutions to meet the needs; the sports car, on the other hand, is a bit beyond the minimum requirements.

If you ask a customer what he needs, what do you expect to hear him say? Will he really clearly define what he needs? What he wants? Or a combination of both? To be most effective you need to understand the difference.

THEORY INTO PRACTICE 26-1

CASE

You are the service advisor at Sunshine Tire & Wheel. A customer arrives on the back of a tow truck with a flat left front tire. She is very concerned because she only has $300 available to spend and she needs a complete new set of four top-of-the-line tires. You know that the top-of-the-line tires retail for $100 each and mounting, balancing, and alignment is an additional $100. You want to keep a satisfied customer but if you meet the stated needs you will have to cut your prices dramatically or risk losing this order and all of her future business.

You decide

Please choose the best option from the list below that meets the customer's needs and explain your reason.

a. Find a way to cut your price (and your profit) to meet her needs by selling her four top-of-the-line tires, mounting and balancing and a 4-wheel alignment in order to keep her business and her goodwill.

b. Tell her that you can meet her needs but that the lowest you can go for the 4 tires and labor is $500 + tax and she will have to take it or leave it.

c. Offer to sell two top-of-the-line tires, mounting, balancing, and aligning the car all at $300 + tax (your normal retail price) along with explaining that you can match these new tires with the same brand and tread pattern as is currently on the car.

Awareness

This is a concept that was briefly introduced in Chapter 25. However, building **awareness** holds a greater level of importance in service industries than it does in many other businesses. As a result it is important that we take more time now to explore it in greater depth.

Awareness
Getting the word out that something exists.

You probably would not be in the business you are in or working for the company that you work for if you did not believe that the company provides goods or services that have value. You know that there is a need (market) for them and the ones that you represent have unique features (value). You know that the market should be beating a path to your doorstep to buy from you. The real question, however, is: do *they* know that? The first goal of marketing is building awareness. You may have the best product at the best price in the most convenient location, but if the market does not know it your business will fail.

Building awareness is getting the word out to the public, and more specifically to your target market, that you exist. Building awareness is letting people know the name of your company and some general idea of what you do. In our case it is announcing to the world that you are out there and are ready and willing to serve the needs of the automotive service market.

You might ask, "Why should I put my efforts into such a general effort? We want business now. They cannot buy our name; we need them to buy our products." Although that is a good point and aims toward your ultimate goal, automotive service customers normally do not jump in their cars and run to a repair shop just because they saw an ad or heard about it on the radio. Their most common motivation is that they have an immediate need—whether that is squeaky brakes or a radio that cuts in and out. Until they have a need your calls for them to become your customer will go unanswered. However, when they finally have a need and have to decide where to go for service you need them to know that you exist and, should therefore be considered as a possible location to take their car for service.

Building awareness is planting the seeds in the minds of the market that you are there. This is essential for every service business because until you are firmly entrenched in their minds you will be overlooked when a need for automotive service arises.

How does a shop build awareness? By obtaining a high degree of general exposure to the potential market. This exposure does not have to be specific but it needs to be consistent. Potential customers need to see you or see something about you often enough for the message that you exist to stick in their mind.

THEORY INTO PRACTICE 26-2

CASE

Unlike most of the exercises we have done in the past, this one is going to be very personal. Every day you pass automotive service shops on your way to school or work.

You decide

Right now take a few minutes to answer the following questions:

1. Please write down the names of the first five auto repair shops that you pass regularly on your way to work or school.
2. What unique things can you remember about each of them?
3. Now, the hard part: Tomorrow as you head out for work or school write down the first five automotive repair shops *that you drive past.* (Please pay particular attention to look for *all* of the shops so that you list the first five and do not miss any regardless of how large or small.)
   a. Are the five that you see the same as the five that you remembered in the first question?
   b. Which ones did you fail to list in the first question?
   c. Why do you think you may have forgotten about the shops that you did not originally list?
   d. If you owned one of those shops that you passed but did not list in the first question, what would you do to increase customer awareness?

Building Identity

Once people are aware that you exist you need them to be able to pick you out of the crowd. The concept behind this is very simple. Those who know you well as a person can easily do this when they see you across the way at the mall or at work. As a competitor in the busy and crowded automotive service market you need to be able to expect your customers to pick your business out of the crowd.

Building **identity** is most commonly done through developing a unique and easily recognizable public appearance that customers can quickly and easily identify that this is you. One of the most common ways to do this is to develop a corporate **logo.** A logo is a specific way of presenting your corporate name consistently so that customers can recognize it at first glance. Just about every large company has invested substantial time and money in developing a logo. These logos present the name of the company in one unique yet consistent design, colors, fonts, and graphics. What does the logo of your bank look like? What colors are in the logo at the grocery store where you shop weekly? What about at the clothing store where you buy most of your clothes? Now, what about at the place where you work?

Identity

Developing a unique and easily recognizable public appearance.

Logo

The name of the company presented in a consistent format—colors, fonts, and graphics.

Using a logo to establish a clear, definable, and consistent identity to the public is very important. Instead of asking people to carefully read the words in an ad, on a billboard, or on your exterior signs they begin to recognize a picture. That picture (your logo) is distinct enough that they can rapidly and at a single glance clearly tell that it is you. This is much akin to recognizing your face in a crowd.

Many companies go beyond just a logo and create an entire corporate visual identity. The logo is the centerpiece of this identity but it may include the color schemes used on their buildings, their advertisements, and even their company stationery. This theme is likely to be carried over into the colors and designs on company vehicles and onto employee uniforms. All of this is an expanded use of the efforts to build a unique and quickly recognizable identity.

A logo is great for visual effect, but how do you carry this concept forward when people cannot see you? What do you do on the radio to maintain this same consistency? The answer is simple. The audio version of a logo is a **tag line.** This is a simple phrase that is consistently used in both print and media advertising and promotion. This phrase is intended to convey some unique features or benefits of your organization that helps you to stand out from the competition. An example might be something like the following: "MicroMax Motors . . . we may be small but we give you maximum value." Can you think of a tag line that

Tag Line

Consistent phrase used in both print and media advertising to promote a product or service.

THEORY INTO PRACTICE 26-3

CASE

An effective tagline helps to put the name of a company in the back of our minds so that when we have a need for that type of product or service we consider them to meet our needs.

You decide

Below is a list of 10 very different products. Take a few minutes and write down the first tag line and company that you can remember for at least five of these categories:

Automobile company: ______________________

Auto parts: ______________________

Bank: ______________________

Beverage: ______________________

Breakfast cereal: ______________________

Clothing: ______________________

Electronics: ______________________

Insurance company: ______________________

Radio station: ______________________

Snack food: ______________________

you have heard on the radio or on TV that has become so common that if you only catch part of the message you know exactly what company the ad is from? Those companies are making effective use of tag lines to build their identity.

Establishing an Image

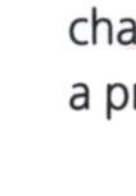

Image
Clear, consistent, and specific attributes or characteristics that define a product or company.

Tag lines have a great value in helping to build identity. However, they go further than just providing an easy means to identify your company. In addition to establishing identity they also help to establish an **image**. Image is a set of clear, consistent, and specific attributes or characteristics that define your company in the consumer's mind. Ask anyone what the first things are that come to mind when you give them the name of a company or a product. Hopefully, if you ask 10 people the responses will be similar. If the responses are similar and they all convey the intended goals and direction of that company then the company is doing a great job of developing, communicating, and living up to their image. If not, they have some serious work to do!

Building an image is clearly not a desire to portray the company or product as something that it is not. The basis for building a clear and consistent public image is to make the public very aware of who you are, what you do, and what sets you apart from the competition in the marketplace. In short, what you do better than everyone else. When people see this demonstrated repeatedly over time it develops into a consistent image of who you are in their minds.

Different companies will actively work to stake out their niche in the market by developing a consistent image through everything that they do. A company that has a simple and plain-looking facility, does not provide the fancier services, and guarantees to meet or beat the lowest price of any competitor in the market is working to build an image of a no frills, low-cost provider.

Some examples of how an automotive repair facility might reinforce its image in promotional materials are listed below.

Price: Best value for your money/Low price guarantee
Convenience: Open late to serve you/extended service hours/we are just around the corner
Quality: Consumer choice award winner/Money back guarantee/10-time award winner

THEORY INTO PRACTICE 26-4

CASE

Each company stakes its identity, its image, and its future on what makes it different.

You decide

Take a minute to write down the name of the automotive company that comes to your mind first when you hear the identifying attribute.

a. Engineering: ______________________
b. High performance: ______________________
c. Reliability: ______________________
d. Fuel economy: ______________________
e. Style: ______________________
f. Luxury: ______________________
g. Value: ______________________

THEORY INTO PRACTICE 26-5

CASE

Your assignment is to find an automotive service ad in some form of local print media (newspaper/flyer/magazine). This exercise is very similar to the one we did in the last chapter, but with a slightly more focused approach to target marketing.

You decide

Please read and look carefully at the ad in front of you. Once you feel that you see what messages the company is trying to communicate to you please answer the following:

a. What techniques and methods did the company use in the ad to promote a unique *identity*?
b. What words, phrases, or other methods did they use to project a unique *image*?

Communicating Your Message

Once you know what you want to say, who you want to say it to, and how you want to say it you need to choose the most efficient communication methods to get the word out. These methods are called media. They fall into two main groups: mass media and personal media. The most commonly used mass media are television, the Internet, newspapers, magazines, direct mailing, radio, and billboards and signage. We discussed the general benefits and limitations of these individual advertising mediums in Chapter 25. You may want to review this information.

Mass media is an effective way to keep your name in front of your current customers and to attract the attention of potential customers in your target market. By effectively choosing the medium to get the message out to all of those who have a need and desire to do business with you it is possible to let people know that you are there in the market (awareness), let them know what is unique about your shop (identity), and why they may want to consider doing business with you rather than with others when they have a need (image).

Another medium for reaching your target market is word of mouth. In Chapter 19 we spoke at great length about the value of satisfied customers and the resulting benefit of having customers who become your vocal advocates. It is important to realize that word of mouth is the most effective, valuable, and lowest cost method of getting your message out. Nothing surpasses the credibility that goes with your current customers telling others about the wonderful experience that they have had doing business with you.

Personal Media
Unsolicited recommendations and referrals from your existing customers.

Personal media is the word-of-mouth unsolicited recommendations and customer referrals open given by your loyal and satisfied customers that you simply cannot buy. However, that does not mean that you are helpless to do anything about it. Although you cannot buy it you can encourage it. Savvy shops encourage their customers to share the good news with their friends and acquaintances. This can be done with a simple suggestion, or even by offering them a special promotion for passing on the good news.

SUMMARY

Being effective in business is not that different from being successful as an individual in life. In both cases it is essential to know who you are, what your strengths are, and how to use them to your best advantage. In the business sense, this is exactly what you must strive to do to define your goals and directions, your audience, and your competition as you move forward to consider and implement any initiative. Once you have built a solid argument to move forward it is then important that you let the world know.

Target marketing is identifying the audience for your product or service and focusing your efforts on reaching that specific group. The goal in building awareness, identity, and image is to differentiate you in the mind of the consumer. Customers must know that you exist so that they will be able to consider you when they have a need (awareness). They must recognize you (identity) when you try to communicate with them through media or signage so that they know that you are trying to attract their business (identity). They must know what sets you apart from all of the others (image) so that they see a reason why they should choose you.

In the final analysis, your goal should be for customers to instantly recognize your company, know who you are and what you do, and have you at the top of their list as the company with whom they prefer to do business. Your job in building your identity and effectively targeting your marketing is to create the environment that makes this possible.

PRACTICING THE PRINCIPLES

1. To be successful in business you need to focus your efforts on meeting the customer's
   a. price.
   b. son-in-law.
   c. needs.
   d. demand.
2. Looking for information that will help you identify your audience, where they are, and how to best reach them is
   a. personal media.
   b. market research.
   c. mass media.
   d. building awareness.
3. The primary audience that has an interest in and ability to purchase your product or service is your primary
   a. target market.
   b. audience.
   c. marketing source.
   d. cause of frustration.
4. If you ask a customer what their requirements are for a product or service they are most likely to tell you their __________, not their __________.
   a. shoe size/sock size.
   b. needs/wants.
   c. height/weight.
   d. wants/needs.
5. A __________ is the name of the company presented in a consistent design, colors, fonts, and graphics.
   a. locus.
   b. picture.
   c. tagline.
   d. logo.
6. ___________ is a set of clear, consistent, and specific attributes or characteristics that define your company in the mind of the consumer.
   a. Awareness.
   b. Your logo.
   c. Image.
   d. Your needs.
7. In a service industry customers do not normally seek you out unless they have an immediate need. It is for that reason that you need to build ____________________ so that they will consider you when that need arises.
   a. customer wants and needs.
   b. your market share.
   c. customer awareness.
   d. your skills and abilities.
8. What is the automotive manufacturer that comes to mind when you think about exotic sports cars? What colors are in their logo?
9. What automotive company comes to mind when you think of tires? What colors are in their logo?
10. List the tagline of any automotive-related manufacturing or service company that you have heard. What company uses this tagline in its advertising?

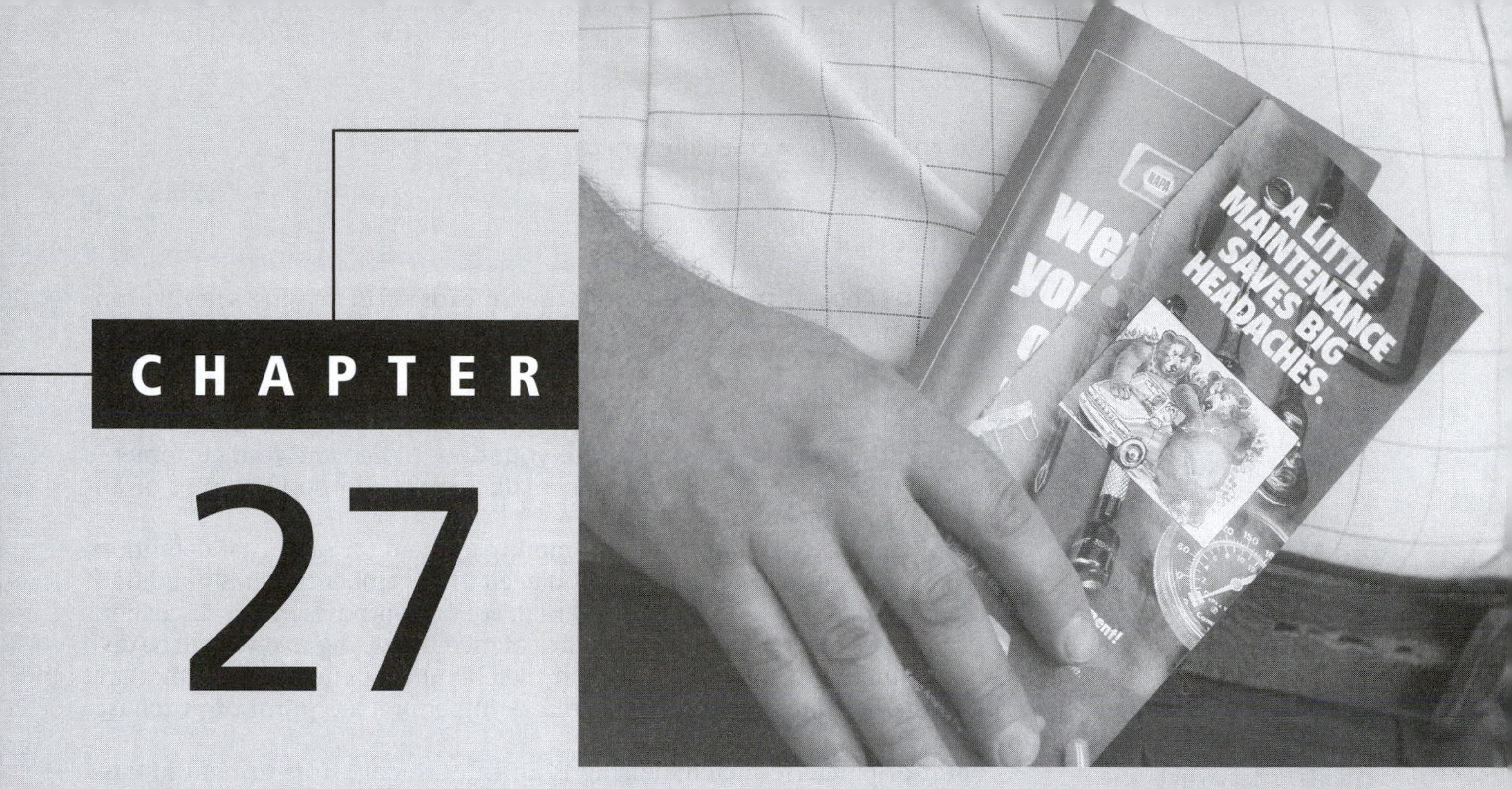

CHAPTER

27

Point-of-Purchase Merchandising

CHAPTER OBJECTIVES

- To examine the concept of point-of-purchase merchandising
- To identify the various methods of merchandising used in retail businesses
- To distinguish those types of merchandising that are commonly used in automotive service
- To identify the unique features and benefits of different merchandising techniques

KEY TERMS

merchandising
point-of-purchase merchandising
signage
package pricing
up-sell
competitive pricing board
product display
impulse items
captive repair items

Introduction

This chapter focuses on a commonly used means of increasing sales within the automotive service shop, merchandising. If you remember, in Chapter 25 we began our discussion by introducing the broad concept of marketing. Marketing was defined as "the complex process that is involved in letting the world know what you have to offer and what value it brings to them so that they will enthusiastically beat a path to your door to become your customer." Point-of-purchase merchandising is a small, yet very important, part of an effective marketing effort.

Merchandising
Displaying and promoting an item for sale.

Point-of-Purchase Merchandising
Efforts to display, promote, and demonstrate the capabilities of a product or service through placement of onsite reminders in a place of business.

Merchandising is, simply put, promoting an item for sale. That definition might initially sound like marketing. You need to remember that it is not different than marketing; it is a part of marketing. For our purposes in this discussion of automotive service applications the area of merchandising that we will be discussing is limited to the most common merchandising efforts, those that are done at the business location. Those marketing efforts are **point-of-purchase merchandising.**

Point-of-purchase merchandising is an intentional effort to remind customers what we have to offer while they are already at our place of business. To be successful in any retail business we need to be sure that our customers know that we are in the marketplace as a possible supplier, what we have to offer, and why they should consider making the purchase from us. Have you ever seen effective point-of-purchase merchandising? What was it? Where?

Some of the most effective point-of-purchase merchandising is so low key yet effective that you are very likely to have become accustomed to it and do not consciously know that it is there. Yet, somehow it keeps on quietly suggesting to you "What about this?" This is an effective use of this medium as a silent salesman that constantly, yet quietly, asks you "By the way, while you are here, do you need one of these?" When is the last time that this question has come to your mind while you were out shopping?

A great deal of the most expert, well-researched, and consistent point-of-purchase merchandising can be found in the big box retail stores. Signs, displays, flashing lights to alert you to specials, and coupons on display as you enter the store are all methods of point-of-purchase merchandising.

The Goal

The vast majority of the customers who enter your service shop have intentionally visited you. Unlike strolling through the mall where they might just be looking around it is highly likely that when they arrive at your shop they have a very specific goal and need in mind. The purpose in using point-of-purchase merchandising is quietly yet effectively raising the customer's awareness of the vast array of other services and products that you have available. You quietly suggest to customers ways that they can do additional business with you while they are already there. This makes it more convenient for them, and it significantly adds to your bottom line.

Merchandising Locations

There are seven areas that are common to most automotive repair shops where effective use of merchandising can help to stimulate customer interest and thus produce increased sales. Good merchandising locations exist both outside and inside of your main shop area.

Some of the exterior locations that can be very effective include the front of your lot along the public road, the exterior of the building area, and at the customer entrance. If your department is a part of a larger company location, as is the case with a dealership or retail store, signage in the other departments can be an effective reminder that will build awareness of the services that you offer.

Once you enter your service area there are abundant opportunities to merchandise and promote your services. Point-of-purchase merchandising can be effectively employed in the service drive area, at the service write-up desk, in the customer waiting area, in the workshop area, and at the cashier's window.

Hopefully, after looking at these lists you are thinking "But that is just about everywhere in the entire place." If you thought that you would be right. Any place that a customer can see, touch, or feel something that may stimulate their interest in considering additional purchases is a point-of-purchase merchandising opportunity.

Signage

Permanent or semipermanent signs at your site serve as reminders to customers of what you have to offer. That ranges from announcing the variety of manufacturers whose products you sell to very specific announcements about current specials and new additions to your product line.

Signs can be used for indirect or direct promotion of your products, services, or even of your reputation. **Signage** encompasses a variety of written communications ranging from directional signs to warnings to reminders. For the purposes of point-of-purchase merchandising your goal is to use this medium as reminders to help promote sales. They can be something as general as a public display of your corporate vision, mission, and goals or as specific as a sign giving notice of a $19.95 Oil Change Special good only today.

Signage
A variety of written communications displayed publicly in a permanent or semipermanent manner.

Signs that identify the use of well-known and respected products and companies that you work with do not directly promote or sell a specific item effectively. Yet, they can be effective by selling your credibility and reputation. They act as silent salesmen that remind customers that you deal with reputable vendors and provide them only with quality parts. It helps to remind them that the service and parts that you provide can be trusted. Through reinforcing the customer's confidence it allows them to become more comfortable in dealing with you, and this results in increased sales opportunities.

This type of signage can often be found in the most public areas of the building: in the service drive, on the building exterior, and throughout the workshop. They may be a permanent illuminated signs from your best known parts providers that are affixed to the outside of your building. The intent is to remind people that they can purchase those products at your store. They can be banners affixed to the walls in the service drive that display the name and logo of a prominent supplier. This signage tells that you deal with good companies. They can be prominently displayed logos or signs located near a prominent piece of shop equipment that helps remind the customer that you use only the best to work on their car.

Menu Boards

A very common use of signage in the service shop is the menu board. It is called a menu board because it is much like what you'll find in a fast-food restaurant. It is a highly visible listing of your most common products or services with their prices prominently displayed. Why post them? The customer already knows what he wants, doesn't he?

The menu board serves a dual purpose. First it clearly states your prices right out in the open. This communicates your willingness to be open and honest about your services and your prices. It also provides a visible reminder of other products and services that customers might want to consider while they are in your shop.

Service menu boards may be used in an automotive repair shop in the same manner that they are used in fast-food restaurants, to prominently display **package pricing** specials. A package price offers a special discount if the customer purchases several common services at the same time. This can be an effective tool to **up-sell** from the customer's initial service request. This will result in the customer purchasing additional work. While the customer is rewarded with a better price and increased convenience the shop is rewarded by increased efficiency, revenue, and profits. We'll address the concept of up-selling in the Chapter 28.

Package Pricing
A special price offered for the purchase of a specified combination of products or services.

Up-Sell
To sell a customer more products or higher priced products than initially requested.

Competitive Pricing Board
A sign displaying a comparison of current prices for common products or services offered by your shop and your major competitors.

A variation of the service menu board that has become common in more aggressive retail establishments is the **competitive pricing board**. This sign clearly shows a comparison of the availability and pricing of common services and repairs at your shop and at those of your primary competitors. The purpose of this board is not simply to suggest service; it is to sell your credibility. By openly displaying your pricing right alongside that of your competitors it helps to dispel customer misconceptions or insecurities about your prices being competitive in the marketplace. This helps to allay customer fears. Finally, it plays a very important role in helping you to effectively sell additional service. Why, you might ask?

Today's price-conscious consumers will typically do some comparison shopping before they decide to make a purchase. As a result of this common habit, customers may be reluctant to make a purchase decision on any item that they were not planning to purchase today. This is due to their uncertainty of the current market price of that item. Without this information they are not sure whether or not they are getting a good deal. However, you can help them to overcome that fear. You can do that 'homework' for them by displaying a competitive pricing menu board . . . thus opening the door to additional sales and increased customer confidence.

More direct sales signage can effectively promote current service specials as a means of stimulating additional sales. Small billboards along the street, below your outdoor company sign, next to the service drive-in door, or alongside the service write-up desk can be used effectively to let the customers know about limited-time offers. They remind your customers that they can get a needed service done at a lower price if they act now.

Product Displays

Signs can effectively remind customers what companies you deal with, what you sell, and your pricing, but nothing gets people's attention better than real examples. No matter how professionally done, a sign that says we sell tires is not as likely to attract serious interest and attention as a **product display** with a real tire. The displayed item generates much greater sensory appeal. You can see it, touch it, feel it, and, in some cases, even smell it. For those who are technically aware, a display can peak their interest as they are able to take a closer look at the real thing. For those who are not so technically inclined, it provides a reminder of what the product is actually like and gives them the opportunity to be able to better understand what you are selling.

Product Display
An exhibit of a product that is available for sale.

In all cases, an effective product display gives you and the product manufacturer the opportunity to present the features and benefits of that product to the customer. It is these features and benefits that build value in the customer's mind and make the purchase a worthwhile investment. Some of the more effective product displays may be combined with free brochures to provide customers with more in-depth information. They can also include cutaway displays of a part of the product that focuses on the unique qualities of that product and sells its value.

In contrast to the glitz and glamour of the display of new equipment and technology, another very useful product display is the failed part display. Some may prefer to steer clear of this type of negative merchandising as being a scare tactic. They can, however, be very effective in explaining to your customers, and especially to your non-technical customers, the importance of taking service and maintenance seriously. Such a display may include photographs of the results of a failure because of a lack of preventative maintenance, such as the inside of an engine that has failed. They may be a comparison of good parts next to failed parts to show real examples of the type of damage and cost that can be incurred by not taking care of your car. Finally, they might be as simple as some examples of failed parts from your shop that are strategically placed in a showcase or on the service desk as a silent reminder of the need for service.

Displays are powerful tools in helping to get your customers thinking about what they need and they help to motivate them to act now. They can provide a gentle and courteous reminder of the service that the customer knows is overdue, they can encourage the customer to approve the service that will soon be due because you are running a special and it is more convenient to do it all in one stop. They can cause the customer to reconsider the potential consequences of putting off a repair that he knows could have expensive consequences if neglected any longer. In all of these examples the intent in effectively merchandising is not to generate unneeded service sales but rather to heighten awareness.

Product displays can be effective in promoting sales of a variety of additional items. A stack of oil filters on the service counter can serve as a reminder to your customer to consider getting an oil change while she is in for this repair visit. Something as simple as a single spark plug can remind a customer of an overdue engine tune-up. Wouldn't a car battery sitting on the service desk provide a good reminder that a long, cold winter is just around the corner?

In addition to reminding customers of products and services that they know you have, product displays also help you to promote other items that customers might never have considered that they could buy from you. Some service shops have expanded into apparel and sports-related merchandising. Racing jackets, shirts, and car models of vehicles that are sponsored by their company or by a major industry partner are common examples. A tastefully done showcase in the customer waiting lounge can effectively make the point that your company offers these items for sale. Another example of this is a display of over-the-counter performance parts. This will let customers know that along with providing service for their car you can also be the supplier to meet their do-it-yourself accessories and parts needs.

Impulse Items

One of the simplest and most effective point-of-purchase merchandising efforts is the one that you've experienced as a child, a teenager, and as an adult every time that you've gone through the checkout lane at your local grocery store. What can you always find lining both sides of the checkout lane as you're waiting impatiently to be checked out and pay your bill? Although you might have correctly answered tabloids, nail clippers, or batteries the most common item is *candy*.

Do you seriously believe that putting an entire display of individual candy bars, gum, and other sugar-filled treats within the reach of a small child who is being held hostage in the seat of a grocery cart for the past hour is by chance? No, it is very intentional. The items that line both sides of the checkout lane are what are called **impulse items.** These are items that are commonly used and wanted by most customers. They are also commonly lower priced items that would not have been the primary reason for a trip to the store.

Impulse Items

Commonly used items that are prominently displayed to promote additional immediate sales that were not the original purpose of the customer's shopping trip.

The intention of impulse purchase merchandising is to quietly say to the customer "Don't forget that you need this *too*." Getting to the *too* part can't be overstated. The intent is getting the customer to purchase a little bit more while they are in your store. It is not to get them to buy something that they really don't want or need, but something that they might not have thought about or remembered unless something or someone had reminded them.

The idea of the candy-lined checkout lane works well in grocery stores but how does that apply in an automotive service shop? There are few types of businesses in which impulse item marketing cannot be effectively used. In an automotive service shop there are three very common areas that can be effectively used for impulse purchase merchandising. They are the service write-up desk/drive area, the cashier's area and the customer waiting area. The use of small displays or signage in each of these areas can effectively remind customers of common additional items that they might want or need that were

THEORY INTO PRACTICE 27-1

CASE

As the new service manager at a brand new shop you want to help spice up the service desk area with some impulse items to help bolster sales. You've met with your service advisors and they've provided you a list of possible items.

You decide

Which of the following items would you choose to display at the service desk to help promote impulse sales? (Hint: you can choose more than 1)

a. windshield wiper inserts.
b. car battery.
c. crankshaft.
d. spark plugs and air filter.
e. crank position sensor.
f. fuel sending unit.

not a part of their original plan that brought them to your store. Examples of these types of items might be windshield washer fluid, snow brushes, or special key chains with your logo on them.

What Should I Merchandise?

You can merchandise any item. However, the most effective focus for merchandising is those items that are commonly known and highly competitive. There is sound reasoning why those items are the most effective targets for merchandising. Let's explore that in more depth.

The idea of merchandising is to get customers thinking about their needs and wants so that they are able to sell themselves on additional services and repairs. This is done in contrast to you taking the time to go through a lengthy presentation to customers to bring up every possible item that they might want or need. Besides, since you're probably not a mind-reader, how could you possibly know about those needs and wants that the customer hasn't shared with you?

Displaying a computer module, although interesting to some, is not likely to be appreciated by the majority of your customers or is it likely to inspire them to buy one. In contrast, most of your customers know what a battery looks like and most of them have heard enough tales about people getting stranded in the winter with a dead battery. Therefore, they know what the item is and can relate to its importance. Thus, this would make a good point-of-purchase item to display as a reminder.

The second important focus for merchandising is focusing on highly competitive items. These are those services and repairs that even the most technically challenged customer regularly reads about in flyers and newspapers. If they are at all sensitive to their need to maintain their car they have some sense of what the price is on the street for these types of parts and services. Therefore, using these items as an intentional subject for your merchandising helps to show that you provide these common services and that they can buy from you, now, here and at a competitive price. We previously spoke about the competitive pricing menu board that can effectively make this point. A simple maintenance menu sign displaying your prices for the most competitive items (oil change/tune up/wheel alignment/tire rotation) can effectively convey this message.

Going back to the impulse items example provided earlier, your local grocer could put fresh artichokes at the checkout line but he doesn't. Why? The most likely reason is that they are not an impulse purchase. That is, they are not an item that most people will commonly want and need and get to the checkout line having forgotten to purchase. Artichokes are more likely a need than a want. They are either needed for a recipe or not. You can't normally say that about a candy bar or two AA batteries. You should focus your efforts on common and competitive items, not on captive repair items. What are captive repair items? Let's discuss that further.

Captive repair items are those items are available only through a very limited number of sources. They are those that cannot normally be provided by a great number of your competitors. Examples might be repair of some computer-related systems on a late model car that requires special tools or equipment. If you are a dealership selling and servicing that make of vehicle, you have a captive market. Similarly, more complex and highly technical

Captive Repair Items

Items are available only through a very limited number of sources.

repairs are not likely to be provided by many of your competitors. Although not totally captive they are semi-captive or low competition repair items.

Customers are unlikely to consider going to the local muffler shop or quick service plaza to have their automatic transmission overhauled or to replace the inner door panel on their new car. These are good examples of captive repair items. Even though there are some other shops that might be capable of doing this repair customers generally won't consider shopping around for these repairs. Further, due to the complexity and broad range of possible repairs and costs it is much more difficult for customers to comparison shop on such an item. Therefore, these are not items that you would want to merchandise.

In effective marketing, the major focus should always be on giving the customer as many reasons as possible why they should choose to do business with you. You do this by promoting features and benefits of the products and services of your organization. The combination of these benefits makes up the total value in the customer's mind. Only when they can consistently feel comfortable that they are getting a better overall value from you than they are from your competitors will you have a loyal, repeat customer. Point-of-purchase merchandising can be a powerful and cost-effective tool in your efforts to continue to reinforce this message to your current customers every time that they pay you a visit.

SUMMARY

In this chapter we have discussed an area of the marketing of your service operations that is critical to your success, point-of-purchase merchandising. Point-of-purchase merchandising includes all efforts that you make to display, promote, and demonstrate your capabilities to your customer through placement of reminders at your facilities.

The three major types of merchandising efforts are through the use of signage, product displays, and impulse item merchandising. These merchandising efforts may be targeted in a general effort to reinforce the attributes and values of your organization or to help directly promote the sale of a specific item. These communication tools serve as a silent salesman to remind customers of items that they want or need and those that they might have forgotten. In addition, it helps to raise their consciousness of items that they might not have even realized that you were ready and willing to provide for them.

The end goal of point-of-purchase merchandising is to promote additional per-customer sales. By doing this through the use of these methods it is possible to suggest additional sales in a low-key, low-pressure way that will not make the customer feel pressured or uncomfortable. After all, it is far better for your long-term relationship when the additional purchase is their idea, not yours—and that is the point.

PRACTICING THE PRINCIPLES

1. Promoting an item for sale is called
   a. promoting.
   b. merchandising.
   c. marketing.
   d. displaying.
2. Effective methods of suggesting the purchase of additional items to customers who are in your shop can be done through
   a. signage.
   b. product displays.
   c. impulse item merchandising.
   d. all of the above.
3. ________________ is the ability to sell a customer more products or higher priced products than they had initially requested.
   a. Add-ons.
   b. Trickery.
   c. Up-selling.
   d. Being a salesperson.

4. ____________________ is a conscious effort to display, promote, and demonstrate the capabilities of a company to customers through placement of onsite reminders.
   a. Point-of-purchase merchandising.
   b. Shameless promotion.
   c. Marketing.
   d. Bragging.

5. A visible display comparing your prices to those of your competition on a variety of common repairs and services is a ______________________.
   a. service menu board.
   b. package pricing guide.
   c. competitive advantage listing.
   d. competitive pricing board.

6. The repair item that would most likely not be a part of a point-of-purchase display is a(n)
   a. oil filter.
   b. windshield wiper blade.
   c. interior trim panel.
   d. battery.

7. A special price offered for the purchase of a specified combination of products or services is called ______________________.
   a. package pricing.
   b. discount pricing.
   c. being competitive.
   d. service merchandising.

Signage can be an affective tool for merchandising. Please list examples of two different types of signs that can be used in an automotive service shop.

8. ____.

9. ____.

10. List three impulse items that you might find on display in an automotive service shop.

CHAPTER

28

Selling Service

CHAPTER OBJECTIVES

- To analyze the relationship of sales per vehicle to profitability
- To examine tools that will help improve sales opportunities in the service drive
- To identify additional sales opportunities in the repair shop
- To demonstrate the importance of focusing on customer repair priorities

KEY TERMS

billable hours
service estimate
checkout time
walkaround
soft-sell
service pricing menu
safety inspection
price leader

Introduction

The survival of an automotive service shop depends upon providing service at an affordable price. It also depends upon the shop's ability to consistently generate a profit. This depends upon more than just generating sales. It is also dependent on how efficient your shop is. The ability of the shop to consistently sell additional needed services to increase overall sales per transaction is a major factor in achieving and maintaining shop efficiency and profitability.

Support Services

There is a major difference in the overall results to the company between selling $1,000 in labor by servicing 20 cars at $50 per transaction and one who generates the same sales by servicing five cars at $200 per transaction. The sales are the same but the net effect on profitability is very different. The reason that they differ is the cost for support services that go into every customer transaction. For every customer that comes into the shop the typical shop provides the following nine support services. These are all necessary activities for which the customer is not charged. The nine support activities are as follows:

1. Greet customer and get their service information.
2. Prepare preliminary estimate.
3. Road test car to verify customer concerns.
4. After diagnosis, prepare detailed estimate.
5. Contact customer and obtain repair approval.
6. Road test car after repairs to verify problem is resolved.
7. Contact customer to notify that car is ready for pickup.
8. Prepare the service bill.
9. Take payment and release vehicle.

The difference in profitability between servicing 20 cars to generate $1,000 and servicing five cars to sell the same amount of service is in the number of times that you need to provide the nine support services and the resulting cost to pay personnel to provide these services. You can dramatically reduce the amount of these indirect expenses and significantly increase the profit earned for the same amount of total sales if you can improve your average sales per vehicle serviced. Once you see the difference between these two examples the answer is obvious, selling additional service per customer and increasing **billable hours** per vehicle is an essential skill that your shop must develop and consistently practice.

Billable Hours
The amount of time directly related to the performance of repairs for which you can charge the customer.

It is important to understand before we proceed with discussing this topic that the shop's focus needs to be more than just selling more service. It needs to be selling more needed service. What is the big difference? The difference is in being honest and ethical and in providing true customer service, not just increased customer sales at all costs. A good customer service representative must strive to be careful to maintain a careful balance where the driving force is to be thorough, yet not oversell. That is, to always base the additional service recommendations on those services that the customer needs and wants. Only in that way is it possible to generate the ultimate goal: additional profit and a satisfied customer.

In the last several chapters we discussed marketing, merchandising, and the importance of promoting service to customers. Now that the customers are in our shop and we have their attention, the way that we handle the sales transaction during their visit will make the difference between success and failure. A major deciding factor is our ability to identify and sell additional needed service and repairs at every opportunity.

Real World Application

While working as service director in big-city shop we were commonly assaulted by competitors who tried to woo our customers away from us by waging price wars for highly competitive repairs. The most common of these was the ever-present cheap oil change ad. The competition was eating into our market share. The big question was "How do we compete and still make money?"

We needed to be price competitive on the oil changes if we did not want to lose those customers. After all, if they went there for an oil change they might decide to stay there for their next alignment, tire rotation, tune up, and so on. However, providing an oil change at a competitive price would result in us losing money *unless* we figured out some other way to generate a profit. We had tried this before and did many oil changes, all at a loss, and really did not want to be busy and lose money. That simply did not make any sense. So, what was the answer? The answer was selling additional service.

I met with the technicians, service advisors, and our parts department and we brainstormed. The one thing that we all agreed on was that we could not afford the risk of losing these long-term customers and the other business that we might lose from them in the future. Yet, we could not afford to lose money on every transaction. The solution was that we all gave a little to make it work. The technicians agreed to take a slight cut in time paid per oil change. The parts department agreed to cut their profit margin on the parts. The service advisors and technicians agreed to make a serious effort to both do a walk-around inspection and a review of the service histories on each vehicle to be sure that they looked for additional needed services on each vehicle. The service department agreed to run an ad in the local newspaper advertising our new competitive oil change pricing and to provide a special bonus to our service advisors and technicians for all additional billable hours sold on any vehicle initially scheduled in for just an oil change.

The result of this collaborative effort was to retain our customers, sell more service per customer transaction, and generate a profit for those vehicles that came in for oil changes that were priced at a loss. A greater long-term benefit was that our technicians and advisors learned how much needed additional service sales they could generate with just a few minutes of checking and our long-term average sales per repair order significantly increased.

Selling in the Service Drive

Selling service begins on the service drive as the service advisor greets the customer when they first arrive. At this point, the customer has made a commitment. He or she has chosen to do some amount of business with your company and demonstrated this by taking the time to make an appointment or even just to drive in unannounced with a service question or need. What you do with this opportunity will make all of the difference as to whether or not you are successful. A part of your success is based on your professional attitude and customer relations skills but just as important is your ability to maximize the financial return on the opportunity that the customer has provided you.

In the following sections we will discuss several of the most common techniques that have been proven to help increase service sales per visit. These techniques are the effective use of the service estimate, the walkaround, maintenance history review, and the use of a service pricing menu.

The Service Estimate

Service Estimate

The preliminary appraisal of the costs to perform maintenance, repairs, and diagnosis given to the customer prior to the start of repair work.

A **service estimate** is a preliminary idea of what the expected service costs will be prior to beginning repairs. However, in most cases vehicles arrive without the customer or the service department having a clear idea of the exact repairs needed. How, then, is it possible to give an accurate and complete estimate? Simply, it is not. Let us talk further about how to effectively prepare estimates. An accurate estimate can be the key to obtaining or losing customer approvals to perform service work.

The first step in estimating the cost of repairs is to determine whether the needed repairs are clearly defined or are uncertain. If, for example, the vehicle is coming in for an oil change it is possible to give a detailed and exact estimate up front. If it is coming in for an oil leak it is most likely that the actual repairs necessary to correct the problem are unknown until further inspection and diagnosis is performed. In cases such as this, the best initial estimate will be to project the time and materials needed to evaluate the situation and to gather a detailed repair estimate. This is commonly called **checkout time.**

Checkout Time

Time and resulting charges related to inspecting and testing to determine the actual cause and actual costs to perform needed repairs.

In a situation where the cause of the problem and needed repairs are to be determined, it is important for the advisor to provide the customer with a realistic estimate of the cost to evaluate the situation and make a complete and accurate diagnosis. It is vitally important that the service personnel make it clear to the customer that this is a charge for diagnosis and that should they choose not to have the repairs done that they will be responsible for these charges. In addition, the customer should be advised that these charges are in addition to those that will be incurred for the actual repairs.

Failure to take the time to obtain approval for a reasonable preliminary estimate for checkout time along with a careful explanation of how that process works is likely to cause difficulties. Without being properly advised that these preliminary charges apply whether or not there is an approval for repairs leaves the shop open to the customer arguing that they did not know that there would be a charge if they declined the repairs. Further, failure to differentiate the checkout charges as costs in addition to the repair costs may leave customers believing that if they approve the repairs the diagnosis will be included in the final repair costs. Misunderstandings about these issues can be financially damaging as well as having a negative affect on customer satisfaction.

Just as it is important to recommend preventative maintenance to every customer, it is important to provide a thorough preliminary estimate. Failure to take the time to provide an estimate that relates to the difficulty of the task at hand is likely to cause problems. If the initial estimate is too low it will require a follow-up call to get additional approval for more money. This may make the customers feel that you are trying to "nickel and dime" them and they may lose confidence in you. On the other hand, overestimating the needed time to arrive at a firm estimate may result in customers feeling that they are being overcharged, which may result in the loss of the sale or, more important, the permanent loss of a customer.

Real World Application

As service director, I found that I started receiving complaints from a group of our senior technicians. They consistently complained that it seemed like they spent more time waiting for approvals for diagnosis and repairs than they did fixing cars. After investigating, it became evident that the vast majority of these complaints trailed back to one service advisor. I asked some questions and looked at some repair orders and I noticed that the initial estimate on almost every one of the repair orders that he wrote up was the same—$25. The estimates were always small—and always the same! How could it be that they all needed the same amount of time? How did he arrive at that figure?

I met with the service advisor in question and expressed my concerns and showed him a variety of examples of the estimates and asked him to explain. He said that he did a better job keeping the customers moving and was able to write up more customers by giving them a quick estimate and then calling them back when he knew more.

I explained to him that it was creating a bottleneck in the shop and dissatisfaction among the technicians. Further, I was concerned that it might cause customer problems when they had to be contacted two and three times asking for more and more money just to finish diagnosing their cars. I directed him to take more time preparing more thorough estimates in relationship to the complexity of the problems that the customers had indicated.

The result was that he wrote up a few less orders each day, but improved his sales and the productivity of the technicians. The percentage of estimates that turned into approved repairs increased. It ended as a win-win situation for all involved.

The Walkaround

Upon greeting the customer in the service drive the advisor can simply be an order-taker or can be a service salesperson. As an order-taker the advisor is in a reactive mode where he simply listens to what the customers says that he wants or needs and provides those services. This type of approach sounds more like a fast-food restaurant than an automotive service shop. However, even the better fast-food restaurants do more than this. They ask the customer if he would like a combination meal, dessert, or to try their new menu item. Why? Because they (or their supervisors, at least) know the value of generating additional sales per customer. A professional automotive service advisor should be expected to do at least that much!

Walkaround
A physical inspection of a vehicle by walking around the entire vehicle looking for indications of additional needed service or repairs.

One of the most effective methods for moving from the position of order-taker to that of service consultant and salesperson is the effective use of the **walkaround.** When the customer arrives, the advisor should make every attempt to move with the customer to their vehicle. Then the process becomes very simple. Let him point out to you exactly what it is that he wants to have done. By doing so, you are able to demonstrate your genuine interest and empathy in the customer's vehicle, his concerns, and his needs. Then, while you are at the car you can do a very simple walkaround.

After the customer has completed his explanation of what is wrong and what he wants you to fix you can then take the lead as you slowly walk completely around the car looking for any telltale signs of other repairs or services that are needed. As you spot these signs you can very easily point them out to the customer. It might seem high-pressure sales to recommend services or repairs from a distance. However, it is much easier to suggest a sale when you are standing next to the broken mirror or worn-out tire, looking at it and putting your hand on it as you inspect it more closely and ask "Would you like me to address this issue too while you are already here?" This technique can help you open the door for adding additional service items to most vehicles that enter your shop and, thus, increase your per-vehicle sales and net profits.

Maintenance History Review

One of the simplest opportunities to up-sell needed service to every customer is the reminder of pending or overdue scheduled maintenance. The manufacturer of every vehicle on the road strongly recommends the value of preventative maintenance. They all spell out a regular schedule for performing that maintenance throughout the life of the vehicle. They even warn owners that failure to do so may reduce the useful life of the vehicle and/or void the warranty. However, it is widely accepted that the vast majority of vehicle owners are not attuned to that information and either are not aware or choose to ignore the warnings. Therefore, the majority of vehicles that come into your shop are likely to be overdue for these simple, affordable, and highly profitable services.

When a customer arrives for service the job responsibility of the service employee to be more than an order-taker, he or she must truly be a service *advisor.* It is the customer's expectation that the service advisor is their technical service expert. Advising customers of upcoming and overdue vehicle maintenance is a primary part of being this expert who is counseling the customer and informing him what he needs to have done and should have done.

Recommending preventative maintenance is one of the easiest items to **soft-sell** to every customer. Even though customers neglect maintenance most of them are aware that there is some care and upkeep that they are expected to do. All that the service advisor needs to do is to be the one to remind them. Many customers intend to have maintenance done but simply forget. Others may be putting it off but realize that they are taking the risk of having a premature failure. That makes these types of sales easy, yet the opportunity is too often missed.

Soft-Sell
A pressure-free approach to selling based on gentle reminders and recommendations.

Service personnel live in a very hectic, fast-paced environment. As such, it is easy for them to forget to do the little things because they are in a hurry to get this customer's vehicle done and get a short break before the next one arrives. Another cause for failure to recommend the full package of maintenance services is due to the advisor's lack of personal belief. That is, the advisor may think that the 30,000-mile service is expensive and, as a result, be hesitant to recommend it to the customer.

Whatever the reason for failing to recommend the preventative maintenance is, there are two compelling reasons why all service personnel need to make these recommendations to all customers every time that they enter the service area. First, as the service experts the customers expect the company personnel to accurately and completely advise them of needed services and repairs. If a premature failure occurs, especially shortly following a trip to your shop, the customer is likely to want to throw some of the blame on the shop. After all, you are the experts. The conversation with the service manager following a failure is likely to sound something like this: "Why didn't you tell me? How was I supposed to know? That is why I spend the money to bring my car to you rather than doing it myself! Can't I depend on you to give me correct advice?"

The second reason for consistently recommending preventative maintenance is job security. That is, we already know that up-selling additional services and repairs increases the shop's productivity and profitability. We also know that preventative maintenance is one of the most often neglected areas in the automotive service industry. Therefore, it is one of the primary means by which a service advisor can significantly contribute to the bottom line through his or her efforts in working with every service customer.

Real World Application

Over the years, there are very few service managers or advisors who have not encountered a story from a customer where a premature major failure has occurred due to lack of preventative maintenance. The following is one of many that I experienced.

A late-model vehicle is towed in with the complaint "engine quit, will not turn over or restart." This vehicle was about 18 months old and had 17,000 miles on it and was still within the manufacturer's basic warranty. Upon inspection it was evident that the engine was seized up due to overheating. The engine would not turn over at all, even with the use of a breaker bar, and looking into the valve cover it was easy to see the discoloration due to severe overheating.

I asked the technician to pull the car into the shop to put it on a lift for a more thorough inspection. I was concerned that this looked like it might be a case of neglect rather than a warranty failure. As soon as the car was up in the air the technician called me to his stall. "Look at this" he said as he pointed to the oil filter. The vehicle still had the original factory-installed oil filter. The filters that come on new engines from the factory are typically distinctively different from those that you can purchase from any store (even from dealerships) and this one had obviously never been changed. I did not want to risk a denied warranty claim.

I called our factory rep and explained what we had found. He declined any warranty assistance. The customer was called and advised of what we had found and I explained further that the manufacturer had been consulted. The customer was advised that there was clear and undisputable evidence of lack of maintenance that voided any warranty coverage for this failure. The customer's immediate response (before "I am going to have to call my lawyer") was "But nobody ever told me that I had to change my oil when I bought this car!"

Fortunately, we conducted regular service advisor training in our shop and had a clear and consistent focus on reviewing customer service files and recommending preventative maintenance. As a result, when the customer called me and, in a very animated conversation, accused the company of never having told him about the need to change the oil it was easy to calmly respond that this could not have been the case. I recounted to the customer our service reminders that we regularly sent him, the service history that we printed on every one of his repair orders, and the regular review of maintenance that the advisors conducted at every visit.

Because of our consistent pattern of reminding customers of needed maintenance in our shop we were not only able to generate a significant amount of increased sales per vehicle, we were even able to dodge a bullet that might have resulted in a legal battle. This is just another way that doing the right thing pays off.

Service Pricing Menu

Service Pricing Menu
A comprehensive quick reference listing common service repairs and pricing.

A valuable tool to help service personnel to accurately and completely provide estimates quickly is a comprehensive **service pricing menu.** This may be in a notebook or be PC-based. In either format, the purpose is to provide a quick reference for the service salesman to be able to identify and accurately quote the cost for the majority of common repairs that the shop performs.

A comprehensive pricing menu is far more than a listing of preventative maintenance items and maintenance packages that you might see on a flyer or on a menu board in the service drive. It lists common light, medium, and even heavy repairs. The menu is commonly organized by vehicle systems (for example engine repair, brakes, electrical, and so on). The purpose of the menu is to give the service salesman a fingertip reference source to save time and improve accuracy. Rather than developing a completely new estimate each and every time a repair is needed, the most common repairs are already recorded. The only additional work that it requires is periodic updating as labor or parts prices change. This provides a tremendous time savings and greatly reduces the chance of errors in pricing estimates.

The comprehensive menu provides two additional benefits. It assures that pricing is consistent for all customers. This helps to assure the credibility of the shop. It provides the service salesman the opportunity to provide useful and accurate information to customers. Rather than simply giving an estimate for checkout time they can also prepare the customer with a range of possible final costs depending on what is found. They are now in the position to give an accurate estimation of the most likely repair based on the symptoms and can get approval to spend up to that limit during the preliminary estimate. This reduces wasted shop time. In addition, the menu information provides the service advisors with information on parts and labor costs that will help them to address customer price inquiries.

Selling in the Shop

So far we have covered most of the opportunities that the shop has to sell service out at the service write-up area. However, the face-to-face interaction between the customer and the service advisor is not the only potential place to sell service nor is the advisor the only one who should be involved in looking for opportunities to sell it. In this section we will focus on the most often neglected area to identify, recommend, and sell service: the opportunities that the technician has in the repair shop. The service technician should always be looking for opportunities to identify additional needed maintenance or repairs. Two methods that can help are the consistent use of a safety inspection along with a general physical inspection to look for telltale signs of problem areas.

Safety Inspection

Having every technician perform a **safety inspection** on every vehicle that comes into the shop can be the most valuable tool for increasing per-vehicle labor and parts sales in any shop. There are four major reasons why an inspection should be mandatory for every vehicle.

Safety Inspection
A visual check of a wide range of systems on the vehicle that could affect vehicle safety or reliability.

1. As the service experts, the customer expects that when their vehicle leaves your care that it is fixed . . . and that includes having informed them of any and all other services or repairs that they need.
2. A failure, even if completely unrelated to those services that had been requested, that occurs shortly after a visit to your shop will almost always be accompanied by the question from the customer "What did you do to my car?"
3. No one has the technical ability or better access to quickly and easily identify additional needs more than the technician who, while driving the car, pulling it into the shop, and working in and under it has the perfect vantage points to find other needed work simply by looking around.
4. Last, and certainly not least important of all, it is the best means to up-sell legitimately needed repairs per vehicle, thus enhancing technician productivity and shop profitability.

Although some shops charge a nominal price for the service inspection, only a percentage of customers are willing to bring their cars in to pay specifically for this service. The potential benefits of this inspection are far greater to the shop if it is carried out on all vehicles by all technicians. In order to do this it is much more marketable as a free customer service that you can promote to all of your customers as "just our little way of showing that we care" to provide them additional peace of mind. Meanwhile it rewards you with additional sales and profits. An example of a free 10-point service inspection worksheet is provided in Figure 28-1.

10 point service inspection
During your visit to your shop we were glad to inspect the following systems for you at no charge.
Please let us know if you have any questions regarding this free service.—*The Service Department*

	CONDITION		
Systems Inspected	**OK**	**Needs Attention**	**Comments**
Fluid levels			
Belts & hoses			
Horn			
Tire condition and inflation pressures			
Front lights (headlamps, front turn signals)			
Rear lights (taillamps, brake lights, turn signals)			
Seat belts			
Hazard flashers			
Exhause system			
Suspension system			

Figure 28-1 Free 10 point service inspection worksheet

Selling for the Entire Shop

Along with all of the technical training and experience that your technicians have they have also worked to develop their ability to spot a problem quickly and accurately. Your job in getting them more involved in selling service is to get them motivated to use those skills on every vehicle that they see. It is not hard to convince a technician who specializes in brakes and suspension work to notice a loose ball joint while the car is up on the lift for a brake job. The technician will get a direct benefit from spotting and doing this extra work. What about the noisy muffler that she notices as she pulls the car into her stall? She does not do exhaust work—and does not want to, either.

Becoming more aware of those things that are not directly related to the work that they have been assigned requires a shift in mindset for most technicians. They need to see themselves as more than individuals; they need to become a part of the departmental service sales team too. This is a value that you should try to instill in all of your employees. After all, if every one of them is looking out for the best interests of the entire team they will all get additional work, earn additional pay, and you will earn additional profits. But what do you do when that type of team spirit is not quite there yet?

In some cases, when trying to instill new habits and values into your workforce, it is necessary to provide a short-term incentive just to prove your point. An example of such an incentive would be to provide a small bonus to each technician for additional work that they identify that is then sold to the customer and performed by others in the shop. This demonstrates the point of the ultimate benefit of everyone doing this for the common good.

THEORY INTO PRACTICE 28-1

CASE

As the service manager you need to continue to find ways to attract more customers or to create a reason for your current customers to stop in a little bit more often. You realize that the most common way to do this is to promote common services as price leaders. A price leader is the practice of significantly lowering the price of a commonly used product or service to attract attention and additional business. It is typical that price leaders are priced at very low profit margins and, in some cases, can even be priced at or below actual cost. With low profit margins or no profit margins how can this be a good business decision? The answer is simply that it is only a good business decision if you can consistently generate enough *additional sales* as a result of this promotion.

You decide

You have just finished running a $49.95 alignment special. A review of repair records indicates that the shop has done 40 alignments during this two-week special. They normally sell this service for $69.95 and pay the technician $50 for labor, a net profit of $19.95 per alignment. A careful review of the repair orders shows that 40 cars came in for alignment *but* 20 of them were regular customers and 20 were new customers. How do you think the company fared as a result of this promotion?

THEORY INTO PRACTICE 28-2

CASE

You are the service manager. Based on your past experiences you decide to try a $49.95 alignment special again this year but with a different twist.

You decide

In this case, you priced the repairs the same and used this opportunity for your service advisors to recommend preventative maintenance and a vehicle walkaround to identify additional needed services. As a result they averaged $50 in additional preventative maintenance sales per vehicle. In addition, all of the technicians did their best to carefully inspect the vehicles for additional needed services and repairs to these 40 additional cars. They identified and were able to sell five complete sets of four tires, along with more than $4,000 in needed suspension and other vehicle repairs. Was the promotion successful?

The Value of Increased Sales per Vehicle

With the example of the alignment special still fresh in your mind, think for a minute about the effect of the two ways of handling the promotion on the technicians, the advisors, and the company. In both exercises the company priced the **price leader** the same. In both scenarios the service advisor took the time to make the appointment, to meet and greet the customer, to write him up for service, to notify him when the car was done. In both scenarios the technician did identical alignments.

Price Leader

A product or service offered at an unusually low price or profit margin to attract customer traffic.

It is obvious that the company generated significant additional sales in the second scenario as a result of up-selling. However, the profits were much greater than just that. Significant additional profits were earned because of the increased efficiencies of simply increasing the sales per vehicle. That is, the advisor spent a similar amount of time with the customers in the first scenario and the second scenario, yet generated substantially more sales and profits with the same efforts in the second scenario. Likewise, the technician took the same amount of time road testing the vehicle and pulling it into the shop in both scenarios but was able to do more productive (and profit-producing) work in the second scenario. Without the additional sales generated from the price leader in the second scenario he would have had to work on one or more additional cars to generate the same amount of labor and parts sales (thus having to spend lost time road testing and pulling those cars in and out). As a result of up-selling he was able to become much more efficient in the use of his time—and generated additional profits for the company.

Some Words of Warning

If you have carefully read the advice that I have been providing in this chapter you know that we have been talking about selling needed services. The idea of up-selling and generating additional sales per repair order can often be so tempting that shops go overboard. That is, they work so hard to push the idea of additional sales per repair order that employees feel compelled to start selling additional services whether or not they are really needed. Let us close this chapter with two important warnings about up-selling service: sell only needed service and focus first on the customer's main concern.

Sell Only Needed Service

It probably is not necessary to remind anyone that customers are skeptics when it comes to automotive service. That is, they are wary that they are going to be sold things that they do not want or that they do not need. Unfortunately, the automotive service industry attracts local and national attention every time someone is caught red-handed overpricing service, selling unwanted or unneeded service, or in any way taking advantage of a customer. You can check the newspapers or the video archives of local exposés or national stories on network television to find incidents like these. They are, without question, ones that you do not want to be involved in.

The best protection from accusations of unethical practices is to be sure that the repairs and services that you recommend are based on sound service practices. That is, recommended maintenance can and should be based on published manufacturer recommendations. Service recommendations should be based on a complete diagnosis performed by a qualified technician. It is my strong advice that any time that you have doubts about your ability to back up your recommendations with these credible resources—simply do not go there! It is not worth jeopardizing your reputation and that of your company over a few dollars.

Focus on the Customer's Main Concern

This may sound like another simple suggestion, but it is extremely critical to customer satisfaction. In the flurry of activity to recommend additional sales at the service desk and then again in the shop it is critically important to keep clearly in mind what the customer's primary concern is. That is, it is essential that you clearly document the customer's primary reason for coming in for service. This item *must* be resolved before addressing any additional maintenance or service items.

The reason why you must take a hard-line approach on this is very simple. The customer has come to you with a problem. Whether it is a seized engine or erratic radio reception, it is something that is of great enough concern to justify them making an appointment and taking the time out of their busy day to get it resolved. Failure to address this issue is, to the customer, a total failure on your part to provide service. Regardless of all that you have done right, if you fail to fix this one item you have failed completely.

If you take the time to look for, sell, and perform other services while the car is in the shop yet ignore the customer's primary concern it will often be taken as an insult by the customer. It may seem petty, but experience has proven time and time again that you must keep your priorities in line with the customer's needs—and if the customer needs you to fix his radio static then you need to be sure that you do that—even if you notice a much more serious and potentially hazardous problem!

SUMMARY

In this chapter we have discussed the importance of selling service. Customers depend upon their service advisors and technicians to be their expert consultants who will provide them with sound advice, guidance, and fair pricing for repairs. It is important that you thoroughly and conscientiously evaluate their vehicle, recommend needed maintenance and services, price service and repairs competitively and complete them on a timely basis to maintain satisfied customers.

While contributing to customer satisfaction, maximizing sales per service transaction has a marked effect on the profitability of any service operation. There are multiple opportunities to sell service in the service drive and in the shop. It is through a concerted team effort on the part of the service salesperson (advisor or manager) and the technicians that you can maximize the service opportunity presented every time a customer drives through your doorway to add to your bottom line.

It is imperative that the focus on increasing sales does not compromise your credibility or that of the shop. You cannot afford to let your drive to sell more compromise your values. You must remember to always and only sell needed service and maintenance. Finally, no matter what the situation, if you are truly focused on providing the best service for your customer you must always be sure to clearly identify their primary concern and make a point to fix that first.

PRACTICING THE PRINCIPLES

1. A free service provided to customers that can be an effective tool in finding addition needed repairs is the
   a. service estimate.
   b. price leader.
   c. safety inspection.
   d. all of the above.
2. A ________________ is a product or service that is specially priced at a lower profit or at a loss with the intention of attracting business.
   a. loser.
   b. price leader.
   c. super special.
   d. total loss.
3. The service advisor can identify additional needed repairs or services easily through the use of ________________.
   a. a walkaround inspection.
   b. a walkabout inspection.
   c. checking the maintenance history.
   d. a and c.
   e. b and c.
4. A service advisor has to carefully explain to the customer that the charges for ________________ are for doing the diagnosis and that the customer will be billed for these charges if they do not approve the repairs.
   a. price leaders.
   b. safety inspections.
   c. checkout time.
   d. service estimate.
5. A ________________ provides the service advisor with a quick-reference source of information listing the current price for parts and labor for common repairs.
   a. service pricing menu.
   b. comprehensive repair estimate.
   c. fast-food menu.
   d. price leader.

6. A service department can dramatically improve its efficiency and profitability by increasing the number of ______________ that it sells per service transaction.

List one of the four reasons why a safety inspection should be done on every vehicle that comes into the shop for service.

7. ______________________________.

List three of the nine support services that a shop generally provides as a part of every service transaction at no charge.

8. ______________________________.

9. ______________________________.

10. ______________________________.

SECTION

9

THE LEGAL ISSUES AND RESPONSIBILITIES

Automotive repair continues to be at or near the top in total number of consumer complaints every year. The importance of automobiles in people's lives is likely to continue, thus making automotive repair one of the most important business transactions that people make in their lifetime. Awareness of and compliance with state and federal regulations is essential to ensure that the manager and the organization are operating within the boundaries of the law. Further, in order to protect employees and the public the manager is required to direct and control compliance to safety regulations. In this section will discuss these two important topics and conclude with a discussion of the how advanced planning can ensure a safe workplace.

CHAPTER 29

Legal Guidelines for Service Operations

CHAPTER OBJECTIVES

- To examine the implications of the repair order as a legal contract
- To identify the major areas of legal responsibilities in customer transactions
- To distinguish the major types of legal actions related to automotive repair
- To examine the requirements and responsibilities for repair and vehicle warranties
- To examine the special laws and systems developed to resolve customer disputes with vehicle repair issues

KEY TERMS

litigious
civil
criminal
contract
small claims court
warranty
subject matter expert
compensatory damages
lemon law
binding arbitration

Introduction

Litigious
Likely to resolve disagreements or disputes by engaging in lawsuits.

We live in a **litigious** society. That is, everything is influenced, affected, and, in some instances, run by the ability of anyone to sue anyone over anything. This is particularly true when dealing in business and, especially in the retail trades. The automobile is typically the second largest purchase that any individual makes during his or her lifetime. That is one of the reasons why it is one of the prime targets for many of these legal actions.

Our society is very independent. People rely upon their ability to move about freely. The automobile is the primary product that provides them this flexibility. People rely upon their cars to get them to work, to an appointment, to the store, to a date, to the doctor, and back home again. No other single product contributes so much to our daily freedom and, thus, is a greater source of frustration and anger when it does not consistently perform its function. When frustrations arise it also becomes a cause for legal action to seek remedy for these situations.

In this chapter we will discuss the legal responsibilities and potential consequences related to our dealings with customers. Consumers are protected from unfair treatment by a variety of state and local laws. Although these laws vary slightly in their standards and legal remedies, they are common in concept across the states and territories of North America, and beyond. We will also explore more adversarial legal encounters addressing repair liability and product liability and the potential avenues of legal recourse open to customers.

Customer Issues

Civil
Related to the code of laws and resulting legal actions developed to protect the rights of the individual and general public.

Criminal
The code of laws developed to punish serious and/or intentional violations of the law.

Consumer rights cover a broad range of expectations that consumers have when they consult an expert and hire that expert to do something on their behalf. As an automotive service shop you are that expert. By taking on that role, there is a broad range of legal responsibilities and related liabilities that assume with each service transaction. Your responsibilities begin with performing workmanlike and quality repair up to responsibility that the vehicle is safe and able to perform its expected function. The legal liability that you assume for your actions ranges from a small claims court fine up to and including **civil** and **criminal** charges and penalties. You are accountable both civilly and criminally for what you promise, what you perform, and all events resulting directly or indirectly from your actions. That is a very large and serious group of responsibilities and, therefore, you must understand them.

The Repair Order

Contract
A binding legal agreement between two or more parties.

The most simple, direct, and common involvement that every service person has with the law is in the preparation of a repair order. It is too commonly overlooked that the repair order is a legal **contract.** It is a two-party agreement that states what both parties agree to. It states what the customer's concerns are. It states what items you are expected to address and resolve. It states what your company's expectations are in return—the price to be paid. It also indicates a timeline for all those events to be completed. Finally, it is on your stationery and is signed and dated by the customer, who acknowledges his acceptance of the terms.

The repair order form, format, and wording are standard for a very important reason; it must comply with state and local codes and laws regulating service transactions. Although these laws vary to some degree from region to region the general information included, as noted earlier, is universal. Taking the time to accurately, completely, and legibly fill out a repair order is an essential and very serious responsibility of every service employee who deals with customers. As with a contract to purchase a house, a car, or any other item, if any disagreement arises about the transaction the foundation for any legal arguments will go back to what is stated in writing in the contract, the repair order.

The typical repair order includes statements of the terms and policies of the company. These are there to ensure that the customer has been duly notified of the conditions of this contract on behalf of the company. Most important for the service employee, there are four areas of important information that must be accurately and completely completed. The first of these areas is customer information. This information will include the name, address, and phone number of the customer. It will also indicate specific contact information for how best to reach the customer during the time that the vehicle is in the shop.

Vehicle information is also an important data source for this contract. The vehicle information includes make, model, color, license plate number, VIN number, and current mileage of the vehicle. The accurate recording of the VIN number, which is unique to every vehicle, and the current mileage can be essential in the event of legal action.

Repair requests are the primary reason for the customer's visit to the shop. Completely and accurately recording the customer's concerns and their requests for service is essential. This information provides your technicians with guidelines for action. Incomplete or inaccurate documentation of the customer's wishes is likely to result in customer complaints. It is for this reason that you should always ask the customer to review what you have written down and verify that this is an accurate and complete explanation of what they want before they leave.

The fourth and final area is the section on the repair order to record customer approvals. This data generally documents three specific and important pieces of data. The customer signature is provided as an overall agreement to the terms of the contract. That is, that he acknowledges that he has read, understood, and accepted the general terms of the contract and that he agrees that the explanation of his concerns and repair requests is thorough and accurate. The second approval, usually initialed by the customer, indicates approval of the initial or preliminary repair estimate. The final approval is the customer's agreement of how he wants to be notified to obtain additional approvals once he has dropped the vehicle off and left the premises. All of these three areas are important and binding legal agreements between the company and the customer. All three are required to comply with most repair order laws. As a result, failure to accurately and completely comply with all of them all of the time can lead to significant disagreements with your customers and, unfortunately, can result in legal action.

— Real World Application

While working as a service director I had become very aware of the legal implications and risks of our repair laws based on the horror stories that I had heard from some of our competitors as they returned from court. I met with my technicians and service advisors several times and tried my utmost to spot-check repair orders and procedures to assure that we were following the law both in spirit and to the letter. I believed that we were doing fine until one day. . . .

The dealership received a summons in the mail. I was called to the general manager's office because this complaint was related to a service problem. When the general manager brought up the customer's name I had no recollection of any problems with the customer or the vehicle. The documentation summoned us to appear in small claims court to defend ourselves in the case of this customer who said that we had not obtained proper approvals for the $385 repairs done on his engine. I checked the records and the repair order documented the date and time when the customer had approved this amount for the repairs via the telephone. I was incensed. The customer was trying to take advantage of us. We had done the job right, we had gotten the proper approvals and my response was, "We are right, let's fight!"

I arrived at court on the appointed date and time armed with the customer's file and all of the supporting documentation. The customer went first and pleaded his case. His main point was that he insisted that we never spoke to him to get the approval for the $385. The magistrate then asked me to explain our position. I responded by citing the date and time noted on the repair order at which the service advisor had documented that approval was given. The customer shouted out that he was not available at that time and was on the road and, thus, could not have given the approval. Somewhat puzzled, I asked, "What phone number did you leave the service advisor as the number to call if an approval was required?" He said that it was his home number and went on to say that he was not at home that day; he was on the road with his work. I asked, "Would your wife have been home during that time?" He said, somewhat sheepishly, "I guess so." I pointed out to both the customer and the magistrate that there was a clearly written note on the hard copy of the repair order where the service advisor had noted "approval given by phone—$385" that also documented the exact date and time that the approval was obtained.

The judge turned to the customer and asked, "Did you check with your wife to see if she may have given the approval?" The customer said nothing and simply shook his head NO. He then tried to argue that it was his car and that he never told them to call his wife. This last-ditch effort to make his point fell short of the mark.

Based on the evidence presented the magistrate dismissed the customer's complaint for the $385. I left the courthouse with a smile on my face. Feeling somewhat shaken by having to go to court at all I felt like the vindicated victor proud of how, unlike some of our competitors, we were doing it all right.

About ten days after the hearing we received the final judgment of the court. In it was a big surprise. It documented the finding in our favor on the customer complaint. In addition, however, it was a letter stating that we were being fined $500 by the state. It went on to explain that after review of the document it was found that the dealership had not complied with all of the laws and regulations of the repair code in that we did not have the customer sign and initial all of the proper boxes on the repair order.

Did we lose? Yes. Did we learn? Yes. In the long run, was it worth it? *Yes.* As a result of this small encounter all of the people that I have worked with since that date have heard "that little story about small claims court" and, as a result, we all are a *lot* more careful about how we handle every customer transaction.

Quality of Repairs

The most general responsibility of any repair shop is to consistently perform repairs that meet or exceed customer expectations—quality repairs. As a business operating in the automotive service industry it is a reasonable expectation of every customer that you are an expert in your field and, as such, regularly perform work to this standard. This includes not only fixing the customer's concern but doing so in a manner that is consistent with accepted industry principles and practices. This means providing a safe and lasting repair at a fair and reasonable price. Any consumer can, and will, question you and your shop if they have concerns that all of these criteria have not been met. It is not uncommon for those who do not feel that they have received what they bargained for to take legal action.

The most common method for customers to take legal action for minor complaints is **small claims court**. Most areas provide an easy, low-cost means for individuals to request a legal hearing before a referee or judge to resolve minor disputes involving items of low monetary value. These courts do not deal in large-ticket civil issues or criminal concerns but are provided strictly to address small misunderstandings. Since most of these courts allow the customer to represent themselves the cost to file and proceed is very low.

Small Claims Court

A local court that deals with minor civil actions. Common features of these courts are that the actions are typically heard by a magistrate or other court-appointed referee, the value of the claim or damages is limited to $1,000 or less, and self-representation is allowed.

As a service manager the small claims court is likely to be your most common direct encounter with the legal system. Examples of complaints that are heard in these courts include being overcharged, not having the work done by the agreed-upon time, poor workmanship, and not following specific repair order laws.

Small claims court, however, is not the customer's only legal recourse. If their dissatisfaction and perception of their loss, damage, or injury exceeds the limitations of a small claims action they have the ability to pursue action for greater penalties and restitution through civil and criminal court actions. Although these actions are more lengthy and expensive in both time and legal fees for both parties the potential findings and penalties are much higher.

Repair Warranty

Consumer protection laws vary from state to state. One commonality, however, is that they all have laws that protect consumers against unfair sales practices. If you are not familiar with the laws in your state and locality you should be. I strongly urge you to get a copy of the federal, state, and local regulations relating to automotive repairs and repair liability, study them, and keep them as a handy reference just in case.

The most commonly cited unfair practice is failure to reasonably **warranty** and correct a premature failure of a repair. The specific minimum guarantee is based on state or local repair warranty codes. In the automotive industry a 90-day/3,000-mile repair warranty has been the national industry standard for the past 20-plus years. Any reputable repair shop or parts supplier expects to provide a money-back guarantee for a failure within this time. The only caveat is for failures due to abuse or negligence.

Warranty

A guarantee of the integrity of a product or service including a commitment to correct problems related to that product or service within a specified time or usage limit.

There is no question that you must offer a warranty and know what your legal responsibilities are in your locality. Failure to comply with these legal requirements will result in expensive legal proceedings. They are difficult to defend except in a clear-cut case of abuse and can garner your shop some very unwanted negative publicity.

Some shops have made a point of turning the requirements for providing a repair guarantee into a marketing benefit. By heavily promoting and honoring a warranty that exceeds the legal minimum standard, even to the point of providing a limited lifetime warranty, they use this to demonstrate their superiority over the competition.

Safety and Reliability

Concerns about the general quality of repairs and compliance with warranty regulations are the most minor legal encounters that you will experience. Questions of the safety and reliability of repairs pose much more serious and potentially damaging legal questions.

There are two areas of concern regarding safety and reliability. They are those related directly to the repairs performed and those related to the overall safety of the vehicle. From the position as the expert in automotive repair your shop takes on the burden of advising the customer from that perspective. As such, there is a responsibility to tell them what the correct repair is and to follow that path. Taking shortcuts resulting in unsafe repairs are a clear violation of the customer's trust in you as the expert. At times this may occur at the specific request of the customer. This, however, does not absolve you of responsibility.

It is not uncommon for a customer to ask if you can do something cheaper. This may be accompanied by requests to bring in their own parts or for you to use rebuilt or junkyard parts. You need to be aware that although these shortcuts may be at the customer's requests, the customer is not the repair expert. You continue to be liable for the quality of the repairs that you do regardless of the circumstances. If you knowingly make repairs that you do not believe are thorough, complete, and up to industry standards you are responsible. You may even encounter liability if you refuse to do a repair.

As the expert in automotive repairs you also have a professional responsibility to advise customers of an unsafe and potentially dangerous condition. Many shops operate under the misconception that if they refuse to work on a vehicle that they have no liability. What if a car comes into your shop and you discover a very unsafe condition, even one that is totally unrelated to the customer's initial service request? What should you do? What are your responsibilities and potential legal liabilities?

Subject Matter Expert
Someone who is generally accepted as having special knowledge or skills in a particular topic area because of training and education.

Because you are the **subject matter expert** you can be held accountable if you allow the customer to take the car back out on the road without clearly advising them that the vehicle is unsafe. The clearest protection that you can, and should, employ if the customer insists on driving his car out after your stern warnings is to put a clear statement on the repair order indicating that the vehicle is unsafe to drive and that the customer has acknowledged acceptance of this warning. To be sure that the customer really understands the risk involved, and to protect yourself, you need to be sure the customer signs this before leaving.

Real World Application

As a service manager I have seen cars come and go that are rusty, neglected, and, in general, a risk to drive. None, however, were quite as clear and obvious as the SUV that came into the shop because it "steered kind of funny." Once the technician had inspected the car he called me over to his stall. He pointed out that the vehicle had obviously been driven hard and that there was evidence of a significant amount of off-roading. Because of all of the worn and loose bushings he really believed that the front end needed extensive and expensive work to be safe to take back out on the road. He suggested that we do it all or tell to the customer that we decline the opportunity to do the work at all. I was all prepared to give the customer a big estimate and the all-or-nothing ultimatum and then he pointed out to me his last and final piece of evidence. The lower control arm on the right side of the front suspension had a large crack in it. It showed evidence of being hit and, frankly, I had never seen one with that much physical damage. It made me think not only about the need for extensive repairs but it also made me think "What if the customer declines? This vehicle is a hazard on the road and at any moment he could lose complete control of steering and get killed and/or kill someone else!"

Following normal procedures the technician gave the estimate to the service advisor so that he could speak to the customer to get approval for the repairs. In addition, however, I made sure that the technician told the advisor that if the customer declined the repairs that I wanted to be notified immediately. As I had feared, the customer declined the repairs. The service advisor came to my office to notify me. The advisor indicated that the customer planned to pick the vehicle up at about 5:30. I immediately called the customer and advised him of the severe damage on the control arm and that the vehicle was unsafe to drive. I further advised him that we strongly advised him not to drive the car and that he should have it towed out of our shop. He said, "It is my car and I will drive it out of there if I want to!" At that point I informed him that we were putting a statement on the repair order that clearly indicated that the vehicle was unsafe to drive and that we recommended that he not operate it until repairs were completed. Further, he was told that we would not release his keys to him until he had signed the statement acknowledging that warning.

When the customer arrived I received a call from the cashier. He wanted his keys and did not want to sign the warning. I met with the customer and explained that we had a legal responsibility and that he needed to understand the potential consequences of driving the vehicle in that condition. He finally agreed to sign the release statement with the promise that he would only drive it slowly and only directly back to his house. I do not know for sure if he did as he promised but I felt a lot better that I had done what I could to protect the customer, other drivers, and the company by catching and directly dealing with this potentially lethal situation.

Civil and Criminal Liability

Almost all legal encounters that you experience in automotive service management will be civil complaints and civil suits. These legal actions will most commonly be for small amounts such as the small claims court examples provided earlier. Some may be for larger amounts. The largest of these will be those asking for replacement of the vehicle and for payment of damages for the loss of time and use of the vehicle.

In the unfortunate case that injuries occur as a result of a failure you may encounter civil actions that are seeking **compensatory damages** for medical expenses and loss of compensation due to injuries. In the most extreme cases this can even include damages for wrongful death. One thing that these civil suits have in common, regardless of their severity and size of settlement, are that they are limited to monetary compensation. Civil responsibility, however, is not the limit of your accountability as a service expert.

Compensatory Damages

A payment or settlement, usually as a result of a legal action, intended to make up for a loss suffered.

As service experts, the liability and responsibilities that technicians and repair shops carry can go beyond that of financial responsibility. The potential exists for criminal liability. Yes, read it again—*criminal liability*. As the one who has been entrusted with the responsibility to perform repairs that meet or exceed industry standards, any instance where a failure occurs could leave you, your employees, and your organization open to criminal charges. A car can become a weapon. It can inflict serious injury up to and including death to its occupants and others around it. Even when this is the case, if you have performed quality repairs the resulting liability will likely only be civil. However, if you knowingly perform (or condone) substandard work or take shortcuts that you know are below standard you are exposing yourself and your company to possible charges of criminal negligence. Just in case you did not realize it, a charge of criminal negligence can result in jail time.

New Vehicle Issues

If you are working in a new car or truck dealership service department there are several unique and important legal situations that you must be aware of and be prepared to address. These are issues related to the manufacturer's warranty and to customer complaints that the car is not meeting its intended purpose. When the frustration with unresolved complaints is very high customers are likely to threaten proceeding with a lemon law lawsuit. However, more common in these situations will be your involvement with binding third-party arbitration. We will now briefly discuss these three areas of legal responsibility.

Manufacturer Warranty

We have discussed the general repair warranty that most localities require that all automotive repair shops offer and honor. If you are working in a dealership there is another type of warranty that you deal with on a daily basis. It is the new vehicle warranty offered by every car manufacturer. As the local manufacturers authorized repair center your shop is responsible (based on the dealership franchise agreement with the manufacturer) to provide service. You are accountable for resolving all customer complaints within the limits of the stated manufacturer warranty.

As a dealership you can make a claim for reasonable reimbursement to the manufacturer for all warranty repairs that you perform. The manufacturer is ultimately responsible that the warranty is upheld. However, you are the local agent that must meet with the customer, evaluate the situation, and take the appropriate action to resolve the customer's complaint if it falls within the warranty. It is important that you fully understand that this is not an option, it is a legal requirement.

Unlike an independent shop, you do not have the choice to decline taking in this type of work. The customer, through their warranty, is guaranteed a resolution to vehicle problems within a stated time and mileage range and you are the local agent responsible to make sure that resolution occurs on a timely basis. You have to act. You have to make the repair. You have to shoulder the responsibility and legal liability that the repairs are done professionally and completely.

Lemon Law

Lemon Law

A law that mandates specific guidelines and requirements for providing vehicle purchasers a settlement (repair, vehicle replacement, or a refund) when they have encountered ongoing and unresolved defects with their vehicle.

Although they are state statutes, I am not aware of any state in the United States that does not currently have an active **lemon law** statute. In general, the concept of all of these statutes is that a customer has a reasonable right for the vehicle that they purchase to be able to meet its intended use. That is, a new vehicle should be able to reliably and consistently transport the customer and be reasonably available to do so on a regular basis. One quick source that can provide you access to the specific Lemon Law statute in your state is through the Web site Lemon Law America (http://www.lemonlawamerica.com/) which has a search feature on its homepage that will direct you there.

Although the responsibility for making a vehicle that meets the intended use requirement falls squarely on the shoulders of the new vehicle manufacturer, as a local service provider you are likely to have customers bringing in vehicles to you that they say are lemons. Further, if you represent a new vehicle manufacturer as a dealership service facility you need to be aware when you hear those two words that you need to be wary, alert, and take appropriate action. Most lemon laws do not apply until the vehicle meets one of two important criteria: (1) the vehicle has been in for the same problem 3 times and it is still unresolved or (2) the vehicle has been out of service for more than 30 days due to a problem. Both of these are bases for claiming that the vehicle does not meet the minimum accepted standards for intended use.

When a customer determines that they want to pursue a lemon law action you are likely to be named in the suit. Your ability and willingness to provide service and the competency of your personnel will be questioned as contributing factors to reaching the lemon law qualifying status. This can, unfortunately, put you in the middle between your customer and your manufacturer. Therefore, customer threats of this nature should never be taken lightly. You should make every attempt to accommodate their needs, resolve their problems, and make sure that you have notified the manufacturer so that they understand the need for their involvement to resolve this situation before it escalates to legal action.

Binding Arbitration

In an effort to work together to reduce the number of legal issues that escalate to formal legal actions, thus clogging up the legal system, consumer protection agencies and the automobile manufacturers have worked together to set up arbitration boards in most states to address these issues in a more informal manner. This method provides the benefits of a speedier resolution and lower costs to proceed. As a result, if you look in the owner's packet of just about any new vehicle sold you will find a brochure providing information about and a way to contact the arbitration board serving in your area of the country.

Binding arbitration is an informal legal process under which the manufacturer agrees to adhere to the decision of an unbiased panel. This panel typically consists of a consumer advocate, a manufacturer's representative, and a neutral technical expert. Although the manufacturer agrees in advance to adhere to the findings of the board, the consumer is not similarly bound. Throughout the process the customer retains the right to proceed with formal legal action if he or she is dissatisfied with the panel's findings.

Binding Arbitration
An informal legal process under which the manufacturer agrees to adhere to the decision of an unbiased panel.

The arbitration board provides an important pre-litigation step in the process of resolving customer complaints. By providing this step that is just short of going to court it saves the manufacturers and you, as their representative, money for legal representation. Due to their fast response time arbitration hearings provide the consumer with a reasonable alternative to lemon law proceedings. Because they provide the customer with a faster and less formal resolution process an important side benefit is that the customer's loyalty to you and the manufacturer will not be as severely damaged.

Whenever a customer complaint reaches the level that the words *legal action* or *lawsuit* are raised it is important that you take these threats seriously. The degree to which you are able to respond swiftly to resolve the complaint will have an impact on your long-term ability to save that customer as yours. You must work to avoid the customer feeling the need for a third party to get involved, whether that is an arbitrator or a judge.

SUMMARY

In this chapter we discussed the most common areas where you, as an automotive service employee, are likely to have direct encounters with the legal system. Every service shop enters into a variety of legal contracts every day of operation as they write up repair orders for their incoming service customers. Every one of these repair orders is a legal and binding contract between your company and your customers.

In bringing their vehicle to you for service the customer has expectations about your abilities and your practices. They come to you because they need a subject matter expert who has the knowledge and skills to fix their automotive problem. As the expert, they expect that you will return the vehicle to them with: (1) a quality repair, (2) at an affordable price, (3) in a timely manner, and (4) with a guarantee that the repair will correct their problem for a reasonable period.

When a customer is dissatisfied with their repair experience and they are unable or unwilling to reach a resolution with the repair shop there are several levels of legal remedies that they may seek. The most common legal recourse is through small claims court. Although this is the most common legal proceeding in repair disputes the process is limited in the dollar value of the issue in question. When the potential loss or damage is great the customer may escalate their legal pleadings to a civil court action. In extreme cases where there is significant bodily or monetary injury or a question of intentional negligence a criminal action can be taken against the shop and involved employees.

There are specific laws and legal procedures that have been developed to protect the rights of automobile purchasers. Lemon laws are state statutes that protect consumers against prolonged and unresolved product problems. They prescribe rules, procedures, and remedies up to and including replacement of the vehicle and full refunds. In an effort to provide customers with an alternative and faster method of dispute resolution, most automotive manufacturers voluntarily offer their customers the opportunity to take their concerns through binding arbitration to quickly resolve all but the most severe product-related disagreements.

PRACTICING THE PRINCIPLES

In Questions 1–5 please match the term in the left column with the best definition provided in the right column. Indicate the letter of the definition on the blank provided to the left of the term.

1. ______ civil	a. an informal legal process involving a panel of experts.
2. ______ arbitration	b. a law that can require buying back a new vehicle.
3. ______ criminal	c. an informal legal procedure heard by a magistrate or referee.
4. ______ small claims	d. a law designed to punish intentional or severe violations.
5. ______ lemon law	e. a law designed to protect the rights and property of individuals.

6. There are four major areas of information that must be completed on a repair order. Which of the following is not one of those four areas?
   a. customer approvals.
   b. current service specials.
   c. vehicle information.
   d. customer information.
   e. repair requests.
7. As a(n) ________________ the customers expect us to have the knowledge and skills to accurately and completely resolve their vehicle problems at a reasonable price.
   a. charitable organization.
   b. subject matter expert.
   c. employee of the company.
   d. magician with a magic wand.
8. As a certified technician who conscientiously works on vehicles and does his best to "fix them right the first time" you could still be taken to ___________ if a customer is dissatisfied with the repairs that you performed.
   a. criminal court, small claims court, or civil court.
   b. small claims court or civil court.
   c. small claims court only.
   d. no court because I tried my best.
9. The "universally accepted" minimum warranty for automotive repair and parts is
   a. lifetime warranty.
   b. 3 years/36,000 miles.
   c. 5 years/50,000 miles.
   d. 90 days/4,000 miles.
   e. 12 months/12,000 miles.
10. If a customer brings a car into your shop and declines the repairs that you recommend you are ____________.
   a. fully responsible for the safety of that vehicle.
   b. still responsible if the vehicle is unsafe and causes harm.
   c. not responsible for future injury or damages since they refused the work.
   d. responsible to make sure the customer knows if the vehicle is unsafe.

CHAPTER

30

Workplace Safety

CHAPTER OBJECTIVES

- To examine the underlying basis of federal workplace safety laws
- To discuss the three major agencies responsible for workplace safety administration
- To recognize the general responsibilities of the employer in providing a safe workplace
- To define the major requirements of the OSHA regulations as they apply to automotive repair shops

KEY TERMS

OSH act of 1970
CCOHS
EASHW
OSHA
general duty clause
emergency action plan
carcinogens
HAZMAT
MSDS
right to know
personal protective equipment
lockout/tagout
MSD

Introduction

As an employer or a supervisor you have a moral, ethical, and legal responsibility to provide a safe workplace for your employees, customers, and neighbors. In an ideal world, business owners would take it upon themselves to assure that these conditions were met without the need for external regulation or threats of penalties. Unfortunately, the rapid economic growth in the 1950s and 1960s resulted in the entry of many entrepreneurs to the market place and rapid expansion of mega-corporations. Fallout of that rapid growth was a lack of understanding and concern for the potential impact that these new enterprises were having on employees, customers, neighbors, and the society in general.

A call from the public gained momentum in the late 1960s for the government to provide protections to every individual and society in general. One of the most far-reaching results of those calls for public protection came in the form of workplace safety legislation. The result of this landmark legislation is still with us today and guides and directs the actions and accountability of business owners and supervisors in the workplace.

Workplace Safety Legislation

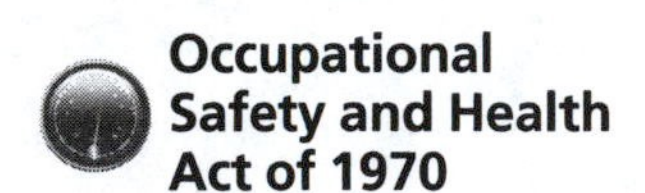

Occupational Safety and Health Act of 1970

The landmark federal workplace safety legislation that created OSHA, NIOSH, and OSHRC to protect workers in the workplace.

In an effort to provide a safe workplace for all workers the **Occupational Safety and Health Act of 1970** (OSH) was signed into law by President Richard Nixon. This bill, nicknamed the "Safety Bill of Rights," was the result of widespread public complaints about the rising injury and death rates on the job. The OSH Act established three new federal agencies

- OSHA, the Occupational Safety and Health Administration, a new agency within the U.S. Department of Labor
- NIOSH, The National Institute for Occupational Safety and Health, to conduct research on occupational safety and health, and
- OSHRC, The Occupational Safety and Health Review Commission, an independent agency to address enforcement actions that are challenged by employers

You may read about and hear about NIOSH and OSHRC on rare occasions in your business dealings. The agency that you will need to be aware of and work with throughout your career on a regular basis in the automotive service industry is OSHA.

CCOHS

The Canadian federal agency responsible for workplace health and safety.

EASHW

The European agency responsible for workplace health and safety.

The movement toward federally mandated and regulated workplace safety is not unique to the United States. In Canada the Canadian Centre for Occupational Health and Safety (**CCOHS**) serves a similar function. In Europe, even though many nations had created their own independent safety agencies they found that they could do more together than they could do alone to resolve the ongoing problems of workplace safety. As a result, in 1996 all of the European nations banded together to form one "super agency" for the same purpose—The European Agency for Safety and Health at Work (**EASHW**). Detailed information is readily available on the Internet for all of these three organizations by going to the following Web sites:

- United States—http://www.osha.gov
- Canada—http://www.ccohs.ca
- Europe—http://osha.europa.eu/OSHA

The purpose and evolution of workplace safety agencies have evolved in the United States, Canada, and Europe over the past 30+ years. As a result, the agencies of today function quite differently than they did at their outset. However, even though their methods have evolved they are just as important for you to understand today in your efforts to manage a successful repair shop. The models and implementation of the workplace safety rules in all three cases are very similar. Let us look at OSHA as an example of the evolution of these agencies and the main features of their regulations and how they affect your work and operation of your shop.

OSHA

When it was initially created, **OSHA** began primarily as an enforcement agency. The relationship between OSHA and workplaces was legendary as an adversarial relationship between business and government. In their effort to "clean up" the unsafe workplaces across the nation the agents of OSHA visited as many worksites as possible. In their wake they left citations, levied heavy fines, and even closed down companies for unsafe practices.

OSHA
The bureau of the U.S. Department of Labor that is primarily responsible for assuring workplace safety and monitoring compliance with federal workplace safety regulations.

The publicity created by the unannounced safety audits by OSHA agents helped to raise awareness in the business community. However, instead of encouraging employers to understand why they should want to improve their workplace so that they would voluntarily comply, it led to one where little change was voluntary. Employers simply tried to hide the truth and lived in constant fear of getting caught. The ability of OSHA to improve the safety of the workplace was limited to the number of agents, the number of visits, and the number of fines that they could levy. OSHA was having minimal impact on improving voluntary compliance from companies.

During the last ten years OSHA has made a dramatic shift in their approach to workplace safety. They have shifted their focus from being an agency of enforcement to one of education, advising, and enforcement. Although enforcement remains a requirement in situations of serious violations and unsafe work conditions, they have shifted their efforts to prevention.

OSHA has found that they can have a greater impact on overall workplace safety if they work with employers rather than against them. With this in mind, they are currently engaged in providing training and consulting services to interested businesses that will help businesses to understand the federal workplace safety regulations and how they can get their company in compliance to those laws. Further, they conduct voluntary non-punitive site inspections to help employers identify areas that may be violations so that they can be remedied before an accident occurs.

This background information should provide you with a general understanding of these safety watchdog agencies, their origins, and their basic relationship with your business. Now, let's take a little bit more time to explore some of the major areas of workplace safety that you must be aware of and involved in to assure that you are providing a safe workplace for your employees. These are the major responsibilities that you have as a supervisor or employer in assuring that your shop complies with these important regulations. These are the standards that you can and will be held legally accountable for. This accountability can be rapid and severe especially in the unfortunate occurrence of a major injury or death in the workplace as the result of a safety violation.

General Duty Clause (GDC)

Before we look at the various areas of responsibility it is important that you have an appreciation of your overarching responsibilities for providing a safe workplace. The best way to clarify your responsibilities is to read and understand this direct excerpt from the Occupational Safety and Health Act. This section is referred to as the **General Duty Clause.** In this section it simply and directly specifies the responsibilities of the employer for providing a safe workplace for employees.

General Duty Clause

The section in the OSHA regulations that specifies the general responsibility of owners and supervisors to provide a safe work environment.

SEC. 5. Duties

---

a. Each employer—
   1. shall furnish to each of his employees employment and a place of employment which are free from recognized hazards that are causing or are likely to cause death or serious physical harm to his employees;
   2. shall comply with occupational safety and health standards promulgated under this Act. 29 USC 654

b. Each employee shall comply with occupational safety and health standards and all rules, regulations, and orders issued pursuant to this Act which are applicable to his own actions and conduct.

—Section 5, Occupational Safety and Health Act of 1970, U.S. Congress, 1970.

Emergency Action Plan (EAP)

As an employer you are required to develop and maintain a formal plan to deal with workplace emergencies and then to clearly communicate that plan to all employees. The intention of this pre-determined plan is to organize the actions of all employees so that they know what their individual roles and responsibilities are in the event of an emergency. An **Emergency Action Plan** (EAP) includes six major elements. These elements are

Emergency Action Plan

The section in the OSHA regulations that specifies that employers develop and maintain a formal plan to deal with workplace emergencies and clearly communicate that plan to all employees.

- An evacuation procedure, including predetermined escape routes.
- Procedures for employees who are required to stay behind to operate and/or shut down critical equipment before they evacuate.
- A procedure to account for all employees after the evacuation has been completed.
- Assignment of medical and rescue responsibilities to those who are to perform them.
- The means for reporting emergencies.
- A listing of individuals and their job titles who can be contacted to provide additional information and clarification on the EAP.

These steps all seem like common sense, but they are too often neglected until a real emergency occurs. During a real emergency the failure to have a clearly marked emergency exit or method for assuring that all employees have escaped the building could result in serious injury or even death. It is exactly for these reasons that the regulations have been developed. You must take very seriously your responsibility to take preventative action to make sure that an accurate and complete EAP exists for your workplace and that every employee knows and understands that plan and their personal responsibilities within it.

Hazardous Material Communication Standard (HAZMAT)

Automotive technicians and body repair personnel use a wide range of chemicals in their work. Chemicals can expose employees and customers to a wide range of hazards. These hazards fall into two major categories: health hazards and physical hazards. Potential health hazards range from minor ones (irritation and sensitization) to severe ones (poisons and **carcinogens**). The physical hazards of chemicals range from their flammability to their corrosiveness and ability to chemically react with other chemicals or compounds. These physical characteristics can create an unsafe work environment. If you have ever worked in or been in an automotive shop it is plain to see that these potential hazards are all around you. These risks exist for those directly using the chemicals (the service technicians), those who are in close proximity to their use (other shop employees) and those who are affected by the work (the service customers). For this reason, the **HAZMAT** standard is one of the most important regulations to help direct your daily operations in an automotive shop.

Carcinogens
Cancer causing agents.

HAZMAT
The Hazardous Material Communication standards of OSHA that require stringent documentation and record-keeping of all dangerous or hazardous materials in the workplace.

There are three major subtopics within the hazardous materials standards that deserve more detailed explanation. These are the Material Safety Data reporting requirements, Right-to-Know, and Cradle-to-Grave responsibility for chemical generators. Because they are all topics that you will regularly encounter in the automotive repair business we need to take the time to discuss them in more detail.

MSDS The Material Safety Data Sheet (**MSDS**) requirement is one of the most fundamental communication tools of the OSHA regulations. Chemical producers, vendors, and users share responsibility under this provision of the law. Producers and vendors are required to provide an MSDS to the purchaser for every product that they sell that contains hazardous chemicals. The user shop is required to have a written hazardous communication program so that all employees are familiar with those chemicals in use and how to obtain that information in an emergency situation.

MSDS
The OSHA requirement for all producers and vendors to provide Material Safety Data Sheets for all hazardous materials in the workplace and for all end-users to have the material available in case of emergency.

The foundation of this system is building and maintaining an organized system of MSDS sheets for every product that contains hazardous chemicals in the shop. Most shops will maintain two complete sets, or books, of MSDS sheets. One must be accessible and clearly marked in the shop area. The second, or backup copy, is usually maintained in a secured office. In the event of an emergency the completeness and accuracy of these records can resolve or even prevent a life-threatening situation.

Right-to-Know Whereas the MSDS requirement deals with the need for all involved parties (chemical manufacturers, distributors, and users) to maintain records of all products sold and in use that contain hazardous chemicals, this regulation addresses the affect of those chemicals on those who are regularly exposed to them, your employees. The **Right-to-Know** regulations require that every individual that is exposed to a chemical in the workplace must be made aware of the existence of that chemical and its potential hazards.

Right-to-Know
The provision of the OSHA regulations that requires that companies inform all employees who are exposed to hazardous chemicals in the workplace.

Fortunately, the regulation and OSHA's involvement goes beyond simply informing the employee that he or she is being exposed to a dangerous substance. It requires that information be provided to the end users so that they can design and provide protection for employees from unnecessary or unsafe levels of exposure.

Some common examples of consistent exposure concerns in the automotive shop would be exposure to asbestos in clutch and brake materials, exposure to body filler dust, or to solvent fumes from paint or cleaners. In all of these cases safety equipment has been developed and is readily available through a variety of sources that will limit employee exposure to these hazardous materials. As a result of the increased awareness of the risks involved with the use of these types of products manufacturers continue to replace many of them with newly developed products that are less toxic.

Real World Application

As a Service Director I always took pride in having a very clean, well-organized shop. We maintained very high standards for our employees and prided ourselves on being good employers. As a result of this we tried to go above and beyond in making sure that we provided a safe workplace. We regularly provided HAZMAT training and all of our OSHA-mandated paperwork was in order. We thought we understood the true importance of these regulations or at least I thought we did until . . .

Our shop had been working on a vehicle that had returned several times for a water leak from the top of the windshield area. We had involved several technicians, the manufacturer, and the local glass company that had removed and reinstalled the windshield so that we could be sure we found any hidden pinholes where water could seep in. We had used every method and product that we could think of to try to stop the leak. Then, all of a sudden, the leak became secondary.

About an hour after the car had left the shop from its most recent multi-day visit to fix the leak I was paged to the phone. I was told that this was an urgent call. When I answered it the man on the other end identified himself as Dr. ________ (I don't remember his name). He informed me that he was an emergency room doctor and that they had a patient (the daughter of the owner of the water leaking car) in the emergency room there. He said that she was having difficulty breathing. He said "I need to know right away exactly what the chemicals are that are in all of the products that you just used on her mother's car. This could be a matter of life or death. I need an answer within the next five to ten minutes."

After I got over the initial shock and panic of being called out of the blue to respond to a life-and-death emergency I swung into action. I paged the shop foreman and the technician who had worked on the car. I told them that I needed to know exactly every item that they had used on that car that day. I told them that the list had to be immediate, accurate, and complete. While they were looking over the repair order and searching their memories to be sure they hadn't left anything out I ran to grab the dealership's MSDS binder.

Together we listed all of the chemicals used. With that information in hand I pulled copies of MSDS sheets for every one of the chemicals that we had used. I quickly faxed the copies of all of the MSDS sheets to the number provided by the emergency room doctor. About a half-hour later I received a return call that the young girl was going to be all right.

We all breathed a sigh of relief . . . but what if we hadn't had the MSDS? What if our records had been incomplete or just one of our vendors had failed to provide us with the complete and accurate information? What if the young girl had been seriously injured as a result of our failure to respond completely and in time to help her? Although I never thought I would experience anything like this firsthand it certainly made OSHA and the MSDS requirements real to me and to our shop. Even though I haven't worked there for quite a while now I'd bet that if there are any employees remaining that were there that day that they still make sure that their MSDS binder is accurate, complete, and available!

Cradle-to-Grave Responsibility A part of the responsibility of the end-user of hazardous materials and chemicals is to make sure that they properly dispose of the byproducts and left over materials. Laws clearly define the proper methods of disposal. Because of the risks of exposure to these items they must be clearly labeled and be removed from your place of business in approved containers. This is most commonly done by a vendor that specializes in the handling and storage of these special materials.

One last, yet extremely important, point needs to be made on the topic of your responsibility for these materials. The federal laws clearly state that the generator of this waste (you) are responsible for it and the damage that it may cause from cradle to grave. That is, you are responsible for it until it is no longer hazardous. This clearly *does not mean* your responsibility ends when you pay a reputable hauler to take it away—as many shops mistakenly believe. You continue to be responsible for it as long as it exists. You can be held responsible for damage resulting from this material many years down the road. This is a responsibility that you cannot sell off to your waste hauler or that they can agree to be assigned as a part of their agreement with you. For this reason you need to pay particular care to work only with vendors that you can trust will do all that they can to assure that future liability issues will never arise.

Personal Protective Equipment (PPE)

Safety and health regulations require that employers provide protection for employees from hazards. Often situations arise in the workplace where a reasonable method does not exist to make changes to the work environment to protect individuals. In these cases, the employer is required to provide **personal protective equipment** that will address concerns of exposure for these individuals.

Personal Protective Equipment

OSHA requirement that employers provide equipment to protect employees from health and physical hazards in the workplace.

Protective equipment provides a reduction in exposure to individuals from exposure to both health hazards (such as chemicals, radioactivity, etc.) and physical hazards (for example, flying objects, excessive heat, etc.). The major areas of personal protective equipment provided for in the regulations are

- eye and face protection
- head protection
- foot and leg protection
- hand and arm protection
- body protection
- hearing protection

Real World Application

The old adage that familiarity breeds contempt is practiced just about every day in many auto repair shops. Because they deal with dangerous chemicals, moving parts, and other hazards forty hours per week every week for years technicians tend to become oblivious to the risk. Although I have always been considered a stickler for detail, over time I must confess that as a service director I started becoming somewhat numb to these regulations and did not pay nearly enough attention until the following incident woke me up:

It started out as a normal day in the shop. One of my top technicians was working just down the line from my office on a car that had been brought in with a charging system problem. Initial tests indicated that the system was overcharging. That should have been nothing but a simple replacement of the voltage regulator . . . until . . . something went terribly wrong.

All of a sudden there was a scurry in the shop and one of the technicians came running into my office. "A battery just blew up in his face," he announced.

(Continued)

I ran from the office and double-checked to make sure that he was OK. By the time I reached his work stall he had already doused himself with tons of water to wash the acid off of his face and his clothing. The focus of the blast of battery acid had hit him directly in his face and eyes.

Quick action by him and fellow employees and the ready access to a wash station had helped him to dilute the acid before it could burn him more than just superficially. But what about his eyes? Fortunately he was one of the few in the shop that took the shop and OSHA rules seriously and he *had* worn the OSHA-mandated safety glasses. There was no doubt in anyone's mind that his decision to follow those rules and wear the glasses had saved his sight.

We were all fortunate. Certainly he was most fortunate because he was most at-risk. However, all of the rest of us in the shop were reminded by this close call of the importance of shop safety and compliance with safety regulations. It proved to us once and for all that these rules are not just there to make life difficult; they *really are* there to protect us all.

Lockout/Tagout

Lockout/Tagout
OSHA requirement that equipment must be disabled and clearly labeled so that it will not unexpectedly start up or operate if it is unsafe to operate or under repair.

Lockout/Tagout provides a requirement to take preventive measures to assure that equipment or machinery will not unexpectedly start up or operate while it is under repair or otherwise unsafe to operate. This provision is most commonly related to the electrical industry where they are required to disable an electrical circuit from being energized while repairs are being made within that circuit. However, this same regulation has several applications within the automotive shop.

Shop operations often require the use of equipment that could cause harm if not in proper operating condition. Some examples range from the small bench-mounted grinder to vehicle lifts. Any time one of these pieces of equipment is malfunctioning there is a responsibility in providing a reasonably safe work environment to disable the equipment and clearly mark it as unsafe to operate.

Still another common example in the automotive repair shop is the need to disable and clearly mark a vehicle that is partially disassembled. Many situations arise where a repair has been halted while waiting on parts or due to a variety of other delays. Wiring may be left loose, fuel lines may be disconnected, suspension parts may be unbolted, or other systems may be left in a state where any attempt to start or operate the vehicle could be hazardous. For these reasons vehicles left in a partial state of repair should be clearly marked to warn everyone of the potential danger.

This simple provision of the law provides for two separate, yet important, elements. First, you are required to lockout the equipment. That is, you are to disable it so that it does not operate. Second, you are required to tagout the equipment. This is the requirement to place a warning on the equipment that it is not to be used. An injury caused by failure to comply with these requirements could be found to be negligence of safety regulations on the part of the shop.

Musculoskeletal Disorders (MSD)

MSD
Chronic physical conditions or injuries that are brought on through specific repetitive activities that are a part of the person's job duties.

One of the more recent additions to OSHA's broad-reaching involvement with workplace safety issues is the introduction of guidelines to prevent musculoskeletal disorders (**MSDs**). Two of the most common MSDs that you have probably heard of are carpal tunnel syndrome and trigger finger. Carpal tunnel is often associated with office personnel and has been linked to prolonged periods of keyboarding without adequate arm support or regular work breaks. Trigger finger, as the name implies, was first identified in policemen and resulted in reduced function of that finger.

In summary, MSD injuries are chronic physical conditions or injuries that are brought on through specific activities that are a part of the person's job duties. As a result, when injury and/or disability results the worker can take action against the employer for damages suffered on the job. Although many of these types of injuries are not immediate or severe in their onset they often become long-term conditions requiring surgical repair or cause permanent disability.

In recent years you have seen more and more about ergonomically designed or ergonomically correct chairs, keyboards, tools, etc. These products are promoting the superiority of their design in helping to prevent or at least reduce the chance of MSDs in the workplace. How does it affect you and what should you do? You need to include this factor in your decisions that you make in purchasing equipment, setting up work stations, and assigning job tasks. The cost to the organization in personal injuries, loss of time, and disability payments make this an important issue that you must be aware of and address. Part of your job as a supervisor is taking reasonable care to minimize risks to your employees and to your company.

Mandatory Safety Training

The OSHA standards indicate that you must comply with the safety regulations and guidelines that govern the workplace. Ignorance is no defense. You and your company are liable for safety issues covered in these codes. However, your responsibility goes beyond you having personal knowledge of the codes and working within them. You are also responsible for having a regular communication program that assures that all of your employees are informed.

The mandatory safety training regulations in the OSHA standards require that all employers provide training to all of their employees. This training is intended to inform employees about the known hazards in their workplace and what they can do to control them. This includes work processes, equipment, and all of the materials used in the workplace. These training and information-sharing requirements have far-reaching implications to you in your role as supervisor. Some of the major responsibilities that you have are to assure that

- No employee undertakes a job until he or she has been trained on how to do it properly and is authorized to perform that job.
- All employees know about all of the equipment and materials that they work with and will come in contact with in the workplace.
- All employees must know what they can do to control hazards and how they should respond when an unsafe or dangerous situation arises.
- No employee performs any job or task that appears unsafe.

From just this short list of responsibilities you can see that your responsibilities, and potential liabilities, under these safety regulations is broad. These training activities are not optional. They are federally mandated and the potential consequences for failure to comply can be swift and severe. It would be a good investment of your time to browse through the OSHA Web page (http://www.osha.gov) and then bookmark it and refer to it regularly as a quick reference to guide your actions.

Mandatory Record Keeping

The final step in complying with OSHA requirements is the need for you to set up and maintain safety and health records of your operations. These include records of all accidents, related injuries, illnesses, and resulting damage or loss of assets. OSHA's stated purpose in requiring these records is to help the business owner or manager have documentation on hand that will help determine causes of injury or damage so that corrective measures can be taken to prevent recurrences.

OSHA spells out a five-step mandatory record-keeping system complete with OSHA-developed forms. The five step system is:

1. Obtain reports on every injury or job-related illness requiring medical treatment beyond basic first aid.
2. Maintain a record of every job-related illness or injury.
3. Maintain a record of all occupational injuries or illnesses.
4. Prepare an annual OSHA summary of illnesses and injuries and post it in the workplace.
5. Maintain these records for at least 5 years.

In the unfortunate event that a major incident occurs in the workplace, federal law requires that it must be reported to OSHA within eight (8) hours of the occurrence. Major incidents are defined as those that result in the hospitalization of three or more employees or any incident resulting in a fatality.

If you are working in an environment where anyone may be exposed to toxic substances or hazardous materials OSHA mandates supplementary reporting of incidents of exposure. The automotive service shop qualifies as such an environment. You work with volatile and potentially dangerous chemicals ranging from gasoline and oil to a variety of solvents and other chemical compounds used in the repair of vehicles on a daily basis. Reporting and record-keeping of exposures and any resulting physical examinations and medical treatments must be maintained in compliance with the five-step system noted above.

SUMMARY

In this chapter we have discussed the major federal health and safety legislation that impacts the operation of all automotive service facilities. The Occupational Safety and Health Act (OSHA) of 1970 is the backbone of this legislation. It addresses safety and health issues both in broad, far-reaching terms as well as in specifics related to common hazards. The legislation charges all employers with the responsibility to provide a safe workplace. However, it goes into much more detail to specify areas of particular concern and spells out actions required by employers in each of these areas.

The first of these areas is the need for all employers to provide an emergency action plan for the workplace and all workers. In addition, OSHA regulations spell out a comprehensive system of identification, labeling, handling, and disposal responsibilities for hazardous wastes. They also cover a wide range of requirements of facilities and equipment necessary to reduce the chances of injury. The regulations also require that employers must train employees in safety procedures and educate them about existing dangers that exist, by nature, in the workplace. Finally, OSHA gives the Federal Government the power to set up an organization to monitor, inspect, and levy penalties on organizations that are found in non-compliance of these regulations.

PRACTICING THE PRINCIPLES

1. Occupational health and safety laws
   a. are very similar in the U.S. and Canada.
   b. have been enacted across all of Europe.
   c. are intended to protect employees.
   d. all of the above.

2. The federally required document that provides detailed information on-site explaining the chemical composition of every hazardous material is
   a. MSDS.
   b. CCOHS.
   c. EASHW.
   d. HAZMAT.

3. Which of the following statements *is not* a requirement of OSHA?
   a. No employee undertakes a job until he or she has been trained how to do it properly.
   b. No employee undertakes a job until he or she is authorized to perform that job.
   c. All employees are solely responsible if they perform any task that appears unsafe.
   d. All employees know the materials they will come in contact with in the workplace.

4. An Emergency Action Plan (EAP) includes all of the following procedures *except*
   a. assigning employees that are required to "stay behind."
   b. accounting for all employees after the evacuation has been completed.
   c. assigning of medical and rescue responsibilities.
   d. none of the above.

5. Based on OSHA regulations, ________________ must know what they can do to control hazards and how they should respond when an unsafe or dangerous situation arises.
   a. the owner of the company.
   b. the direct supervisor.
   c. all employees.
   d. properly trained employees.

Please match the term from the column on the left with the best definition provided in the list to the right.

___ 6. personal protective equipment	a. disabling unsafe equipment
___ 7. lockout/tagout	b. safety responsibility of business owner
___ 8. general duty clause	c. special clothing that is provided
___ 9. right to know	d. notify employees of hazardous materials
___ 10. emergency action plan	e. posted map of nearest exits

INDEX

N

O

P

Q

R

S

T

U

V

W

Z